GREAT
CANADIAN
PLANT GUIDE

PLANT HARDINESS ZONES

KEY

0a	4a
0b	4b
1a	5a
1b	5b
2a	6a
2b	6b
3a	7a
3b	7b
	8a

Davis Strait

Foxe Basin

Iqaluit

Hudson Strait

LABRADOR SEA

D

A

Hudson Bay

0a

NEWFOUNDLAND & LABRADOR

James Bay

La Grande Rivière

Labrador City

St. John's

Newfoundland

QUEBEC

Corner Brook

0b

ARIO

Albany

1a

Lac Mistassini

Gulf of St. Lawrence

1b

Jonquière · Chicoutimi

PRINCE EDWARD ISLAND

Charlottetown

St. Maurice

Saguenay

2a

NEW BRUNSWICK

Moncton

NOVA SCOTIA

Lake Superior

Charlesbourg

Québec

2b

Fredericton

Saint John

Dartmouth

3a

Trois-Rivières

Laval

Halifax

3b

Sudbury

North Bay

Gatineau

Sherbrooke

4a

Sault Ste. Marie

Montreal

4b

OTTAWA

5a

Peterborough

Kingston

ATLANTIC OCEAN

Oshawa

Lake Huron

Kitchener

Toronto

Lake Ontario

Lake Michigan

London

Hamilton

St. Catharines

5b

Sarnia

6a

Windsor

6b

Lake Erie

GREAT CANADIAN PLANT GUIDE

3rd edition

Editor-in-Chief **TREVOR COLE**

Project Editor Caroline Reed
Project Art Editor Elaine Hewson
Senior Editor Helen Fewster
Senior Art Editor Joanne Doran
Managing Editor Esther Ripley
Managing Art Editor Alison Donovan
Production Editors Joanna Byrne, Luca Frassinetti
Production Controller Mandy Inness
Publisher Jonathan Metcalf
Associate Publisher Liz Wheeler
Art Director Peter Luff

Canadian Publishing Team
Editor-in-Chief Trevor Cole
Project Editor Barbara Campbell

DK India
Editors Divya Chandhok, Nidhilekha Mathur
Senior DTP Designer Pushpak Tyagi

Third Canadian Edition, 2012
12 13 14   10 9 8 7 6 5 4 3 2 1
001—183442—Mar/2012

Dorling Kindersley is represented in Canada by Tourmaline Editions Inc.
662 King Street West, Suite 304, Toronto ON M5V 1M7

First published in Great Britain in 1998 by Dorling Kindersley
Publishers Limited, 80 Strand, London WC2R ORL
This revised edition published in 2012
Copyright © 1998, 2000, 2003, 2007, 2012 Dorling Kindersley Limited
All rights reserved

Library and Archives Canada Cataloguing in Publication
Great Canadian plant guide / editor-in-chief, Trevor Cole. -- 3rd Canadian ed.
Includes index.
ISBN 978-1-55363-177-4

1. Plants, Ornamental--Canada. 2. Flowers--Canada.
3. Gardening--Canada. I. Cole, Trevor J.
SB453.3.C2G73 2012   635.9'0971   C2011-904011-5

Printed and bound in Singapore by Star Standard

DK books are available at special discounts when purchased in bulk for corporate sales,
sales promotions, premiums, fund-raising, or educational use. For details, please contact
specialmarkets@tourmaline ca.

Discover more at
www.dk.com

Contents

INTRODUCTION

Gardeners today have plenty of choice when buying plants. Not only are plant breeders constantly producing new and exciting cultivars, but plants are now more widely available in garden centers and nurseries as well as in do-it-yourself superstores. In less traditional plant-buying situations, information and advice may not be readily available or reliable. It is perhaps no wonder, then, that gardeners sometimes find choosing the right plant a bewildering business.

The *Great Canadian Plant Guide* was conceived to help gardeners select outstanding and reliable plants for their garden, whatever their level of expertise and experience, and whatever the site. While all of the plants in this book are suitable for some region of Canada, they are not all hardy. Some are tender and are grown as annuals or houseplants.

However, these recommendations refer only to the plants themselves, and not to those who produce them. It is impossible to guarantee the quality of plants offered for sale by any nursery, garden center, store or website, and here gardeners must exercise a degree of common sense and good judgment in selecting the best plants to take home. The following pages include guidance on recognizing healthy, well-grown plants and bulbs, and how to choose them wisely and get them off to a good start.

CHOOSING FOR YOUR GARDEN

Selecting plants appropriate to your site and soil is essential, and each plant in the *A–Z of Plants* has its preferences indicated. Well-prepared soil, fertilizing, mulching, and, in dry conditions, watering in the early stages are also important for the well-being of most plants (although in *The Planting Guide* you will find plants to grow in poor soil or dry sites). Entries in the *A–Z* include basic care for the plant concerned, along with specific hints and tips on topics such as pruning and siting, and on winter protection where hardiness is borderline. By following this advice, the plants you choose using the *Great Canadian Plant Guide* should get off to a great start and continue to perform well.

Ever-widening plant choice Exotic flowers, such as this blue poppy (*Meconopsis grandis*), may tempt the gardener, but check the conditions they require before buying.

USING THE GUIDE

The *Great Canadian Plant Guide* is designed to help you choose plants in two different ways.

THE A–Z OF PLANTS

Here, over 1,000 full plant entries are given, illustrated with photographs. Consult this section to find details about a plant, whether you have read its name on a label in a garden center, or have noted it down from a plant catalog, magazine article, or website. Each entry tells you what type of plant it is, how it grows, what its ornamental features are, and how to care for it. For quick reference, symbols (right) summarize its main requirements.

THE PLANTING GUIDE

This section provides "shopping lists" of plants for every purpose, whether practical, such as a group of plants for a damp, shady site, or for themed plantings, such as a selection of plants to attract birds into your garden. Page references are given for plants with entries and portraits elsewhere. Hundreds of plants not pictured are also recommended.

Plant sirens (facing page)
Garden centers and nurseries feature a wide range of plants to tempt gardeners.

SYMBOLS USED IN THE GUIDE

Soil Moisture Preferences/Tolerances
◊ Well-drained soil
◑ Moist soil
● Wet soil

Sun/Shade Preferences/Tolerances
☼ Full sun
☀ Partial shade: either dappled shade or shade for part of the day
☀ Full shade

Hardiness Zones
* Depending on the cultivar

Hardiness Zones
These are given (as Z4, for example) for all plants in this book, except for tender plants, for which the minimum temperature is given, and annuals (including some perennials commonly grown as annuals). Many subtropical plants that tolerate temperatures slightly below freezing are indicated as being tender. Hardiness zones are intended only as a guide. They are affected by many factors, especially altitude, slope, and exposure. Areas in a garden near the boundary of a zone may be warmer or cooler than indicated depending on the specific microclimate. Walls, hedges, and buildings give shelter from winds and may enable slightly more tender plants to survive. The hardiness of perennials is particularly complex and often depends more on a reliable, persistent snow cover than on the minimum winter temperature.

THE PLANTS IN THE GUIDE

The range of plants—well over 2,000—featured in the *Great Canadian Plant Guide* has been carefully chosen to provide the best selection from among all the different types of plant, and for many of the situations for which plants may be required. Many of the plants in this book are readily available from local sources throughout Canada, although gardeners in places not easily served by local nurseries and garden centers will need to do some research (including looking through mailorder catalogs, doing web searches, and networking with members of garden clubs and specialized plant societies) to track down many of these plants.

WHAT IS A GREAT PLANT?

Calling a plant "great" is, admittedly, the result of a combination of subjective and objective appraisals of a plant, whether on the part of an individual or a committee of experts. It must be remembered that a plant that performs exceedingly well as a great garden plant in one part of North America may be a miserable failure in the rest of the continent, or it may be a noxious weed. Similarly, any "great" plant put into a garden situation not to its liking will fail, if not immmediately, then eventually. The perception of an individual plant, genus, or even entire group of plants as "great" can also come and go upon the whims of current gardening trends and fads.

Geranium 'Kashmir White' Plants that are versatile and easily grown are noteworthy for sheer garden value.

Camellia x williamsii 'Brigadoon' Choice forms of familiar and unusual plants are in this book.

Hydrangea macrophylla 'Altona' The best selections of many garden stalwarts are recommended.

Generally, though, a great garden plant that withstands the test of time will meet the following criteria:

• It is excellent for ornamental use, either outdoors (in the open ground or in a container) or under cover

• It is of good constitution, being neither frail and weak nor overly vigorous to the point of being invasive or weedy

• It is available in the horticultural trade, whether locally or through mail order

• It is not particularly susceptible to any pest or disease

• It does not require any highly specialized care other than providing the appropriate conditions for the type of plant or individual plant concerned (for example, acidic soil)

• It should not be subject to an unreasonable degree of reversion in its vegetative or floral characteristics.

To explain this last point simply, many plants with unusual characteristics differing from the species, such as double flowers or variegated leaves, have often been propagated from a single plant or part of a plant—a natural mutation or "sport"—that has appeared spontaneously. Plants bred from sports—especially when raised from seed—are liable to show only the normal leaf color or flower form. It takes several generations of careful and controlled propagation for the special feature to be stable enough for plants to be recognized and registered with a distinct cultivar name (which is usually chosen by the breeder) and then offered for sale. Many never retain the special feature when grown from seed and therefore can be reproduced only by vegetative methods such as cuttings or grafting.

Prunus laurocerasus This evergreen is handsome year-round, both as a specimen shrub and as a hedge.

Anemone blanda '**White Splendour**' Floriferous cultivars for every site and season are included in this book.

Cornus alba '**Spaethii**' Plants that are grown for their variegated foliage should not be prone to excessive reversion.

NONPICTURED PLANTS

The Planting Guide section at the back of the book presents (in list form) hundreds of trees, shrubs, climbers, perennials, bulbs, and other plants that could not be pictured and that are suitable for a specific site or garden situation. These lists do not pretend to be exhaustive, but they do present a representative cross-section of plants to consider. The lists also contain plants that are pictured; these are cross-referenced to the appropriate pages.

In some categories of plant, notably annuals (particularly those for summer bedding, such as impatiens, petunias, and salvias) and in some perennial genera, new cultivars appear so rapidly, often superseding others offered for sale, that producers, retailers, and gardeners alike are hard pressed to keep up with developments. In order to give a wider choice in these somewhat underrepresented categories, the *Great Canadian Plant Guide* includes, in *The Planting Guide*, selected cultivars that have proved their reliability over the years.

Putting plants to the test
Trials at public gardens and at display gardens at seed companies help select the best forms for gardeners.

FINDING PLANTS BY NAME

The botanical, or so-called "Latin," names for plants are used throughout this book, simply because these are the names that gardeners will find on plant tags and in publications. These names are also international, transcending any language barriers or regional variation.

To the uninitiated, plant nomenclature may seem confusing, and sometimes plant names appear to be very similar. Also, plant nomenclature is by no means static: plant names, whether scientific or vernacular, are subject to constant revision. Sometimes this is in response to scholarly research, whereby a genus may be split up and given several new names (for example, the genus *Chrysanthemum* is now several genera); other times it is a marketing technique to create new interest for an already established plant. Some plants have synonyms—older or alternative names—by which they may sometimes be referred to: the *Great Canadian Plant Guide* gives synonyms for a number of plants. A brief guide to plant nomenclature can be found on pp.24–25. Many common names for plants or plant types that feature in the *Guide* are also given, both in the *A–Z of Plants* and in the Index.

SHOPPING FOR GOOD PLANTS

The first step in ensuring that your garden will be full of healthy plants is to choose and buy carefully.

WHERE TO BUY

Plants can be found for sale in a variety of situations today. Generally, you should buy plants only when you feel sure that the plants offered are actually what they say they are, that they have been well grown, and are not going to bring any pests and diseases into your garden.

PLANTS BY MAIL

Buying plants by mail order or from nursery websites is one of the easiest (and most addictive!) ways of obtaining particular plants. It gives you a huge choice, and also offers access to specialized nurseries that concentrate on certain plant groups or genera and that may not be open to visitors. You can track down almost any specimen from the comfort of your own home, and, provided someone is at home to receive it, it should be delivered in perfect health. Mail-order nurseries are usually happy to replace any plant damaged in transit. Often, the plants will arrive with their roots surrounded with soil mix or peat (otherwise bare-root). They are best planted out soon after receipt.

WHEN TO BUY

Trees, shrubs, and roses that are available as bare-root specimens are almost always deciduous. Woody plants with roots balled and burlapped may be deciduous or evergreen. Many are available only in the dormant season; they are ideally purchased in late fall or early spring and should be planted as soon as possible.

Container-grown plants are now extremely popular and are offered for sale throughout the planting season. However, the traditional planting times of spring and fall, when conditions are not extreme, are still the best. Plants should not be put into near-freezing or baked, dry soil; instead, keep them in their containers until conditions improve.

In colder climates, reliably hardy plants can be planted in fall. Spring is the time to put in plants of borderline hardiness and to buy bedding plants. Beware of buying them too early, however tempting they look after the dark, bare days of winter. Bedding sold in early and mid-spring is intended to be bought by people with greenhouses and cold frames, where plants can grow under cover until all danger of frost has passed. If you plant out bedding too early in the season, you risk losing it to late frost.

YOUR SHOPPING LIST

Whether you are starting a new garden from scratch, replacing a casualty, or simply wanting to add extra touches to a shady corner or a half barrel, informed choice is the

Well-grown plants for sale Healthy, clearly labeled plants in neat, well-kept surroundings are a good indication of excellent nursery care.

key to buying the right plants, which are also the very best and healthiest.

There are many factors to consider about your garden (see pp.16–17) and, equally, buying tips that will help you make the best choice from the selection of plants offered (see pp.18–19). Many gardeners prefer to set out with specific plants in mind. However, no one can deny that impulse buys are one of gardening's great pleasures—and with the *Great Canadian Plant Guide* at hand, you will be able to obtain just the right plants for your garden and avoid expensive mistakes.

CHOOSING THE RIGHT PLANTS

Although there are ways to get around many of plants' climatic and soil requirements, you will avoid extra work and expense by choosing plants well suited to the conditions your garden offers.

HARDINESS

Most of us garden in areas that experience frost and cold (including plenty of snow) in winter. Choose plants that are generally known to be adapted to your area by checking the hardiness zone ranges given in this book. Providing good growing conditions throughout the season helps promote survival, including appropriate winter and summer mulches such as pine boughs and light straw. Optimism is no substitute for action if plants

Extending the range
Container growing may be the answer for gardeners who covet plants with special soil needs, like these acid-loving azaleas, that their open gardens cannot meet.

are to survive in a particular region, yard, or microclimate, such as a low, poorly drained spot, an unusually hot and dry corner, or an exposed north-facing hillside.

SUN AND SHADE

It is well worth observing your garden to see how much sun the different areas receive at different times of the day and year. For good growth and the best display of features such as colored foliage, always match plants' sun and shade requirements.

YOUR SOIL

Most plants can tolerate soil that falls short of perfect, and many survive in harsh conditions. But it is always preferable—and far more labor-saving—to choose plants that suit your soil, rather than manipulate your soil to suit plants, by adding, for example, peat or lime. The effect never lasts and is now also considered environmentally inadvisable—local insects, birds and other fauna may be unable or unwilling to feed on such plants. It is, however, important to add nutrients to the soil. By regularly applying compost or manure to your soil, you not only add nutrients but improve soil texture.

Determining your soil acidity (or its reverse, alkalinity), measured by units known as pH values, is important. Most plants tolerate a broad range of pH values around neutral, but some groups have specifically evolved to be suited by soil that is either definitely acidic or definitely alkaline. Choose plants that will enjoy your soil, or if you really covet specialized plants, grow them in containers in a soil mix that meets their needs.

DRAINAGE

The expression "well-drained yet moisture-retentive" is one of the most widely used yet seemingly baffling expressions in gardening. However, it is not such a contradiction in terms as it seems. What it applies to is a soil that in composition is not dominated by pebbles or grains of sand, which cannot hold water, nor clay, which binds up and retains water in a solid gluey mass. It is the presence of well-decomposed organic material that enables soil to hold moisture *and* air simultaneously, so that both are readily available to plants. Incorporating well-decomposed organic matter (see p.21) is the most useful way to improve soil texture, either for an entire area or as plants are planted.

CHOOSING A HEALTHY PLANT

Try to resist buying plants that are in poor condition, even if it is the sole example offered of a plant you really want. Nursing a pathetic specimen could take an entire growing season, and, with container-grown plants now so widely available it is likely that you will find a healthier specimen later on, that can be planted right away. In practice, however, few gardeners can resist taking pity on a neglected or undernourished plant—but you must always harden your heart to those showing signs of pest infestation or disease. You risk importing problems that could spread to other plants.

should always have been raised in containers, and not hastily uprooted from a nursery bed or field and potted up. There should be no sign of roots at the surface.

Look at the base of the pot for protruding roots, a sign that the plant is potbound (has been in its container for too long). Always lift the pot to make sure roots have not grown out underneath the pot, another sign of a badly potbound specimen. Crowded roots do not penetrate the surrounding soil readily after planting, and the plant will not establish well.

WHAT TO BUY

Plants offered for sale should be clearly labeled, healthy, undamaged, and free from pests and diseases. Inspect the plant thoroughly for signs of neglect. With balled-and-burlapped plants, check that the root ball is firm and evenly moist, with the netting or burlap intact. Containerized plants

Leaves are glossy and healthy

Early pruning has produced an attractive shape

Roots are well grown but not crowded

Good specimen This well-grown skimmia has a substantial root ball that is in good proportion to the bushy top growth.

Healthy bulb A sound neck, tunic (the papery outer covering) and basal plate (where the roots grow) all recommend this bulb to the buyer.

Sound, firm basal plate

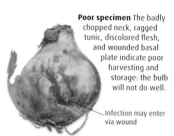

Poor specimen The badly chopped neck, ragged tunic, discolored flesh, and wounded basal plate indicate poor harvesting and storage: the bulb will not do well.

Infection may enter via wound

HEALTHY GROWTH

Strong top growth is another key factor. Avoid plants with pale or yellowing foliage, damaged shoot tips, or etiolated growth (soft, pale, overextended, and weak-looking shoots). Look at the soil surface: it should not be covered in weeds, mosses, or liverworts.

With herbaceous plants, small healthy specimens are cheaper than large ones and will soon grow once planted. Groups of three or five plants often look better than single specimens. With all types of herbaceous plants, including young annuals and bedding plants, pick out the stockiest, bushiest specimens, with (if appropriate) plenty of flower buds, rather than open flowers.

PLANT SHAPE AND FORM

When buying trees and shrubs, which are to make a long-lasting contribution to your garden, choose plants with a well-balanced branch framework and with top growth that is in proportion to the rootball or pot. A stocky, multistemmed plant usually makes the best well-rounded shrub, while young trees with a single trunk should have just that, right from the start. A one-sided shrub may of course be acceptable for wall-training, but will put on more growth from the base, and thus cover space better, if its shoot tips are pruned after planting.

BUYING BULBS

Buy bulbs (see above) as if they were onions you were intending to cook—reject any that are soft, discolored, diseased, or damaged. While it is not ideal, there is no harm in buying bulbs that have begun to sprout a little, as long as the bulbs are planted soon afterward.

PREPARING THE SOIL

While the best plants for your garden are those suited to the growing conditions available, most soils can be improved to extend the range of plants that can be grown.

IDENTIFYING YOUR SOIL TYPE

Investigating your soil to discover just what its qualities are is one of the most useful things you can do to ensure thriving plants. Generally, soil will be either sandy or have a clay texture, or somewhere between the two. If your soil has a light, loose texture and drains rapidly, it is probably sandy. Sandy soil has a rough, gritty feel when rubbed and makes a characteristic rasping, scraping sound against the blade of a spade. Although easy to dig, it is low in fertility. Clay soil is heavy, sticky, cold, easy to mold when wet, and can become waterlogged. It is difficult to work but is often very fertile. A good mix of the two—a "medium loam"—is ideal.

To further establish which plants will be best suited by your soil, you can determine its pH value (to what degree it is acidic or alkaline) and the levels of various nutrients it contains using simple testing kits available at most garden centers.

CLEARING WEEDS

In a new garden, or in a previously uncultivated area, the first task is to clear away any debris and weeds. This step is essential, since weeds will compete with your plants for light, moisture, and nutrients. For perennial weeds, an alternative to laborious hand-clearing is to spray the ground in the season before planting with a systemic herbicide that will kill their roots. This is best done in early summer, when weeds are growing strongly. Some provinces and municipalities have banned the use of pesticides for cosmetic purposes, so they will not be available in these areas.

Isolated perennial weeds can be forked out carefully, removing all root fragments. Annual weeds may be hoed out immediately before planting.

WORKING THE SOIL

Digging or forking over the soil helps break down compacted areas and increase aeration, which encourages good plant growth. The deeper you dig the better, but never bring poor-quality subsoil up to the surface: plants need all the nourishment that the darker, more

Digging with ease The correct tools and technique make digging more comfortable, and safer for your back. Test the weight and height of a spade before buying, and always keep your back straight when using it.

Forking over Drive the fork into the ground, then lift and turn the fork over to break up and aerate soil. Spread a layer of organic matter over the soil first so that it is incorporated into the soil as you work.

nutritious topsoil can give them. If you need to dig deeply, remove the topsoil, fork over the subsoil, then put the topsoil back in.

Dig heavy clay soils in late fall. The weathering effects of frost and cold over the winter helps improve the soil's texture by breaking it down into smaller pieces. Avoid digging wet soil as this damages the soil structure. Incorporate soil amendments as you go.

ADDING SOIL AMENDMENTS

Digging and forking will improve soil texture to some extent, but to really bring a soil to life, the addition of a soil amendment is invaluable. The drainage, aeration (the ability to store oxygen, which is important for

healthy root development), fertility and moisture-holding properties of most soil types can be improved simply by adding well-rotted organic matter. This is best done in the season before planting, to allow the soil to settle. Well-rotted manure, compost, and leafmold (shredded leaves that have been partly composted) enhance the moisture retention of a sandy soil and improve nutrient levels. Applied regularly, they improve the structure of clay soil. Clay soils can be further opened up by the addition of coarse sand to a depth of at least 12in (30cm). Organic mulches of bark, cocoa shells, or wood chips are also eventually broken down into the soil.

PLANTING

Careful planting saves both time and money, and well-chosen plants positioned in optimum conditions will perform well and should resist attack from pests and diseases.

PREPLANTING PLANNING

Before planting, check the potential heights and spreads of plants to ensure that you leave the correct distances between them. When designing plant groups, consider different plants' season of interest, including their appearance in winter.

WHEN TO PLANT

In most areas, the best planting seasons are fall and spring. Fall planting allows plants to establish quickly before the onset of winter, since the soil is still warm and moist enough to permit root growth. Spring planting is better in cold areas for plants that are not reliably hardy.

Perennials can be planted at any time of the year, except during extreme conditions. They should grow rapidly and usually perform well within their first year. To reduce stress on a perennial when

Basic planting Soak plants well in a bucket of water. Position the plant so that the root ball surface is flush with soil level, then fill around the sides.

Settling the soil Backfill the hole, gently firming the soil to ensure good contact with the roots. Water in well, then add a layer of mulch over the root area.

planting during dry or hot weather, prune off its flowers and the largest leaves before planting. In full, hot sun, shade the plant for a few days.

PLANTING TECHNIQUES

For container-grown or balled-and-burlapped plants, dig a hole about twice the size of the rootball. If necessary, water the hole in advance to ensure that the surrounding soil is thoroughly moist. Carefully remove the plant from its pot and gently tease out the roots with your fingers. Check that the plant is at the correct depth, then backfill the hole with a mix of compost, fertilizer, and soil. Firm the soil, then water thoroughly to settle it around the roots. Apply a mulch around, but not touching, the plant base to aid moisture retention and suppress weeds.

For bare-root plants, the planting technique is essentially the same, but ensure that the roots never dry out before replanting. Dig holes in advance, and, in case of delay, heel the plants in or store in moist sand or compost until replanting. Bare-root plants need a planting hole wide enough to accommodate their roots when fully spread, and deep enough to ensure the final soil level will be the same as it was in the pot or nursery. After planting, press the soil gently to firm.

WALL SHRUBS AND CLIMBERS

Always erect supports before planting. Plant wall shrubs and climbers at least 10in (25cm) from walls and fences so that the roots are not in a rain shadow, and lean the plant slightly inward toward the wall. Fan out the main shoots and attach them firmly to their support. Shrubs and nonclinging climbers will need further tying in as they grow; the shoots of twining climbers may also need gentle guidance.

ANNUALS AND BEDDING

To ensure that these plants look their best for the little time that they are in flower, a moist soil and regular deadheading are essential. Bedding plants need regular feeding throughout the growing season, especially in containers, but many annuals flower best in soil that is not overly fertile. Many annuals are available as seedling "plugs," which should be grown on under cover. When planted, the well-developed root system suffers little damage, ensuring rapid growth.

PLANTING BULBS

In general, bulbs can be planted at between three and five times their own depth. Plant small bulbs quite shallowly; those of bigger plants such as large tulips more deeply.

UNDERSTANDING PLANT NAMES

All plants in the *Great Canadian Plant Guide* are listed by their current botanical names. The basic unit of plant classification is the species, with a two-part name correctly given in italic text: the first part is the genus, and the second part is the species name, or "epithet."

GENUS

A group of one or more plants that share a wide range of characteristics, such as *Chrysanthemum* or *Rosa*, is known as a genus. A genus name is quite like a family name, because it is shared by a group of individuals that are all closely related. Hybrid genera (crosses between plants derived from two genera, such as x *Cupressocyparis*), are denoted by the x symbol before the genus name.

SPECIES

A group of plants capable of breeding together to produce similar offspring are known as a species. In a two-part botanical name, the species epithet distinguishes a species from other plants in the same genus, rather like a given name. A species epithet usually refers to a particular feature of that species, such as *tricolor* (of three colors), or it may refer to the person who first discovered the plant.

SUBSPECIES, VARIETY, AND FORMA

Naturally occurring variants of a species—subspecies, variety, or forma—are given an additional name in italics, prefixed by "subsp.," "var.," or "f.". All of these are concerned with minor

Genus/Species *Malus floribunda* is in the same genus as apples. Its species name means "mass of flowers."

Variety *Dictamnus albus* var. *purpureus* has purplish flowers instead of the white of the species.

Hybrid The x symbol after the genus name in *Osmanthus* x *burkwoodii* denotes its hybrid status.

subdivisions of a species, differing slightly in their botanical structure or appearance.

HYBRIDS

If different species within the same genus are cultivated together, they may cross-breed, giving rise to hybrids sharing attributes of both parents. This process is exploited by gardeners who wish to combine the valued characteristics of two distinct plants. The new hybrid is then increased by propagation. An example is *Camellia* x *williamsii*, which has the parents *C. japonica* and *C. saluensis*.

CULTIVARS

Variations of a species that are selected or artificially raised are given a vernacular name. This appears in single quotation marks after the species name. Some

cultivars are also registered with trademark names, often used commercially instead of the valid cultivar name. If the parentage is obscure or complex, the cultivar name may directly follow the generic name—*Iris* 'Muse's Visit'. In a few cases, particularly roses, the plant is known by a popular selling name, which is not the correct cultivar name; in this guide, the popular name is listed before the cultivar name, as in *Rosa* BONICA 'Meidomonac'.

GROUPS AND SERIES

Several very similar cultivars may, for convenience, be classified in named Groups or Series that denote their similarities. Sometimes, they can be a deliberate mixture of cultivars of the same overall character but with flowers in different colors.

Cultivar The species parentage of plants like *Osteospermum* 'Buttermilk' is complex and therefore not given.

Cultivar or species *Ophiopogon planiscapus* 'Nigrescens' is an unusual form cultivated for its black leaves.

Seed series *Antirrhinum majus* Sonnet Series is a mixture of brightly colored cultivars for summer bedding.

ANNUALS AND BEDDING PLANTS

Some of the finest bedding plants you can buy are listed in this section, together with advice on where and how to grow them for the best effect. Using these plants will enable you to map out a wide range of designs, including the quiet, colorful, minimilist, subtropical, and formal. There are additional bedding plants in the A—Z section of this book.

◄ *Abutilon* 'Souvenir de Bonn'

Flowering maple is a showy shrub for a large container or a temporary border display. It has cream-margined leaves and hanging orange flowers. Shelter over winter in a frost-free place.

CULTIVATION: *Grow in well-drained, fertile, soil-based potting medium, in full sun. Minimum temperature 40°F (4°C).*

☼ ◊ ◊ Z9   ↕↔to 10ft (3m)

Agastache foeniculum 'Golden Jubilee' ►

Bushy anise hyssop creates a mound of golden green foliage topped by long-lasting, scented purple flowers from midsummer. Good for borders.

CULTIVATION: *Provide fertile, well-drained soil, in full sun.*

☼ ◊ Z6   ↕24in (60cm) ↔12in (30cm)

◄ *Ageratum houstonianum* 'Blue Lagoon'

Forming a low mound, ageratums are ideal edging for summer displays. 'Blue Lagoon' has rich blue-purple flowers, borne in profusion throughout summer.

CULTIVATION: *Grow in fertile, moist but well-drained soil, with sun and shelter.*

☼ ◊ ◊ Annual   ↕↔6–12in (15–30cm)

◀ *Ageratum houstonianum* 'Shell Pink Hawaii'

With its light pink flowers, this short, compact floss flower forms a mound of color and creates an effective mix with white and blue forms.

CULTIVATION: *Grow in fertile, moist but well-drained soil, with sun and shelter.*

☼ ◊ Annual ↕↔6–12in (15–30cm)

Amaranthus caudatus ▶

The bushy, upright growth of love-lies-bleeding produces fun, eye-catching, reddish-purple summer tassels, up to 24in (60cm) long, which make good cut flowers. Best against a wall.

CULTIVATION: *Provide moderately fertile, humus-rich, moist soil, in full sun.*

☼ ◊ Annual
↕3–5ft (1–1.5m) ↔18–30in (45–75cm)

◀ *Anagallis monellii* subsp. *linifolia*

The short, free-branching blue pimpernel, from the Mediterranean, is prolifically covered by (usually) blue flowers in summer. It makes an excellent show in pots and hanging baskets.

CULTIVATION: *Grow in moderately fertile, moist but not wet soil, in a sunny place.*

☼ ◊ ◊ Z7 ↕8in (20cm) ↔16in (40cm)

A

◀ *Antirrhinum majus* Sonnet Series

These snapdragons bear fragrant, two-lipped flowers all summer in mixed or single colors. They are good for summer bedding and as cut flowers. Deadhead to prolong flowering.

CULTIVATION: *Grow in well-drained, fertile soil, in full sun.*

☼ ◊ Z8
‡12–24in (30–60cm) ↔12in (30cm)

Atriplex hortensis var. *rubra* ▶

Valued for its attractive blood- or purple-red foliage, this plant contrasts boldly with adjacent white flowers. Remove the flower buds as they diminish the effect.

CULTIVATION: *Grow in well-drained, dry, poor to average soil, in full sun.*

☼ ◊ Annual
‡to 4ft (1.2m) ↔12in (30cm)

◀ *Begonia* 'Peardrop'

The dark, pointed leaves of this compact begonia set off the peachy flowers beautifully. The plant's rounded shape lends itself to a range of container plantings. It flowers all summer. Will overwinter at minimum temperature 55°F (13°C).

CULTIVATION: *Grow in well-drained, fertile potting medium, out of direct sun.*

☼ ◊ ◐ Tender ‡↔10in (25cm)

◄ *Bellis perennis*

A winter annual, planted in fall for spring bloom. The white flowers, with yellow centers, are often tinged pink. Many named forms are available with white, pink, or red; single or double flowers.

CULTIVATION: *Grow in well-drained, moderately fertile soil, in full sun or part shade.*

☼ ☀ ◊ Z6 ↕↔2–8in (5–20cm)

◄ *Beta vulgaris* 'Bright Lights'

A variety of edible Swiss chard, these plants have variously colored stems, including red, pink, gold, and orange, and large, green or bronze leaves. Grow with other vegetables or in borders.

CULTIVATION: *Grow in fertile, moist but well-drained soil, in sun or light shade.*

☼ ☀ ◊ ◔ Biennial, grown as annual
↕20in (50cm) ↔18in (45cm)

Bidens ferulifolia 'Golden Eye' ►

The bright yellow, late summer flowers on long thin stems, with fernlike foliage, make it a good choice for tumbling out of hanging baskets, pots, and over low walls.

CULTIVATION: *Provide fairly fertile, moist but well-drained soil, in full sun.*

☼ ◊ ◔ Z9
↕9–12in (23–30cm) ↔indefinite

◀ *Brachyscome iberidiflora* Bravo Mix

A mix of Swan River daisies, mainly in white, blue, and violet. Good in summer pots and windowboxes, for edging paths, and in rock gardens.

CULTIVATION: *Grow in light, fertile, well-drained soil, in a sunny position.*

☼ ◊ Annual
‡10in (25cm) ↔9in (23cm)

Brassica oleracea cultivars ▶

Ornamental cabbages make fun plants for the front of a border, especially in fall or winter when the leaf colours intensify in the cold. Not for eating.

CULTIVATION: *Provide fertile, well-drained soil, with plenty of sun.*

☼ ◊ Grown as an annual
‡24in (60cm) ↔10in (25cm)

◀ *Briza maxima*

The small seedheads of greater quaking grass add a gentle touch to cottage gardens in summer, and turn from red or purple to beige. When planted in drifts, the heads clearly sway in the breeze.

CULTIVATION: *Any soil, provided it is well-drained, with full sun.*

☼ ◊ Annual
‡18–24in (45–60cm) ↔10in (25cm)

◀ *Browallia speciosa*

A mounded plant covered with clusters of blue, white, or violet flowers for much of the summer. There are several named forms, some with two-toned flowers.

CULTIVATION: *Grow in well-drained, fertile soil, in full sun; or in part shade where summers are humid.*

☼ ◐ ◊ Annual
‡8–12in (20–30cm) ↔10in (25cm)

Calendula 'Fiesta Gitana' ▶

This dwarf, fast-growing marigold produces double flowerheads in orange or yellow in spring and fall. The leaves are hairy and aromatic. May self-seed.

CULTIVATION: *Grow in well-drained, poor to moderately fertile soil, in sun or partial shade. Deadhead regularly to prolong flowering.*

☼ ◐ ◊ Annual
‡to 12in (30cm) ↔12–18in (30–45cm)

◀ *Callistephus chinensis* Ostrich Plume Series

China asters perk up the late summer to fall border with their mainly pink and red blooms. Water well in dry spells and deadhead to promote more buds; good for cut flowers.

CULTIVATION: *Provide moist, well-drained, fertile soil, in full sun.*

☼ ◊ Annual
‡to 24in (60cm) ↔12in (30cm)

◀ *Canna* 'President'

Red, resembling gladiolus, late summer flowers are perched above large, paddlelike, blue-green leaves. Good in subtropical schemes, and as a focal point surrounded by annuals. Lift tubers in fall and store in a frost-free location.

CULTIVATION: *Best in fertile soil, in full sun. Water well over summer.*

☼ ◊ ◑ Tender
↕4ft (1.2m) ↔20in (50cm)

Canna 'Striata' ▶

A striking, late-summer combination of orange flowers above the large, yellow green leaves with vivid yellow veins. Plant where it will allow the sun to shine through the foliage.

CULTIVATION: *Provide fertile soil, full sun, and water well. Minimum temperature 32°F (0°C).*

☼ ◊ ◑ Tender
↕5ft (1.5m) ↔20in (50cm)

◀ *Catharanthus roseus* 'Pacific Punch'

The excellent Pacifica range of Madagascar periwinkles produce colorful spring flowers, 'Punch' being red, white, or rose-red. Use as border gap fillers, or in pots and hanging baskets.

CULTIVATION: *Provide average, well-drained soil, in full sun. Minimum temperature 41°F (5°C).*

☼ ◊ Tender   ↕↔12–14in (30–35cm)

◀ *Celosia spicata* 'Flamingo Feather'

This coxcomb gives a lovely show of light pink summer flowers, which gradually fade to off-white, on upward-pointing spikes. They make excellent cut flowers, fresh or dry. Deadhead for more flowers.

CULTIVATION: *Best in moist, well-drained fertile soil, in full sun, in a sheltered site.*

☼ ◊ ◖ Annual
↕24–36in (60–90cm) ↔18in (45cm)

Centaurea cyanus Florence Series ▶

Compact plants offer plentiful cherry red, pink, or white summer flowers, good for cutting. Sow in drifts in cottage or wild gardens, or plant in patio pots.

CULTIVATION: *Grow in average, well-drained soil, in bright sun.*

☼ ◊ Annual
↕to 14in (35cm) ↔to 10in (25cm)

◀ *Clarkia amoena* Azalea Hybrids

The semidouble, azalea-like summer flowers, with a satin texture, appear in clusters at the ends of leafy shoots. Grow plenty of spare plants, cutting them for flower arrangements.

CULTIVATION: *Grow in average, slightly acid, well-drained soil, in bright light.*

☼ ◑ ◊ ◖ Annual
↕12in (30cm) ↔10in (25cm)

C

◀ *Clarkia amoena* Satin Series

With a short, bushy habit, the plants have summer flowers 2in (5cm) wide in various colors, often with an attractive white margin or contrasting center. Very effective at the front of an island bed.

CULTIVATION: *Provide average, slightly acid, well-drained soil, in bright light.*

☼ ◑ ◊ ◖ Annual
‡to 8in (20cm) ↔12in (30cm)

Cleome hassleriana 'Helen Campbell' ▶

The white spider flower has stiffly upright, spiny stems and is topped by unusual, beautiful flowers. Grow cleomes in bold groups in the middle of a border, giving plenty of impact.

CULTIVATION: *Provide light, fertile, well-drained soil, in a sunny position.*

☼ ◊ Annual ‡to 5ft (1.5m) ↔18in (45cm)

◀ *Cleome hassleriana* 'Rose Queen'

A good choice for pastel-colored schemes or for softening bold arrangements, 'Rose Queen' has characteristic stiff, spiny stems and is topped by deep pink flowers.

CULTIVATION: *Provide light, fertile, well-drained soil, in a sunny position.*

☼ ◊ Annual
‡to 5ft (1.5m) ↔18in (45cm)

◀ *Cleome hassleriana* 'Violet Queen'

The reddish violet form of the spider flower is equally effective in a one-colored group or in a mix with white and pink cleomes. For slightly shorter plants, don't sow seed until mid-spring.

CULTIVATION: *Provide light, fertile, well-drained soil, in a sunny position.*

☼ ◊ Annual ‡to 5ft (1.5m) ↔18in (45cm)

Cobaea scandens ▶

An extraordinarily vigorous climber, the cup-and-saucer vine needs a large space, and a strong support to cling onto. The fleshy, bell-shaped flowers turn from creamy green to purple.

CULTIVATION: *Provide light, fertile, well-drained soil, in a sheltered sunny position. Minimum temperature 41ºF (5ºC).*

☼ ◊ ◗ Tender ‡12–15ft (4–5m)

◀ *Consolida ajacis*

The delphinium-like larkspur makes a free-and-easy cottage garden plant. The stiff, upright stems have densely packed flower spikes in a range of colours in summer. Beware of slugs and snails.

CULTIVATION: *Grow in light, fertile, well-drained soil, in full sun.*

☼ ◊ Annual
‡12–48in (30–120cm) ↔9–12in (23–30cm)

◀ *Convolvulus tricolor* 'Royal Ensign'

A good choice in rock gardens, border gap-filler, and for hanging baskets, this ornamental bindweed has a prolific show of short-lived, deep blue flowers in summer, which close up at night.

CULTIVATION: *Best in poor to average, well-drained soil, with full sun and shelter.*

☼ ◊ Annual   ↕↔12in (30cm)

Coreopsis tinctoria ▶

The loose, open habit and sunny yellow petals, brown-red at the base, with a dark red eye in the center, make tickseed an excellent summer annual. Grow in a sunny border.

CULTIVATION: *Provide fertile, well-drained soil, in full sun or semi-shade.*

☼ ◑ ◊ Annual
↕to 4ft (1.2m) ↔12–18in (30–45cm)

◀ *Cosmos bipinnatus* Sonata Series Mixed

A good choice for exposed gardens and the front of a border, Sonata Mixed freely branches and is liberally covered by red, pink, or white flowers in summer above thin stems with fine leaves.

CULTIVATION: *Grow in average, moist but well-drained soil, in full sun.*

☼ ◊ ◒ Annual   ↕↔to 12in (30cm)

◄ *Crepis rubra*

Hawk's beard has slightly arching stems with long-lasting, small, pinkish red flowers from spring on, above a ground-hugging rosette of leaves. Plant at the front of a border and in pots.

CULTIVATION: *Grow in well-drained soil, in full sun.*

☼ ◊ Annual
↕16in (40cm) ↔6in (15cm)

Dianthus nanus '**Magic Charms**' ►

Giving a low-level mix of sweet-scented reds, pinks, and whites, 'Magic Charms' is ideal for pots, borders, rock gardens, and for growing alongside a path.

CULTIVATION: *Grow in well-drained soil, in full sun.*

☼ ◊ Z7, but short-lived
↕12in (90cm) ↔12in (30cm)

◄ *Diascia* CORAL BELLE

Twinspurs, named for their spurred flowers, are useful trailing perennials for temporary edging or hanging baskets. CORAL BELLE bears a profusion of salmon-pink flowers on wiry stems all summer.

CULTIVATION: *Grow in moist but well-drained, fertile soil, in sun.*

☼ ◊ ◑ Z7   ↕6in (15cm) ↔12in (30cm)

F

◄ *Felicia amelloides* 'Santa Anita'

This blue daisy, with white-marked, bright green foliage, is a rounded, evergreen subshrub. Large, daisylike flowers, open from late spring to fall. Good in containers.

CULTIVATION: *Grow in well-drained, fairly fertile soil, in sun. Dislikes damp. Minimum temperature 37ºF (3ºC).*

☼ ◊ Tender   ↕↔12–24in (30–60cm)

Fuchsia 'Patio Princess' ►

Bearing pendulous pink and white flowers all summer, this upright fuchsia is good for patio pots. Pinch out shoots to encourage bushiness. With care, tender fuchsias can be overwintered indoors.

CULTIVATION: *Grow in moist but well-drained soil, with some shade. Minimum temperature 35ºF (2ºC).*

☼ ◑ ◊ ◖ Tender   ↕↔12in (30cm) or more

◄ *Gaillardia* 'Kobold'

A lively choice for the front of borders in need of perking up. The flowers have a red eye, and yellow-edged red petals. Good for cutting. Flowers appear throughout summer. Short-lived unless divided frequently.

CULTIVATION: *Best in fertile, well-drained soil, and full sun.*

☼ ◊ Z3   ↕↔12in (30cm)

◀ *Helianthus annuus* 'Russian Giant'

A fun, shooting-up giant of a sunflower, which can be grown in an avenue, flanking a path, or a children's garden. Leave the seeds for the birds, and beware of slugs and snails in spring.

CULTIVATION: *Provide humus-rich, moist, well-drained soil, in full sun.*

☼ ◊ ◊ Annual
‡to 11ft (3.5m) ↔ to 18in (45cm)

Helianthus annuus 'Velvet Queen' ▶

'Velvet Queen' has unusual, attractive reddish flowers with dark centers. Grow at the back of a border to contrast with shorter white and yellow plants.

CULTIVATION: *Provide humus-rich, moist, well-drained soil, in full sun.*

☼ ◊ ◊ Annual
‡5ft (1.5m) ↔ to 18in (45cm)

◀ *Helichrysum petiolare* 'Variegatum'

A trailing, evergreen foliage shrub, this plant is useful in container or basket displays as a foil for flowering plants. Pinch prune to encourage bushiness.

CULTIVATION: *Grow in moist but well-drained soil, in sun. Minimum temperature 35°F (2°C).*

☼ ☀ ◊ ◊ Tender
‡to 20in (50cm) ↔ 6ft (2m) or more

H

◄ *Hesperis matronalis* var. *albiflora*

Sweet rocket is an invaluable, tall, sweetly scented, informal biennial, which freely self-seeds, for the wild or cottage garden. It effectively contrasts with formal shapes, like box topiary.

CULTIVATION: *Grow in fertile, moist but well-drained soil, in sun or semi-shade.*

☼ ☀ ◊ ◊ Z4
‡36in (90cm) ↔18in (45cm)

Iberis umbellata Fairy Series ►

The abundant, colorful, spring to summer flowers, in white, pink, and purple, are invaluable for pots, gaps in patio paving, and the front of borders.

CULTIVATION: *Best in poor to moderate, moist but well-drained soil, in full sun.*

☼ ◊ ◊ Annual
‡12in (30cm) ↔to 9in (23cm)

◄ *Impatiens* New Guinea Hybrids

A first-rate choice for summer-long color, these busy Lizzies come in a wide range of bright hues, some with eye-catching, variegated foliage. Superb potted plants and gap-fillers between shrubs.

CULTIVATION: *Grow in humus-rich, moist but well-drained soil, in semi-shade. Minimum temperature 41°F (5°C).*

☼ ◊ ◊ Tender ‡14in (35cm) ↔12in (30cm)

◀ *Ipomoea nil* 'Scarlet O'Hara'

A bright red-flowering, vigorous, climbing morning glory that is equally effective when spiraling around a wigwam of stakes, up a trellis, or threading through adjacent shrubs. Usually grown as an annual.

CULTIVATION: *Provide moderately fertile, well-drained soil, in a sunny position.*

☼ ◊ Tender ‡to 15ft (5m) or more

Ipomoea quamoclit ▶

From tropical South America, the star glory has pretty, fernlike leaves and small, showy, flowers, which are usually bright scarlet but can sometimes be white. Provide a trellis-like support.

CULTIVATION: *Best in moderately fertile, well-drained soil, in full sun. Minimum temperature 50°F (10°C).*

☼ ◊ Annual ‡6ft (2m) or more

◀ *Lantana* 'Radiation'

Wonderfully vibrant flowerheads are produced all summer above the wrinkled, dark green leaves of this prickly subshrub. Use it for containers in sun. Overwinter indoors.

CULTIVATION: *Grow in moist but well-drained soil, in sun. Feed monthly. Minimum temperature 50°F (10°C).*

☼ ◊ ◓ Tender
‡18–24in (45–60cm) ↔10in (25cm)

L

◀ *Linaria maroccana* 'Northern Lights'

Good for cut flowers, 'Northern Lights' has long-lasting summer flowers in a wide range of colors. It is excellent in informal drifts in cottage and Mediterranean-style gardens.

CULTIVATION: *Provide moderately fertile, light, well-drained soil, in full sun.*

☼ ◊ Annual ‡24in (60cm) ↔6in (15cm)

Linum grandiflorum 'Rubrum' ▶

A flamboyant, summer gap-filler, 'Rubrum' has a regular supply of bright crimson flowers with a dark eye. It makes a smart, lively contrast when mixed with the pure white form, 'Bright Eyes'.

CULTIVATION: *Best in moderately fertile, humus-rich, sharp-draining soil, in sun.*

☼ ◊ Annual ‡to 18in (45cm) ↔6in (15cm)

◀ *Lobelia erinus* Cascade Series Mixed

A good choice for hanging baskets, windowboxes, or tubs, with the trailing, flowering stems spilling over the sides from summer to fall. Alternatively, let them soften the edge of a path.

CULTIVATION: *Best in deep, fertile, moist soil, in sun or partial shade.*

☼ ☀ ◊ Annual ‡↔6in (15cm)

◄ *Lobularia maritima* 'Carpet of Snow'

An extremely useful plant for growing in the gaps of brick paths and patio paving. 'Carpet of Snow' produces attractive clumps of white flowers in summer. Alternate it with 'Navy Blue'.

CULTIVATION: *Grow in light, moderately fertile, well-drained soil, in full sun.*

☼ ◊ Annual
‡4in (10cm) ↔12in (30cm)

Lunaria annua 'Munstead Purple' ►

This purple-flowered honesty adds a free-and-easy look to informal borders. The papery seedheads can be picked for dried arrangements, or left to self-seed.

CULTIVATION: *Grow in fertile, moist but well-drained soil, in sun or semi-shade.*

☼ ☀ ◊ ◑ Annual
‡36in (90cm) ↔12in (30cm)

◄ *Lunaria annua* 'Variegata'

A popular cottage garden annual, this honesty has cream-edged leaves and reddish-purple flowers. They are followed by papery seedheads, which can be used in dried arrangements.

CULTIVATION: *Provide fertile, moist but well-drained soil, in sun or semi-shade.*

☼ ☀ ◊ ◑ Annual
‡36in (90cm) ↔12in (30cm)

M

◀ *Malope trifida*

Looking like a bushy hollyhock, the annual mallow has pale to dark purple-red flowers from summer to fall, and can be squeezed into most gaps in the middle ranks of the border. Good for cottage gardens.

CULTIVATION: *Best in average, moist but well-drained soil, in bright sun.*

☼ ◐ ◌ ◑ Annual
↕ to 36in (90cm) ↔ 9in (23cm)

Matthiola longipetala subsp. *bicornis* ▶

Valued for its rich perfume, night-scented stock is best planted under windows or around seats. Its small summer flowers are pink, mauve, or purple.

CULTIVATION: *Best in average, moist but well-drained soil, with some shelter.*

☼ ◌ ◑ Annual
↕ 14in (35cm) ↔ 9in (23cm)

◀ *Mimulus aurantiacus*

This domed or sprawling, evergreen shrub bears open trumpet-shaped, yellow, orange, or dark red flowers from late summer to fall. May be overwintered in a greenhouse.

CULTIVATION: *Best in well-drained soil, in full sun. Often short-lived, but easily propogated by cuttings in mid-summer.*

☼ ◌ Z8   ↕↔ 3ft (1m)

◀ *Mirabilis jalapa*

The four o'clock flower opens in late afternoon on summer days (but will stay closed in cloudy weather). It has a gentle, citrus scent and often different-colored flowers on the same plant. Grow in pots or borders. Lift tubers in fall and store at 45°F (7°C).

CULTIVATION: *Best in average, well-drained soil, in full sun; water well.*

☼ ◊ Tender   ↕↔24in (60cm) or more

Mirabilis jalapa 'Red Glow' ▶

Similar to *M. jalapa* (above), except that 'Red Glow' has bright red, open flowers set against rich green leaves. When the flowers open in sunny weather they emit a sweet scent.

CULTIVATION: *Provide average, well-drained soil, in full sun; water well.*

☼ ◊ Tender   ↕↔24in (60cm)

◀ *Myosotis sylvatica* 'Blue Ball'

A compact forget-me-not, it has ball-shaped azure blue flowers from spring to early summer, and makes a relaxed, informal background to tall tulips in red, yellow, white, and blue. A biennial that flowers the second spring.

CULTIVATION: *Best in average to poor, moist but well-drained soil, in sun or partial shade.*

☼ ☼ ◊ ◊ Z4   ↕↔6in (15cm)

◀ *Nemesia strumosa* 'Sundrops'

The bright mix of colors includes warm apricot, cream, and shades of red, pink, and orange on compact, bushy plants. They give a good show in early and midsummer in borders and patio pots.

CULTIVATION: *Grow in average, moist but well-drained, slightly acidic soil, in sun.*

☼ ◊ ◊ Annual ‡↔10in (25cm)

Nemophila menziesii 'Penny Black' ▶

With white-rimmed, dark purple summer flowers, 'Penny Black' adds a strong note to white plantings, and tubs with vivid colours. Once established, it self-seeds.

CULTIVATION: *Grow in fertile, moist but well-drained soil, in sun or light shade.*

☼ ☀ ◊ ◊ Annual
‡8in (20cm) ↔12in (30cm)

◀ *Nicandra physalodes*

The free-branching, fast-growing South American shoo-fly has a long supply of violet-blue flowers from summer to fall. These are followed by round green berries in a papery coat, which are good for winter dried arrangements.

CULTIVATION: *Grow in fertile, moist but well-drained soil, in full sun.*

☼ ◊ Annual
‡to 36in (90cm) ↔12in (30cm)

Nicotiana x *sanderae* Domino Series ◄

The summer flowers—which come in a wide color range, including bicolored—provide a useful change in scale from the bigger, bolder nicotianas, and are equally suited to informal settings.

CULTIVATION: *Provide fertile, moist but well-drained soil, in sun or semi-shade.*

☼ ☀ ◊ ◑ Annual
↕↔12–18in (30–45cm)

Nolana paradoxa 'Blue Bird' ►

Bright and punchy, the dark blue flowers (sometimes purple or purple-blue) make a highly effective block planting with other summer annuals.

CULTIVATION: *Grow in any moderately fertile, well-drained soil, in full sun.*

☼ ◊ Annual
↕8–10in (20–25cm) ↔to 24in (60cm)

◄ *Osteospermum* 'Whirligig'

Cape daisies make fine bedding plants that flower all summer, closing at night and in dull weather. 'Whirligig' has quilled petals that may revert if the weather gets too hot and dry.

CULTIVATION: *Grow in moist but well-drained soil, in sun. Minimum temperature 45°F (7°C).*

☼ ◊ ◑ Tender ↕↔14in (35cm)

◀ *Papaver nudicaule* 'Flamenco'

The pastel pink flowers of this poppy have white-fluted edges, and when planted in large numbers produce beautiful drifts of summer color. Excellent in "natural plantings."

CULTIVATION: *Grow in deep, fertile, well-drained soil, in a sunny site.*

☼ ◊ Z3 ‡20in (50cm) ↔6in (15cm)

Papaver nudicaule 'Meadow Pastels' ▶

This wide-ranging mix of pastel and bicolored summer flowers, on strong, sturdy stems, add a natural touch. They contrast well with geometric shapes.

CULTIVATION: *Best in deep, fertile, well-drained soil, in a sunny site.*

☼ ◊ Z3 ‡24in (60cm) ↔8in (20cm)

◀ *Papaver rhoeas* 'Mother of Pearl'

An excellent choice for a soft, pastel-colored scheme. The delicate shades include lilac, blue, peach, pink, white, and gray. A dark green background will help bring out the summer colors.

CULTIVATION: *Provide deep, fertile, well-drained soil, in a sunny site.*

☼ ◊ Annual
‡12in (30cm) ↔6in (15cm)

◀ *Pennisetum setaceum* 'Rubrum'

Fountain grass is an impressive upright container or bedding plant. Its beautifully fluffy red flower spikes arch over the deep purple foliage in late summer. It tolerates drought.

CULTIVATION: *Grow in well-drained soil, in open, sunny conditions. Minimum temperature 36°F (2°C).*

☼ ◔ ◊ Tender ↕↔36in (90cm)

Petunia 'Prism Sunshine' ▶

A good choice for a bright flash of summer color in borders and hanging baskets, this petunia has large yellow flowers, which gradually fade to cream. Will withstand light frosts.

CULTIVATION: *Provide light, well-drained soil in full sun, and a sheltered position.*

☼ ◊ Annual
↕9–12in (23–30cm) ↔12–36in(30–90cm)

◀ *Petunia* Surfinia Hybrids

Surfinias are a good choice for hanging baskets, as they are trailing, vigorous, and free-branching with medium-sized flowers that can withstand rain.

CULTIVATION: *Provide light, well-drained soil, in full sun, and wind-shelter.*

☼ ◊ Annual
↕9–16in (23–40cm) ↔12–36in (30–90cm)

R

◀ ***Ricinus communis*
'Carmencita'**

The soaring caster oil plant has a
splayed-open shape with reddish-purple
leaves and bright red summer flowers
followed by attractive seedheads.
Underplant with dark red dahlias.

CULTIVATION: *Provide fertile, humus-rich,
well-drained soil, on a sunny site.*

☼ ◊ Annual   ↕to 6ft (2m) ↔3ft (1m)

***Rudbeckia hirta*
'Prairie Sun'** ▶

This free-flowering perennial is
best grown in massed planting.
The striking green-eyed yellow flowers
in late summer attract butterflies.

CULTIVATION: *Provide quite fertile, fairly
moist soil, in sun to light shade.*

☼ ☀ ◊ ◊ Z3   ↕3ft (90cm) ↔1ft (30cm)

◀ ***Salpiglossis sinuata*
Casino Series**

These upright annuals freely produce
a contrasting display of funnel-shaped,
prominently veined flowers throughout
summer and fall. Colors range from blue
and purple to red, yellow, or orange.

CULTIVATION: *Grow in moist but well-
drained, fertile soil, in sun.*

☼ ◊ ◊ Annual
↕to 24in (60cm) ↔to 12in (30cm)

◀ *Salvia farinacea* 'Strata'

'Strata' has bicolored, clear blue and white flowers in summer and fall, making a striking contrast. It is very useful in mixed plantings with red and yellow flowers, and in containers.

CULTIVATION: *Best in average, humus-rich, well-drained but moist soil, in sun.*

☼ ◊ Annual
‡2ft (60cm) ↔ to 1ft (30cm)

Sanvitalia procumbens 'Orange Sprite' ▶

With a long flowering period in summer and a loose trailing habit, this orange-yellow, dark-eyed creeping zinnia adds an effective touch to hanging baskets and pots, or if left to mound up on the soil.

CULTIVATION: *Grow in average, humus-rich, well-drained soil, in full sun.*

☼ ◊ Annual ‡4in (10cm) ↔14in (35cm)

◀ *Scaevola aemula*

The fairy fan flower is a vigorous trailing plant ideal for edging, a container or basket. It bears a profusion of pretty blue flowers, although purplish and mauve varieties are available. Feed biweekly.

CULTIVATION: *Grow in moist but well-drained, fertile soil, in a well-lit position. Minimum temperature 41°F (5°C).*

☼ ☼ ◊ ◊ Tender ‡↔to 20in (50cm)

◀ *Schizanthus pinnatus* 'Hit Parade'

Very pretty, orchid-like, pink flowers with yellow throats almost cover the ferny foliage of this plant for a long season from spring to fall. Pinch back growth to encourage bushiness.

CULTIVATION: *Grow in moist but well-drained soil, in sun.*

☼ ◊ ◗ Annual
‡8–20in (20–50cm) ↔10–12in (25–30cm)

Senecio cineraria 'Silver Dust' ▶

This mound-forming evergreen shrub is mainly grown for its attractive, lacy silver foliage. It bears insignificant daisylike, yellow flowers in midsummer. Ideal for summer bedding schemes.

CULTIVATION: *Grow in well-drained, fertile soil, in sun. Nip out flower buds if desired.*

☼ ◊ Z8   ‡↔12in (30cm)

◀ *Solenostemon (Coleus) scutellarioides* Wizard Series

These compact, vivid plants have superb leaves, which can be red, pink, black, and white, often with a contrasting leaf margin. Remove any flowers.

CULTIVATION: *Best in humus-rich, moist but well-drained soil, in bright light.*

☼ ☀ ◊ ◗ Annual   ‡↔to 8in (20cm)

◀ *Tagetes erecta* 'Gold Coins'

African marigolds are very reliable border or container annuals with plenty of summer flowers above the dark green, ferny foliage. 'Gold Coins' has yellow pompom flowers. Deadhead to promote flowering.

CULTIVATION: *Grow in moist but well-drained soil, in sun or partial shade.*

☼ ☀ ◊ ◊ Annual
‡32in (80cm) ↔20in (50cm)

Tagetes 'Naughty Marietta' ▶

A high-impact annual with flowers appearing from late spring to early fall, with bright, striking colors. The petals are deep yellow with a maroon-red flash toward the base.

CULTIVATION: *Best in moderately fertile, well-drained soil, in full sun.*

☼ ◊ Annual   ‡↔12–16in (30–40cm)

◀ *Tagetes patula* 'Striped Marvel'

With a bushy, uniform height, these clearly striped plants with a large eye give a prolific summer show. Equally good for bedding schemes and cut flower displays.

CULTIVATION: *Best in moderately fertile, well-drained soil, in full sun.*

☼ ◊ Annual   ‡↔24–30in (60–75cm)

◀ *Thunbergia alata* Suzie Hybrids

The yellow, orange, or white flowers have a contrasting dark eye, and appear from summer to fall. It can easily be trained up a support or allowed to spread over adjacent shrubs.

CULTIVATION: *Grow in fertile, moist but well-drained soil, in a sunny site.*

☼ ◊ ◑ Annual ‡5–8ft (1.5–2m)

Torenia fournieri ▶ Clown Series

Injecting extra interest into summer bedding, the Clown Series comes in white, lavender-blues, purples, and pinks, with orchidlike petal patterning.

CULTIVATION: *Grow in fertile, moist but well-drained soil, in partial shade.*

☼ ◊ ◑ Annual
‡8–10in (20–25cm) ↔6–9in (15–23cm)

◀ *Tropaeolum majus* 'Alaska Salmon Orange'

A dwarf, bushy nasturtium, it has yellow to red flowers and light green leaves with creamy white markings. Gives a reliable show of summer color at the front of borders and in pots.

CULTIVATION: *Grow in average, moist but well-drained soil, in full sun.*

☼ ◊ ◑ Annual
‡12in (30cm) ↔to 18in (45cm)

◄ *Verbena* Romance Series

A colorful trailing verbena, ideal for hanging baskets, it flowers from early summer to the first frosts in a range of pastels. Nip out the young growing tips to make it bushier and more floriferous.

CULTIVATION: *Grow in average, well-drained soil, in full sun. Minimum temperature 35°F (2°C).*

☼ ◊ ◖ Tender ‡6in (15cm) ↔3ft (90cm)

Viola Princess Series ►

Known as winter pansies for their hardiness to frost, these short-lived perennials flower well from spring and into summer. The flowers come in a mixture of colours and are ideal for containers or baskets.

CULTIVATION: *Grow in moist but well-drained soil, in a well-lit position.*

☼ ◐ ◊ ◖ Z6 ‡↔to 12in (30cm)

◄ *Zinnia* x *hybrida* 'Profusion Cherry'

Zinnias produce an abundance of summer flowers on compact, free-branching plants which thrive in beds, borders, and containers. 'Profusion Mixed' also has white and orange flowers.

CULTIVATION: *Provide fertile, humus-rich, well-drained soil, in full sun.*

☼ ◊ Annual ‡12–15in (30–38cm) ↔6in (15cm)

THE
A–Z OF
PLANTS

Attractive and reliable plants for every garden, and for every part of the garden, can be found in this section. However much their ornamental features and season(s) of interest appeal to you, always check hardiness, eventual size, and site and soil requirements before you buy.

Abelia 'Edward Goucher'

This semi-evergreen shrub with arching branches bears glossy, dark green leaves that are bronze when young. Trumpet-shaped, lilac-pink flowers appear from summer to fall. Like most abelias, it is suitable for a sunny border.

CULTIVATION: *Grow in well-drained, fertile soil, in sun with shelter from cold winds. Remove dead or damaged growth in spring, cutting some of the older stems back to the ground after flowering to promote new growth.*

☼ ◊ Z6 ↕5ft (1.5m) ↔6ft (2m)

Abelia floribunda

An evergreen shrub with arching shoots, from which tubular, bright pink-red flowers hang in profuse clusters in early summer. The leaves are oval and glossy dark green. Ideal for a sunny border. Where marginally hardy, grow in a sheltered position or provide a deep winter mulch.

CULTIVATION: *Grow in well-drained, fertile soil, in full sun with shelter from cold, drying winds. Prune older growth back after flowering, removing any dead or damaged growth in spring.*

☼ ◊ Z8 ↕10ft (3m) ↔12ft (4m)

Abelia x *grandiflora*

A rounded, semi-evergreen shrub bearing arching branches. Cultivated for its attractive, glossy dark green leaves and profusion of fragrant, pink-tinged white flowers that are borne from midsummer to fall. Suitable for a sunny border.

CULTIVATION: *Grow in well-drained, fertile soil, in full sun with shelter from cold, drying winds. Prune back older growth back after flowering, and remove damaged growth in spring.*

☼ ◊ Z6 ↕10ft (3m) ↔12ft (4m)

Abutilon megapotamicum

The trailing abutilon is a semi-evergreen shrub bearing pendulous, bell-shaped, red and yellow flowers from summer to fall. The oval leaves are bright green and heart-shaped at the base. Where marginal or not hardy, train against a warm wall or grow in a conservatory.

CULTIVATION: *Best in well-drained, moderately fertile soil, in full sun. Remove any wayward shoots during late winter or early spring.*

☼ ◊ Z8 ↕↔6ft (2m)

Abutilon vitifolium 'Veronica Tennant'

A fast-growing, upright, deciduous shrub that may attain the stature of a small, bushy tree. Masses of large, pink, bowl-shaped flowers hang from the thick, gray-felted shoots in early summer. The softly gray-hairy leaves are sharply toothed. 'Tennant's White', with pure white flowers, is also recommended.

CULTIVATION: *Grow in well-drained, moderately fertile soil, in full sun. Prune young plants after flowering to encourage a good shape; do not prune established plants.*

☼ ◊ Z8   ↕15ft (5m) ↔8ft (2.5m)

Acacia baileyana 'Purpurea'

The Bailey acacia is a fast-growing small tree or multitrunked shrub with feathery, bluish-gray foliage. It bears clusters of small fragrant yellow pompon flowers from winter to spring. 'Purpurea' has darker foliage most noticeable in new growth.

CULTIVATION: *Grows best in well-drained, neutral to acid soil, in full sun. Drought tolerant. Remove leader to encourage shrubby habit. Minimum temperature 35°F (2°C).*

☼ ◊ Tender
↕to 35ft (11m) ↔15–30ft (5–10m)

Acaena microphylla

This summer-flowering, mat-forming
perennial bears heads of small,
dull red flowers with spiny bracts
that develop into decorative burrs.
The finely divided, mid-green leaves
are bronze-tinged when young
and evergreen through most winters.
Good for a rock garden, trough,
or raised bed.

CULTIVATION: *Grow in well-drained soil,
in full sun or partial shade. Pull out
rooted stems around the main plant to
restrict spread.*

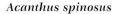 ☼ ☽ ◊ Z7   ↕2in (5cm) ↔24in (60cm)

Acanthus spinosus

Bear's breeches is a striking,
architectural perennial bearing long,
arching, dark green leaves that have
deeply cut and spiny edges. From late
spring to midsummer, pure white,
two-lipped flowers with purple bracts
are borne on tall, sturdy stems; they
are good for cutting and drying. Grow
in a spacious border.

CULTIVATION: *Best in deep, well-drained,
fertile soil, in full sun or partial shade.
Provide plenty of space to display its
architectural merits.*

 ☼ ☽ ◊ Z6   ↕5ft (1.5m) ↔24in (60cm)

Acer griseum

The paperbark maple is a slow-growing, spreading, deciduous tree valued for its peeling orange-brown bark. The dark green leaves, divided into three leaflets, turn orange to red and scarlet in fall. Tiny yellow flowers are carried in hanging clusters during early or mid-spring, followed by brown, winged fruits.

CULTIVATION: *Grow in moist but well-drained, fertile soil, in sun or partial shade. In summer only, remove shoots that obscure the bark on the trunk and lower parts of the main branches.*

☼ ☀ ◊ Z6   ↕↔30ft (10m)

Acer grosseri var. hersii

This variety of the snakebark maple with boldly green- and white-streaked bark is a spreading to upright, deciduous tree. The three-lobed, triangular, bright green leaves turn orange or yellow in fall. Hanging clusters of tiny, pale yellow flowers appear in spring, followed by pink-brown, winged fruits.

CULTIVATION: *Grow in moist but well-drained, fertile soil, in full sun or partial shade. Shelter from cold winds. Remove shoots that obscure the bark on the trunk and main branches in summer.*

☼ ☀ ◊ Z6b   ↕↔50ft (15m)

Acer japonicum **'Aconitifolium'**

A deciduous, bushy tree or large shrub bearing deeply lobed, mid-green leaves that turn brilliant dark red in fall. It is very free-flowering, producing upright clusters of conspicuous, reddish-purple flowers in mid-spring, followed by brown, winged fruits. 'Vitifolium' is similar, not so free-flowering but with fine fall color.

CULTIVATION: *Grow in moist but well-drained, fertile soil, in partial shade. Where marginally hardy, mulch around the base in fall. Remove badly placed shoots in summer only.*

☀ ◐ ○ Z6   ↕15ft (5m) ↔20ft (6m)

Acer negundo **'Flamingo'**

Round-headed, deciduous tree with pink-margined, oval leaflets which turn white in summer. With regular pruning it can be grown as a shrub; this also produces larger leaves with an intensified color. Flowers are tiny and inconspicuous. Plain-leaved var. *violaceum* has glaucous shoots and long tassels of violet flowers.

CULTIVATION: *Grow in any moist but well-drained, fertile soil, in full sun or partial shade. For larger leaves and a shrubby habit, cut back to a framework every 1 or 2 years in winter. Remove any branches with all-green leaves.*

☀ ◐ ○ Z5b   ↕50ft (15m) ↔30ft (10m)

Japanese Maples (*Acer palmatum*)

Cultivars of *Acer palmatum*, the Japanese maple, are mostly small, round-headed, deciduous shrubs, although some, such as 'Sango-kaku', will grow into small trees. They are valued for their delicate and colorful foliage, which often gives a beautiful display in fall. The leaves of 'Butterfly', for example, are variegated gray-green, white, and pink, and those of 'Osakazuki' turn a brilliant red before they fall. In mid-spring, hanging clusters of small, reddish-purple flowers are produced, followed by winged fruits later in the season. Japanese maples are excellent for gardens of any size.

CULTIVATION: *Grow in moist but well-drained, fertile soil, in sun or partial shade. Restrict pruning and training to young plants only; remove badly placed or crossing shoots in summer to develop a well-spaced branch network. Keep pruning to a minimum on established plants.*

☼ ☀ ◊ Z5–6*

‡↔15ft (5m)

‡10ft (3m) ↔5ft (1.5m)

‡6ft (2m) ↔10ft (3m)

‡6ft (2m) ↔10ft (3m)

1 *Acer palmatum* 'Bloodgood' **2** *A. palmatum* 'Butterfly' **3** *A. palmatum* 'Chitose-yama'
4 *A. palmatum* 'Garnet'

‡15ft (5m) ↔12ft (4m)

MORE CHOICES

'Burgundy Lace' Very deeply cut red-purple leaves, 4m (12ft) tall and widely spreading.

var. *coreanum* 'Korean Gem' Green leaves turning crimson-scarlet in fall.

var. *dissectum* 'Crimson Queen' (see p.588)

var. *dissectum* (see p.662)

var. *dissectum* 'Inabe-Shidare' Deeply divided purple-red leaves.

'Seiryû' (see p.662)

‡↔30ft (6m)

7

‡↔5ft (1.5m)

‡20ft (6m) ↔15ft (5m)

5 *A. palmatum* 'Linearilobum' **6** *A. palmatum* 'Osakazuki' **7** *A. palmatum* 'Red Pygmy' **8** *A. palmatum* 'Sango-kaku' (*syn.* 'Senkaki')

Acer pensylvanicum 'Erythrocladum'

This striped maple is an upright, deciduous tree. Its leaves are bright green, turning clear yellow in fall. In winter, brilliant pink or red young shoots make a fiery display; they become orange-red with white stripes as they mature. Hanging clusters of small, greenish-yellow flowers in spring are followed by winged fruits. Best grown as a specimen tree.

CULTIVATION: *Grow in fertile, moist but well-drained soil, in sun or part shade. Remove crossing or damaged shoots in summer only.*

☼ ☀ ◊ Z2b   ‡40ft (12m) ↔30ft (10m)

Acer platanoides 'Crimson King'

Like *Acer platanoides*, the Norway maple, this cultivar is a large, spreading, deciduous tree. It is grown for its dark red-purple leaves, which deepen to dark purple as they mature. The foliage is preceded in spring by clusters of small, red-tinged yellow flowers. These develop into winged fruits. A colorful specimen tree.

CULTIVATION: *Grow in fertile, moist but well-drained soil, in sun or partial shade. Prune in summer only, to remove any crossing, crowded, or unhealthy growth.*

☼ ☀ ◊ Z4b   ‡80ft (25m) ↔50ft (15m)

Acer platanoides '**Drummondii**'

This is a much smaller, more spreading deciduous tree than the Norway maple, and is as broad as it is tall. Its leaves have a wide, pale green to cream margin and color well in fall. In spring, clusters of yellow flowers appear; from these later develop winged fruits. An attractive specimen tree for a medium-sized garden.

CULTIVATION: *Grow in fertile, moist but well-drained soil, in sun or partial shade. Prune in summer only, to remove any crossing, crowded, or unhealthy growth.*

☼ ☀ ◊ Z5   ↕↔30–40ft (10–12m)

Acer pseudoplatanus '**Brilliantissimum**'

This small, slow-growing cultivar of sycamore maple is a spreading, deciduous tree with a dense head. It bears colorful, five-lobed leaves that turn from salmon-pink to yellow then dark green as they mature. Hanging clusters of tiny, yellow-green flowers appear in spring, followed by winged fruit. An attractive maple for smaller gardens.

CULTIVATION: *Grow in any soil, in sun or partial shade. Tolerates exposed sites. Prune in summer to develop well-spaced branches and a clear trunk.*

☼ ☀ ◊ Z5b   ↕20ft (6m) ↔25ft (8m)

Acer rubrum 'October Glory'

This cultivar of the red, or swamp, maple is a round-headed to open-crowned, deciduous tree with glossy dark green foliage, turning bright red in early fall. The upright clusters of tiny red flowers in spring are followed by winged fruits. A fine specimen tree for a larger garden.

CULTIVATION: *Grow in any fertile, moist but well-drained soil, although best fall color is seen in acidic soil. Choose a site with full sun or in partial shade, and restrict pruning to summer to remove any crossing or congested branches.*

☀ ◑ ◊ Z3b   ↕70ft (20m) ↔30ft (10m)

Acer tataricum subsp. *ginnala*

The Amur maple is a rounded, bushy, deciduous tree with slender, arching branches and glossy bright green leaves, very deeply lobed; in fall, these become a deep, rich bronze-red. In spring, it bears upright clusters of cream flowers, from which develop red, winged fruits. Best as a specimen tree.

CULTIVATION: *Grow in any fertile, moist but well-drained soil, in full sun or in partial shade. Restrict pruning to summer to remove any crossing or congested branches, if necessary.*

☀ ◊ Z1b   ↕30ft (10m) ↔25ft (8m)

Achillea ageratifolia

This small yarrow is a fast-growing, creeping perennial, forming mats of silvery, hairy leaf rosettes above which, in summer, small white flowerheads stand on upright stems. Grow at the front of a sunny border or in a rock or scree garden, or in planting spaces in a paved area.

CULTIVATION: *Grow in any moderately fertile, free-draining soil, in sun. Divide plants that have spread too widely or become straggly in spring or fall. Deadhead to encourage further flowers.*

☼ ◊ Z3b
‡2–3in (5–8cm) ↔to 18in (45cm)

Achillea 'Coronation Gold'

This cultivar of yarrow is a clump-forming perennial that bears large, flat heads of golden yellow flowers from midsummer to early fall. The luxuriant, evergreen, fernlike leaves are silver-gray, complementing the flower color (contact may aggravate skin allergies). Excellent for a mixed or herbaceous border, and for cutting and drying.

CULTIVATION: *Grow in moist but well-drained soil, in an open site in full sun. Divide large or congested clumps to maintain vigor.*

☼ ◊ ◊ Z3
‡30–36in (75–90cm) ↔18in (45cm)

Achillea filipendulina 'Gold Plate'

A strong-growing, clump-forming and upright, evergreen perennial with gray-green leaves. Flat-headed clusters of bright golden yellow flowers are borne on strong stems from early summer to early fall; they make good cut flowers. Grow in a mixed or herbaceous border. Contact with the foliage may aggravate skin allergies.

CULTIVATION: *Grow in moist but well-drained soil in an open, sunny site. To maintain good performance, divide clumps when large and congested.*

☼ ◊ ◊ Z3　‡4ft (1.2m) ↔18in (45cm)

Achillea 'Heidi'

This charming rose-pink yarrow is shorter than most, which makes it useful in mixed plantings or in tight spaces. Flat, dish-like flowerheads appear through midsummer and attract pollinators, including butterflies. Flower stems need little support.

CULTIVATION: *Grow in any moist but well-drained soil, in sun. Remove old flowerheads to promote rebloom. Divide large clumps in spring or fall.*

☼ ◊ ◊ Z4
‡18in (45cm) ↔18in (45cm or more)

Achillea 'Moonshine'

A clump-forming, evergreen perennial with narrow, feathery, gray-green leaves. Light yellow flowerheads with slightly darker centers appear from early summer to early fall in flattish clusters; they dry well for arrangements. Excellent for mixed borders and for informal, wild, or cottage-style plantings.

CULTIVATION: *Grow in well-drained soil in an open, sunny site. Divide every 2 or 3 years in spring to maintain vigor.*

☼ ◊ Z3b ‡↔24in (60cm)

Achillea 'Paprika' (Galaxy Series)

This is a vigorous yarrow yielding flat clusters of rich red flowers with white centers, which look striking in mixed borders. This tough plant tolerates drought and heat and makes good cut flowers. Beneficial insects flock to the flowers.

CULTIVATION: *Grow in moist but well-drained soil, in sun, ideally through a support. Remove old flowerheads to promote rebloom. Divide large clumps in spring or fall.*

☼ ◊ ◊ Z4 ‡24in (60cm) ↔24in (60cm) or more

Aconitum 'Bressingham Spire'

A compact perennial producing very upright spikes of hooded, deep violet flowers from midsummer to early fall. The leaves are deeply divided and glossy dark green. Ideal for woodland or borders in partial or dappled shade. For lavender flowers on a slightly taller plant, look for *A. carmichaelii* 'Kelmscott'. All parts of these plants are poisonous.

CULTIVATION: *Best in cool, moist, fertile soil, in partial shade, but will tolerate most soils and full sun. The tallest stems may need staking.*

☼ ☀ ◊ Z3b
‡36–39in (90–100cm) ↔12in (30cm)

Actaea simplex 'Brunette'

A useful late-season-bloomer, this clump-forming perennial is ideal for a shade or woodland garden. In late summer to fall, spiky pink flowerheads bloom on slender stems above the attractive dark purple-brown foliage. Formerly listed in the genus *Cimicifuga*.

CULTIVATION: *Grow in moist, fertile soil in partial shade. Enrich soil with organic matter. Divide large clumps in spring.*

☼ ◊ Z4
‡to 4ft (1.2m) ↔24in (60cm) or more

Actinidia kolomikta

A vigorous, deciduous climber with large, deep green leaves that are purple-tinged when young and develop vivid splashes of white and pink as they mature. Small, fragrant, white flowers appear in early summer. Female plants produce small, egg-shaped, yellow-green fruits, but only if a male plant is grown nearby. Train against a wall or up into a tree.

CULTIVATION: *Best in well-drained, fertile soil. For best fruiting, grow in full sun with protection from strong winds. Tie in new shoots as they develop, and remove badly placed shoots in summer.*

☼ ◊ Z4   ↕15ft (5m)

Adiantum pedatum

A deciduous relative of the maidenhair fern bearing long, mid-green fronds up to 14in (35cm) tall. These have glossy dark brown or black stalks that emerge from creeping rhizomes. There are no flowers. *A. aleuticum* is very similar and also recommended; var. *subpumilum* is a dwarf form of this fern, only 6in (15cm) tall. Grow in a shady border or light woodland.

CULTIVATION: *Best in cool, moist soil, in deep or partial shade. Remove old or damaged fronds in early spring. Divide and replant rhizomes every few years.*

☼ ☀ ◊ Z4   ↔12–16in (30–40cm)

Adiantum venustum

The Himalayan maidenhair fern has black-stalked, triangular, mid-green fronds, beautifully divided into many small leaflets. The new foliage is bright bronze-pink when it emerges in late winter to early spring from creeping rhizomes. It is evergreen above 14°F (-10°C). Decorative groundcover for a woodland garden or shady border.

CULTIVATION: *Grow in moderately fertile, moist but well-drained soil, in partial shade. Remove old or damaged fronds in spring, and divide the rhizomes every few years in early spring.*

☀ ◊ ◊ Z6   ‡6in (15cm) ↔indefinite

Aeonium haworthii

A succulent subshrub with slender branches, each crowned by a neat rosette of bluish green, fleshy leaves with red margins. Clusters of pale yellow to pinkish-white flowers are borne in spring. It is a popular pot plant for conservatories and porches.

CULTIVATION: *Under glass, grow in standard cactus soil mix in filtered light, and allow the mix to dry out between waterings. Outdoors, grow in moderately fertile, well-drained soil, in partial shade. Minimum temperature 50°F (10°C).*

☀ ◊ Tender   ‡↔24in (60cm)

Aeonium 'Zwartkop'

An upright, succulent subshrub with few branches, each tipped by a rosette of black-purple leaves. Large, pyramid-shaped clusters of bright yellow flowers appear in late spring. Makes an unusually colored pot plant. *A. arboreum* 'Atropurpureum' is similarly striking.

CULTIVATION: Grow in standard cactus soil mix in filtered light under glass, allowing the mix to dry out between waterings. Outdoors, grow in reasonably fertile, well-drained soil, in partial shade. Minimum temperature 50°F (10°C).

☼ ◊ Tender ↔ to 6ft (2m)

Aesculus carnea 'Briotii'

This cultivar of red horsechestnut is a spreading tree, admired in early summer for its large, upright cones of dark rose-red flowers. The dark green leaves are divided into 5–7 leaflets. The flowers are followed by spiny fruits. For larger gardens, look for the sunrise horsechestnut, *A.* x *neglecta* 'Erythroblastos', to 30ft (10m; Z6b), or the red buckeye, *A. pavia*, to 15ft (5m; Z5b).

CULTIVATION: Grow in deep, fertile, moist but well-drained soil, in full sun or partial shade. Remove dead, diseased or crossing branches during winter.

☼ ◐ ◊ ◔ Z5b
↕ 70ft (20m) ↔ 50ft (15m)

Aesculus parviflora

A large, thicket-forming, deciduous shrub, closely related to the horse-chestnut, that bears large-lobed, dark green leaves. The foliage is bronze when young, turning yellow in fall. Upright white flowerheads, up to 12in (30cm) tall, appear in mid-summer, followed by smooth-skinned fruits.

CULTIVATION: *Grow in moist but well-drained, fertile soil, in sun or partial shade; it will not grow in wet ground. If necessary, restrict spread by pruning stems to the ground after leaf fall.*

☼ ☀ ◊ ◗ Z4b   ‡10ft (3m) ↔15ft (5m)

Aethionema 'Warley Rose'

A short-lived, evergreen or semi-evergreen, compact shrub bearing clusters of bright pink, cross-shaped flowers in late spring and early summer. The small, narrow leaves are blue-gray. For flowers of a much paler pink, look for *A. grandiflorum*, very similar if a little taller. Aethionemas are ideal for a rock garden or on a wall.

CULTIVATION: *Best in well-drained, fertile, alkaline soil, but tolerates poor, acidic soils. Choose a site in full sun.*

☼ ◊ Z5   ‡↔6–8in (15–20cm)

Agapanthus campanulatus subsp. *patens*

A vigorous, clump-forming perennial bearing round heads of bell-shaped, light blue flowers on strong, upright stems during late summer and early fall. The narrow, strap-shaped, grayish-green leaves are deciduous. Useful in borders or large containers.

CULTIVATION: *Grow in moist but well-drained, fertile soil or soil mix, in full sun. Water freely when in growth, and sparingly in winter.*

☼ ◊ Z8
↕18in (45cm) ↔12in (30cm)

Agapanthus 'Loch Hope'

Large heads of deep blue flowers held on tall stems above the foliage make this clump-forming plant an excellent late-summer perennial. The strap-shaped foliage dies back in winter. Clumps expand and eventually take up a lot of space. 'Loch Hope' is a sturdy cultivar.

CULTIVATION: *Grow in moist but well-drained, fertile soil or pots of soil-based growing medium in full sun. Divide large clumps in spring. Protect with mulch in cold winters.*

☼ ◊ ◊ Z7
↕to 5ft (1.5m) ↔24in (60cm) or more

Agave victoriae-reginae

A tender, succulent perennial bearing basal rosettes of triangular, dark green leaves with white marks. The central leaves curve inward, each tipped with a brown spine. Upright spikes of creamy white flowers appear in summer. A good specimen plant: where not hardy, grow in containers for summer display, taking it under cover for winter shelter.

CULTIVATION: *Best in sharply drained, moderately fertile, slightly acidic soil, or standard cactus soil mix. Site in full sun. Minimum temperature 35°F (2°C).*

☼ ◊ Tender   ‡↔to 20in (50cm)

Ageratina altissima 'Chocolate'

White snakeroot is a clump-forming perennial suitable for sun or part shade. Its finely toothed leaves are deep brown. Bears terminal clusters of small creamy white flowers in late summer; these attract pollinators. May be listed as *Eupatorium rugosum* in some catalogs.

CULTIVATION: *Best in reasonably moist, fertile soil; site in part shade in warm regions. Divide in spring, as necessary.*

☼ ◑ ◊ Z4
‡3–4ft (90–120cm) ↔1–2ft (30–60cm) or more

Ajuga reptans '**Atropurpurea**'

This evergreen perennial makes an excellent groundcover, spreading freely over the soil surface by means of rooting stems. Dark blue flowers are borne in whorls along the upright stems during late spring and early summer. The glossy leaves are deep bronze purple. *A. reptans* 'Catlin's Giant' has similarly colored leaves. Invaluable for border edging under shrubs and vigorous perennials.

CULTIVATION: *Best in moist but well-drained, fertile soil, but tolerates most soils. Site in sun or partial shade.*

☼ ☼ ◊ ◑ Z3 ‡6in (15cm) ↔3ft (1m)

Alchemilla mollis

Lady's mantle is a drought-tolerant, clump-forming, tallish groundcover perennial that produces sprays of tiny, bright greenish yellow flowers from early summer to early fall; these are ideal for cutting and dry well for winter arrangements. The pale green leaves are rounded with crinkled edges. It looks well in a wildflower garden; for a rock garden, *A. erythropoda* is similar but smaller, with blue-tinged leaves.

CULTIVATION: *Grow in any moist but well-drained, organic soil, in an open, sunny site. Deadhead soon after flowering: it self-seeds very freely.*

☼ ◊ ◑ Z4b
‡24in (60cm) ↔30in (75cm)

Tall Ornamental Onions (*Allium*)

These onions grown for garden display are bulbous perennials from the genus *Allium*; their attractive flowerheads are excellent for a mixed border, especially grouped together. The tiny summer flowers are usually massed into dense, rounded or hemispherical heads—like those of *A. giganteum*—or they may hang loosely, like the yellow flowers of *A. flavum*. When crushed, the strap-shaped leaves release a pungent aroma; they are often withered by flowering time. The seedheads tend to dry out intact, standing well into fall and continuing to look attractive. Some alliums self-seed and will naturalize.

CULTIVATION: *Grow in fertile, well-drained soil, in full sun to simulate their dry native habitats. Plant bulbs 2–4in (5–10cm) deep in fall; divide and replant older clumps at the same time or in spring. Where marginally hardy, provide a thick winter mulch for* A. cristophii *and* A. caeruleum.

☼ ◊ Zones vary

‡3ft (1m) ↔ 6in (15cm)

MORE CHOICES

A. carinatum subsp. *pulchellum* Purple flowers. 12–18in (30–45cm) tall. Z3
A. cernuum 'Hidcote' Nodding pink flowers.
A. hollandicum Purplish pink flowers, 3ft (1m) tall, very similar to 'Purple Sensation'. Z4

‡24in (60cm) ↔ 1in (2.5cm)

1 *Allium* 'Beau Regard' (Z7) **2** *A. caeruleum* (Z4b)

‡12–24in (30–60cm) ↔ 7in (18cm)

‡to 14in (35cm) ↔ 2in (5cm)

‡5–6ft (1.5m–2m) ↔ 6in (15cm)

‡4ft (1.2m) ↔ 6in (15cm)

‡32in (80cm) ↔ 8in (20in)

‡3ft (1m) ↔ 3in (7cm)

‡24in (60cm) ↔ 4in (10cm)

3 *A. cristophii* (Z5) **4** *A. flavum* (Z3) **5** *A. giganteum* (Z5) **6** *A.* 'Gladiator' (Z6b)
7 *A.* 'Globemaster' (Z5) **8** *A. hollandicum* 'Purple Sensation' (Z4)
9 *A. sphaerocephalum* (Z3)

Small Ornamental Onions (*Allium*)

These alliums are summer-flowering, bulbous perennials for the front of a border or rock garden. They form clumps as they establish; some, such as *A. moly*, will self-seed. The flowers are borne in clustered heads which may be large or small; those of *A. karataviense* can be 3in (8cm) across, despite its small stature. Flower colors range from bright gold to purple, blue, and pale pink. The seedheads are attractive, too, lasting well into winter. The strap-shaped leaves are often withered by flowering time. Those of ornamental chives, such as *A. schoenoprasum* 'Pink Perfection' and the very similar 'Black Isle Blush', are edible.

CULTIVATION: *Best in well-drained, organic soil, in full sun. Plant bulbs 2–4in (5–10cm) deep in fall; divide and replant old or crowded clumps in fall or spring. Provide a thick, dry winter mulch for* A. karataviense *where marginally hardy.*

☼ ◊ Zones vary

‡ 4–10in (10–25cm) ↔ 4in (10cm)

‡ 6–10in (15–25cm) ↔ 2in (5cm)

‡ 2–8in (5–20cm) ↔ 1¼in (3cm)

‡ 12–24in (30–60cm) ↔ 2in (5cm)

1 *Allium karataviense* (Z4) **2** *A. moly* (Z3) **3** *A. oreophilum* (Z4)
4 *A. schoenoprasum* 'Pink Perfection' (Z3)

Alnus glutinosa 'Imperialis'

This attractive cultivar of the black alder is a broadly conical tree with deeply dissected, lobed, mid-green leaves. Groups of yellow-brown catkins emerge in late winter, followed by small oval cones in summer. This is a beautiful foliage tree, particularly good close to water because it tolerates poor, wet soil.

CULTIVATION: *Thrives in any moderately fertile, moist but not waterlogged soil, in full sun. Prune after leaf fall, if necessary, to remove any damaged or crossing branches.*

☼ ◊ Z4   ‡80ft (25m) ↔15ft (5m)

Aloe vera

This fast-growing, tender succulent is a popular house plant. It forms clumps of thick, lance-shaped, bright green fleshy leaves. Yellow flowers bloom on spikes in regions where it is hardy. The clear gel inside the leaves can be used to soothe mild burns and skin irritations.

CULTIVATION: *Grow in a well-drained potting medium in containers indoors, or outdoors in summer, watering as needed. Divide clumps as necessary; rooting new plants is easy. Minimum temperature 50°F (10°C).*

☼ ◊ ◊ Tender
‡24in (60cm) ↔indefinite

Alonsoa warscewiczii

This species of maskflower is a compact, bushy perennial, grown for its bright scarlet, sometimes white, flowers. These are on display from summer to fall amid the dark green leaves. Useful as summer bedding or in a mixed border, it also provides good cut flowers.

CULTIVATION: *Outdoors, grow in any fertile, well-drained soil, in full sun, or in soil-based potting mix if grown in a container. Water moderately.*

☼ ◊ Tender
‡18–24in (45–60cm) ↔12in (30cm)

Alstroemeria 'Apollo'

This border perennial has long-lasting, yellow-centered, lily-like white flowers with red flecks in midsummer. They make an excellent cut flower, but wear gloves, since the sap can irritate. Dwarf varieties are good for containers.

CULTIVATION: *Grow in light, well-drained soil, in full sun. In cold areas, plant deeply in spring and mulch in winter to protect the crown from frost.*

☼ ◊ Z8   ‡3ft (1m) ↔36in (90cm)

Amelanchier x *grandiflora* 'Ballerina'

A spreading, deciduous tree grown for its profusion of white spring flowers and colorful fall foliage. The glossy bronze-tinted leaves become mid-green in summer, then red and purple in fall. Its sweet, juicy red fruits ripen to purplish black in summer. They are edible cooked or fresh, and are attractive to birds.

CULTIVATION: *Grow in moist but well-drained, fertile, neutral to acidic soil, in full sun or partial shade. Allow shape to develop naturally; only minimal pruning is necessary, in winter.*

☼ ☼ ◊ ◊ Z4　　‡20ft (6m) ↔25ft (8m)

Amelanchier lamarckii

A many-stemmed, upright, deciduous shrub bearing leaves that are bronze when young, maturing to dark green in summer, then brilliant red and orange in fall. Hanging clusters of white flowers are produced in spring. The ripe, purple-black fruits that follow are edible cooked or fresh, and are attractive to birds. Also known as *A. canadensis*.

CULTIVATION: *Grow in moist but well-drained, organic, neutral to acidic soil, in sun or partial shade. Develops its shape naturally with only minimal pruning when dormant in winter.*

☼ ☼ ◊ ◊ Z4　　‡30ft (10m) ↔40ft (12m)

Amsonia hubrichtii

The star-shaped, light blue, flowers of bluestar create a cool spring accent. This southern U.S. native has feathery, light green foliage that turns burnished gold in fall. It attracts butterflies, making it ideal for wildflower and woodland gardens.

CULTIVATION: *This clump-former tolerates all types of soil pH, average to clay soils, and partial shade. To discourage floppy growth, plant in full sun and well-drained soil of average fertility.*

☼ ☀ ◐ Z5b ‡3ft (1m) ↔4ft (1.2m)

Anaphalis triplinervis 'Sommerschnee'

A clump-forming perennial carrying pale gray-green, white-woolly leaves. The tiny yellow flowerheads, surrounded by brilliant white bracts, appear during mid- and late summer in dense clusters; they are excellent for cutting and drying. Provides good foliage contrast in borders that are too moist for the majority of other gray-leaved plants.

CULTIVATION: *Grow in any reasonably well-drained, moderately fertile soil that does not dry out in summer. Choose a position in full sun or partial shade.*

☼ ☀ ◐ Z3 ‡32–36in (80–90cm) ↔18–24in (45–60cm)

Anchusa azurea 'Loddon Royalist'

An upright, clump-forming perennial that is much-valued in herbaceous borders for its spikes of intensely dark blue flowers. These are borne on branching stems in early summer, above the lance-shaped and hairy, mid-green leaves arranged at the base of the stems. For a rock garden, *A. cespitosa* looks similar in miniature, only 2–4in (5–10cm) tall.

CULTIVATION: *Grow in deep, moist but well-drained, fertile soil in sun. Often short-lived, but easily propagated by root cuttings. If growth is vigorous, may need staking.*

☀ ◊ Z3b   ‡36in (90cm) ↔24in (60cm)

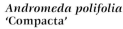

Andromeda polifolia 'Compacta'

Bog rosemary has leathery, linear leaves that resemble those of the herb rosemary. It thrives in cool, moist conditions and bears hanging clusters of pink bell-shaped flowers in spring and early summer. This compact form grows well in shaded rock gardens. Mulch with leaf mold in spring.

CULTIVATION: *Grow in part shade in moist, well-drained, acid soil enriched with plenty of organic matter; will tolerate full sun in regions with cool summers.*

☀ ☼ ◊ ◆ Z2   ‡to 12in (30cm) ↔to 8in (20cm)

Androsace carnea subsp. *laggeri*

An evergreen, cushion-forming perennial that bears small clusters of tiny, cup-shaped, deep pink flowers with yellow eyes, in late spring. The pointed, mid-green leaves are arranged in tight rosettes. Rock jasmines grow wild in alpine turf and rock crevices, making them ideal for rock gardens or troughs. *A. sempervivoides* has scented flowers, ideal for a raised bed.

CULTIVATION: *Grow in moist but sharply drained, gritty soil, in full sun. Provide a topdressing of grit or gravel to keep the stems and leaves dry.*

☼ ◊ Z4b   ‡2in (5cm) ↔6in (15cm)

Anemone blanda 'White Splendour'

A spreading, spring-flowering perennial that soon forms clumps of stems growing from knobby tubers. The solitary, upright, flattish white flowers, with pink-tinged undersides, are borne above oval, dark green leaves divided into delicately lobed leaflets. Excellent for naturalizing in sunny or shaded sites with good drainage. Mix it with 'Radar', with white-centered magenta flowers, or 'Ingramii', with deep blue flowers.

CULTIVATION: *Grow in well-drained soil that is rich in organic matter. Choose a position in full sun or partial shade.*

☼ ☀ ◊ Z5   ↕↔6in (15cm)

Anemone hupehensis 'Hadspen Abundance'

Upright, woody-based, late-flowering border perennial that spreads by shoots growing from the roots. Reddish pink flowers, with petal margins that gradually fade to white, are borne on branched stems during mid- and late summer. The deeply divided, long-stalked, dark green leaves are oval and sharply toothed. *A. hupehensis* 'Prinz Heinrich' is similar but spreads more vigorously.

CULTIVATION: *Grow in moist, fertile, organic soil, in sun or partial shade. Provide a mulch where marginal.*

☼ ☀ ◊ ◗ Z3
‡24–36in (60–90cm) ↔16in (40cm)

Anemone x *hybrida* 'Honorine Jobert'

This upright, woody-based perennial with branched, wiry stems is an invaluable long-flowering choice for late summer to mid-fall, when single, cupped white flowers, with pink-tinged undersides and golden yellow stamens, are borne above divided, mid-green leaves. (For pure white flowers without a hint of pink, look for Géante des Blanches'.) It can be invasive.

CULTIVATION: *Grow in moist but well-drained, moderately fertile, organic soil, in sun or partial shade.*

☼ ☀ ◊ ◗ Z4
‡4–5ft (1.2–1.5m) ↔indefinite

Anemone nemorosa 'Robinsoniana'

A vigorous, carpeting perennial that produces masses of large, star-shaped, pale lavender-blue flowers on maroon stems from spring to early summer, above deeply divided, mid-green leaves that die down in midsummer. Excellent for underplanting or a woodland garden; it naturalizes with ease. 'Allenii' has deeper blue flowers; choose 'Vestal' for white flowers.

CULTIVATION: *Grow in loose, moist but well-drained soil that is rich in organic matter, in light, dappled shade.*

☀ ◊ Z5
‡3–6in (8–15cm) ↔12in (30cm) or more

Anemone ranunculoides

This spring-flowering, spreading perennial is excellent for naturalizing in damp woodland gardens. The large, solitary, buttercup-like yellow flowers are borne above the "ruffs" of short-stalked, rounded, deeply lobed, fresh green leaves.

CULTIVATION: *Grow in moist but well-drained, organic soil, in semi-shade or dappled sunlight. Tolerates drier conditions when dormant in summer.*

☀ ◊ ◐ Z5
‡2–4in (5–10cm) ↔to 18in (45cm)

Antennaria microphylla

A mat-forming, semi-evergreen
perennial carrying densely white-
hairy, spoon-shaped, gray-green
leaves. In late spring and early
summer, heads of small, fluffy,
rose-pink flowers are borne on
short stems. Use in a rock garden,
as a low groundcover at the front
of a border, or in crevices in walls
or paving. The flowerheads dry well
for indoor decoration.

CULTIVATION: *Best in well-drained soil
that is no more than moderately fertile.
Choose a position in full sun.*

☼ ◊ Z4   ↕2in (5cm) ↔18in (45cm)

Anthemis punctata
subsp. *cupaniana*

A mat-forming, evergreen perennial
that produces a flush of small but
long-lasting, daisylike flowerheads in
early summer, and a few blooms later
on. The white flowers with yellow
centers are borne singly on short
stems, amid dense, finely cut, silvery
gray foliage that turns dull gray-green
in winter. Excellent for border edges.

CULTIVATION: *Grow in well-drained soil,
in a sheltered, sunny position. Cut back
after flowering to maintain vigor.*

☼ ◊ Z7   ↕12in (30cm) ↔18in (45cm)

Aquilegia canadensis

A lovely woodland or border plant with an airy habit, Canadian columbine bears nodding red and yellow, spurred flowers from late spring into early summer. The nectar-loaded spurs lure bumblebees, hummingbirds, and butterflies. Its attractive fernlike foliage is bluish green.

CULTIVATION: *Grow in any moist but well-drained soil in dappled shade. Propagate by seed; self sows.*

☼ ◐ ◊ Z3
‡to 36in (90cm) ↔12in (30cm)

Aquilegia vulgaris 'Nivea'

An upright, vigorous, clump-forming perennial, sometimes sold as MUNSTEAD WHITE, bearing leafy clusters of nodding, short-spurred, pure white flowers in late spring and early summer. Each grayish-green leaf is deeply divided into lobed leaflets. Attractive in light woodland or in a herbaceous border; plant with soft blue *Aquilegia* 'Hensol Harebell' for a luminous mix in light shade.

CULTIVATION: *Best in moist but well-drained, fertile soil. Choose a position in full sun or partial shade.*

☼ ◐ ◊ Z3
‡36in (90cm) ↔18in (45cm)

Aquilegia vulgaris 'Nora Barlow'

This upright, vigorous perennial is much valued for its leafy clusters of funnel-shaped, double, pompon flowers. These are pink and white with pale green petal tips and appear from late spring to early summer. The grayish-green leaves are deeply divided into narrow lobes. Nice in herbaceous borders and cottage garden-style plantings.

CULTIVATION: *Grow in moist but well-drained, fertile soil. Position in an open, sunny site.*

☼ ◊ Z3   ‡36in (90cm) ↔18in (45cm)

Arabis procurrens 'Variegata'

A mat-forming, evergreen or semi-evergreen perennial bearing loose clusters of cross-shaped white flowers on tall, slender stems during late spring. The narrow, mid-green leaves, arranged into flattened rosettes, have creamy white margins and are sometimes pink-tinged. Useful in a rock garden.

CULTIVATION: *Grow in any well-drained soil, in full sun. Remove completely any stems with plain green leaves.*

☼ ◊ Z5b
‡2–3in (5–8cm) ↔12–16in (30–40cm)

Aralia elata 'Variegata'

The variegated Japanese angelica tree is deciduous, with a beautiful, exotic appearance. The large leaves are divided into leaflets irregularly edged with creamy white. Flat clusters of small white flowers appear in late summer, followed by round black fruits. Suitable for a shady border or wooded streambank in a large garden. Less prone to suckering than the plain-leaved *Aralia elata*.

CULTIVATION: *Grow in fertile, organic, moist soil, in sun or part shade. Remove any branches with all-green foliage in summer. Needs a sheltered site; strong winds can damage leaves.*

☼ ◊ Z5 ↕↔15ft (5m)

Araucaria heterophylla

The Norfolk Island pine is a grand, cone-shaped conifer valued for its geometrical shape and unusual branches of whorled foliage. The scalelike leaves are tough, light green. There are no flowers. An excellent, fast-growing tree, normally grown as a house plant but may overwinter in a sheltered zone 9.

CULTIVATION: *Grow in moderately fertile, moist but well-drained soil in an open site with shelter from cold, drying winds. Tolerates partial shade when young.*

☼ ◊ ◊ Tender
↕80–150ft (25–45m) ↔20–25ft (6–8m)

Arbutus x *andrachnoides*

This strawberry tree is a broad, sometimes shrubby tree, with peeling, red-brown bark. The mid-green leaves are finely toothed and glossy. Clusters of small white flowers are borne from fall to spring, only rarely followed by fruits. Excellent for a large shrub border, or as a specimen tree.

CULTIVATION: *Grow in fertile, well-drained soil rich in organic matter, in a sheltered but sunny site. Protect from cold winds, even when mature, and keep pruning to a minimum, in winter if necessary. It tolerates alkaline soil.*

☼ ◊ Z8　　　　　↕↔25ft (8m)

Arbutus unedo

The strawberry tree is a spreading, evergreen tree with attractive, rough, shredding, red-brown bark. Hanging clusters of small, urn-shaped white flowers, which are sometimes pink-tinged, open during fall as the previous season's strawberry-like red fruits ripen. The glossy deep green leaves are shallowly toothed. Excellent for a large shrub border, with shelter from wind.

CULTIVATION: *Best in well-drained, fertile, organic, acidic soil. Tolerates slightly alkaline conditions. Choose a sheltered site in sun. Prune low branches in spring, but keep to a minimum.*

☼ ◊ Z7　　　　　↕↔25ft (8m)

Arctostaphylos uva-ursi

Bearberry is a hardy, low-growing evergreen with glossy small leaves. Clusters of small pink or white, nectar-rich flowers appear in summer, followed by red berries and bronze foliage. Use as a groundcover for rock gardens and borders. 'Vancouver Jade' has arching branches and pink flowers.

CULTIVATION: *Grow in open areas with well-drained, acidic soil, and full sun. Tolerates drought and coastal conditions.*

☼ ☀ ◐ Z1 ↕4in (10cm) ↔to 15ft (5m)

Arenaria montana

This sandwort is a low-growing, spreading, vigorous, evergreen perennial freely bearing shallowly cup-shaped white flowers in early summer. The small, narrowly lance-shaped, grayish-green leaves on wiry stems form loose mats. Easily grown in wall or paving crevices, or in a rock garden.

CULTIVATION: *Grow in sandy, moist but sharply drained, poor soil, in full sun. Must have adequate moisture.*

☼ ◊ Z3 ↕³/₄–2in (2–5cm) ↔12in (30cm)

Argyranthemum 'Jamaica Primrose'

A bushy, evergreen perennial that bears daisylike, primrose-yellow flowerheads with darker yellow centers throughout summer above fernlike, grayish-green leaves. Where not hardy, grow as summer bedding or in containers, bringing under cover for the winter. 'Cornish Gold'—shorter, with flowers of a deep yellow—is also recommended.

CULTIVATION: *Grow in well-drained, fairly fertile soil or soil mix, in a warm, sunny site. Pinch out shoot tips to encourage bushiness. Minimum temperature 35°F (2°C).*

☼ ◊ Tender   ↕3½ft (1.1m) ↔3ft (1m)

Argyranthemum 'Vancouver'

This compact, summer-flowering, evergreen subshrub is valued for its double, daisylike pink flowerheads with rose-pink centers and fernlike, gray-green leaves. Suits a mixed or herbaceous border; where marginal, grow as summer bedding or in containers that can be sheltered over winter.

CULTIVATION: *Grow in well-drained, fairly fertile soil, in sun. Pinch out growing tips to encourage bushiness. Minimum temperature 35°F (2°C).*

☼ ◊ Tender
↕36in (90cm) ↔32in (80cm)

Armeria juniperifolia

This tiny, hummock-forming, evergreen subshrub bears small, purplish pink to white flowers that are carried in short-stemmed, spherical clusters during late spring. The small, linear, gray-green leaves are hairy and spine-tipped and are arranged in loose rosettes. Native to mountain pastures and rock crevices, it is ideal for a rock garden or trough. Also known as *A. caespitosa*.

CULTIVATION: *Grow in well-drained, poor to moderately fertile soil, in an open position in full sun.*

☼ ◊ Z4
‡2–3in (5–8cm) ↔to 6in (15cm)

Armeria juniperifolia 'Bevan's Variety'

A compact, cushion-forming, evergreen subshrub that bears small, deep rose-pink flowers. These are carried in short-stemmed, rounded clusters during late spring, over the loose rosettes of small and narrow, pointed, gray-green leaves. Suits a rock garden or trough; for the front of the border, look for *Armeria* 'Bee's Ruby', a similar plant growing to 12in (30cm) tall, with chivelike flowerheads.

CULTIVATION: *Grow in well-drained, poor to moderately fertile soil. Choose an open site in full sun.*

☼ ◊ Z5   ‡2in (5cm) ↔6in (15cm)

Artemisia ludoviciana 'Silver Queen'

An upright, bushy, clump-forming, semi-evergreen perennial bearing narrow, downy leaves, sometimes jaggedly toothed; silvery white when young, they become greener with age. White-woolly plumes of brown-yellow flowers are borne from mid-summer to fall. Indispensable in a silver-themed border. 'Valerie Finnis' is also worthy; its leaves have more deeply cut edges.

CULTIVATION: *Grow in well-drained soil, in an open, sunny site. Cut back in spring for best foliage effect.*

☼ ◊ Z4
‡30in (75cm) ↔24in (60cm) or more

Artemisia 'Powis Castle'

A vigorous, shrubby, woody-based perennial forming a dense, billowing clump of finely cut, aromatic, silver-gray leaves. Sprays of insignificant, yellow-tinged silver flowerheads are borne in late summer. Excellent in a rock garden or border.

CULTIVATION: *Grow in well-drained, fertile soil, in full sun. Will die back in heavy, poorly drained soils and may be short-lived. Cut to the base in fall to maintain a compact habit.*

☼ ◊ Z5b
‡24in (60cm) ↔36in (90cm)

Arum italicum subsp. *italicum* 'Marmoratum'

This unusual bulbous plant bears cream-veined, deep green, glossy leaves, creamy flowers, and spiky clusters of berrylike fruits. The fruits appear in fall, ripening from green to red as winter progresses. As they fade, foliage begins to emerge. Plant at the edge of shade gardens among early bulbs, such as snowdrops. Note: the fruits are poisonous.

CULTIVATION: *Plant tubers in summer or fall in moist but well-drained, humus-rich soil. Plant in part or dappled shade; may tolerate full sun in cool regions.*

☼ ◐ ◊ ◑ Z6
‡12in (30cm) ↔6in (15cm)

Aruncus dioicus

Goatsbeard forms arresting clumps of rich green foliage from which loose and arching clusters of creamy or greenish-white flowers emerge in the first half of summer.It is a graceful woodland plant suited to a shady, damp site, such as a pond edge. It tolerates full sun in cool regions, as long as the soil remains moist. Plants may self sow.

CULTIVATION: *Grow in moist, fertile soil, in sun or shade. Cut flower stems back hard in fall.*

☼ ◐ ◊ ◖ Z3   ‡6ft (2m) ↔4ft (1.2m)

Asplenium scolopendrium

The hart's tongue fern has irregular crowns of shuttlecock-like, tongue-shaped, leathery, bright green fronds, to 16in (40cm) long. Heart-shaped at the bases, they often have wavy margins, markedly so in the cultivar 'Crispum Bolton's Nobile'. On the undersides of mature fronds, rust-colored spore cases are arranged in a herringbone pattern. Good in alkaline soil.

CULTIVATION: *Grow in moist but well-drained, organic, preferably alkaline soil with added grit, in partial shade.*

☼ ◐ ◊ ◖ Z7
‡18–28in (45–70cm) ↔24in (60cm)

Aster alpinus

This spreading, clump-forming perennial is grown for its mass of daisylike, purplish-blue or pinkish-purple flowerheads with deep yellow centers. These are borne on upright stems in early and midsummer above short-stalked, narrow, mid-green leaves. A low-growing aster, it is suitable for the front of a border or in a rock garden. Several outstanding cultivars are available.

CULTIVATION: *Grow in well-drained, moderately fertile soil, in sun. Mulch annually after cutting back in fall.*

☼ ◊ Z4
‡10in (25cm) ↔18in (45cm)

Aster amellus 'King George'

A clump-forming, bushy perennial bearing loose clusters of large, daisylike, violet-blue flowerheads with yellow centers that open from late summer to fall. The rough, mid-green leaves are hairy and lance-shaped. An invaluable late-flowering border plant; other recommended cultivars include 'Framfieldii' (lavender-blue flowers), 'Jacqueline Genebrier' (bright red-purple), and 'Veilchenkönigen' (deep purple).

CULTIVATION: *Grow in open, well-drained, moderately fertile soil, in full sun. Thrives in alkaline conditions.*

☀ ◊ Z4   ↕↔18in (45cm)

Aster 'Andenken an Alma Pötschke'

This upright clump-forming perennial carries sprays of large, daisylike, bright salmon-pink flowerheads with yellow centers from late summer to mid-fall, on stiff stems above rough, stem-clasping, mid-green leaves. Good for cutting, or in late-flowering displays. *A. novae-angliae* 'Harrington's Pink' is similar, with paler flowers.

CULTIVATION: *Grow in moist but well-drained, fertile, well-cultivated soil, in sun or semi-shade. Divide and replant every third year to maintain vigor and flower quality. May need staking.*

☀ ☀ ◊ Z4   ↕4ft (1.2m) ↔24in (60cm)

Aster x *frikartii* 'Mönch'

This upright, bushy perennial provides a continuous show of long-lasting, daisylike, lavender-blue flowerheads with orange centers during late summer and early fall. The dark green leaves are rough-textured and oblong. A useful plant for adding cool tones to a late summer or fall display, as is the very similar 'Wunder von Stäfa'.

CULTIVATION: *Best in well-drained, moderately fertile soil. Position in an open, sunny site. Mulch annually after cutting back in late fall.*

☼ ◊ Z4
↕28in (70cm) ↔14–16in (35–40cm)

Aster laterflorus var. *horizontalis*

A clump-forming, freely branching perennial bearing clusters of daisylike, sometimes pink-tinged white flowerheads with darker pink centers, from midsummer to mid-fall. The slender, hairy stems bear small, lance-shaped, mid-green leaves. An invaluable late-flowerer for a mixed border.

CULTIVATION: *Grow in moist but well-drained, moderately fertile soil, in partial shade. Keep moist in summer.*

☼◐ ◊ Z4   ↕24in (60cm) ↔12in (30cm)

Aster 'Little Carlow'

A clump-forming, upright perennial that produces large clusters of daisylike, violet-blue flowers with yellow centers, in early and mid-fall. The dark green leaves are oval to heart-shaped and toothed. Valuable for fall displays; the flowers cut and dry very well. Closely related to *A. cordifolius* 'Chieftain' (mauve flowers) and 'Sweet Lavender' (Z4).

CULTIVATION: *Best in moist, moderately fertile soil, in partial shade, but tolerates well-drained soil, in full sun. Mulch annually after cutting back in late fall. May need staking.*

☀ ☀ ◊ ◊ Z5
‡36in (90cm) ↔18in (45cm)

Astilbe × crispa 'Perkeo'

A summer-flowering, clump-forming perennial, low-growing compared with other astilbes, that bears small, upright plumes of tiny, star-shaped, deep pink flowers. The stiff, finely cut, crinkled, dark green leaves are bronze-tinted when young. Suitable for a border or rock garden; the flowers color best in light shade. 'Bronce Elegans' is another good, compact astilbe for where space is limited.

CULTIVATION: *Grow in reasonably moist, fertile soil that is rich in organic matter. Choose a position in partial shade.*

☀ ◊ Z3b ‡8in (15–20cm) ↔6in (15cm)

Astilbe 'Fanal'

A leafy, clump-forming perennial grown for its long-lasting, tapering, feathery heads of tiny, dark crimson flowers in early summer; they later turn brown, keeping their shape well into winter. The dark green leaves, borne on strong stems, are divided into several leaflets. Grow in a damp border or woodland garden, or use for waterside plantings. 'Brautschleier' is similar, with creamy white flower plumes.

CULTIVATION: *Grow in moist, fertile, preferably organic soil. Choose a position in full sun or partial shade.*

☼ ☀ ◐ ◊ Z3b
‡24in (60cm) ↔18in (45cm)

Astilbe 'Sprite'

A summer-flowering, leafy, clump-forming dwarf perennial that is suitable for waterside plantings. The feathery, tapering plumes of tiny, star-shaped, shell pink flowers arch elegantly over a mass of broad, mid-green leaves composed of many narrow leaflets. *Astilbe* 'Deutschland' has the same arching (as opposed to upright) flower plumes, in cream.

CULTIVATION: *Grow in reliably moist, fertile soil that is rich in organic matter. Choose a site in partial shade.*

◐ ◊ Z3b   ‡20in (50cm) ↔3ft (1m)

Astrantia major 'Sunningdale Variegated'

A clump-forming perennial bearing attractive, deeply lobed, basal leaves that have unevenly variegated, creamy yellow margins. From early summer, domes of tiny, green or pink, often deep purple-red flowers with star-shaped collars of pale pink bracts, are carried on wiry stems. Thrives in a moist border, woodland garden, or on a stream bank.

CULTIVATION: *Grow in any moist but well-drained, fertile soil. Needs full sun to obtain the best leaf coloring.*

☼ ◊ Z5
‡12–36in (30–90cm) ↔18in (45cm)

Astrantia maxima

Sometimes known as Hattie's pincushion, this mat-forming perennial produces domed, rose-pink flowerheads with star-shaped collars of papery, greenish-pink bracts, on tall stems during summer and fall. The mid-green leaves are divided into three toothed lobes. Flowers are good for cutting and drying for use in cottage-style arrangements.

CULTIVATION: *Grow in any moist, fertile, preferably organic soil, in sun or semi-shade. Tolerates drier conditions.*

☼ ◐ ◊ ◊ Z5
‡24in (60cm) ↔12in (30cm)

Athyrium filix-femina

The lady fern has much divided, light green, deciduous fronds that are borne like upright shuttlecocks, about 3ft (1m) long, arching outward with age. Frond dissection is very varied, and the stalks are sometimes red-brown. Useful for shaded sites, such as a woodland garden. Its cultivars 'Frizelliae' and 'Vernoniae' have unusual, distinctive fronds.

CULTIVATION: *Grow in moist, fertile, neutral to acidic soil enriched with leaf mold or compost. Choose a shaded, sheltered site.*

☀ ◊ Z4
‡to 4ft (1.2m) ↔24–36in (60–90cm)

Aubrieta 'Red Cascade' (Cascade series)

In common with other aubrietas, this variety forms a spreading mat of mid-green foliage that bursts into flower each spring. Aubrietas are good groundcovers and are effective spilling over dry stone walls and raised beds. They are also well suited to rock gardens. The smallish, four-petalled flowers are bright red.

CULTIVATION: *Grow in moderately fertile, well-drained, preferably neutral to alkaline soil, in full sun. Trim back after flowering to keep compact.*

☀ ◊ Z4
‡6in (15cm) ↔3ft (1m) or more

Aucuba japonica 'Crotonifolia' (female)

This variegated form of Japanese laurel is a rounded, evergreen shrub with large, glossy, dark green leaves boldly speckled with golden yellow. Upright clusters of small purplish flowers are borne in mid-spring, followed by red berries in fall. Ideal for dense, semi-formal hedging.

CULTIVATION: *Grow in any but waterlogged soil, in full sun for best foliage color, or in shade. Plant with male cultivars to ensure good fruiting. Tolerates light pruning at any time; cut back in spring to promote bushiness.*

☼ ☀ ◊ ◊ Z7   ↕↔10ft (3m)

Aurinia saxatilis

An evergreen perennial that forms dense clusters of bright yellow flowers in late spring that give rise to its common name, gold dust. The flowers of its cultivar 'Citrinus', also recommended, are a more lemony yellow. The oval, hairy, gray-green leaves are arranged in clumps. Ideal for rock gardens, walls, and banks. Also sold as *Alyssum saxatilis*.

CULTIVATION: *Grow in moderately fertile soil that is reliably well drained, in a sunny site. Cut back after flowering to maintain compactness.*

☼ ◊ Z3   ↕8in (20cm) ↔12in (30cm)

Ballota pseudodictamnus

An evergreen subshrub that forms mounds of rounded, yellow-gray-green leaves on upright, white-woolly stems. Whorls of small, white or pinkish white flowers, each enclosed by a pale green funnel, are produced in late spring and early summer.

CULTIVATION: *Grow in poor, very well-drained soil, in full sun with protection from excessive winter moisture. Cut back in early spring to keep compact.*

☀ ◊ Z9   ‡18in (45cm) ↔24in (60cm)

Baptisia australis

Blue false indigo is a gently spreading, upright perennial with a long season of interest. The bright blue-green leaves, on gray-green stems, are divided into three oval leaflets. Spikes of indigo-blue flowers, often flecked white or cream, open throughout early summer. The dark gray seed pods can be dried for winter decoration.

CULTIVATION: *Grow in deep, moist but well-drained, fertile, preferably neutral to acidic soil, in full sun. Once planted, it is best left undisturbed.*

☀ ◊ Z3b   ‡5ft (1.5m) ↔24in (60cm)

Begonias with Decorative Foliage

These perennial begonias are typically grown as annuals for their large, usually asymmetrical, ornamental leaves that are available in a variety of colors. For example, there are lively leaves of 'Merry Christmas' outlined with emerald green, or there is the more subtle, dark green, metallic foliage of *B. metallica*. Some leaves are valued for their unusual patterns; *B. masoniana* is appropriately known as the iron-cross begonia. Under the right conditions, 'Thurstonii' may reach shrublike proportions, but most, like 'Munchkin', are more compact. Grow as summer bedding, in a conservatory, or as house plants.

CULTIVATION: *Grow in fertile, well-drained, neutral to acidic soil or soil mix, in light dappled shade. Promote compact, leafy growth by pinching out shoot tips during the growing season. When in growth, feed regularly with a nitrogen-rich fertilizer. Minimum temperature 59°F (15°C).*

☀ ◊ Tender

1
↕↔2ft (60cm)

↕20in (50cm) ↔18in (45cm)

1 *Begonia listada* **2** *B. masoniana*

‡8in (25cm) ↔12in (30cm)

‡36in (90cm) ↔24in (60cm)

‡8in (20cm) ↔10in (25cm)

‡30cm (12in) ↔45cm (18in)

‡6ft (2m) ↔18in (45cm)

‡8in (20cm) ↔10in (25cm)

3 *B.* 'Merry Christmas' **4** *B. metallica* **5** *B.* 'Munchkin'
6 *B.* 'Silver Queen' **7** *B.* 'Thurstonii' **8** *B.* 'Tiger Paws'

Flowering Begonias

Usually grown outdoors as annuals, these bold-flowered begonias are very variable in size and shape, offering a range of summer uses to the gardener. For specific information on growth habit, check the label or ask advice when buying. Upright or compact begonias, such as 'Pin Up' or the Olympia series, are ideal for summer bedding; for containers and hanging baskets, there are pendulous or trailing varieties such as 'Illumination Orange'. Begonias can also be grown as house plants. The flowers also come in a wide variety of sizes and colors; they are either single or double and appear in loose clusters throughout summer.

CULTIVATION: *Fertile, organic, neutral to acidic soil or soil mix with good drainage. Flowers are best in partial shade; they suffer in direct sun. When in growth, give a balanced fertilizer. Many will not survive below 59°F (15°C).*

☀ ◊ Tender

‡ to 18in (45cm) ↔ to 14in (35cm)

‡↔ to 16in (40cm)

‡8in (20cm) ↔ 8–9in (20–22cm)

‡24in (60cm) ↔ 12in (30cm)

1 *B.* 'Alfa Pink' **2** *Begonia* 'All Round Dark Rose Green Leaf'
3 *B.* 'Expresso Scarlet' **4** *B.* 'Illumination Orange'

‡to 14in (35cm) ↔ to 12in (30cm)

‡30in (75cm) ↔ 24in (60cm)

‡↔ 12in (30cm)

‡↔ to 8in (20cm)

‡24in (60cm) ↔ 18in (45cm)

‡10in (25cm) ↔ 8in (20cm)

‡30in (75cm) ↔ 18in (45cm)

5 *B.* 'Inferno Apple Blossom' **6** *B.* 'Irene Nuss' **7** *B.* 'Nonstop'
8 *B.* 'Olympia White' **9** *B.* 'Orange Rubra' **10** *B.* 'Pin Up'
11 *B. sutherlandii*

Bellis perennis 'Pomponette'

This double-flowered form of the English daisy is usually grown as a biennial for spring bedding. Pink, red, or white flowerheads with quill-shaped petals appear from late winter to spring, above the dense clumps of spoon-shaped, bright green leaves. 'Dresden China' and 'Rob Roy' are other recommended selections.

CULTIVATION: *Grow in well-drained, moderately fertile soil, in full sun or partial shade. Deadhead to prolong flowering and to prevent self-seeding.*

☼ ☀ ◊ Z5b   ↕↔4–8in (10–20cm)

Berberis darwinii

The Darwin barberry is a vigorous, arching, evergreen shrub that carries masses of small, deep golden orange flowers on spiny stems from mid- to late spring; these are followed by blue berries in fall. The leaves are glossy dark green and spiny. Use as a vandal-resistant or barrier hedge.

CULTIVATION: *Grow in any but water-logged soil, in full sun or partial shade with shelter from cold, drying winds. Trim after flowering, if necessary.*

☼ ☀ ◊ ◊ Z7
↕10ft (3m) or more ↔10ft (3m)

Berberis x *ottawensis* '**Superba**'

This spiny, rounded, deciduous, spring-flowering shrub bears clusters of small, pale yellow, red-tinged flowers that are followed by red berries in fall. The red-purple leaves turn crimson before they fall. Effective as a specimen shrub or in a mixed border.

CULTIVATION: *Grow in almost any well-drained soil, preferably in full sun. Thin out dense growth in midwinter.*

☼ ◊ ♦ Z5   ↕↔8ft (2.5m)

Berberis x *stenophylla* '**Corallina Compacta**'

While *Berberis stenophylla* is a large, arching shrub, ideal for informal hedging, this cultivar of it is tiny: a small, evergreen shrub bearing spine-tipped, deep green leaves on arching, spiny stems. Quantities of tiny, light orange flowers appear from mid-spring, followed by small, blue-black berries.

CULTIVATION: *Best in fertile, organic soil that is reliably drained, in full sun. Cut back hard after flowering.*

☼ ◊ Z6b   ↕↔to 12in (30cm)

Berberis thunbergii 'Bagatelle'

A very compact, spiny, spring-flowering, deciduous shrub with deep red-purple leaves that turn orange and red in fall. The pale yellow flowers are followed by glossy red fruits. Good for a rock garden. *B. thunbergii* 'Atropurpurea Nana', (also sold as 'Crimson Pygmy'), is another small purple-leaved barberry, up to 24in (60cm) tall.

CULTIVATION: *Grow in well-drained soil, in full sun for best flower and foliage color. Thin out dense, overcrowded growth in mid- to late winter.*

☼ ◊ Z4b ↕12in (30cm) ↔16in (40cm)

Berberis thunbergii 'Rose Glow'

A compact, spiny, deciduous shrub with reddish-purple leaves that gradually become flecked with white as the season progresses. Tiny, pale yellow flowers appear in mid-spring, followed by small red berries. Good as a barrier hedge.

CULTIVATION: *Grow in any but water-logged soil, in full sun or partial shade. Cut out any dead wood in summer.*

☼ ☀ ◊ ◊ Z4b
↕6ft (2m) or more ↔6ft (2m)

Berberis verruculosa

A slow-growing, compact, spring-flowering barberry that makes a fine evergreen specimen shrub. The cup-shaped, golden yellow flowers are carried amid the spine-tipped, glossy dark green leaves on spiny, arching stems. Oval to pear-shaped black berries develop in fall.

CULTIVATION: *Best in well-drained, organic, fertile soil, in full sun. Keep pruning to a minimum.*

☼ ◊ Z7   ↔5ft (1.5m)

Berberis wilsoniae

A very spiny, semi-evergreen, arching shrub forming dense mounds of gray-green foliage that turns red and orange in fall. Clusters of pale yellow flowers in summer are followed by coral-pink to pinkish-red berries. Makes a good barrier hedge. Avoid seed-grown plants; they may be inferior hybrids.

CULTIVATION: *Grow in any well-drained soil, in sun or partial shade. Flowering and fruiting are best in full sun. Thin out dense growth in midwinter.*

☼ ◐ ◊ Z6b   ↕3ft (1m) ↔6ft (2m)

Bergenia 'Ballawley'

This clump-forming, evergreen perennial, one of the first to flower in spring, bears bright crimson flowers that are carried on sturdy red stems. The leathery, oval leaves turn bronze-red in winter. Suits a woodland garden, or plant in groups to edge a mixed border. *B. cordifolia* 'Purpurea' has similarly colored leaves, with deep magenta flowers.

CULTIVATION: *Grow in any well-drained soil, in full sun or light shade. Shelter from cold winds. Mulch in fall.*

☼ ☀ ◊ ◊ Z3b
‡to 24in (60cm) ↔24in (60cm)

Bergenia 'Silberlicht'

An early-flowering, clump-forming, evergreen perennial bearing clusters of cup-shaped white flowers, often flushed pink, in spring. (For pure white flowers on a similar plant, look for 'Bressingham White', or for deep pink, 'Morgenröte'.) The mid-green leaves are leathery, with toothed margins. Good underplanting for shrubs, which give it some winter shelter.

CULTIVATION: *Grow in any well-drained soil, in full sun or partial shade. Shelter from cold winds to avoid foliage scorch. Provide a mulch in fall.*

☼ ☀ ◊ ◊ Z3b
‡12in (30cm) ↔20in (50cm)

Betula nigra

The river birch is a tall, conical to spreading, deciduous tree with glossy, mid- to dark green, diamond-shaped leaves. It has shaggy, red-brown bark that peels in layers on young trees; on older specimens, the bark becomes blackish or gray-white and develops cracks. Yellow-brown male catkins are conspicuous in spring. Makes a fine specimen tree. 'Heritage' is a superior selection.

CULTIVATION: *Grow in moist but well-drained, moderately fertile soil, in full sun. Remove any damaged, diseased, or dead wood in late fall.*

☼ ◊ Z3   ↕60ft (18m) ↔40ft (12m)

Betula pendula 'Youngii'

Young's weeping birch is a deciduous tree with an elegant, weeping habit. The yellow-brown male catkins appear in early spring before the triangular leaves; the foliage turns golden yellow in fall. An attractive tree for a small garden, more dome-shaped than 'Tristis', 'Lacianata', or other popular weeping birches; growing wider than it is tall.

CULTIVATION: *Any moist but well-drained soil, in an open, sunny site. Keep pruning to a minimum; remove any shoots on the trunk in late fall.*

☼ ◊ Z2   ↕25ft (8m) ↔30ft (10m)

Betula utilis var. *jacquemontii*

The West Himalayan birch is an open, broadly conical, deciduous tree with smooth, peeling white bark. Catkins are a feature in early spring, and the dark green leaves turn rich golden yellow in fall. Plant where winter sun will light up the bark, particularly brilliantly white in the cultivars 'Silver Shadow', 'Jermyns', and 'Grayswood Ghost'.

CULTIVATION: *Grow in any moist but well-drained soil, in sun. Remove any damaged or dead wood from young trees in late fall; once established, keep pruning to a minimum.*

☼ ◊ Z4b ⬍50ft (15m) ↔23ft (7.5m)

Blechnum chilense

This South American plant is a striking evergreen that forms large clumps of leathery, ribbed fronds, which are covered with large scales when new. It makes an excellent house or conservatory plant that grows well in sun or shade, but needs frequent watering. The native *B.spicant* (deer fern) is widely available, requires an acidic soil, and is hardy to zone 5.

CULTIVATION: *Grow in a deep container in a neutral to acid soil mix enriched with organic matter. It forms a spreading colony and propagates easily by division. Minimum temperature 41°F (5°C).*

☼ ☀ ☀ ◊ ◊ Tender
⬍to 6ft (1.8m) ↔indefinite

Brachyglottis 'Sunshine'

A bushy, mound-forming, evergreen shrub bearing oval leaves that are silvery gray when young, becoming dark green with white-felted undersides as they develop. Daisylike yellow flowers appear from early to midsummer. Some gardeners prefer it as a foliage plant, pinching it or snipping off the flower buds before they open. Thrives in coastal sites.

CULTIVATION: *Grow in any well-drained soil, in a sunny, sheltered site. Trim back after flowering. Responds well to hard pruning in spring.*

☼ ◊ Tender
‡3–5ft (1–1.5m) ↔6ft (2m) or more

Bracteantha Bright Bikini Series

These strawflowers are upright annuals or short-lived perennials with papery, double flowers in red, pink, orange, yellow, and white from late spring to fall. The leaves are gray-green. Use to edge a border, or grow in a windowbox; flowers are long-lasting and cut and dry well. For single colors rather than a mixture, try 'Frosted Sulphur' (lemon yellow), 'Silvery Rose', and 'Reeves Purple'.

CULTIVATION: *Grow in moist but well-drained, moderately fertile soil. Choose a position in full sun.*

☼ ◊ Tender   ‡↔12in (30cm)

Brunnera macrophylla 'Hadspen Cream'

This clump-forming perennial with attractive foliage is ideal as a groundcover in borders and among deciduous trees. In mid- and late spring, upright clusters of small, bright blue flowers appear above heart-shaped leaves, plain green in *Brunnera macrophylla*, but with irregular, creamy white margins in this attractive cultivar.

CULTIVATION: *Grow in moist but well-drained, organic soil. Choose a position that is cool and lightly shaded.*

☼ ◐ ◊ ◊ Z3b
‡18in (45cm) ↔24in (60cm)

Buddleja alternifolia

A dense, deciduous shrub carrying slender, arching branches. Fragrant, lilac-purple flowers are produced in neat clusters during early summer among the narrow, gray-green leaves. Makes a good wall shrub or can be trained with a single, clear trunk as a striking specimen tree. Attractive to beneficial insects.

CULTIVATION: *Best in alkaline soil but can be grown in any soil that is well drained, in full sun. Cut stems back to strong buds after flowering; responds well to hard pruning in spring.*

☼ ◊ Z4b   ‡↔12ft (4m)

Buddleja davidii

All cultivars of *B. davidii*, the butterfly bush, are fast-growing, deciduous shrubs with a wide range of flower colors. As the popular name suggests, the flowers attract butterflies and other beneficial garden insects in profusion. The long, arching shoots carry lance-shaped, mid- to gray-green leaves, up to 10in (25cm) long. Conical clusters of bright, fragrant flowers, usually about 12in (30cm) long, are borne at the end of arching stems from summer to fall; those of 'Royal Red' are the largest, up to 20in (50cm) long. These shrubs respond well to hard pruning in spring, which keeps them a compact size for a small garden.

CULTIVATION: *Grow in well-drained, fertile soil, in sun. Restrict size and encourage better flowers by pruning back hard to a low framework each spring. To prevent self-seeding, cut spent flowerheads back to a pair of leaves or sideshoots; this may also result in a second period of bloom.*

☼ ◊ Z5

‡10ft (3m) ↔15ft (5m)

‡10ft (3m) ↔15ft (5m)

‡10ft (3m) ↔15ft (5m)

1 *B. davidii* 'Empire Blue' **2** *B. davidii* 'Royal Red' **3** *B. davidii* 'White Profusion'

Buddleja globosa

The orange ball tree is a deciduous or semi-evergreen shrub bearing, unusually for a buddleja, round clusters of tiny, orange-yellow flowers that appear in early summer. The lance-shaped leaves are dark green with woolly undersides. This large shrub is prone to becoming bare at the base and does not respond well to pruning, so grow toward the back of a mixed border.

CULTIVATION: *Best on well-drained, alkaline soil, in a sunny position with shelter from cold winds. Pruning should be kept to a minimum, or the next year's flowers will be lost.*

☼ ◊ Z8   ↕↔15ft (5m)

Buddleja 'Lochinch'

A compact, deciduous shrub, very similar to a *Buddleja davidii* (see p.125), bearing long spikes of lilac-blue flowers from late summer to fall. The leaves are downy and gray-green when young, becoming smooth and developing white-felted undersides as they mature. Very attractive to butterflies.

CULTIVATION: *Grow in any well-drained, moderately fertile soil, in sun. Cut back all stems close to the base each year as the buds begin to swell in spring.*

☼ ◊ Z7   ↕8ft (2.5m) ↔10ft (3m)

Buxus sempervirens 'Elegantissima'

This variegated form of the common boxwood is a rounded, dense, evergreen shrub bearing small and narrow, glossy bright green leaves edged with cream. The flowers are of little significance. Responding well to trimming, it is very good as an edging plant or for use as a low hedge. 'Latifolia Maculata' (Z6) is also variegated, with yellow leaf markings.

CULTIVATION: *Grow in any well-drained soil, in sun or light shade. Trim in spring and summer; overgrown shrubs respond well to hard pruning in late spring.*

☼ ☀ ◊ Z5b   ↕↔5ft (1.5m)

Buxus sempervirens 'Suffruticosa'

A very dense, slow-growing boxwood bearing small, evergreen, glossy, bright green leaves. Widely used as an edging plant or for clipping into precise shapes. During late spring or early summer, inconspicuous but fragrant flowers are produced. Excellent as a hedge.

CULTIVATION: *Grow in any well-drained, fertile soil, in sun or semi-shade. The combination of dry soil and full sun can cause scorching. Trim hedges in summer; overgrown specimens can be pruned hard in late spring.*

☼ ☀ ◊ Z6   ↕3ft (1m) ↔5ft (1.5m)

Calamagrostis brachytricha

Feather reed grass is a handsome plant with tall, upright stems of narrow flowering plumes in late summer. These open and fade to silvery gray tinged with pink as the season progresses, lasting well into winter. This is a useful plant for both the summer and winter garden, and looks best planted in drifts. It forms neat clumps of arching foliage.

CULTIVATION: *Grow in any fertile, moist but well-drained soil, in sun or partial shade. Cut back old flowerheads in late winter.*

☀ ◐ ◊ ❍ Z4
‡to 5ft (1.5m) ↔24in (60cm)

Callicarpa bodinieri var. *giraldii* 'Profusion'

An upright, deciduous shrub grown mainly for its long-lasting fall display of shiny, beadlike, deep violet berries. The large, pale green, tapering leaves are bronze when they emerge in spring, and pale pink flowers appear in summer. Brings a long season of interest to a shrub border; for maximum impact, plant in groups.

CULTIVATION: *Grow in any well-drained, fertile soil, in full sun or dappled shade. Cut back hard in spring to remove winter kill and to keep compact.*

☀ ◐ ◊ Z6b   ‡10ft (3m) ↔8ft (2.5m)

Callirhoe involucrata

Commonly called purple poppy mallow or wine cups, this tough, heat-tolerant North American native perennial is a ground-hugging mallow family member that bears cup-shaped, magenta flowers in summer. Use it to line rock walls or as a groundcover on sloping or infertile sites

CULTIVATION: *Grow in medium to dry, well-drained, or rocky soil, in full sun. A long tap root makes transplanting difficult, but it self-sows in ideal conditions. No serious pests or diseases, but can suffer crown rot in moist conditions.*

☼ ◊ Z5b ‡to 9in (23cm) ↔3ft (1m)

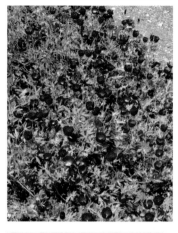

Callistemon citrinus 'Splendens'

This attractive cultivar of the crimson bottlebrush is an evergreen shrub, usually with arching branches. Dense spikes of brilliant red flowers appear in spring and summer, amid the gray-green, lemon-scented leaves, which are bronze-red when young. Grow in a container and bring indoors for the winter.

CULTIVATION: *Best in well-drained, fertile, neutral to acidic soil, in full sun. Pinch out tips of young plants to promote bushiness. Tolerates hard pruning in spring.*

☼ ◊ Tender
‡6–25ft (2–8m) ↔5–20ft (1.5–6m)

Calluna vulgaris

Cultivars of *C. vulgaris* are upright to spreading, fine-leaved heathers. They make excellent evergreen groundcover plants if weeds are suppressed before planting. Dense spikes of bell-shaped flowers appear from midsummer to late fall, in shades of red, purple, pink, or white; 'Kinlochruel' is quite distinctive with its double white flowers in long clusters. Seasonal interest is extended into winter by cultivars with colored foliage, such as 'Robert Chapman' and 'Beoley Gold'. Heathers are very attractive to bees and other beneficial insects and make good companions to dwarf conifers.

CULTIVATION: *Best in well-drained, organic, acidic soil, in an open, sunny site, to recreate their native moorland habitats. Trim off flowered shoots in early spring with shears; remove overly long shoots wherever possible, cutting back to their point of origin below the flower cluster.*

☼ ◊ Z5–6*

‡10in (25cm) ↔14in (35cm)   ‡14in (35cm) ↔to 30in (75cm)   ‡10in (25cm) ↔16in (40cm)

‡10in (25cm) ↔26in (65cm)

1 *C. vulgaris* 'Beoley Gold' **2** *C. vulgaris* 'Darkness' **3** *C. vulgaris* 'Kinlochruel'
4 *C. vulgaris* 'Robert Chapman'

Caltha palustris

The marsh marigold is a clump-forming, aquatic perennial that thrives in a bog garden or at the margins of a stream or pond. Cup-shaped, waxy, bright golden yellow flowers appear on tall stems in spring, above the kidney-shaped, glossy green leaves. For cheerful double flowers, look for the cultivar 'Flore Pleno'.

CULTIVATION: *Best in boggy, rich soil, in an open, sunny site. Tolerates root restriction in aquatic containers in water no deeper than 9in (23cm), but prefers shallower conditions.*

☼ ◑ Z3
↕4–16in (10–40cm) ↔18in (45cm)

Camellia 'Inspiration'

A dense, upright, evergreen shrub or small tree bearing masses of saucer-shaped, semidouble, deep pink flowers from mid-winter to late spring. The dark green leaves are oval and leathery. Good for the back of a border or as a specimen shrub.

CULTIVATION: *Best in moist but well-drained, fertile, neutral to acidic soil, in partial shade with shelter from cold, drying winds. Mulch around the base with shredded bark. After flowering, prune back young plants to encourage a bushy habit and a balanced shape.*

◐ ◊ ◑ Z8   ↕12ft (4m) ↔6ft (2m)

Camellia japonica

These long-lived and elegant, evergreen shrubs or small trees for gardens with acidic soil are very popular in shrub borders, woodland gardens, or standing on their own in the open ground or in containers. The oval leaves are glossy and dark green; they serve to heighten the brilliance of the single to fully double flowers in spring. Single and semidouble flowers have a prominent central boss of yellow stamens. Most flowers are suitable for cutting, but blooms may be spoiled by late frosts.

CULTIVATION: *Grow in moist but well-drained, organic, acidic soil, in partial shade. Choose a site sheltered from early morning sun, cold winds, and late frosts. Do not plant too deeply; the top of the root ball must be level with the firmed soil. Maintain a mulch 2–3in (5–7cm) deep of leaf mold or shredded bark. Little pruning is necessary, although moderate trimming of young plants will help produce a balanced shape.*

☀ ◐ ◌ Z8

1 ‡15ft (5m) ↔25ft (8m) **2** ‡28ft (9m) ↔25ft (8m) **3** ‡28ft (9m) ↔25ft (8m)

4 ‡6ft (2m) ↔3ft (1m) **5** ‡28ft (9m) ↔25ft (8m) **6** ‡28ft (9m) ↔25ft (8m)

1 *Camellia japonica* 'Adolphe Audusson' **2** 'Alexander Hunter' **3** 'Berenice Boddy'
4 'Bob's Tinsie' **5** 'Coquettii' **6** 'Elegans'

MORE CHOICES

'Akashigata' Deep pink flowers.
'Bob Hope' Dark red.
'C. M. Hovey' Crimson scarlet
'Doctor Tinsley' Pinkish white.
'Grand Prix' Bright red with yellow stamens
'Hagoromo' Pale pink
'Masayoshi' White with red marbling.
'Miss Charleston' Ruby red.
'Nuccio's Gem' White.

7

‡28ft (9m) ↔25ft (8m)

8

‡28ft (9m) ↔25ft (8m)

9

‡28ft (9m) ↔25ft (8m)

10

‡28ft (9m) ↔25ft (8m)

11

‡28ft (9m) ↔25ft (8m)

12

‡28ft (9m) ↔25ft (8m)

13

‡28ft (9m) ↔25ft (8m)

14

‡28ft (9m) ↔25ft (8m)

7 *Camellia japonica* 'Gloire de Nantes' **8** 'Guilio Nuccio' **9** 'Jupiter' (*syn.* 'Paul's Jupiter')
10 'Lavinia Maggi' **11** 'Mrs D. W. Davis' **12** 'R. L. Wheeler' **13** 'Rubescens Major'
14 'Tricolor'

Camellia 'Lasca Beauty'

An open, upright shrub greatly valued for its very large, semidouble, pale pink flowers, which appear in mid-spring. They stand out against the dark green foliage. Grow in a cool greenhouse, and move outdoors to a partially shaded site in early summer where not hardy.

CULTIVATION: *Grow in acidic potting mix in bright filtered light. Water freely with soft water when in growth; more sparingly in winter. Apply a balanced fertilizer once in mid-spring and again in early summer.*

☀ ◊ ◊ Z8
↕6–15ft (2–5m) ↔5–10ft (1.5–3m)

Camellia 'Leonard Messel'

This spreading, evergreen shrub with oval, leathery, dark green leaves is one of the hardiest camellias available. It produces an abundance of large, flattish to cup-shaped, semidouble, clear pink flowers from early to late spring. Excellent in a shrub border.

CULTIVATION: *Best in moist but well-drained, fertile, neutral to acidic soil. Position in semi-shade with shelter from cold, drying winds. Maintain a mulch of shredded bark or leafmold around the base. Pruning is rarely necessary.*

☀ ◊ ◊ Z8   ↕12ft (4m) ↔10ft (3m)

Camellia 'Mandalay Queen'

This large, widely branching shrub bears deep rose-pink, semidouble flowers in spring. The broad, leathery leaves are dark green. Best grown in a cool greenhouse, but move it outdoors in summer.

CULTIVATION: *Best in acidic potting mix with bright, filtered light. Water freely with soft water when in growth, more sparingly in winter. Apply a balanced fertilizer in mid-spring and again in early summer.*

☀ ◊ ◖ Z8 ‡to 50ft (15m) ↔15ft (5m)

Camellia sasanqua 'Narumigata'

An upright shrub or small tree valued for its late display of fragrant, single-petaled white flowers in mid- to late fall. The foliage is dark green. Makes a good hedge, though where marginally hardy it does better against a warm, sunny wall. *C. sasanqua* 'Crimson King' is a very similar shrub, with red flowers.

CULTIVATION: *Grow in moist but well-drained, organic, acidic soil, and maintain a thick mulch. Choose a site in full sun or partial shade, with shelter from cold winds. Tolerates hard pruning after flowering.*

☀ ☀ ◊ ◖ Z8 ‡20ft (6m) ↔10ft (3m)

Camellia x *williamsii*

Cultivars of *C. x williamsii* are strong-growing, evergreen shrubs that are much valued for their bright, lustrous foliage and the unsurpassed elegance of their roselike flowers that range from pure white to crimson. Most flower in mid- and late spring, although 'Anticipation' and 'Mary Christian' begin to flower in late winter. These plants make handsome specimens for a cool conservatory or shrub border, and 'J.C. Williams', for example, can be trained against a wall. Avoid sites exposed to morning sun to prevent damage to buds and flowers.

CULTIVATION: *Best in moist but well-drained, acidic to neutral soil, in partial shade. Shelter from frost and cold winds, and mulch with shredded bark. Prune young plants after flowering to promote bushiness; wall-trained shrubs should be allowed to develop a strong central stem.*

☼ ◐ ◊ ◊ Z8

1
‡12ft (4m) ↔ 6ft (2m)

2
‡10ft (3m) ↔ 8ft (2.5m)

3
‡15ft (5m) ↔ 8ft (2.5m)

1 *C. x williamsii* 'Anticipation' **2** *C. x williamsii* 'Brigadoon' **3** *C. x williamsii* 'Donation'

4 ↕↔12ft (4m)

5 ↕12ft (4m) ↔8ft (2.5m)

6 ↕12ft (4m) ↔8ft (2.5m)

7 ↕12ft (4m) ↔8ft (2.5m)

8 ↕12ft (4m) ↔8ft (2.5m)

9 ↕↔10ft (3m)

4 *C.* × *williamsii* 'George Blandford' **5** *C.* × *williamsii* 'Joan Trehane' **6** *C.* × *williamsii* 'J.C. Williams' **7** *C.* × *williamsii* 'Mary Christian' **8** *C.* × *williamsii* 'Saint Ewe' **9** *C.* × *williamsii* 'Water Lily'

Campanula cochleariifolia

Fairies' thimbles is a low-growing, rosette-forming perennial bearing, in midsummer, abundant clusters of open, bell-shaped, mauve-blue or white flowers. The bright green leaves are heart-shaped. It spreads freely by means of creeping stems and can be invasive. Particularly effective if allowed to colonize areas of gravel, paving crevices, or the tops of dry walls.

CULTIVATION: *Prefers moist but well-drained soil, in sun or partial shade. To restrict spread, pull up unwanted plants.*

☼ ☀ ◊ Z3
‡to 3in (8cm) ↔to 20in (50cm) or more

Campanula glomerata 'Superba'

A fast-growing, clump-forming perennial carrying dense heads of large, bell-shaped, purple-violet flowers in summer. The lance-shaped to oval, mid-green leaves are arranged in rosettes at the base of the plant and along the stems. Excellent in herbaceous borders or informal, cottage-style gardens.

CULTIVATION: *Best in moist but well-drained, neutral to alkaline soil, in sun or semi-shade. Cut back after flowering to encourage a second flush of flowers.*

☼ ☀ ◊ ◊ Z3
‡30in (75cm) ↔3ft (1m) or more

Campanula lactiflora 'Loddon Anna'

An upright, branching perennial producing sprays of large, nodding, bell-shaped, soft lilac-pink flowers from midsummer above mid-green leaves. Makes an excellent border perennial but may need staking in an exposed site. Mixes well with the white-flowered 'Alba', or the deep purple 'Prichard's Variety'.

CULTIVATION: *Best in moist but well-drained, fertile soil, in full sun or partial shade. Trim after flowering to encourage a second, although less profuse, flush of flowers.*

☼ ☀ ◊ ◊ Z3
↕4–5ft (1.2–1.5m) ↔24in (60cm)

Campanula portenschlagiana

The Dalmatian bellflower is a robust, mound-forming, evergreen perennial with long, bell-shaped, deep purple flowers from mid- to late summer. The leaves are toothed and mid-green. Good in a rock garden or on a sunny bank. May become invasive. *Campanula poschkarskyana* can be used in a similar way; look for the recommended cultivar 'Stella'.

CULTIVATION: *Best in moist but well-drained soil, in sun or partial shade. Very vigorous, so plant away from smaller, less robust plants.*

☼ ☀ ◊ Z3
↕to 6in (15cm) ↔20in (50cm) or more

Campsis x tagliabuana 'Madame Galen'

Woody-stemmed climber that will cling with aerial roots against a wall, fence, or pillar, or up into a tree. From late summer to fall, clusters of trumpet-shaped, orange-red flowers open among narrow, toothed leaves. For yellow flowers, choose *C. radicans* f. *flava* (Z5b).

CULTIVATION: *Prefers moist but well-drained, fertile soil, in a sunny, sheltered site. Tie in new growth until the allotted space is covered by a strong framework. Prune back hard each winter to promote bushiness.*

☼ ◊ ◑ Z6　　　↕30ft (10m) or more

Cardiocrinum giganteum

The giant lily is a spectacular, summer-flowering, bulbous perennial with trumpet-shaped white flowers that are flushed with maroon-purple at the throats. The stems are thick and the leaves broadly oval and glossy green. It needs careful siting and can take up to seven years to bloom. Grow in woodland or in a sheltered border in shade.

CULTIVATION: *Best in deep, moist but well-drained, reliably cool, organic soil, in semi-shade. Intolerant of hot or dry conditions. Slugs can be a problem.*

☼ ◊ Z7
↕5–12ft (1.5–4m) ↔18in (45cm)

Carex elata 'Aurea'

Bowles' golden sedge is a colorful, tussock-forming, deciduous perennial for a moist border, bog garden, or the margins of a pond or stream. The bright leaves are narrow and golden yellow. In spring and early summer, small spikes of relatively inconspicuous, dark brown flowers are carried above the leaves. Often sold as *C.* 'Bowles' Golden'.

CULTIVATION: *Grow in moist or wet, reasonably fertile soil. Position in full sun or partial shade.*

 ☼ ☀ ◑ ◐ Z5
‡to 28in (70cm) ↔18in (45cm)

Carex oshimensis 'Evergold'

A very popular, evergreen, variegated sedge, bright and densely tufted with narrow, dark green, yellow-striped leaves. Spikes of tiny, dark brown flowers are borne in mid- and late spring. Tolerates freer drainage than many sedges and is suitable for a mixed border.

CULTIVATION: *Needs moist but well-drained, fertile soil, in sun or partial shade. Remove dead leaves in summer.*

☼ ☀ ◐ Z6b
‡12in (30cm) ↔14in (35cm)

Carpenteria californica

This summer-flowering, evergreen shrub bears large, fragrant, white flowers with showy yellow stamens. The glossy, dark green leaves are narrowly oval. It is suitable for wall-training, which overcomes its sometimes sprawling habit. Where marginally hardy, protect it by growing it on a sheltered wall.

CULTIVATION: *Grow in well-drained soil, in full sun with shelter from cold winds. In spring, remove branches that have become exhausted by flowering, cutting them back to their bases.*

☼ ◊ Z8　　　　　　↕↔6ft (2m)

Caryopteris x *clandonensis* 'Heavenly Blue'

A compact, upright, deciduous shrub grown for its clusters of intensely dark blue flowers that appear in late summer and early fall. The irregularly toothed leaves are gray-green.

CULTIVATION: *Grow in well-drained, moderately fertile, light soil, in full sun. Prune all stems back hard to low buds in late spring. A woody framework will develop, which should not be cut into.*

☼ ◊ Z6　　　　　　↕↔3ft (1m)

Cassiope 'Edinburgh'

A heatherlike, upright, evergreen shrub producing nodding, bell-shaped flowers in spring; these are white with small, greenish-brown outer petals. The scalelike, dark green leaves closely overlap along the stems. Good in a rock garden (not among limestone) or a peat bed. *C. lycopoides* (Z8) has very similar flowers but is mat-forming, almost prostrate, only 3in (8cm) tall.

CULTIVATION: *Grow in reliably moist, organic, acidic soil, in partial shade. Trim after flowering.*

☀ ◑ Z3b   ↔to 10in (25cm)

Catalpa bignonioides 'Aurea'

This bright-leaved variety of southern catalpa is a superb foliage plant, which can be cultivated either as a specimen tree or at the back of a mixed border. In a border, cut it back to a stump each year, and it will respond with luxuriant foliage. The yellowish-green, deciduous, heart-shaped leaves are tinted bronze when young. White flower clusters in spring give rise to long, bean-like pods.

CULTIVATION: *Grow in fertile, moist but well-drained soil, in sun.*

☀ ◊ ◑ Z5b   ↔30ft (10m)

Ceanothus 'Autumnal Blue'

A vigorous, evergreen shrub that produces a profusion of tiny but vivid, rich sky blue flowers from late summer to fall. The leaves are broadly oval and glossy dark green. One of the hardiest of the evergreen ceanothus, it is suitable in an open border as well as for informal training on walls; especially where marginally hardy.

CULTIVATION: *Grow in well-drained, moderately fertile soil, in full sun with shelter from cold winds. Tip-prune young plants in spring, and trim established plants after flowering.*

☼ ◊ Z8   ↕↔10ft (3m)

Ceanothus 'Blue Mound'

This mound-forming, late spring-flowering ceanothus is an evergreen shrub carrying masses of rich dark blue flowers. The leaves are finely toothed and glossy dark green. Ideal as a groundcover, for cascading over banks or low walls, or in a large, sunny rock garden. *Ceanothus* 'Burkwoodii' and 'Italian Skies' can be used similarly.

CULTIVATION: *Grow in well-drained, fertile soil, in full sun. Tip-prune young plants and trim established ones after flowering, in midsummer.*

☼ ◊ Z8   ↕5ft (1.5m) ↔6ft (2m)

Ceanothus x *delileanus* 'Gloire de Versailles'

This deciduous ceanothus is a fast-growing shrub. From midsummer to early fall, large spikes of tiny, pale blue flowers are borne amid broadly oval, finely toothed, mid-green leaves. 'Topaze' (Z9) is similar, with dark blue flowers. They benefit from harder annual pruning than evergreen ceanothus.

CULTIVATION: *Grow in well-drained, fairly fertile, light soil, in sun. Tolerates alkaline soil. In spring, shorten the previous year's stems by half or more, or cut right back to a low framework.*

☼ ◊ Z8   ↕↔5ft (1.5m)

Ceanothus thyrsiflorus var. *repens*

This low and spreading ceanothus is a mound-forming, evergreen shrub bearing rounded clusters of tiny blue flowers in late spring and early summer. The leaves are dark green and glossy. A good shrub to clothe a sunny or slightly shaded bank, provide the protection of a warm, sunny site where marginal.

CULTIVATION: *Best in light, well-drained, fertile soil, in sun or light shade. Trim back after flowering to keep compact.*

☼ ◑ ◊ Z8   ↕3ft (1m) ↔8ft (2.5m)

Ceratostigma plumbaginoides

A spreading, woody-based, sub-shrubby perennial bearing clusters of brilliant blue flowers in late summer. The oval, bright green leaves, carried on upright, slender red stems, become red-tinted in fall. Good for a rock garden, and also suitable as a groundcover.

CULTIVATION: *Grow in moist but well-drained, moderately fertile soil. Choose a sheltered site in full sun or partial shade. Cut back stems to the ground in late winter or early spring.*

☼ ☀ ◊ Z6
‡to 18in (45cm) ↔ to 12in (30cm) or more

Cercidiphyllum japonicum

The katsura tree is fast growing, spreading tree with small, heart-shaped, mid-green leaves. New leaves emerge bronze but are at their best in fall, when they turn to pale yellow, orange, red, or pink; at this time, the tree also exudes a delicious caramel scent. The best foliage colors are seen on trees in neutral to acid soils.

CULTIVATION: *Grow in fertile, moist but well-drained soil, with plenty of depth for the roots. Water regularly until established and during extended droughts.*

☼ ☀ ◊ ◊ Z5
‡to 70ft (20m) ↔ to 50ft(15m)

Cercis canadensis '**Forest Pansy**'

The eastern redbud is remarkable for pale pink flowers that adorn trunk and branches in spring before the heart-shaped leaves emerge. This selection has red-purple foliage that turns purple and gold in fall. The deciduous tree will develop a rounded shape, spreading as wide as it is tall. Dark gray beanpods develop in fall and sometimes remain into winter.

CULTIVATION: *Adaptable to different soils, but thrives in moist, well drained, organic rich sites; mature trees will tolerate some drought. Fertilize during growing season.*

☀ ◐ ◊ Z6   ↔15ft (5m)

Cercis siliquastrum

The Judas tree is a handsome, broadly spreading, deciduous tree that gradually develops a rounded crown. Clusters of pealike, bright pink flowers appear on the previous year's wood, either before or with the heart-shaped leaves in mid-spring. The foliage is bronze when young, maturing to dark blue-green, then to yellow in fall. Flowering is best after a long, hot summer.

CULTIVATION: *Grow in deep, reliably well-drained, fertile soil, in full sun or light dappled shade. Prune young trees to shape in early summer, removing any frost-damaged growth.*

☀ ◐ ◊ Z7   ↔30ft (10m)

Chaenomeles speciosa 'Moerloosei'

A fast-growing and wide-spreading, deciduous shrub bearing large white flowers, flushed dark pink, in early spring. Tangled, spiny branches bear oval, glossy dark green leaves. The flowers are followed in fall by apple-shaped, aromatic, yellow-green fruits. Use as a free-standing shrub or train against a wall.

CULTIVATION: *Grow in well-drained, moderately fertile soil, in full sun for best flowering, or light shade. If wall-trained, shorten sideshoots to 2 or 3 leaves in late spring. Free-standing shrubs require little pruning.*

☼ ☼ ◊ Z5b   ‡8ft (2.5m) ↔15ft (5m)

Chaenomeles x *superba* 'Crimson and Gold'

This spreading, deciduous shrub bears masses of dark red flowers with conspicuous golden yellow anthers from spring until summer. The dark green leaves appear on the spiny branches just after the first bloom of flowers; these are followed by yellow-green fruits. Useful as a groundcover or low hedging.

CULTIVATION: *Grow in well-drained, fertile soil, in sun. Trim lightly after flowering; shorten sideshoots to 2 or 3 leaves if grown against a wall.*

☼ ◊ Z5   ‡3ft (1m) ↔6ft (2m)

Lawson Cypresses (*Chamaecyparis lawsoniana*)

Cultivars of *C. lawsoniana* are popular evergreen conifers, available in many different shapes, sizes, and foliage colors. All have red-brown bark and dense crowns of branches that droop at the tips. The flattened sprays of dense, aromatic foliage, occasionally bearing small, rounded cones, make the larger types of Lawson cypress very suitable for thick hedging, such as bright blue-gray 'Pembury Blue', or golden yellow 'Lane'. Use compact cultivars in smaller gardens such as 'Ellwoodii' (to 10ft/3m) and 'Ellwood's Gold'; dwarf upright types such as 'Chilworth Silver' make eye-catching feature plants for containers, rock gardens, or borders.

CULTIVATION: *Grow in moist but well-drained soil, in sun. They tolerate alkaline soil but not exposed sites. Trim regularly from spring to fall; do not cut into older wood. To train as formal hedges, pruning must begin on young plants.*

☀ ◊ Z6

‡5ft (1.5m) ↔24in (60cm) ‡to 130ft (40m) ↔to 15ft (5m) ‡to 50ft (15m) ↔6-15ft (2-5m)

1 *C. lawsoniana* 'Ellwood's Gold' **2** *C. lawsoniana* 'Lanei Aurea'
3 *C. lawsoniana* 'Pembury Blue'

Chamaecyparis nootkatensis 'Pendula'

This large and drooping conifer develops a gaunt, open crown as it matures. Hanging from the arching branches are evergreen sprays of dark green foliage with small, round cones that ripen in spring. Its unusual habit makes an interesting feature for a large garden.

CULTIVATION: *Best in full sun, in moist but well-drained, neutral to slightly acidic soil; will also tolerate dry, alkaline soil.*

☼ ◊ ◊ Z5
‡to 100ft (30m) ↔ to 25ft (8m)

Chamaecyparis obtusa 'Nana Gracilis'

This dwarf form of Hinoki cypress is an evergreen, coniferous tree with a dense pyramidal habit. The aromatic, rich green foliage is carried in rounded, flattened sprays, bearing small cones that ripen to yellow-brown. Useful in a large rock garden, particularly to give Oriental style. 'Nana Aurea' (Z5b) looks very similar but grows to only half the size.

CULTIVATION: *Grow in moist but well-drained, neutral to slightly acidic soil, in full sun. Also tolerates dry, alkaline soil. Regular pruning is not necessary.*

☼ ◊ Z5b
‡10ft (3m) ↔6ft (2m)

Chamaecyparis pisifera 'Boulevard'

A broad, evergreen conifer that develops into a conical tree with an open crown. The soft, blue-green foliage is borne in flattened sprays with angular green cones, maturing to brown. Very neat and compact in habit; this makes an excellent specimen tree for poorly drained, damp soil.

CULTIVATION: *Grow in reliably moist, preferably neutral to acidic soil, in full sun. No regular pruning is required.*

☼ ◐ ◆ Z4b ‡30ft (10m) ↔15ft (5m)

Chamaerops humilis

The European fan palm is a bushy foliage plant with several shaggy, fibrous stems topped by fan-like leaves with spiny stalks. Unspectacular flowers appear from spring. It will survive only short spells just below freezing so in colder climates is best grown in a cool greenhouse or in a container that can be moved under cover in winter.

CULTIVATION: *Grow in well-drained, reasonably fertile soil, in sun. To grow in containers, choose a soil-based growing medium and fertilize monthly in summer. Minimum temperature 45°F (7°C).*

☼ ◑ ◊ Tender
‡6–10ft (2–3m) ↔3–6ft (1–2m)

Chimonanthus praecox '**Grandiflorus**'

Wintersweet is a vigorous, upright, deciduous shrub grown for the fragrant flowers borne on its bare branches in winter; on this cultivar they are large, cup-shaped, and deep yellow with maroon stripes inside. The leaves are mid-green. Suitable for a shrub border or for training against a sunny wall.

CULTIVATION: *Grow in well-drained, fertile soil, in a sunny, sheltered site. Best left unpruned when young so that mature flowering wood can develop. Cut back flowered stems of wall-trained plants in spring.*

☼ ◊ Z7　　　‡12ft (4m) ↔10ft (3m)

Chionodoxa luciliae

Glory of the snow is a small, bulbous perennial bearing star-shaped, clear blue flowers with white eyes in early spring. The glossy green leaves are usually curved backward. Grow in a sunny rock garden, or naturalize under deciduous trees. Sometimes referred to as *C. gigantea* of gardens. *C. forbesii* (Z3) is very similar, with more erect leaves.

CULTIVATION: *Grow in any well-drained soil, with a position in full sun. Plant bulbs 3in (8cm) deep in fall.*

☼ ◊ Z3　　　‡6in (15cm) ↔1¹/₄in (3cm)

Choisya ternata

Mexican orange blossom is a fast-growing, rounded, evergreen shrub valued for its attractive foliage and fragrant flowers. The aromatic, dark green leaves are divided into three. Clusters of star-shaped white flowers appear in spring. A fine, pollution-tolerant shrub for town gardens, but prone to frost damage in exposed sites. 'Aztec Pearl' is similar, its flowers perhaps not quite as fragrant.

CULTIVATION: *Grow in well-drained, fairly fertile soil, in full sun. Naturally forms a well-shaped bush without pruning. Cutting back flowered shoots encourages a second flush of flowers.*

☼ ◊ Z8   ↕↔8ft (2.5m)

Choisya ternata 'Sundance'

This slower-growing, bright yellow-leaved variety of Mexican orange blossom is a compact, evergreen shrub. The aromatic leaves, divided into three leaflets, are a duller yellow-green if positioned in shade. Flowers are rare.

CULTIVATION: *Best in well-drained, fertile soil, in full sun for the best leaf color. Provide shelter from cold winds. Trim wayward shoots in summer, removing any frost-damaged shoots in spring.*

☼ ◊ Z8   ↕↔8ft (2.5m)

Garden Chrysanthemums

These upright, bushy perennials are a mainstay of the late border, with bright, showy flowerheads traditionally used for display and cutting. The lobed or feathery leaves are aromatic and bright green. They flower from late summer to mid-fall, depending on the cultivar; very late-flowering cultivars are best raised under glass in colder climates (see p.157). The flower form, often many-petaled, varies from the daisylike 'Pennine Alfie' to the blowsy, reflexed blooms of 'George Griffith'. Lift in fall and store over winter in frost-free conditions. Plant out after any risk of frost has passed.

CULTIVATION: *Grow in moist but well-drained, neutral to slightly acidic soil enriched with well-rotted manure, in a sunny, sheltered site. Stake tall flower stems. Apply a balanced fertilizer when in growth, until flower buds begin to show.*

☼ ◊ ◑ Z4–8*

1 ‡4ft (1.2m) ↔30in (75cm) 2 ‡4ft (1.2m) ↔30in (75cm) 3 ‡3ft (1m) ↔24-30in (60-75cm)

4 ‡20in (50cm) ↔10in (25cm) 5 ‡↔24in (60cm) 6 ‡3¹/₂ft (1.1m) ↔24-30in (60-75cm)

1 *Chrysanthemum* 'Amber Enbee Wedding' 2 *C.* 'Amber Yvonne Arnaud' 3 *C.* 'Angora' 4 *C.* 'Bravo' 5 *C.* 'Bronze Fairie' 6 *C.* 'Cherry Nathalie'

‡3½ft (1m) ↔ 24–30in (60–75cm)

‡30in (90cm) ↔ 12in (30cm)

‡4½–5ft (1.3–1.5m) ↔ 30in (75cm)

‡4ft (1.2m) ↔ 30in (75cm)

‡30in (90cm) ↔ 12in (30cm)

‡24in (60cm) ↔ 12in (30cm)

‡30in (90cm) ↔ 12in (30cm)

‡4ft (1.2m) ↔ 30in (75cm)

‡4ft (1.2m) ↔ 30in (75cm)

7 *C.* 'Eastleigh' **8** *C.* 'Flo Cooper' **9** *C.* 'George Griffiths' **10** *C.* 'Madeleine'
11 *C.* 'Mancetta Bride' **12** *C.* 'Mavis' **13** *C.* 'Myss Madi' **14** *C.* 'Pennine Alfie'
15 *C.* 'Pennine Flute'

16 ‡28in (70cm) ↔ 10in (30cm)

17 ‡25in (65cm) ↔ 12in (30cm)

18 ‡4ft (1.2m) ↔ 24–30in (60–75cm)

19 ‡3ft (1m) ↔ 18in (45cm)

20 ‡4ft (1.2m) ↔ 30in (75cm)

21 ‡↔ 24in (30–60cm)

22 ‡4ft (1.2m) ↔ 24–30in (60–75cm)

23 ‡34in (85cm) ↔ 18in (45cm)

24 ‡4ft (1.2m) ↔ 30in (75cm)

25 ‡4ft (1.2m) ↔ 24–30in (60–75cm)

MORE CHOICES

'Margaret' Pink, with
reflexed petals.
'Max Riley' Yellow.
'Pennine Signal' Scarlet.
'Yellow Pennine Oriel'
Sprays of small yellow
flowers.

16 *Chrysanthemum* 'Pennine Lace' **17** *C.* 'Pennine Marie' **18** *C.* 'Pennine Oriel'
19 *C.* 'Primrose Allouise' **20** *C.* 'Purple Pennine Wine' **21** *C.* 'Salmon Fairie'
22 *C.* 'Salmon Margaret' **23** *C.* 'Southway Swan' **24** *C.* 'Wendy' **25** *C.* 'Yvonne Arnaud'

Late-Flowering Chrysanthemums

This group of herbaceous perennials comes into flower from fall into winter, which means that the protection of a greenhouse during this time is essential in cold areas. None can tolerate frost, but they can be moved outdoors during summer. The showy flowerheads come in a wide range of shapes and sizes and are available in a blaze of golds, bronzes, yellows, oranges, pinks, and reds. Protection from the elements enables perfect blooms for exhibition to be nurtured. Grow late-flowering chrysanthemums in containers or in a greenhouse border.

CULTIVATION: *Best in a good soil-based potting mix, kept slightly moist at all times, in bright, filtered light. Stake plants as they grow, and give liquid fertilizer until flower buds begin to form. Ensure adequate ventilation and a min. temp. of 50°F (10°C). In frost-free areas, grow outdoors in fertile, moist but well-drained soil, in full sun.*

☼ ◊ ♦ Z4–8*

‡4ft (1.2m) ↔24in (60cm)

‡5ft (1.5m) ↔24in (60cm)

‡4¹⁄₂ft (1.4m) ↔24in (60cm)

MORE CHOICES

'Apricot Shoesmith Salmon'
'Bronze Cassandra'
'Dark Red Mayford Perfection'
'Pink Gin' Light purple.
'Rose Mayford Perfection'
'Rynoon' Light pink.

‡4ft (1.2m) ↔30–39in (75–100cm)

‡4ft (1.2m) ↔24–30in (60–75cm)

1 *Chrysanthemum* 'Beacon' **2** *C.* 'Golden Cassandra'
3 *C.* 'Roy Coopland' **4** *C.* 'Satin Pink Gin' **5** *C.* 'Yellow John Hughes'

Chrysogonum virginianum

This spring-flowering perennial is native to woodland and makes a good garden plant in a similar location. The bright yellow flowers have darker veins, and plants begin to bloom while still small in early spring. The hairy, bright green leaves are spade- to heart-shaped and persist until fall but may be evergreen in mild areas. The variety 'Pierre' flowers for a longer time and forms larger plants.

CULTIVATION: *Grow in a shaded location under trees or tall shrubs in a moist soil rich in humus. Water during prolonged dry spells*

☀ ◊ Z3   ‡10in (25cm) ↔20in (50cm)

Cistus x *aguilarii* 'Maculatus'

This fast-growing, evergreen shrub bears large, solitary white flowers for a few weeks in early and midsummer. At the center of each flower is a mass of bright golden yellow stamens surrounded by five crimson blotches. The lance-shaped leaves are sticky, aromatic, and bright green. Excellent on a sunny bank or in containers.

CULTIVATION: *Grow in well-drained, poor to moderately fertile soil, in a sunny, sheltered site. Tolerates alkaline soil. If necessary, trim lightly (not hard) in early spring or after flowering. Minimum temperature 41°F (5°C).*

☀ ◊ Tender   ‡↔4ft (1.2m)

Cistus x purpureus

This summer-flowering, rounded, evergreen shrub bears few-flowered clusters of dark pink flowers with maroon blotches at the base of each petal. The dark green leaves are borne on upright, sticky, red-flushed shoots. Good in a large rock garden, on a sunny bank, or in a container.

CULTIVATION: *Grow in well-drained, poor to moderately fertile soil. Choose a sheltered site in full sun. Tolerates alkaline soil. Can be trimmed lightly after flowering; avoid hard pruning.*

☼ ◊ Z7　　　　↔3ft (1m)

Claytonia virginica

Spring beauty is a native species that forms carpets of flowers in early spring. The color is variable from white to mid-pink, but all the blooms have dark pink veins radiating from the center. It makes a good garden plant in a well-drained soil. Given the right conditions, it will self-seed and just a few plants will soon form a large colony.

CULTIVATION: *Grow in a well-drained, gritty, humus-rich soil in full sun with protection from winter moisture.*

☼ ◊ Z4　　↕12in (30cm) ↔8in (20cm)

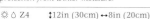

Early-flowering Clematis

The early-flowering species clematis are valued for their showy displays during spring and early summer. They are generally deciduous climbers with mid- to dark green, divided leaves. The flowers of the earliest species to bloom are usually bell-shaped; those of the later *C. montana* types are either flat or saucer-shaped. Flowers are often followed by decorative seedheads. Many clematis, especially *C. montana* types, are vigorous and will grow very quickly, making them ideal for covering featureless or unattractive walls. Allowed to grow through deciduous shrubs, they may flower before their host comes into leaf.

CULTIVATION: *Grow in well-drained, fertile, organic soil, in full sun or semi-shade. The roots and base of the plant should be shaded. Immediately after flowering, tie in young growth carefully and prune out shoots that exceed the allotted space.*

☼ ◑ ◊ Z1–6 as noted

‡6–10ft (2–3m) ↔1.5m (5ft)

‡2–3m (6–10ft) ↔5ft (1.5m)

‡30ft (10m) ↔12ft (4m)

MORE CHOICES

C. 'White Columbine' White flowers. Z4

C. 'Helsingborg' Deep blue and brown. Z3

C. cirrhosa var. *balearica* and *C. cirrhosa* 'Freckles' Cream flowers speckled with pinkish brown. Z5

‡30ft (10m) ↔6–10ft (2–3m)

‡15ft (5m) ↔6–10ft (2–3m)

1 *Clematis* 'Frances Rivis' (Z4) **2** *C.* 'Markham's Pink' (Z1) **3** *C. montana* var. *grandiflora* (Z6) **4** *C. montana* var. *rubens* (Z6) **5** *C. montana* var. *rubens* 'Tetrarose' (Z5)

Mid-season Clematis

The mid-season, mainly hybrid clematis are twining and deciduous climbers, bearing an abundance of stunning flowers throughout the summer months. Their flowers are large, saucer-shaped, and outward-facing, with a plentiful choice of shapes and colors. Toward the end of the summer, blooms may darken. The leaves are pale to mid-green and divided into several leaflets. Mid-season clematis look very attractive scrambling through other shrubs, especially if they bloom before or after their host. Topgrowth may be damaged in severe winters, but plants are usually quick to recover.

CULTIVATION: *Grow in well-drained, fertile, organic soil, with the roots in shade and the heads in sun. Pastel flowers may fade in sun; better in semi-shade. Mulch in late winter, avoiding the immediate crown. Cut back older stems to strong buds in late winter, and tie in young growth carefully.*

☼ ◑ ◊ Z2–4*

1
‡8ft (2.5m) ↔3ft (1m)

2
‡8ft (2.5m) ↔3ft (1m)

3
‡6–10ft (2–3m) ↔3ft (1m)

1 *Clematis* 'Bees' Jubilee' **2** *C.* 'Doctor Ruppel' **3** *C.* 'Elsa Späth'

‡to 10ft (3m) ↔3ft (1m)

6
‡8ft (2.5m) ↔3ft (1m)

7
‡8ft (2.5m) ↔3ft (1m)

8
‡10ft (3m) ↔3ft (1m)

9
‡8ft (2.5m) ↔3ft (1m)

10
‡10ft (3m) ↔3ft (1m)

11
‡8ft (2.5m) ↔3ft (1m)

12
‡6–10ft (2–3m) ↔3ft (1m)

5 *C.* 'Fireworks' **6** *C.* 'Gillian Blades' **7** *C.* 'H. F. Young' **8** *C.* 'Henryi'
9 *C.* 'Lasurstern' **10** *C.* 'Marie Boisselot' **11** *C.* 'Miss Bateman' **12** *C.* 'Nelly Moser'

‡6–10ft (2–3m) ↔3ft (1m)

‡6–10ft (2–3m) ↔3ft (1m)

‡6ft (2m) ↔3ft (1m)

‡6ft (2m) ↔3ft (1m)

MORE CHOICES

'Lord Nevill' Deep blue
flowers with purple-red
anthers.
'Mrs Cholmondely'
Lavender; brown anthers.
'Will Goodwin' Pale blue
with yellow anthers.

‡6–10ft (2–3m) ↔3ft (1m)

‡6–10ft (2–3m) ↔3ft (1m)

13 *C.* 'Niobe' **14** *C.* 'Richard Pennell' **15** *C.* 'Royalty'
16 *C.* 'Silver Moon' **17** *C.* 'The President' **18** *C.* 'Vyvyan Pennell'

Late-flowering Clematis

Many large-flowered hybrid clematis flower from mid- to late summer, when the season for the *C. viticella* types, characterized usually by smaller but more profuse flowers, also begins. These are followed by other late-flowering species. They may be deciduous or evergreen, with an enormous variety of flower and leaf shapes and colors. Many, like 'Perle d'Azur', are vigorous and will cover large areas of wall or disguise unsightly buildings. Some develop decorative, silvery-gray seedheads that last well into winter. With the exception of 'Bill Mackenzie', most look good when trained up into small trees.

CULTIVATION: *Grow in organic, fertile soil with good drainage, with the base in shade and the upper part in sun or partial shade. Mulch in late winter, avoiding the crown. Each year in early spring, cut back hard before growth begins.*

☼ ☼ ◊ Z2–4*

1
‡12ft (4m) ↔ 5ft (1.5m)

2
‡22ft (7m) ↔ 6–10ft (2–3m)

3
‡8ft (2.5m) ↔ 5ft (1.5m)

1 *C.* 'Alba Luxurians' **2** *C.* 'Bill Mackenzie' **3** *C.* 'Duchess of Albany'

4 ‑10ft (2–3m) ↔ 3ft (1m)

7 ↕ 10ft (3m) ↔ 5ft (1.5m)

5 ‑10–15ft (3–5m) ↔ 5ft (1.5m)

6 ↕ 10ft (3m) ↔ 3ft (1m)

8 ↕ 10ft (3m) ↔ 3ft (1m)

9 ↕ 10ft (3m) ↔ 3ft (1m)

10 ↕ 10ft (3m) ↔ 3ft (1m)

11 ↕ 10ft (3m) ↔ 3ft (1m)

12 ↕ 20–22ft (6–7m) ↔ 6–10ft (2–3m)

4 *C.* 'Comtesse de Bouchaud' **5** *C.* 'Etoile Violette' **6** *C.* 'Jackmanii' **7** *C.* 'Madame Julia Correvon' **8** *C.* 'Minuet' **9** *C.* 'Perle d'Azur' **10** *C.* 'Venosa Violacea' **11** *C. viticella* Purpurea Plena Elegans' **12** *C. rehderiana* (Z6)

Clianthus puniceus

Lobster claw is an evergreen, woody-stemmed, climbing shrub with scrambling shoots. Drooping clusters of clawlike, brilliant red flowers appear in spring and early summer. (The cultivar 'Albus' has pure white flowers.) The mid-green leaves are divided into many oblong leaflets. Suitable for wall-training. It grows nicely under glass where not hardy.

CULTIVATION: *Grow in well-drained, fairly fertile soil, in sun with shelter from wind. Pinch-prune young plants to promote bushiness; otherwise, keep pruning to a minimum.*

☼ ◊ Z8 ↕12ft (4m) ↔10ft (3m)

Codonopsis convolvulacea

A slender, herbaceous, summer-flowering climber with twining stems that bears delicate, bell- to saucer-shaped, soft blue-violet flowers. The leaves are lance-shaped to oval and bright green. Grow in a herbaceous border or woodland garden, scrambling through other plants.

CULTIVATION: *Grow in moist but well-drained, light, fertile soil, ideally in dappled shade. Provide support or grow through neighboring shrubs. Cut to the base in spring.*

☼ ◊ ◊ Z5 ↕to 6ft (2m)

Colchicum speciosum 'Album'

While *Colchicum speciosum*, the fall crocus, has pink flowers, this cultivar is white. A cormous perennial, it produces thick, weather resistant, goblet-shaped, snow-white blooms in fall; its narrow, mid-green leaves appear in spring and die down in early summer. Grow at the front of a border, at the foot of a bank, or in a rock garden. All parts are highly toxic if ingested.

CULTIVATION: *Grow in moist but well-drained soil, in full sun. Plant bulbs in late summer, 4in (10cm) below the surface of soil that is deep and fertile.*

☼ ◊ Z4   ↕7in (18cm) ↔4in (10cm)

Convallaria majalis

Lily-of-the-valley is a creeping perennial bearing small, very fragrant white flowers that hang from arching stems in late spring or early summer. The narrowly oval leaves are mid- to dark green. An excellent groundcover plant for woodland gardens and other shady areas, although it will spread rapidly under suitable conditions.

CULTIVATION: *Grow in reliably moist, fertile, organic, leafy soil in deep or partial shade. Topdress with leaf mold in fall.*

☼ ☼ ◊ Z2   ↕9in (23cm) ↔indefinite

Convolvulus cneorum

This compact, rounded, evergreen shrub bears masses of funnel-shaped shining white flowers with yellow centers that open from late spring to summer. The narrowly lance-shaped leaves are silvery green. Excellent as a larger plant in a rock garden, or on a sunny bank. Where not hardy, grow in a container and move into a cool greenhouse in winter.

CULTIVATION: *Grow in gritty, very well-drained, poor to moderately fertile soil, in a sunny, sheltered site. Trim back after flowering, if necessary.*

☼ ◊ Z8   ‡↔36in (90cm)

Convolvulus sabatius

A small, trailing perennial bearing trumpet-shaped, vibrant blue-purple flowers from summer into early fall. The slender stems are clothed with small, oval, mid-green leaves. Excellent in crevices between rocks; where marginally hardy, it is best grown in containers with shelter under glass during the winter. Sometimes seen as *C. mauritanicus.*

CULTIVATION: *Grow in well-drained, gritty, poor to moderately fertile soil. Provide a sheltered site in full sun.*

☼ ◊ Z8   ‡6in (15cm) ↔20in (50cm)

Coreopsis verticillata 'Moonbeam'

In late summer and fall, the light-green, feathery leaves of 'Moonbeam' are smothered by star-shaped, lemon yellow, daisy shaped flowers. A useful plant, this small, drought-resistant perennial is suited to edging sidewalks, driveways, and beds.

CULTIVATION: *This delicate-looking perennial is extremely cold hardy, drought, and deer resistant. It grows in poor to average soil, and full sun.*

 ☼ ◊ ◗ Z3 ↕↔to 18in (46cm)

Cornus alba 'Sibirica'

A deciduous shrub that is usually grown for the winter effect of its bright coral-red, bare young stems. Small clusters of creamy white flowers appear in late spring and early summer amid oval, dark green leaves that turn red in fall. Particularly effective in a waterside planting or any situation where the winter stems show off well.

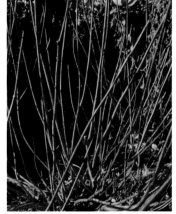

CULTIVATION: *Grow in any moderately fertile soil, in sun. For the best stem effect, cut back hard and feed every spring once established, although this will be at the expense of the flowers.*

 ☼ ◊ ◗ Z2 ↕↔10ft (3m)

Cornus alba 'Spaethii'

A vigorous and upright, deciduous shrub bearing bright green, elliptic leaves that are margined with yellow. It is usually grown for the effect of its bright red young shoots in winter. In late spring and early summer, small clusters of creamy white flowers appear amid the foliage Very effective wherever the stems show off well in winter.

CULTIVATION: *Grow in any moderately fertile soil, preferably in full sun. For the best stem effect, but at the expense of any flowers, cut back hard and feed each year in spring, once established.*

☼ ◊ Z2   ‡to 12ft (4m) ↔to 18ft (5m)

Cornus florida 'Cherokee Chief'

This small, showy tree has an attractive, rounded crown and produces red flowers with white bracts in spring; red fruits and reddish leaves in fall. Break-resistant branches need little pruning, making it ideal near patios, in beds for spring and fall color, or in a lawn as a specimen.

CULTIVATION: *Shade from afternoon sun; grow in fertile, well-drained, clay or sandy soil. In wet areas, plant in a raised bed. Irrigate during drought. It resists verticillium wilt.*

☼ ☼ ◊ Z6   ‡20ft (6m) ↔25ft (8m)

Cornus kousa var. chinensis

This broadly conical, deciduous tree with flaky bark is valued for its dark green, oval leaves that turn an impressive, deep crimson-purple in fall. The early summer flowers have long white bracts, fading to red-pink. An effective specimen tree, especially in a woodland setting. *C. kousa* 'Satomi' has even deeper fall color and pink flower bracts.

CULTIVATION: *Best in well-drained, fertile, organic, neutral to acidic soil, in full sun or partial shade. Keep pruning to a minimum.*

☀ ☀ ◊ Z5b ‡22ft (7m) ↔15ft (5m)

Cornus mas

The Cornelian cherry is a vigorous and spreading, deciduous shrub or small tree. Clusters of small yellow flowers provide attractive late winter color on the bare branches. The oval, dark green leaves turn red-purple in fall, giving a display at the same time as the fruits ripen to red. Particularly fine as a specimen tree for a woodland garden.

CULTIVATION: *Tolerates any well-drained soil, in sun or partial shade. Pruning is best kept to a minimum.*

☀ ☀ ◊ Z4b ‡↔15ft (5m)

Cornus sericea 'Flaviramea'

This vigorous, deciduous shrub makes a bright display of its bare yellow-green young shoots in winter, before the oval, dark green leaves emerge in spring. Clusters of white flowers appear in late spring and early summer. The leaves redden in fall. Excellent in a bog garden or in wet soil near water.

CULTIVATION: *Grow in reliably moist soil, in full sun. Restrict spread by cutting out 1 in 4 old stems annually. Prune all stems hard and feed each year in early spring for the best display of winter stems.*

☼ ◊ Z1b ‡6ft (2m) ↔12ft (4m)

Correa backhouseana

The Australian fuchsia is a dense, spreading, evergreen shrub with small clusters of tubular, pale red-green or cream flowers during late fall to late spring. The hairy, rust-red stems are clothed with oval, dark green leaves. Where not hardy, grow against a warm wall or overwinter in frost-free conditions. *Correa* 'Mannii', with red flowers, is also recommended.

CULTIVATION: *Grow in well-drained, fertile, acidic to neutral soil, in full sun. Trim back after flowering, if necessary.*

☼ ◊ Tender
‡3–6ft (1–2m) ↔5–8ft (1.5–2.5m)

Cortaderia selloana 'Aureolineata'

This pampas grass, with rich yellow-margined, arching leaves that age to dark golden yellow, is a clump-forming, evergreen perennial. Feathery plumes of silvery flowers appear on tall stems in late summer. The flowerheads can be dried for decoration. Also known as 'Gold Band'.

CULTIVATION: *Grow in well-drained, fertile soil, in full sun. In late winter, cut out all dead foliage and remove the previous year's flower stems: wear gloves to protect hands from the sharp foliage.*

☼ ◊ Z7
↕to 7ft (2.2m) ↔5ft (1.5m) or more

Cortaderia selloana 'Sunningdale Silver'

This sturdy pampas grass is a clump-forming, evergreen, weather-resistant perennial. In late summer, silky plumes of silvery cream flowers are borne on strong, upright stems above the narrow, arching, sharp-edged leaves. Where marginal, protect the crown with a winter mulch.

CULTIVATION: *Grow in well-drained, fertile, not too heavy soil, in full sun. Remove old flower stems and any dead foliage in late winter: wear gloves to protect hands from the sharp foliage.*

☼ ◊ Z7
↕10ft (3m) or more ↔to 8ft (2.5m)

Corydalis solida '**George Baker**'

A low, clump-forming, herbaceous perennial bearing upright spires of deep salmon-rose flowers. These appear in spring above the delicate, finely cut, grayish-green leaves. Excellent in a rock garden or in an alpine house.

CULTIVATION: *Grow in sharply drained, moderately fertile soil or soil mix. Site in full sun, but tolerates some shade.*

☼ ☀ ◊ Z5
↕ to 10in (25cm) ↔ to 8in (20cm)

Corylopsis pauciflora

This deciduous shrub bears hanging, catkinlike clusters of small, fragrant, pale yellow flowers on its bare branches during early to mid-spring. The oval, bright green leaves are bronze when they first emerge. Often naturally well-shaped, it makes a beautiful shrub for sites in dappled shade. The flowers may be damaged by frost.

CULTIVATION: *Grow in moist but well-drained, organic, acidic soil, in partial shade with shelter from wind. Allow room for the plant to spread. The natural shape is easily spoiled, so prune only to remove dead wood.*

☀ ◊ ◊ Z7   ↕ 5ft (1.5m) ↔ 8ft (2.5m)

Corylus avellana 'Contorta'

The corkscrew hazel is a deciduous shrub bearing strongly twisted shoots that are particularly striking in winter; they can also be useful in flower arrangements. Winter interest is enhanced later in the season with the appearance of pale yellow catkins. The mid-green leaves are almost circular and toothed.

CULTIVATION: *Grow in any well-drained, fertile soil, in sun or semi-shade. Once established, the twisted branches tend to become congested and may split, so thin out in late winter.*

☼ ☼ ◊ Z5   ‡↔50ft (15m)

Corylus maxima 'Purpurea'

The purple filbert is a vigorous, open, deciduous shrub that, left unpruned, will grow into a small tree. In late winter, purplish catkins appear before the rounded, purple leaves emerge. The edible nuts ripen in fall. Effective as a specimen tree, in a shrub border, or as part of a woodland planting.

CULTIVATION: *Grow in any well-drained, fertile soil, in sun or partial shade. For the best leaf effect, but at the expense of the nuts, cut back hard in early spring.*

☼ ☼ ◊ Z5   ‡20ft (6m) ↔15ft (5m)

Cosmos bipinnatus 'Sonata White'

A branching but compact annual bearing single, saucer-shaped white flowers with yellow centers from summer to fall at the tips of upright stems. The leaves are bright green and feathery. Excellent for exposed gardens. The flowers are good for cutting.

CULTIVATION: *Grow in moist but well-drained, fertile soil, in full sun. Deadhead to prolong flowering.*

☼ ◊ ◊ Annual   ‡↔12in (30cm)

Cotinus coggygria 'Royal Purple'

This deciduous shrub is grown for its rounded, red-purple leaves that turn a brilliant scarlet in fall. Smoke-like plumes of tiny, pink-purple flowers are produced on older wood, but only in areas with long, hot summers. Good in a shrub border or as a specimen tree; where space permits, plant in groups.

CULTIVATION: *Grow in moist but well-drained, fairly fertile soil, in full sun or partial shade. For the best foliage effect, cut back hard to a framework of older wood each spring, before growth begins.*

☼ ☀ ◊ ◊ Z5   ‡↔15ft (5m)

Cotinus 'Grace'

A fast-growing, deciduous shrub or small tree carrying oval, purple leaves that turn a brilliant, translucent red in late fall. The smokelike clusters of tiny, pink-purple flowers appear in abundance only during hot summers. Effective on its own or in a border. For green leaves during the summer but equally brilliant fall foliage color, look for *Cotinus* 'Flame'.

CULTIVATION: *Grow in moist but well-drained, reasonably rich soil, in sun or partial shade. The best foliage is seen after hard pruning each spring, just before new growth begins.*

☼ ☀ ◐ ◑ Z4b ‡20ft (6m) ↔15ft (5m)

Cotoneaster atropurpureus 'Variegatus'

This compact, low-growing shrub, sometimes seen as *C. horizontalis* 'Variegatus', has fairly inconspicuous red flowers in summer, followed in fall by a bright display of orange-red fruits. The small, oval, white-margined, deciduous leaves also give fall color, turning pink and red before they drop. Effective as a groundcover or in a rock garden.

CULTIVATION: *Grow in well-drained, moderately fertile soil, in full sun. Tolerates dry soil and partial shade. Pruning is best kept to a minimum.*

☼ ☀ ◐ Z5
‡18in (45cm) ↔36in (90cm)

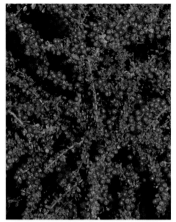

Cotoneaster conspicuus 'Decorus'

A dense, mound-forming, evergreen shrub that is grown for its shiny red berries. These ripen in fall and will often persist until late winter. Small white flowers appear amid the dark green leaves in summer. Good in a shrub border or under a canopy of deciduous trees.

CULTIVATION: *Grow in well-drained, moderately fertile soil, ideally in full sun, but tolerates shade. If necessary, trim lightly to shape after flowering.*

☼ ☀ ◊ Z7
↕5ft (1.5m) ↔ 6–8ft (2–2.5m)

Cotoneaster horizontalis

A deciduous shrub with spreading branches that form a herringbone pattern. The tiny, pinkish-white flowers, which appear in summer, are attractive to bees. Bright red berries ripen in fall, and the glossy, dark green leaves redden before they fall. Good as a groundcover, but most effective when grown flat up against a wall.

CULTIVATION: *Grow in any but water-logged soil. Site in full sun for the best berries, or in semi-shade. Keep pruning to a minimum; if wall-trained, shorten outward-facing shoots in late winter.*

☼ ☀ ◊ ◊ Z5   ↕3ft (1m) ↔5ft (1.5m)

Cotoneaster lacteus

This dense, evergreen shrub has arching branches that bear clusters of small, cup-shaped, milky white flowers from early to midsummer. These are followed by brilliant red berries in fall. The oval leaves are dark green and leathery, with gray-woolly undersides. Ideal for a wildlife garden, since it provides food for bees and birds; also makes a good windbreak or informal hedge.

CULTIVATION: *Grow in well-drained, fairly fertile soil, in sun or semi-shade. Trim hedges lightly in summer, if necessary; keep pruning to a minimum.*

☼ ☀ ◊ Z8   ↕↔12ft (4m)

Cotoneaster simonsii

An upright, deciduous or semi-evergreen shrub with small, cup-shaped white flowers in summer. The bright orange-red berries that follow ripen in fall and persist well into winter. Fall color is also seen in the glossy leaves, which redden from dark green. Good for hedging and can also be clipped fairly hard to a semi-formal outline.

CULTIVATION: *Grow in any well-drained soil, in full sun or partial shade. Clip hedges to shape in late winter or early spring, or allow to grow naturally.*

☼ ☀ ◊ Z7   ↕10ft (3m) ↔6ft (2m)

Cotoneaster sternianus

This graceful, evergreen or semi-evergreen shrub bears arching branches that produce clusters of pink-tinged white flowers in summer, followed by a profusion of large, orange-red berries in fall. The gray-green leaves have white undersides. Good grown as a hedge.

CULTIVATION: *Grow in any well-drained soil, in sun or semi-shade. Trim hedges lightly after flowering, if necessary; pruning is best kept to a minimum.*

☼ ◑ ◊ Z6b   ↔10ft (3m)

Cotoneaster x *watereri* 'John Waterer'

A fast-growing, evergreen or semi-evergreen shrub or small tree valued for the abundance of red berries that clothe its branches in fall. In summer clusters of white flowers are carried among the lance-shaped, dark green leaves. Good on its own or at the back of a shrub border.

CULTIVATION: *Grow in any but water-logged soil, in sun or semi-shade. When young, cut out any badly placed shoots to develop a framework of well-spaced branches. Thereafter, keep pruning to an absolute minimum.*

☼ ◑ ◊ ◗ Z8   ↔15ft (5m)

Crambe cordifolia

A tall, clump-forming, vigorous
perennial grown for its stature and
its fragrant, airy, billowing sprays of
small white flowers, which are very
attractive to bees. These are borne
on strong stems in summer above
the large, elegant, dark green leaves.
Magnificent in a mixed border, but
allow plenty of space.

CULTIVATION: *Grow in any well-drained,*
preferably deep, fertile soil, in full sun
or partial shade. Provide shelter from
strong winds.

☀ ◐ ◊ Z5   ↕8ft (2.5m) ↔5ft (1.5m)

Crataegus laevigata
'Paul's Scarlet'

This rounded, thorny, deciduous
tree is valued for its long season
of interest. Abundant clusters of
double, dark pink flowers appear from
late spring to summer, followed in fall
by small red fruits. The leaves, divided
into three or five lobes, are a glossy
mid-green. Particularly useful for a
city, coastal, or exposed garden. In
colder regions, grow *C.* x *mordenensis*
'Toba' (Z3).

CULTIVATION: *Grow in any but water-*
logged soil, in full sun or partial shade.
Pruning is best kept to a minimum.

☀ ◐ ◊ ◑ Z6   ↕↔25ft (8m)

Crataegus x *lavalleei* 'Carrierei'

This vigorous hawthorn is a broadly spreading, semi-evergreen tree with thorny shoots and leathery green leaves that turn red in late fall and persist into winter. Flattened clusters of white flowers appear in early summer, followed in fall by round, red fruits that persist into winter. Tolerates pollution, so it is good for an urban garden. Often offered as simply *C.* x *lavallei.*

CULTIVATION: *Grow in any but water-logged soil, in full sun or partial shade. Pruning is best kept to a minimum.*

☼ ◐ ◊ ◗ Z5 ↕22ft (7m) ↔30ft (10m)

Crinodendron hookerianum

The lantern tree is an upright, evergreen shrub, so-called because of its large, scarlet to carmine-red flowers that hang from the upright shoots during late spring and early summer. The leaves are narrow and glossy dark green. It dislikes alkaline soils.

CULTIVATION: *Grow in moist but well-drained, fertile, organic, acidic soil, in partial shade with protection from cold winds. Tolerates a sunny site if the roots are kept cool and shaded. Trim lightly after flowering, if necessary. Minimum temperature 45ºF (7ºC).*

☼ ◊ Tender ↕20ft (6m) ↔15ft (5m)

Crinum x *powellii* 'Album'

A sturdy, bulbous perennial bearing clusters of up to ten large, fragrant, widely flared, pure white flowers on upright stems in late summer and fall. *C. x powellii* is equally striking, with pink flowers. The strap-shaped leaves, to 5ft (1.5m) long, are mid-green and arch over. Where marginal, choose a sheltered site and protect the dormant bulb over winter with a deep, dry mulch.

CULTIVATION: *Grow in deep, moist but well-drained, fertile, organic soil in full sun with shelter from frost and cold, drying winds.*

☼ ◊ Z8 ‡5ft (1.5m) ↔12in (30cm)

Crocosmia x *crocosmiiflora* 'Solfatare'

This clump-forming perennial produces spikes of funnel-shaped, apricot-yellow flowers on arching stems in midsummer. The bronze-green, deciduous leaves are strap-shaped, emerging from swollen corms at the base of the stems. Excellent in a border; the flowers are good for cutting.

CULTIVATION: *Grow in moist but well-drained, fertile, organic soil, in full sun. Provide a dry mulch over winter.*

☼ ◊ Z6
‡24–28in (60–70cm) ↔3in (8cm)

Crocosmia 'Lucifer'

A robust, clump-forming perennial with swollen corms at the base of the stems. These give rise to pleated, bright green leaves and, in summer, arching spikes of upward-facing red flowers. Particularly effective at the edge of a shrub border or by water.

CULTIVATION: *Grow in moist but well-drained, moderately fertile, organic soil. Site in full sun or dappled shade.*

☼ ☀ ◊ ◊ Z5
‡3–4ft (1–1.2m) ↔3in (8cm)

Crocosmia masoniorum

A robust, late-summer-flowering perennial bearing bright vermilion, upward-facing flowers. These are carried above the dark green foliage on arching stems. The flowers and foliage emerge from a swollen, bulblike corm. Thrives in coastal gardens. Where marginally hardy, grow in the shelter of a warm wall.

CULTIVATION: *Best in moist but well-drained, fairly fertile, organic soil, in full sun or partial shade. In cold areas, provide a dry winter mulch.*

☼ ☀ ◊ Z8
‡4ft (1.2m) ↔3in (8cm)

Spring-flowering Crocus

Spring-flowering crocus are indispensable dwarf perennials, since they bring a welcome splash of early spring color into the garden. Some cultivars of *C. sieberi*, such as 'Tricolor' or 'Hubert Edelstein', bloom even earlier, in late winter. The goblet-shaped flowers emerge from swollen, underground corms at the same time as or just before the narrow, almost upright foliage. The leaves are mid-green with silver-green central stripes and grow markedly as the blooms fade. Very effective in drifts at the front of a mixed or herbaceous border, or in massed plantings in rock gardens or raised beds.

CULTIVATION: *Grow in gritty, well-drained, poor to moderately fertile soil, in full sun. Water freely during the growing season, and apply a low-nitrogen fertilizer each month. C. corsicus must be kept completely dry over summer. Can be naturalized under the right growing conditions.*

☼ ◊ Z3 (*C. corsicus* Z7)

‡3–4in (8–10cm) ↔ 1½in (4cm)

‡3in (7cm) ↔ 2in (5cm)

‡2–3in (5–8cm) ↔ 1in (2.5cm)

‡2–3in (5–8cm) ↔ 1in (2.5cm)

‡2–3in (5–8cm) ↔ 1in (2.5cm)

1 *C. corsicus* **2** *C. chrysanthus* 'E.A. Bowles' **3** *C. sieberi* 'Albus' **4** *C. sieberi* 'Tricolor' **5** *C. sieberi* 'Hubert Edelsten'

Fall-flowering Crocus

These crocus are invaluable for their late-flowering, goblet-shaped flowers with showy interiors. They are dwarf perennials with underground corms that give rise to the foliage and fall flowers. The leaves are narrow and mid-green with silver-green central stripes, appearing at the same time or just after the flowers. All types are easy to grow in the right conditions and look excellent when planted in groups in a rock garden. Rapid-spreading crocus, such as

C. ochroleucus, are useful for naturalizing in grass or under deciduous shrubs.
C. banaticus is effective planted in drifts at the front of a border, but do not allow it to become swamped by larger plants.

CULTIVATION: *Grow in gritty, well-drained, poor to moderately fertile soil, in full sun. Reduce watering during the summer for all types except* C. banaticus, *which prefers damper soil and will tolerate partial shade.*

☼ ◊ Z4 (*C. ochroleucus* Z5–8)

1 ↕4in (10cm) ↔2in (5cm)

2 ↕4in (10cm) ↔2in (5cm)

3 ↕2½–3in (6–8cm) ↔2in (5cm)

4 ↕3in (8cm) ↔1in (2.5cm)

5 ↕2in (5cm) ↔1in (2.5cm)

6 ↕4–5in (10–12cm) ↔1½in (4cm)

1 *C. banaticus* **2** *C. goulimyi* **3** *C. kotschyanus*
4 *C. medius* **5** *C. ochroleucus* **6** *C. pulchellus*

Cryptomeria japonica 'Bandai-sugi'

Japanese cedars are reliable evergreens with foliage color that varies with the seasons, turning from mid-green in summer to bronze in winter. 'Bandai-sugi' is relatively small and develops into a rounded shrub; plant a row to create a hedge.

CULTIVATION: *Grow in moist but well-drained soil, enriched with organic matter, in a sheltered site in sun or partial shade. No formal pruning is necessary.*

☼ ☀ ◊ ◊ Z6 ↕↔6ft (2m)

Cryptomeria japonica 'Elegans Compacta'

This small, slow-growing conifer looks good in a heather bed or rock garden with other dwarf conifers. It has feathery sprays of slender, soft green leaves, which turn a rich bronze-purple in winter. Mature trees usually have a neat cone shape.

CULTIVATION: *Grow in any well-drained soil, in full sun or partial shade. Needs no formal pruning, but to renovate ungainly trees, cut back to within 28in (70cm) of ground level, in spring.*

☼ ☀ ◊ Z6 ↕6–12ft (2–4m) ↔6ft (2m)

x *Cupressocyparis leylandii* 'Gold Rider'

Leyland cypress trees develop a classic narrow pyramidal form, but are renowned for their vigor and will grow quickly to a great height if left untrimmed. 'Gold Rider', however, is a restrained form with attractive bright yellow-green, evergreen foliage. It would make a good, thick hedge for screening or as a windbreak.

CULTIVATION: *Grow in any deep, well-drained soil. The foliage color is best in full sun. Trim regularly.*

☀ ◐ ◊ ◐ Z7　　‡↔10ft (3m) or more

x *Cupressocyparis leylandii* 'Haggerston Grey'

This popular cultivar of the Leyland cypress is a fast-growing coniferous tree with a tapering, columnar shape. It has dense, gray-green foliage and will establish quickly planted as a screen or windbreak.

CULTIVATION: *Grow in deep, well-drained soil in full sun or partial shade. Needs no formal pruning, unless grown as a hedge, when it should be trimmed 2 or 3 times during the growing season.*

☀ ◐ ◊ Z7
‡to 120ft (35m) ↔to 15ft (5m)

...yananthus lobatus

...spreading, mat-forming perennial ...own for its late summer display ...bright blue-purple, broadly funnel- ...aped flowers, on single stems with ...iry brown calyces. The leaves are ...shy and dull green, with deeply ...t lobes. Perfect in a rock garden ...trough.

...LTIVATION: Grow in poor to moderately ...rtile, moist but well-drained soil, ...eferably neutral to slightly acidic, ...d rich in organic matter. Choose a ...e in partial shade.

◌ ◐ ◊ Z6b   ‡2in (5cm) ↔12in (30cm)

...yclamen cilicium

...tuberous perennial valued for ...s slender, nodding, white or pink ...owers, borne in fall and often into ...inter among patterned, rounded or ...eart-shaped, mid-green leaves. This ...egant plant needs a warm and dry ...ummer, when it is dormant, and ...n cool-temperate climates it may ...e better grown in a cool greenhouse, ...r under trees or shrubs, to avoid ...xcessive summer moisture.

...LTIVATION: Grow in moderately fertile, ...well-drained soil enriched with organic ...atter, in partial shade. Mulch annually ...ith leafmold after flowering when the ...aves wither.

◐ ◊ Z6   ‡2in (5cm) ↔3in (8cm)

Cyclamen coum
Pewter Group

This winter- to spring-flowering,
tuberous perennial is excellent for
naturalizing beneath trees or shrubs
The compact flowers have upswept
petals that vary from white to shade
of pink and carmine-red. These
emerge from swollen, underground
tubers at the same time as the
rounded, silver-green leaves. Provid
a deep, dry mulch where marginal.

CULTIVATION: *Grow in gritty, well-draine
fertile soil that dries out in summer, in su
or light shade. Mulch annually when the
leaves wither.*

☼ ◐ ◊ Z5
‡2–3in (5–8cm) ↔ 4in (10cm)

Cyclamen hederifolium

A fall-flowering, tuberous perennial
bearing shuttlecock-like flowers that
are pale to deep pink and flushed
deep maroon at the mouths. The
ivylike leaves, mottled with green
and silver, appear after the flowers
from a swollen, underground tuber.
It self-seeds freely, forming extensiv
colonies under trees and shrubs,
especially where protected from
summer rainfall.

CULTIVATION: *Grow in well-drained, fertil
soil, in sun or partial shade. Mulch each
year after the leaves wither.*

☼ ◐ ◊ Z7
‡4–5in (10–13cm) ↔ 6in (15cm)

ynara cardunculus

e cardoon is a clump-forming,
atuesque, late-summer-flowering
rennial that looks very striking in
order. The large, thistlelike purple
owerheads, which are very attractive
bees, are carried above the deeply
vided, silvery leaves on thick, gray-
olly stems. The flowerheads dry
ell for indoor display. When blanched,
e leaf stalks can be eaten. Can be
own as an annual where not hardy.

LTIVATION: *Grow in any well-drained,
rtile soil, in full sun with shelter from
ld winds. For the best foliage effect,
move the flower stems as they emerge.*

☼ ◊ Z8   ↕5ft (1.5m) ↔4ft (1.2m)

ytisus battandieri

neapple broom develops a loose
nd open-branched habit. It is a
emi-evergreen shrub bearing
ense clusters of pineapple-scented,
right yellow flowers from early to
idsummer. The silver-gray leaves,
ivided into three, make an attractive
ackdrop to herbaceous and mixed
lantings. Best by a sunny wall in
old areas. The cultivar 'Yellow Tail'
s recommended.

LTIVATION: *Grow in any well-drained, not
oo rich soil, in full sun. Very little pruning
s necessary, but old wood can be cut out
fter flowering to be replaced with strong,
oung growth. Resents transplanting.*

☼ ◊ Z7b   ↕↔15ft (5m)

Cytisus x *beanii*

This low-growing and semi-trailing, deciduous, spring-flowering shrub carries an abundance of pealike, rich yellow flowers on arching stem The leaves are small and dark green It is a colorful bush for a rock garder or raised bed and is also effective if allowed to cascade over a wall. *Cytisus* x *ardoinei* (Z7) is similar but slightly less spreading where space is limited.

CULTIVATION: *Grow in well-drained, poor to moderately fertile soil, in full sun. Trin lightly after flowering, but avoid cutting into old wood.*

☼ ◊ Z5　　‡24in (60cm) ↔3ft (1m

Cytisus x *praecox* 'Allgold'

This compact, deciduous shrub is smothered by a mass of pealike, dark yellow flowers from mid- to late spring. The tiny, gray-green leaves are carried on arching stems. Suitabl for a sunny shrub border or large roc garden. 'Warminster' is very similar, with paler, cream-yellow flowers.

CULTIVATION: *Grow in well-drained, acidic to neutral soil, in sun. Pinch out the growing tips to encourage bushiness, then cut back new growth by up to two-thirds after flowering; avoid cutting into old wood. Replace old, leggy specimens.*

☼ ◊ Z5b　　‡4ft (1.2m) ↔5ft (1.5m

Daboecia cantabrica 'Bicolor'

This straggling, heatherlike shrub bears slender spikes of urn-shaped flowers from spring to fall. They are white, pink, or beet-red, sometimes striped with two colors. The leaves are small and dark green. Good in a heather bed or among other acidic-soil-loving plants. 'Waley's Red', with glowing magenta flowers, is also recommended.

CULTIVATION: *Best in sandy, well-drained, acidic soil, in full sun; tolerates neutral soil and some shade. Clip lightly in early spring to remove spent flowers; do not cut into old wood.*

☀ ☼ ◊ Z6 ↕18in (45cm) ↔24in (60cm)

Daboecia cantabrica 'William Buchanan'

This compact, heatherlike shrub bears spikes of bell-shaped, purple-crimson flowers from late spring to mid-fall. The narrow dark green leaves have silver-gray undersides. Good with other acidic-soil-loving plants, or among conifers in a rock garden. Plant with 'Silverwells', more ground-hugging, with white flowers.

CULTIVATION: *Grow in well-drained, sandy, acidic to neutral soil, preferably in sun, but tolerates light shade. Trim in early to mid-spring to remove old flowers, but do not cut into old wood.*

☀ ☼ ◊ Z6 ↕18in (45cm) ↔24in (60cm)

Dahlias

Dahlias are showy, deciduous perennials, grown as annuals in cold climates, with swollen underground tubers that must be stored in frost-free conditions in climates with cold winters. They are valued for their massive variety of brightly colored flowers that bloom from midsummer to fall, when many other plants are past their best. The leaves are mid- to dark green and divided. Very effective in massed plantings, wherever space allows: in small gardens, choose from a variety of dwarf types to fill gaps in border displays, or grow in containers. The flowers are ideal for cutting.

CULTIVATION: *Best in well-drained soil, in sun. Lift tubers and store over winter. Plant out tubers once the danger of frost has passed. Feed with high-nitrogen fertilizer every week in early summer. Taller varieties need staking. Deadhead to prolong flowering.*

☼ ◊ Tender

1 ‡3½ft (1.1m) ↔18in (45cm)

2 ‡3½ft (1.1m) ↔24in (60cm)

3 ‡24in (60cm) ↔18in (45cm)

4 ‡4ft (1.2m) ↔24in (60cm)

5 ‡3½ft (1.1m) ↔24in (60cm)

1 *D.* 'Bishop of Llandaff' **2** *D.* 'Clair de Lune'
3 *D.* 'Fascination' (dwarf) **4** *D.* 'Hamari Accord' **5** *D.* 'Conway'

6

‡ 1.2m (4ft) ↔ 60cm (24in)

7

‡ 1.1m (3½ft) ↔ 60cm (24in)

8

‡ 1.2m (4ft) ↔ 60cm (24in)

9

3ft (1m) ↔ 18in (45cm)

10

‡ ↔ 18–20in (45–50cm)

11

3½ft (1.1m) ↔ 24in (60cm)

12

‡ 3½ft (1.1m) ↔ 24in (60cm)

13

‡ 24in (60cm) ↔ 18in (45cm)

14

‡ 4ft (1.2m) ↔ 24in (60cm)

15

‡ 4ft (1.2m) ↔ 24in (60cm)

6 *D.* 'Hamari Gold' **7** *D.* 'Hillcrest Royal' **8** *D.* 'Kathryn's Cupid' **9** *D.* 'Rokesley Mini'
10 *D.* 'Sunny Yellow' (dwarf) **11** *D.* 'So Dainty' **12** *D.* 'Wootton Cupid'
13 *D.* 'Yellow Hammer' (dwarf) **14** *D.* 'Zorro' **15** *D.* 'Wootton Impact'

Daphne bholua 'Gurkha'

An upright, deciduous shrub bearing clusters of strongly fragrant, tubular, white and purplish pink flowers on its bare stems in late winter. They open from deep pink-purple buds and are followed by round, black-purple fruits. The lance-shaped leaves are leathery and dark green. A fine plant for a winter garden. All parts are highly toxic if ingested.

CULTIVATION: *Grow in well-drained but moist soil, in sun or semi-shade. Mulch to keep the roots cool. Best left unpruned. Minimum temperature 35ºF (2ºC).*

☼ ◐ ◊ Tender
↕6–12ft (2–4m) ↔5ft (1.5m)

Daphne tangutica Retusa Group

These evergreen, dwarf forms of *D. tangutica*, sometimes listed simply as *D. retusa,* are valued for their clusters of very fragrant, white to purple-red flowers that are borne during late spring and early summer. The lance-shaped leaves are glossy and dark green. Useful in a large rock garden, shrub border, or mixed planting. All parts are toxic.

CULTIVATION: *Grow in well-drained, moderately fertile, organic soil that does not dry out, in full sun or dappled shade. Pruning is not necessary.*

☼ ◐ ◊ Z7   ↕↔30in (75cm)

Darmera peltata

A handsome, spreading perennial,
sometimes included in the genus
Peltiphyllum, that forms an imposing,
umbrella-like clump with large, round,
mid-green leaves, to 24in (60cm)
across, that turn red in fall. The foliage
appears after the compact clusters of
star-shaped, white to bright pink,
spring flowers. Ideal for a bog garden
or by the edge of a pond or stream.

CULTIVATION: *Grow in reliably moist,
moderately fertile soil, in sun or partial
shade; tolerates drier soil in shade.*

☼ ☼ ◊ Z6   ↕6ft (2m) ↔3ft (1m)

Davidia involucrata

Dove tree is named for the showy,
large, white flower bracts that adorn
the branches in mid- to late spring.
To be seen at its best, it needs to grow
as a free-standing specimen. When
not in flower, this deciduous tree is
less remarkable, but has a pleasing
conical shape and bright green,
heart-shaped leaves. The peeling
bark is orange-brown.

CULTIVATION: *Grow in moist but well-
drained, fertile soil, in sun or partial shade.*

☼ ☼ ◊ ◊ Z7   ↕50ft (15m) ↔30ft (10m)

Delphiniums

Delphiniums are clump-forming perennials cultivated for their towering, spectacular spikes of, shallowly cup-shaped, spurred, single or double flowers. These appear in early to midsummer and are available in a range of colors from creamy whites through lilac-pinks and clear sky blues to deep indigo-blue. The toothed and lobed, mid-green leaves are arranged around the base of the stems. Grow tall delphiniums in a mixed border or island bed with shelter to prevent them from being blown over in strong winds; shorter ones do well in a rock garden. The flowers are good for cutting.

CULTIVATION: *Grow in well-drained, fertile soil, in full sun. For quality blooms, feed weekly with a balanced fertilizer in spring, and thin out the young shoots when they reach 3in (7cm) tall, Most cultivars need staking. Remove spent flower spikes, and cut back all growth in fall.*

☼ ◊ Z4

  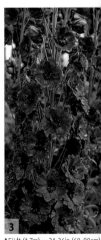

1 ↕5½ft (1.7m) ↔24–36in (60–90cm)   2 ↕6ft (2m) ↔24–36in (60–90cm)   3 ↕5½ft (1.7m) ↔24–36in (60–90cm)

1 *Delphinium* 'Blue Nile' 2 *D.* 'Bruce' 3 *D.* 'Cassius'

‡to 6ft (2m) ↔ 24–36in (60–90cm)

5

‡to 5ft (1.5m) ↔ 24–36in (60–90cm)

‡5½ft (1.7m) ↔ 24–36in (60–90cm)   ‡6ft (2m) ↔ 24–36in (60–90cm)   ‡5½ft (1.7m) ↔ 24–36in (60–90cm)

4 *D.* 'Claire' **5** *D.* 'Conspicuous'
6 *D.* 'Emily Hawkins' **7** *D.* 'Fanfare' **8** *D.* 'Giotto'

MORE CHOICES

The following Pacific Giant series can be raised from seed but are not long lived.

'Blue Jay' Brilliant blue with white eye.

'Galahad' Large white.

'Guinevere' Lavender pink.

'King Arthur' Violet with white eye.

'Summer Skies' Pale blue shades.

'Black Knight' Deep violet.

'Astolat' Pale pink to raspberry with dark eye.

Magic Fountain Mix A dwarf strain that grows 24in (60cm) tall and needs no staking.

9
‡ to 6ft (2m) ↔ 24–36in (60–90cm)

10
‡ to 5ft (1.5m) ↔ 24–36in (60–90cm)

11
‡ 5ft (1.5m) ↔ 24–36in (60–90cm)

9 *D.* 'Kathleen Cooke' **10** *D.* 'Langdon's Royal Flush' **11** *D.* 'Lord Butler'

12 ‡6ft (2m) ↔30in (75cm)

13 ‡5ft (1.5m) ↔24–36in (60–90cm)

14 ‡to 5ft (1.5m) ↔24–36in (60–90cm)

17 ‡4ft (1.2m) ↔24–36in (60–90cm)

15 ‡to 5ft (1.5m) ↔30in (75cm)

16 ‡5ft (1.5m) ↔24–36in (60–90cm)

18 ‡5½ft (1.7m) ↔24–36in (60–90cm)

12 *D.* 'Mighty Atom' **13** *D.* 'Our Deb' **14** *D.* 'Rosemary Brock' **15** *D.* 'Sandpiper'
16 *D.* 'Sungleam' **17** *D.* 'Thamesmead' **18** *D.* 'Walton Gemstone'

Deschampsia cespitosa 'Goldtau'

Tufted hairgrass is a compact, semi-evergreen, clump-forming grass that bears clusters of airy yellow flowers above the foliage in midsummer. Forming neat mounds of deep-green, narrow leaves, it is suited to mass plantings, as edgings, or groundcovers.

CULTIVATION: *Grow in full sun to part shade, average to moist soil. Withstands periods of heat if soil is kept moist.*

☼ ☀ ◊ Z4 ↕↔30in (75cm)

Deutzia x *elegantissima* 'Rosealind'

This compact, rounded, deciduous shrub bears profuse clusters of small, deep carmine-pink flowers. These are carried from late spring to early summer amid the oval, dull green leaves. Very suitable for a mixed border.

CULTIVATION: *Grow in any well-drained, fertile soil that does not dry out, in full sun or partial shade. Tip-prune when young to encourage bushiness; after flowering, thin out by cutting some older stems back to the ground.*

☼ ☀ ◊ Z7 ↕4ft (1.2m) ↔5ft (1.5m)

Border carnations (*Dianthus*)

This group of *Dianthus* are annuals or evergreen perennials of medium height, suitable for mixed or herbaceous borders. They are grown for their mid-summer flowers, which are good for cutting. Each flower stem bears five or more double flowers to 3in (8cm) across, with no fewer than 25 petals. These may be of one color only, as in 'Golden Cross'; gently flecked, like 'Grey Dove'; or often with white petals margined and striped in strong colors. Some have clove-scented flowers. The linear leaves of all carnations are blue-gray or gray-green with a waxy bloom.

CULTIVATION: *Ideal in well-drained, neutral to alkaline soil enriched with well-rotted manure or compost; apply a balanced fertilizer in spring. Plant in full sun. Provide support in late spring using thin stakes or twigs, or wire rings. Deadhead to prolong flowering and maintain a compact plant habit.*

☼ ◊ Z6b

1 18–24in (45–60cm) ↔ 18in (45cm)

2 18–24in (45–60cm) ↔ 18in (45cm)

3 18–24in (45–60cm) ↔ 18in (45cm)

4 18–24in (45–60cm) ↔ 18in (45cm)

5 18–24in (45–60cm) ↔ 18in (45cm)

6 18–24in (45–60cm) ↔ 18in (45cm)

1 *Dianthus* 'David Russell' **2** *D.* 'Devon Carla' **3** *D.* 'Golden Cross'
4 *D.* 'Grey Dove' **5** *D.* 'Ruth White' **6** *D.* 'Spinfield Wizard'

Pinks (*Dianthus*)

Summer-flowering pinks belong, like carnations, to the genus *Dianthus* and are widely grown for their charming, often clove-scented flowers and narrow, blue-gray leaves. They flower profusely over long periods; when cut, the stiff-stemmed blooms last exceptionally well. Thousands are available, usually in shades of pink, white, carmine, salmon, or mauve with double or single flowers; they may be plain (self), marked with a contrasting color or laced around the margins. Most are

excellent border plants; tiny alpine pinks such as 'Pike's Pink' and magenta 'Joan's Blood' are well suited to a rock garden or raised bed.

CULTIVATION: *Best in well-drained, neutral to alkaline soil, in an open, sunny site. Alpine pinks need very sharp drainage. Feed with a balanced fertilizer in spring. Deadhead all types to prolong flowering and to maintain a compact habit.*

☼ ◊ Z5–7*

1 ‡10–18in (25–45cm) ↔16in (40cm)
2 ‡10–18in (25–45cm) ↔16in (40cm)
3 ‡10–18m (25–45cm) ↔16in (40cm)
4 ‡10–18in (25–45cm) ↔16in (40cm)
5 ‡10–18in (25–45cm) ↔16in (40cm)
6 ‡10–18in (25–45cm) ↔16in (40cm)

1 *Dianthus* 'Becky Robinson' **2** *D.* 'Devon Pride' **3** *D.* 'Doris'
4 *D.* 'Gran's Favourite' **5** *D.* 'Haytor White' **6** *D.* 'Houndspool Ruby'

‡10–18in (25–45cm) ↔16in (40cm)

‡3–4in (8–10cm) ↔8in (20cm)

‡10–18in (25–45cm) ↔16in (40cm)

‡10–18in (25–45cm) ↔16in (40cm)

‡10–18in (25–45cm) ↔16in (40cm)

‡10–18in (25–45cm) ↔16in (40cm)

MORE CHOICES

D. alpinus The original alpine pink, with pale-flecked pink flowers.
D. alpinus 'Joan's Blood' Dark-centered deep pink flowers.
'Bovey Belle' Clove-scented, fuchsia-pink.
'Coronation Ruby' Clove-scented, pink flowers with ruby flecks.
'Inschriach Dazzler' Alpine pink with fringed carmine flowers.
'Valda Wyatt' Clove-scented, double lavender flowers.

‡3–4in (8–10cm) ↔18in (20cm)

‡10–18in (25–45cm) ↔16in (40cm)

‡10–18in (25–45cm) ↔16in (40cm)

‡10–18in (25–45cm) ↔16in (40cm)

7 *D.* 'Kathleen Hitchcock' **8** *D.* 'La Bourboule' **9** *D.* 'Monica Wyatt' **10** *D.* 'Natalie Saunders' **11** *D.* 'Oakwood Romance' **12** *D.* 'Oakwood Splendour' **13** *D.* 'Pike's Pink' **14** *D.* 'Suffolk Pride' **15** *D.* 'Trisha's Choice' **16** *D.* 'White Joy'

Diascia barberae 'Blackthorn Apricot'

A mat-forming perennial bearing loose spikes of apricot flowers. These are produced over a long period from summer to fall above the narrowly heart-shaped, mid-green leaves. Good in a rock garden, at the front of a mixed border, or on a sunny bank. *D. barberae* 'Fisher's Flora' and 'Ruby Field' are also recommended.

CULTIVATION: *Grow in moist but well-drained, fertile soil, in full sun. Where not hardy, overwinter young plants under glass.*

☼ ◊ Z7
‡10in (25cm) ↔ to 20in (50cm)

Diascia rigescens

This trailing perennial is valued for its tall spires of salmon-pink flowers. These appear above the mid-green, heart-shaped leaves during summer. Excellent in a rock garden or raised bed, or at the front of a border. Where marginally hardy, grow at the base of a warm, sunny wall.

CULTIVATION: *Grow in moist but well-drained, fertile, organic soil. Site in full sun. Where marginally hardy, overwinter young plants under glass.*

☼ ◊ Z6b   ‡12in (30cm) ↔20in (50cm)

Dicentra spectabilis

Bleeding heart is an elegant, mound-forming perennial. In spring, it bears rows of distinctive hanging, red-pink, heart-shaped flowers on arching stems. The leaves are deeply cut and mid-green, and they die back completely in early summer. A beautiful plant for a shady border or woodland garden.

CULTIVATION: *Grow in reliably moist, fertile, organic, neutral or slightly alkaline soil. Prefers a site in partial shade, but it tolerates full sun.*

☼ ◑ ◊ Z3   ↕18in (45cm) ↔3ft (1m)

Dicentra spectabilis 'Alba'

This white-flowered form of bleeding heart is otherwise very similar to the species (above), so to avoid possible confusion, purchase plants during the flowering period. The leaves are deeply cut and light green, and the heart-shaped flowers are borne along arching stems in spring.

CULTIVATION: *Grow in reliably moist but well-drained soil that is enriched with well-rotted organic matter. Prefers partial shade, but tolerates full sun.*

☼ ◑ ◊ Z3   ↕18in (45cm) ↔3ft (1m)

Dicentra 'Stuart Boothman'

A spreading perennial that bears heart-shaped pink flowers along the tips of arching stems during late spring and summer. The very finely cut foliage is fernlike and gray-green. Very attractive for a shady border or woodland planting.

CULTIVATION: *Best in moist but well drained, organic, neutral to slightly alkaline soil, in partial shade. Divide and replant clumps in early spring, after the leaves have died down.*

☼ ◊ ◊ Z3b
↕12in (30cm) ↔16in (40cm)

Dicksonia antarctica

Tree ferns have fibrous trunks topped by a tuft of large, feathery, bright green fronds, up to 10ft (3m) in length. Slow growing Tasmanian tree fern is a fine specimen for a cool conservatory. Of the several types of tree fern available, this is perhaps the hardiest.

CULTIVATION: *Grow in humus-rich, moist, neutral to acid soil, in full or partial shade. In mild-winter areas, wrap the trees to protect them from frost. Minimum temperature 50°F (10°C).*

☼ ☼ ◊ Tender
↕to 12ft (4m) or more ↔12ft (4m)

Dictamnus albus var. *purpureus*

This herbaceous perennial bears upright spikes of purple flowers in early summer, above the highly aromatic, light green leaves. Striking in a mixed or herbaceous border.

CULTIVATION: *Grow in any dry, well-drained, moderately fertile soil, in full sun or partial shade.*

☼ ◐ ◊ Z3

‡16–36in (40–90cm) ↔24in (60cm)

Digitalis x *mertonensis*

An evergreen, clump-forming, short-lived perennial grown for its spires of flared, strawberry pink flowers that are borne from late spring to early summer. The leaves are dark green and lance-shaped. A beautiful plant for mixed or herbaceous borders or woodland plantings. The dusky pink cultivar 'Raspberry' is also recommended.

CULTIVATION: *Best in moist but well-drained soil, in partial shade, but tolerates full sun and dry soil.*

☼ ◐ ◊ ◊ Z3

‡36in (90cm) ↔12in (30cm)

Digitalis purpurea f. *albiflora*

This ghostly form of the common foxglove is a tall biennial producing robust, stately spires of tubular, pure white flowers during summer. The coarse, lance-shaped leaves are bright green. A lovely addition to a woodland garden or mixed border. May be sold as *D. purpurea* 'Alba'.

CULTIVATION: *Grow in moist but well-drained soil, in partial shade, but also tolerates dry soil in full sun.*

☼ ☀ ◐ ◊ Z4
‡3–6ft (1–2m) ↔24in (60cm)

Disanthus cercidifolius

This medium-sized, rounded shrub is an underused garden plant with excellent fall color. The heart-shaped leaves turn various shades of orange, red, purple, and yellow before they fall. Mildly fragrant red flowers appear in fall. Protect from late spring frosts.

CULTIVATION: *Grow in moist but well-drained, slightly acid soil, in partial sun or light shade. Choose a sheltered site; hard frosts in late spring may kill the plant if they occur after buds emerge.*

☼ ◊ ◐ Z7 ‡↔10ft (3m)

Dodecatheon meadia f. album

This herbaceous perennial is valued for its open clusters of creamy white flowers with strongly reflexed petals. These are borne on arching stems during mid- to late spring, above the rosettes of oval, pale green, toothed leaves. Suits a woodland or shady rock garden; flowering is followed by a period of dormancy. *D. dentatum* (Z8) is similar but is only half the height; is ideal for a small rock garden.

CULTIVATION: *Grow in moist, organic soil, in partial shade. May be prone to slug and snail damage in spring.*

❀ ◊ Z5 ‡16in (40cm) ↔10in (25cm)

Dryopteris filix-mas

The male fern is a deciduous foliage perennial forming large clumps of lance-shaped, mid-green fronds that emerge from a thick, scaly crown in spring. Ideal for a shady border or corner, by the side of a stream or pool, or in woodland. 'Cristata', with crested fronds, is a handsome cultivar.

CULTIVATION: *Grow in reliably moist, organic soil. Site in partial shade with shelter from cold, drying winds.*

❀ ◊ Z3b ‡↔3ft (1m)

Dryopteris wallichiana

Wallich's wood fern is a deciduous foliage perennial with a strongly upright, shuttlecock-like habit. The fronds are yellow-green when they emerge in spring, becoming dark green in summer. A fine architectural specimen for a moist, shady site.

CULTIVATION: *Best in damp soil that is rich in organic matter. Choose a sheltered position in partial shade.*

☼ ◊ Z6b   ↕3ft (1m) ↔30in (75cm)

Eccremocarpus scaber

The Chilean glory flower is a fast-growing, scrambling climber with clusters of brilliant orange-red, tubular flowers in summer. The leaves are divided and mid-green. Grow as a climbing annual to clothe an arch or pergola, or up into a large shrub, or as a trailing annual.

CULTIVATION: *Grow in free-draining, fertile soil, in a sheltered, sunny site. Cut back to within 12–24in (30–60cm) of the base in spring.*

☼ ◊ Tender
↕10–15ft (3–5m) or more ↔8in (20cm)

Echinacea purpurea 'Magnus'

Coneflowers are popular late summer perennials, and there are now many new colors available. The daisy-like flowers have a raised, textured center or "cone". They come into bloom at a time when many other summer perennials are flagging, extending the summer season. 'Magnus' has large, purple-pink flowers with orange cones.

CULTIVATION: *Grow in any deep, well-drained soil in sun. Enrich the soil with organic matter before planting. Divide plants in spring, as needed.*

❋ ◊ ◊ Z3b   ↕↔24in (60cm)

Echinops ritro

This globe thistle is a compact perennial forming clumps of eye-catching flowerheads, metallic blue at first, turning a brighter blue as the flowers open. The leathery green leaves have white-downy undersides. Excellent for a wild garden. The flowers dry well if cut before fully open. *E. bannaticus* 'Taplow Blue' (Z4) makes a good substitute for *E. ritro*, although it may grow a little taller.

CULTIVATION: *Grow in well-drained, poor to moderately fertile soil. Site in full sun, but tolerates partial shade. Deadhead to prevent self-seeding.*

❋ ❋ ◊ Z3
↕24in (60cm) ↔18in (45cm)

Elaeagnus x *ebbingei* 'Gilt Edge'

A large, dense, evergreen shrub grown for its oval, dark green leaves that are edged with rich golden yellow. Inconspicuous yet highly scented, creamy white flowers are produced in fall. Makes an excellent, fast-growing, well-shaped specimen shrub; it can also be planted as an informal hedge.

CULTIVATION: *Grow in well-drained, fertil soil, in full sun. Dislikes very alkaline soil. Trim to shape in late spring; completely remove any shoots with plain green leaves as soon as seen.*

☀ ◊ Z7   ‡↔12ft (4m

Elaeagnus pungens 'Maculata'

This large, evergreen foliage shrub bears oval, dark green leaves that are generously splashed in the centre with dark yellow. Small but very fragrant flowers are produced from mid-autumn, followed by red fruits. Tolerates coastal conditions.

CULTIVATION: *Best in well-drained, fairly fertile soil, in sun. Dislikes very alkaline soil. Trim lightly in spring, as needed. Remove completely any shoots with plain green leaves as soon as seen.*

☀ ◊ Z7   ‡12ft (4m) ↔15ft (5m)

Elaeagnus 'Quicksilver'

A fast-growing shrub with an open habit bearing small yellow flowers in summer, followed by yellow fruits. The silver, deciduous leaves are lance-shaped and are carried on silvery shoots. Makes an excellent specimen shrub, or it can be planted to great effect with other silver-leaved plants. May be known as *E. angustifolia* var. *caspica*.

CULTIVATION: *Grow in any but alkaline soil that is fertile and well-drained, in full sun. Tolerates dry soil and coastal winds. Keep pruning to a minimum.*

☼ ◊ Z2b   ↕↔12ft (4m)

Enkianthus campanulatus

A spreading, deciduous shrub grown for its dense, hanging clusters of bell-shaped, creamy yellow flowers in late spring. The dull green leaves turn to a fine orange-red fall display. Suits an open site in a woodland garden; can become treelike with age. *E. cernuus* var. *rubens* (Z6), with deep pink flowers, is more suited to a small garden, at only 8ft (2.5m) tall.

CULTIVATION: *Grow in reliably moist but well-drained, peaty or organic, acidic soil. Best in full sun, but tolerates some shade. Keep pruning to a minimum.*

☼ ☀ ◊ ◊ Z5b   ↕↔12–15ft (4–5m)

Epimedium x perralchicum

A robust, clump-forming, evergreen perennial that produces spikes of delicate, bright yellow flowers above the glossy dark green foliage in mid- and late spring. The leaves are tinged bronze when young. Very useful as a groundcover under trees or shrubs.

CULTIVATION: *Grow in moist but well-drained, moderately fertile, organic soil in, partial shade. Provide shelter from cold, drying winds.*

☀ ◊ ◊ Z4   ‡16in (40cm) ↔24in (60cm)

Epimedium x rubrum

A compact perennial bearing loose clusters of pretty crimson flowers with yellow spurs, in spring. The divided leaves are tinted bronze-red when young, aging to mid-green, the reddening in fall. Clump together to form drifts in a damp, shady border or woodland garden. *E. grandiflorum* 'Rose Queen' is very similar.

CULTIVATION: *Grow in moist but well-drained, moderately fertile, organic soil, in partial shade. Cut back old, tattered foliage in late winter so that the flowers can be seen in spring.*

☀ ◊ ◊ Z3   ‡↔12in (30cm)

Epimedium x *youngianum* 'Niveum'

A clump-forming perennial that bears dainty clusters of small white flowers in late spring. The bright green foliage is bronze-tinted when young and, despite being deciduous, persists well into winter. Makes a good groundcover in damp, shady borders and woodland areas.

CULTIVATION: *Grow in moist but well-drained, fertile, organic soil, in partial shade. In late winter, cut back old, tattered foliage so that the new flowers can be seen in spring.*

◊ ◊ Z4
8–12in(20–30cm) ↔12in (30cm)

Eranthis hyemalis

Winter aconite is one of the earliest spring-flowering bulbs, bearing buttercup-like, bright yellow flowers. These sit on a ruff of light green leaves, covering the ground from late winter until early spring. Ideal for naturalizing beneath deciduous trees and large shrubs, as is 'Guinea Gold', with similar flowers and bronze-green leaves.

CULTIVATION: *Grow in moist but well-drained, fertile soil that does not dry out in summer. Best in dappled shade.*

☀ ◊ ◊ Z4   ‡3in (8cm) ↔2in (5cm)

Erica arborea var. **alpine**

This tree heath is an upright shrub, much larger than other heathers, densely clothed with clusters of small, honey-scented white flowers from late winter to late spring. The evergreen leaves are needlelike and dark green. A fine centerpiece for a heather garden.

CULTIVATION: *Grow in well-drained, ideally sandy, acidic soil, in an open, sunny site. Tolerates alkaline conditions. Cut back young plants in early spring by about two-thirds to promote bushy growth; in later years, pruning is unnecessary. Tolerates hard renovation pruning.*

☼ ◊ Z8 ‡6ft (2m) ↔3ft (1m)

Erica x *veitchii* '**Exeter**'

An upright, open, evergreen shrub that bears masses of highly scented, tubular to bell-shaped white flowers from midwinter to spring. The needlelike leaves are bright green. Good in a large rock garden with conifers or as a focal point among low-growing heathers.

CULTIVATION: *Grow in sandy soil that is well-drained, in sun. Best in acidic soil, but tolerates slightly alkaline conditions. When young, cut back by two-thirds in spring to encourage a good shape; reduce pruning as the plant gets older.*

☼ ◊ Z8 ‡6ft (2m) ↔26in (65cm)

Early-flowering Ericas

e low-growing, early flowering
aths are evergreen shrubs valued
r their urn-shaped flowers in winter
d spring. The flowers come in white
d a wide range of pinks, bringing
valuable early interest during the
nter months. This effect can be
derlined by choosing cultivars with
lorful foliage; *E. erigena* 'Golden
dy', for example, has bright golden
llow leaves (Z7), and *E. carnea*
oxhollow' carries yellow, bronze-
ped foliage that turns a deep orange

in cold weather (Z4). Excellent as a
groundcover, either in groups of the
same cultivar or with other heathers
and dwarf conifers.

CULTIVATION: *Grow in open, well-drained,
preferably acidic soil, but tolerate alkaline
conditions. Choose a site in full sun. Cut
back flowered stems in spring to remove
most of the previous year's growth; cultivars
of* E. erigena *may be scorched by frost, so
remove any affected growth in spring.*

☼ ◊ Z4–7*

‡5in (15cm) ↔10in (25cm)   ‡6in (15cm) ↔16in (40cm)   ‡6in (15cm) ↔18in (45cm)

‡6in (15cm) ↔14in (35cm)   ‡12in (30cm) ↔24in (60cm)   ‡12in (30cm) ↔16in (40cm)

E. carnea 'Ann Sparkes' **2** *E. carnea* 'Foxhollow' **3** *E. carnea* 'Springwood White'
E. carnea 'Vivellii' **5** *E.* × *darleyensis* 'Jenny Porter' **6** *E. erigena* 'Golden Lady'

Late-flowering Ericas

Mostly low and spreading in form, the summer-flowering heaths are fully hardy, evergreen shrubs. They look well on their own or mixed with other heathers and dwarf conifers. Flowers are borne over a very long period; *E. x stuartii* 'Irish Lemon' starts in late spring, and cultivars of *E. ciliaris* and *E. vagans* bloom well into fall. Their season of interest can be further extended by choosing types with colorful foliage; the young shoots of *E. williamsii* 'P.D. Williams' are tipped with yellow in spring, and the golden foliage of *E. cinerea* 'Windlebrooke' turns a deep red in winter.

CULTIVATION: *Grow in well-drained, acidic soil, although* E. vagans *and* E. williamsii *tolerate alkaline conditions. Choose an open site in full sun. Prune or shear lightly in early spring, cutting back to strong shoots below the flower clusters.*

☼ ◊ *ciliaris* and *cinerea* Z6; all others Z5

1 ‡9in (22cm) ↔35cm (14in)

2 ‡to 16in (40cm) ↔18in (45cm)

3 ‡8in (20cm) ↔20in (50cm)

4 ‡10in (25cm) ↔20in (50cm)

5 ‡6in (15cm) ↔18in (45cm)

1 *E. ciliaris* 'Corfe Castle' **2** *E. ciliaris* 'David McClintock' **3** *E. cinerea* 'Eden Valley'
4 *E. cinerea* 'C.D. Eason' **5** *E. cinerea* 'Windlebrooke'

‡10in (25cm) ↔ 20in (50cm)

‡8in (20cm) ↔ 12in (30cm)

0in (25cm) ↔ 18in (45cm)

12in (30cm) ↔ 20in (50cm)

‡10in (25cm) ↔ 20in (50cm)

‡12in (30cm) ↔ 18in (45cm)

6in (15cm) ↔ 12in (30cm)

‡8in (20cm) ↔ to 34in (85cm)

‡12in (30cm) ↔ 18in (45cm)

6 *E. cinerea* 'Fiddler's Gold' 7 *E. × stuartii* 'Irish Lemon' 8 *E. tetralix* 'Alba Mollis'
9 *E. vagans* 'Birch Glow' 10 *E. vagans* 'Lyonesse' 11 *E. vagans* 'Mrs D.F. Maxwell'
12 *E. vagans* 'Valerie Proudley' 13 *E. watsonii* 'Dawn' 14 *E. × williamsii* 'P.D. Williams'

Erigeron karvinskianus

This carpeting, evergreen perennial with gray-green foliage produces an abundance of yellow-centered, daisylike flowerheads in summer. The outer petals are initially white, maturing to pink and purple. Ideal for wall crevices or cracks in paving. Sometimes sold as *E. mucronatus*.

CULTIVATION: *Grow in well-drained, ferti. soil. Choose a site in full sun, ideally wit. some shade at midday.*

☼ ◊ Z6
‡6–12in (15–30cm) ↔3ft (1m) or mor.

Erinus alpinus

The fairy foxglove is a tiny, short-lived, evergreen perennial producing short spikes of pink, purple, or white daisylike flowers in late spring and summer. The lance- to wedge-shaped leaves are soft, sticky, and mid-green. Ideal for a rock garden or in crevices in old walls. 'Mrs Charles Boyle' is a recommended cultivar.

CULTIVATION: *Grow in light, moderately fertile soil that is well-drained. Tolerates semi-shade, but best in full sun.*

☼ ◖ ◊ Z3b   ‡3in (8cm) ↔4in (10cm

Eryngium alpinum

This spiky, upright, thistlelike perennial bears cone-shaped, purple-blue flowerheads in summer; these are surrounded by prominent, feathery bracts. The deeply toothed, mid-green leaves are arranged around the base of the stems. An excellent textural plant for a sunny garden. The flowerheads can be cut, and they dry well for arrangements.

CULTIVATION: *Grow in free-draining but not too dry, poor to moderately fertile soil, in full sun. Choose a site not prone to excessive winter moisture.*

◊ Z3   ‡28in (70cm) ↔18in (45cm)

Eryngium x oliverianum

An upright, herbaceous perennial bearing cone-shaped, bright silver-blue flowerheads with a flat ring of silvery, daggerlike bracts around the base, produced from midsummer to early fall, above spiny-toothed, dark green leaves. Longer-lived than its parent *E. giganteum*, and an essential architectural addition to a dry, sunny border with a theme of silver- or gray-leaved plants.

CULTIVATION: *Grow in free-draining, fairly fertile soil, in full sun. Choose a site without excessive winter moisture.*

☼ ◊ Z4   ‡36in (90cm) ↔18in (45cm)

Eryngium x *tripartitum*

This delicate but spiky, upright perennial bears conelike heads of tiny, metallic blue flowers in late summer and fall. The flowerheads sit on a ring of pointed bracts and are carried above rosettes of gray-green foliage on the tips of wiry, blue-tinted stems. The flowers dry well if cut before fully open.

CULTIVATION: *Grow in free-draining, moderately fertile soil. Choose a position not prone to excessive winter moisture, in full sun. Trim lightly after flowering to prevent legginess.*

☼ ◊ Z4
‡24–36in (60–90cm) ↔20in (50cm)

Erysimum 'Bowles' Mauve

This vigorous, shrubby wallflower is one of the longest-flowering of all perennials. It forms a rounded, evergreen bush of narrow, gray-green leaves and produces dense spikes of small, four-petaled, rich mauve flowers all year, most freely in spring and summer. An excellent border plant that benefits from the shelter of a warm wall where not fully hardy.

CULTIVATION: *Grow in any well-drained, preferably alkaline soil, in full sun. Trim lightly after flowering to keep compact. Often short-lived, but easily propagated by cuttings in summer.*

☼ ◊ Z4 ‡30in (75cm) ↔24in (60cm)

Erysimum 'Wenlock Beauty'

A bushy, evergreen perennial that produces clusters of bluish-pink and salmon, bronze-shaded flowers from early to late spring. The lance-shaped leaves are softly hairy and mid-green. Good for early-season color in a sunny rock garden or dry wall; where marginally hardy, choose a warm, sheltered spot.

CULTIVATION: *Grow in poor or fairly fertile, ideally alkaline soil that has good drainage, in full sun. Trim lightly after flowering to keep compact.*

☼ ◊ Z6   ↕↔18in (45cm)

Erythronium dens-canis

The European dog's-tooth violet is a woodland or mountain meadow plant in the wild and thrives in damp, part-shady conditions in the garden. Its paired, mid-green leaves with variable bronze marking emerge from a bulbous rootstock. From spring to early summer, slender stems rise from the foliage with delicate white, pink, or lilac pendent flowers with reflexed tepals. Effective planted in drifts.

CULTIVATION: *Plant bulbs in fall in humus-rich soil in dappled shade. Keep bulbs slightly damp in storage and plant at least 4in (10cm) deep.*

 ◊ Z4
4–6in (10–15cm) ↔ 4in (10cm)

Erythronium 'Pagoda'

This very vigorous, clump-forming, bulbous perennial is related to the dog's tooth violet, *E. dens-canis*, and, like it, looks good planted in groups under deciduous trees and shrubs. Clusters of pale sulfur yellow flowers droop from slender stems in spring above the large, oval, bronze-mottled glossy dark green leaves.

CULTIVATION: *Grow in moist but well-drained soil rich in organic matter. Choose a position in partial shade.*

☼ ◐ ◊ ◊ Z4
‡6–14in (15–35cm) ↔4in (10cm)

Escallonia 'Apple Blossom'

A compact, evergreen shrub carrying dense, glossy dark foliage and, from early to midsummer, a profusion of small, pink-flushed white flowers. Valuable in a shrub border, it can also be grown as a hedge, barrier, or windbreak. Very useful in coastal areas, if prevailing winds are not harshly cold. *E.* 'Donard Seedling', also usually readily available, looks similar, and is a little hardier.

CULTIVATION: *Grow in any well-drained, fertile soil, in full sun. In especially cold areas, shelter from wind. Cut out old or damaged growth after flowering.*

☼ ◊ Z8
‡↔8ft (2.5m)

Escallonia 'Iveyi'

A vigorous, upright, evergreen shrub bearing large clusters of fragrant, pure white flowers from mid- to late summer. The rounded leaves are glossy dark green. Grow in a shrub border, or use as a hedge where winters are reliably mild; the foliage often takes on bronze tints in cold weather, but choose a sheltered position where marginally hardy.

CULTIVATION: *Grow in any fertile soil with good drainage, in full sun with shelter from cold, drying winds. Remove damaged growth in fall, or in spring if flowering finishes late.*

☼ ◊ Z8   ↕↔10ft (3m)

Escallonia 'Langleyensis'

This graceful, semi-evergreen shrub produces abundant clusters of small, rose-pink flowers. These are borne from early to midsummer above the oval, glossy bright green leaves. Thrives in relatively mild coastal gardens as an informal hedge or in a shrub border.

CULTIVATION: *Best in well-drained, fertile soil, in a sunny site. Protect from cold, drying winds where marginal. Cut out dead or damaged growth after flowering; old plants can be renovated by hard pruning in spring.*

☼ ◊ Z8   ↕6ft (2m) ↔10ft (3m)

Eschscholzia caespitosa

A tufted annual bearing a profusion of scented, bright yellow flowers in summer. The blue-green leaves are finely divided and almost threadlike. Suitable for a sunny border, rock garden, or gravel patch. The flowers close up in dull weather.

CULTIVATION: *Grow in well-drained, poor soil. Choose a site in full sun. For early flowers the following year, sow seed directly outdoors in fall.*

☼ ◊ Annual   ‡↔to 6in (15cm

Eschscholzia californica

The California poppy is a mat-forming annual with cup-shaped flowers borne on slender stems throughout summer. Colors are mixed, including white, red, or yellow, but most are usually orange. The cultivar 'Dali' flowers in scarlet only. The leaves are finely cut and grayish-green. Grow in a sunny border or rock garden; the flowers last well when cut.

CULTIVATION: *Best in light, poor soil with good drainage, in full sun. For early flowers the following year, sow seed directly outdoors in fall.*

☼ ◊ Annual
‡12in (30cm) ↔6in (15cm)

Eucalyptus gunnii

The cider gum is a vigorous, evergreen tree useful as a fast-growing feature in a new garden. The new yellow- to grayish-green bark is revealed in late summer as the old, whitish-green layer is shed. Young plants have rounded, gray-blue leaves; on adult growth they are lance-shaped. Protect where marginally hardy with a winter mulch, especially when young.

CULTIVATION: *Grow in well-drained, fertile soil, in sun. To keep compact, and for the best display of young foliage, cut back hard each spring.*

☼ ◊ Z8
‡40–80ft (10–25m) ↔20–50ft (6–15m)

Eucalyptus pauciflora subsp. niphophila

The snow gum is a handsome, silvery, evergreen tree with open, spreading branches and attractively peeling, white and gray bark. Young leaves are oval and dull blue-green; on mature stems they are lance-shaped and deep blue-green. The flowers are less significant. Popularly grown as a shrub, pruned back hard at regular intervals.

CULTIVATION: *Grow in well-drained, fertile soil, in full sun. For the best display of young foliage, cut back hard each year in spring.*

☼ ◊ Z8
‡↔to 20ft (6m)

Eucryphia x *nymansensi* 'Nymansay'

A columnar, evergreen tree that bears clusters of large, fragrant, glistening white flowers with yellow stamens. These are borne in late summer to early fall amid the oval, glossy dark green leaves. Makes a magnificent flowering specimen tree. For very sheltered gardens in Z8 only.

CULTIVATION: *Grow in well-drained, reliably moist soil, preferably in full sun with shade at the roots, but will tolerate semi-shade. Shelter from cold winds. Remove damaged growth in spring.*

☼ ◐ ◌ ◊ Z8 ‡50ft (15m) ↔15ft (5n

Euonymus alatus

The burning bush is a dense, deciduous shrub with winged stems, much value for its spectacular fall display; small purple and red fruits split to reveal orange seeds as the oval, deep green foliage turns to scarlet. The flowers are much less significant. Excellent in a shrub border or light woodland. The fruits are poisonous. 'Compactus' is a dwarf version of this shrub, only half its height.

CULTIVATION: *Grow in any well-drained, fertile soil. Tolerates light shade, but fruiting and fall color are best in full sun. Keep pruning to a minimum.*

☼ ☀ ◊ Z3 ‡6ft (2m) ↔10ft (3m

Euonymus europaeus 'Red Cascade'

A treelike, deciduous shrub that produces colorful fall foliage. Inconspicuous flowers in early summer are followed by rosy red fruits that split to reveal orange seeds. The oval, mid-green leaves turn scarlet-red at the end of the growing season. The fruits are toxic.

CULTIVATION: *Grow in any fertile soil with good drainage, but thrives on alkaline soil. Tolerates light shade, but fruiting and fall color are best in full sun. Two or more specimens are required to guarantee a good crop of fruits. Very little pruning is necessary.*

☀ ☀ ◊ Z4   ‡10ft (3m) ↔8ft (2.5m)

Euonymus fortunei 'Emerald 'n' Gold'

A small and scrambling, evergreen shrub that will climb if supported. The bright green, oval leaves have broad, bright golden yellow margins and take on a pink tinge in cold weather. The spring flowers are insignificant. Use to fill gaps in a shrub border, or wall-train.

CULTIVATION: *Grow in any but water-logged soil. The leaves color best in full sun, but tolerates light shade. Trim in mid-spring. Trained up a wall, it may reach a height of up to 15ft (5m).*

☀ ☀ ◊ ◊ Z5   ‡24in (60cm) or more ↔36in (90cm)

Euonymus fortunei 'Silver Queen'

A compact, upright or scrambling, evergreen shrub that looks most effective when grown as a climber against a wall or up into a tree. The dark green leaves have broad white edges that become pink-tinged in prolonged cold. The greenish-white flowers in spring are insignificant.

CULTIVATION: *Grow in any but water-logged soil, in sun or light shade. Leaf color is best in full sun. Trim shrubs in mid-spring. Allowed to climb, it can grow up to 20ft (6m) tall.*

☼ ☀ ◑ ◊ Z5 ‡8ft (2.5m) ↔5ft (1.5m)

Eupatorium maculatum

Named for a legendary Native American healer, Joe Pye weed is a tall perennial that bears clusters of dusky pink flowers in midsummer. These attract hummingbirds, bees, and butterflies. Handsome seedheads persist into winter. Plant in groups, at the back of the border, or interspersed with ornamental grasses. 'Gateway' is a highly rated compact form. Sometimes listed as *Eupatoriadelphus maculatus* var. *maculatus*.

CULTIVATION: *Very hardy; grows best in average to moist, fertile soil, in full sun. Tolerates part sun. Divide when needed.*

☼ ☀ ◊ Z3b ‡to 9ft (3m) ↔to 3ft (1m)

Euphorbia amygdaloides var. *robbiae*

Mrs. Robb's bonnet, also known simply as *E. robbiae*, is a spreading, evergreen perennial bearing open heads of yellowish-green flowers in spring. The long, dark green leaves are arranged in rosettes at the base of the stems. Particularly useful in shady areas. Can be invasive.

CULTIVATION: *Grow in well-drained but moist soil, in full sun or partial shade. Tolerates poor, dry soil. Dig up invasive roots to contain spread. The milky sap can irritate skin.*

☼ ◐ ◊ ◖ Z6
‡30–32in (75–80cm) ↔12in (30cm)

Euphorbia characias subsp. *wulfenii* 'John Tomlinson'

This billowing, shrubby perennial bears larger flowerheads than others of the same species. The flowers are bright yellow-green, without dark eyes, and are borne in rounded heads above the narrow, gray-green leaves. Where marginally hardy, it is best grown at the base of a warm, sunny wall.

CULTIVATION: *Grow in light soil that has good drainage, in full sun. Shelter from cold winds. Cut the flowered stems back to the base in fall; wear gloves, since the milky sap can irritate skin.*

☼ ◊ Z8
↕↔4ft (1.2m)

Euphorbia x *martinii*

This upright, clump-forming, evergreen subshrub bears spikes of yellow-green flowers with very distinctive, dark red nectar glands. These are carried on red-tinged shoots from spring to mid-summer, above lance-shaped, mid-green leaves that are often tinged purple when young. A choice plant with an architectural look for a hot, dry site.

CULTIVATION: *Grow in well-drained soil, in a sheltered, sunny site. Deadhead after flowering, wearing gloves to protect hands from the milky sap that may irritate skin.*

☼ ◊ Z6 ↕↔3ft (1m

Euphorbia myrsinites

A small, evergreen perennial bearing sprawling stems that are densely clothed with a spiral arrangement of fleshy, elliptic, blue-green leaves. Clusters of yellow-green flowers brighten the tips of the stems in spring. Excellent in a dry, sunny rock garden, or trailing over the edge of a raised bed.

CULTIVATION: *Grow in well-drained, light soil, in full sun. Deadhead after flowering; it self-seeds freely. Wear gloves to avoid contact with the milky sap, which is a potential skin irritant.*

☼ ◊ Z4 ↕4in (10cm) ↔to 12in (30cm)

Euphorbia polychroma

This evergreen perennial forms a neat, rounded clump of softly hairy, mid-green foliage. It is covered with clusters of brilliant greenish-yellow flowers over long periods in spring. Excellent with spring bulbs, in a border or light woodland. Tolerates a wide range of soil types. Its cultivar 'Major' grows a little taller.

CULTIVATION: *Grow in either well-drained, light soil, in full sun, or moist, organic soil, in light dappled shade. Deadhead after flowering. The milky sap can irritate skin.*

☼ ◐ ◊ ◊ Z4

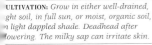

‡16in (40cm) ↔24in (60cm)

Euphorbia schillingii

This vigorous, clump-forming perennial that, unlike many euphorbias, dies back in winter, bears clusters of long-lasting yellowish-green flowers from midsummer to mid-fall. The lance-shaped leaves are dark green and have pale green or white central veins. Ideal for lighting up a woodland planting or shady wild garden.

CULTIVATION: *Grow in reliably moist, organic soil, in light dappled shade. Deadhead after flowering. The milky sap can irritate skin.*

☼ ◐ Z8   ‡3ft (1m) ↔12in (30cm)

Exochorda x *macrantha* 'The Bride'

A dense, spreading, deciduous shrub grown for its gently arching habit an abundant clusters of fragrant, pure white flowers. These are borne in lat spring and early summer amid the oval, fresh green leaves. An elegant foil to other plants in a mixed border

CULTIVATION: *Grow in any well-drained soil, in full sun or light dappled shade. Does not like shallow, alkaline soil. Very little pruning is necessary.*

☼ ☀ ◊ Z5   ‡6ft (2m) ↔10ft (3m

Fagus sylvatica 'Dawyck Gold'

This golden-foliage selection of deciduous European beech is more upright and conical than the standard beech. The vivid golden leaves unfurl in spring and early summer, mellowing to pale green as the season progresses. In fall, the leaves begin to yellow before dropping. When grown as a clipped hedge, the dried, coppery leaves persist through winter.

CULTIVATION: *Grow in any well-drained soil, in sun or partial shade. Leaf color is best in partial shade. Remove dead, diseased, or crossing branches in winter.*

☼ ☀ ◊ ◊ Z5b   ‡60ft (18m) ↔22ft (7m)

Fargesia nitida

Fountain bamboo is a slow-growing perennial that forms a dense clump of upright, dark purple-green canes. In the second year after planting, cascades of narrow, dark green leaves are produced from the top of the clump. Handsome in a wild garden; to restrict spread, grow in a large container. May be sold as *Sinarundinaria nitida*. *F. murielae* (Z5b) is equally attractive, similar but with yellow stems and brighter leaves.

CULTIVATION: *Grow in reliably moist, fertile soil, in light dappled shade. Shelter from cold, drying winds.*

☼ ◑ ◊ Z5
↕ to 15ft (5m) ↔ 15ft (5m) or more

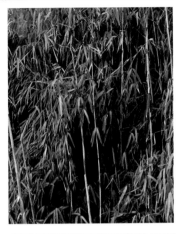

x *Fatshedera lizei*

The tree ivy is a mound-forming, evergreen shrub cultivated for its large, handsome, glossy dark green, ivylike leaves. Small white flowers appear in fall. Excellent in shady areas; where marginally hardy, grow in a sunny, sheltered site. Given support, it can be trained against a wall; it also makes a fine house- or conservatory plant. Look for cream-edged 'Variegata'.

CULTIVATION: *Best in moist but well-drained, fertile soil, in sun or partial shade. No regular pruning is required. Tie in to grow against a support.*

☼ ◑ ◊ ◊ Z7b
↕ 4–6ft (1.2–2m) ↔ 10ft (3m)

Fatsia japonica

The Japanese aralia is a spreading, evergreen shrub grown for its large, palm-shaped, glossy green leaves. Broad, upright clusters of rounded, creamy white flowerheads appear in fall. An excellent architectural plant for a shady border. Tolerates atmospheric pollution and thrives in sheltered city gardens. 'Variegata' has cream-edged leaves.

CULTIVATION: *Grow in any well-drained soil, in sun or shade. Provide shelter from cold winds and hard frosts. Little pruning is required, except cutting wayward shoots and damaged growth in spring.*

☼ ☀ ◊ Z7b   ↕↔5–12ft (1.5–4m)

Festuca glauca 'Blaufuchs'

This bright blue fescue is a densely tufted, evergreen, perennial grass. It is excellent in a border or rock garden as a foil to other plants. Spikes of not particularly striking, violet-flushed, blue-green flowers are borne in early summer, above the foliage. The narrow, bright blue leaves are its chief attraction.

CULTIVATION: *Grow in dry, well-drained, poor to moderately fertile soil, in sun. For the best foliage color, divide and replant clumps every 2 or 3 years.*

☼ ◊ Z3b   ↕↔12in (30cm)

Ficus carica 'Brown Turkey'

The common fig is remarkable for its large, lobed, bright green leaves and its heavy crop of edible fruit. These tend to ripen fully only in regions with long, hot summers. Figs can be grown as specimen trees, as multistemmed shrubs, and trained against a sunny wall. Where not hardy, grow them in a container that can be wintered indoors.

CULTIVATION: *Grow in moist but well-drained soil, in sun. Protect emerging figs from late frosts in spring. Remove a few of the oldest stems each year.*

☼ ◊ ◑ Z6b
↕10ft (3m) or more ↔12ft (4m) or more

Filipendula purpurea

An upright, clump-forming perennial that looks well planted in groups to form drifts of elegant, dark green foliage. Feathery clusters of red-purple flowers are carried above the leaves on purple-tinged stems in summer. Suitable for a waterside planting or bog garden; can also be naturalized in damp woodland.

CULTIVATION: *Grow in reliably moist, moderately fertile, organic soil, in partial shade. Can be planted in full sun where the soil does not dry out.*

☼ ☀ ◐ ◑ Z3b
↕4ft (1.2m) ↔24in (60cm)

Filipendula rubra 'Venusta'

A vigorous, upright perennial that produces feathery plumes of tiny, soft pink flowers on tall branching stems in midsummer. The large, dark green leaves are jaggedly cut into several lobes. Excellent in a bog garden, in moist soil by the side of water, or in a damp wild garden.

CULTIVATION: *Grow in reliably moist, moderately fertile soil, in partial shade. Thrives in wet or boggy soil, where it will tolerate full sun.*

☀ ◐ ◗ ♦ Z3
↕6–8ft (2–2.5m) ↔4ft (1.2m)

Forsythia x intermedia 'Lynwood Variety'

A vigorous, deciduous shrub with upright stems that arch slightly at the tips. Its golden yellow flowers appear in profusion on bare branches in early spring. Mid-green, oval leaves emerge after flowering. A reliable shrub for a mixed border or as an informal hedge. May only flower below snow-line at limits of hardiness.

CULTIVATION: *Grow in well-drained, fertile soil, in full sun. Tolerates partial shade, although flowering will be less profuse. On established plants, cut out some old stems after flowering.*

☀ ◐ ◊ Z6 ↕↔10ft (3m)

Forsythia suspensa

This upright, deciduous shrub,
sometimes called golden bell, is less
bushy than *F.* x *intermedia* (see facing
page, below), with more strongly
arched stems. It is valued for the
nodding, bright yellow flowers that
open on its bare branches from early
to mid-spring. The leaves are oval
and mid-green. Good planted on its
own, as an informal hedge, or in a
shrub border.

CULTIVATION: *Best in well-drained, fertile
soil, ideally in full sun; flowering is less
spectacular in shade. Cut out some of
the older stems on established plants
after flowering.*

✳ ☀ ◊ Z5b   ↔10ft (3m)

Fothergilla major

This slow-growing, upright shrub
bears spikes of bottlebrush-like,
fragrant white flowers in late spring.
It is also valued for its blaze of fall
foliage. The deciduous leaves are
glossy dark green in summer, then
turn orange, yellow, and red before
they fall. An attractive addition to a
shrub border or in light woodland.

CULTIVATION: *Best in moist but well-
drained, acidic, organic soil. Choose a
position in full sun for the best flowers
and fall color. Requires very little pruning.*

✳ ◊ Z5b   ↕8ft (2.5m) ↔6ft (2m)

Fremontodendron 'California Glory'

A vigorous, upright, semi-evergreen shrub producing large, cup-shaped, golden yellow flowers from late spring to mid-fall. The rounded leaves are lobed and dark green. Excellent for wall-training in a cool conservatory or when grown in a large container.

CULTIVATION: *Best in well-drained, poor t moderately fertile, neutral to alkaline soil in sun. Shelter from cold winds. Best wit no pruning, but wall-trained plants can be trimmed in spring.*

☼ ◊ Tender   ↕20ft (6m) ↔12ft (4n

Fritillaria imperialis 'Rubra'

This red-flowered variety of the crown imperial bears tall upright stems in early summer, topped by clusters of hanging bell flowers above whorls of fresh green foliage. A bunch of narrow leaves forms a tuft above the flowers. This is an impressively tall perennial for a larg border. Plant bulbs in late summer. The species form has orange flowers.

CULTIVATION: *Grow in a sunny border in fertile, well-drained soil. Mulch with manure as flowers fade.*

☼ ◊ ◑ Z5
↕5ft (1.5m) ↔to 3ft (1m) or more

Fritillaria meleagris

The snake's head fritillary is a bulbous perennial that naturalizes well in grass where summers are cool and damp. The drooping, bell-shaped flowers are pink, pinkish purple, or white, and are strongly checkered. They are carried singly or in pairs during spring. The narrow leaves are gray-green. There is a white-flowered form, f. *alba*, which is also recommended.

CULTIVATION: *Grow in any moist but well-drained, organic soil, in full sun or light shade. Divide and replant bulbs in late summer.*

☀ ◐ ◊ ❉ Z3
12in (30cm) ↔ 2–3in (5–8cm)

Fritillaria pallidiflora

In late spring, this robust, bulbous perennial bears bell-shaped, foul-smelling flowers above the gray-green, lance-shaped leaves. They are creamy yellow with green bases, checkered brown-red inside. Suits a rock garden or border in areas with cool, damp summers. Naturalizes easily in damp meadows.

CULTIVATION: *Grow in moist but well-drained, moderately fertile soil, in sun or partial shade. Divide and replant bulbs in late summer.*

☀ ◐ ◊ ❉ Z3
16in (40cm) ↔ 2–3in (5–8cm)

Hardier Fuchsias

The hardier fuchsias are wonderfully versatile shrubs: as well as being useful in mixed borders and as flowering hedges, they can be trained as espaliers or fans against warm walls, or grown as free-standing standards or pillars. Hanging flowers, varying in form from single to double, appear throughout summer and into fall. Where marginally hardy, these fuchsias will lose some or all of their topgrowth during winter. They are fast to recover, however, and most will retain their leaves if overwintered in a cool greenhouse or temperatures stay above 39°F (4°C).

CULTIVATION: *Grow in well-drained but moist, fertile soil. Choose a position in sun or semi-shade with shelter from cold winds. Provide a deep winter mulch. Pinch-prune young plants to encourage a bushy habit. In early spring, remove winter-damaged stems; cut back healthy growth to the lowest buds.*

☼ ◑ ◊ ◐ Z8b

1 ↕↔30–36in (75–90cm)

2 ↕12in (30cm) ↔18in (45cm)

3 ↕↔3–3¹⁄₂ft (1–1.1m)

4 ↕6–10ft (2–3m) ↔3–6ft (1–2m)

5 ↕↔6–12in (15–30cm)

6 ↕to 10ft (3m) ↔6–10ft (2–3m)

1 *F.* 'Genii' **2** *F.* 'Lady Thumb' **3** *F.* 'Mrs Popple'
4 *F.* 'Riccartonii' **5** *F.* 'Tom Thumb' **6** *F. magellanica* 'Versicolor'

Tender Fuchsias

The tender fuchsias are flowering shrubs that require at least some winter protection in cold climates. The compensation for this extra care is an increased range of beautiful summer flowers for the garden, greenhouse, and conservatory. All can be grown out of doors in the summer months and make superb patio plants when grown in containers, whether pinch-pruned into dense bushes or trained as columns or standards. Shelter tender fuchsias in a greenhouse or cool conservatory over the winter months; the tender species fuchsias, including 'Thalia', need a minimum temperature of 50°F (10°C) at all times.

CULTIVATION: *Grow in moist but well-drained, fertile soil or soil mix, in sun or partial shade. Pinch-prune young plants to promote bushiness, and trim after flowering to remove spent blooms. Prune back to an established framework in early spring.*

☼ ☀ ◊ ◊ Tender

1 ↔12–24in (30–60cm)

2 ‡to 24in (60cm) ↔to 18in (45cm)

3 ‡to 12ft (4m) ↔3–4ft (1–1.2m)

Fuchsia 'Annabel' **2** *F.* 'Billy Green' **3** *F. boliviana* var. *alba*

‡↔18–30in (45–75cm)

‡to 36in (90cm) ↔to 30in (75cm)

‡to 36in (90cm) ↔to 24in (60cm)

‡5ft (1.5m) ↔to 32in (80cm)

‡to 18in (45cm) ↔to 24in (60cm)

‡to 18in (75cm) ↔to 24in (60cm)

4 *Fuchsia* 'Celia Smedley' **5** *F.* 'Checkerboard' **6** *F.* 'Coralle'
7 *F. fulgens* **8** *F.* 'Joy Patmore' **9** *F.* 'Leonora'

‣12–24in (30–60cm)

‡to 18in (45cm) ↔18in (45cm)

‡to 30in (75cm) ↔to 24in (60cm)

‡to 24in (60cm) ↔30m (75cm)

‡↔18–36in (45–90cm)

24in (60cm) ↔18in (45cm)

MORE CHOICES

'Brookwood Belle' Cerise and white flowers.
'Pacquesa' Red and red-veined white.
'Winston Churchill' Lavender and pink.

0 *F.* 'Mary' **11** *F.* 'Nellie Nuttall' **12** *F.* 'Royal Velvet'
3 *F.* 'Snowcap' **14** *F.* 'Swingtime' **15** *F.* 'Thalia'

Trailing Fuchsias

Fuchsia cultivars with a trailing or spreading habit are the perfect plants to have trailing over the edge of a tall container, windowbox, or hanging basket, where their pendulous flowers will be shown to great effect. They bloom continuously throughout summer and into early fall and can be left in place undisturbed right up until the end of the season. After this, they are best discarded and new plants bought the following year. An alternative, longer-lived planting is to train trailing fuchsias into attractive weeping standards for container plantings, but they must be kept frost-free in winter.

CULTIVATION: *Grow in fertile, moist but well- drained soil or soil mix, in full sun or partial shade. Shelter from cold, drying winds. Little pruning is necessary, except to remove wayward growth. Regularly pinc out the tips of young plants to encourage bushiness and a well-balanced shape.*

☼ ☀ ◊ ◑ Tender

‡6–12in (15–30cm) ↔18in (45cm)

‡6–12in (15–30cm) ↔18in (45cm)

‡18in (45cm) ↔24in (60cm)

‡to 24in (60cm) ↔30in (75cm)

1 *F.* 'La Campanella' **2** *F.* 'Golden Marinka' **3** *F.* 'Jack Shahan' **4** *F.* 'Lena'

Gaillardia 'Dazzler'

bushy, short-lived perennial that ars large, daisylike flowers over a ng period in summer. These have llow-tipped, bright orange petals rrounding an orange-red center. e leaves are soft, lance-shaped, d mid-green. Effective in a sunny, ixed or herbaceous border; the owers are good for cutting.

ULTIVATION: *Grow in well-drained, t too fertile soil, in full sun. May need king. Often short-lived, but can be nvigorated by division in winter.*

○ △ Z3
24–34in (60–85cm) ↔18in (45cm)

Galanthus elwesii

his robust snowdrop is a bulbous erennial that produces slender, oney-scented, pure white flowers late winter, above the bluish-reen foliage. The inner petals have reen markings. Good for borders d rock gardens; naturalizes easily light woodland.

ULTIVATION: *Grow in moist but well-rained, organic soil that does not dry ut in summer. Choose a position partial shade.*

☼ ◐ ◊ Z4
4–6in (10–15cm) ↔3in (8cm)

Galanthus 'Magnet'

This tall snowdrop is a vigorous bulbous perennial bearing drooping pear-shaped, pure white flowers during late winter and early spring; the inner petals have a deep green, V-shaped mark at the tips. The strap-shaped, gray-green leaves are arranged around the base of the plant. Good for naturalizing in grass or in a woodland garden.

CULTIVATION: *Grow in moist but well-drained, fertile soil that does not dry out in summer. Choose a position in partial shade.*

☼ ◊ ◊ Z4　　‡8in (20cm) ↔3in (8cm)

Galanthus nivalis 'Flore Pleno'

This double-flowered form of the common snowdrop, *G. nivalis*, is a robust, bulbous perennial. Drooping, pear-shaped, pure white flowers appear from late winter to early spring, with green markings on the tips of the inner petals. The narrow leaves are gray-green. Good for naturalizing under deciduous trees or shrubs.

CULTIVATION: *Grow in reliably moist but well-drained, fertile soil, in light shade. Divide and replant every few years after flowering to maintain vigor.*

☼ ◊ ◊ Z3　　‡↔4in (10cm)

alanthus 'S. Arnott'

his honey-scented snowdrop, which
as even larger flowers than 'Magnet'
acing page, above), is a fast-growing,
lbous perennial. Nodding, pear-
aped, pure white flowers appear
late winter to early spring and have
green, V-shaped mark at the tip of
ch inner petal. The narrow leaves
re gray-green. Good for a rock
rden or raised bed. 'Atkinsii' is also
commended, similar to this one.

ULTIVATION: *Grow in moist but well-*
ained, fertile soil, in dappled shade.
ep reliably moist in summer. Divide
d replant clumps after flowering.

❄ ◊ ◊ Z4   ‡8in (20cm) ↔3in (8cm)

Garrya elliptica 'James Roof'

his silk-tassel bush is an upright,
vergreen shrub, becoming treelike
ith age. It is grown for its long,
lver-gray catkins, which dangle
om the branches in winter and
rly spring. The leaves are dark
ea green and have wavy margins.
xcellent in a shrub border, against
shady wall, or as hedging; tolerates
oastal conditions.

ULTIVATION: *Grow in well-drained,*
noderately fertile soil, in full sun or
artial shade. Tolerates poor, dry soil.
rim after flowering, as necessary.

❄ ☀ ◊ Z8   ↔12ft (4m)

Gaultheria mucronata 'Mulberry Wine' (female)

This evergreen, spreading shrub, sometimes included in *Pernettya*, is much valued for its fall display of large, rounded, magenta to purple berries that show off well against the toothed, glossy dark green leaves. Small white flowers are borne throughout summer.

CULTIVATION: *Grow in reliably moist, peaty, acidic to neutral soil, in partial shade or full sun. Plant close to male varieties to ensure a reliable crop of berries. Chop away spreading roots with a spade to restrict the overall size.*

☼ ☀ ◊ Z7　　　　↕↔4ft (1.2m)

Gaultheria mucronata 'Wintertime' (female)

An evergreen, spreading shrub, sometimes included in the genus *Pernettya*, bearing large, showy white berries that persist well into winter. Small white flowers are borne from late spring into early summer. The glossy dark green leaves are elliptic to oblong and toothed.

CULTIVATION: *Grow in reliably moist, acidic to neutral, peaty soil. Best in light shade, but tolerates sun. Plant close to male varieties to ensure a good crop of berries. Dig out spreading roots as necessary to restrict the overall size.*

☼ ☀ ◊ Z7　　　　↕↔4ft (1.2m)

...ultheria procumbens

...eckerberry is a creeping shrub that
...rs drooping, urn-shaped, white or
...k flowers in summer, followed by
...matic scarlet fruits. As these
...ally persist until spring, they give
...ter color. The glossy, dark green
...ves have a strong fragrance when
...shed, giving the plant its other
...mmon name, winter-green. Good
...oundcover in shade.

...LTIVATION: *Grow in acidic to neutral,
...ty, moist soil in partial shade; full
... is tolerated only where the soil is
...ays moist. Trim after flowering.*

❍ Z4
...n (15cm) ↔ 3ft (1m) or more

...aura lindheimeri

...all, clump-forming perennial with
...sal leaves and slender stems. From
...e spring to fall, it bears loose spires
... pinkish white buds that open in the
...orning into white flowers. A graceful
...ant for a mixed border, tolerating
...th heat and drought.

...LTIVATION: *Grow in fertile, moist but
...ell-drained soil, ideally in full sun,
...t some part-day shade is tolerated.
...necessary, divide clumps in spring.*

: ◊ ❍ Z6
...o 5ft (1.5m) ↔ 36in (90cm)

Gazanias

These useful summer bedding plants are vigorous, spreading perennials usually grown as annuals. They are cultivated for their long display of large and very colorful, daisylike flowers. They close in dull or cool weather. Flowers may be orange, white, golden yellow, beige, bronze, or bright pink, often with striking contrasting central zones of one or two other colors. Hybrid selections with variously colored flowerheads are also popular. The lance-shaped leaves are dark green with white-silky undersides. Gazanias grow well in containers and tolerate coastal conditions.

CULTIVATION: *Grow in light, sandy, well-drained soil, in full sun. Remove old or faded flowerheads to prolong flowering. Water freely during the growing season. The plants will die back on arrival of the first frosts.*

☼ ◊ Z8

MORE CHOICES

G. Chansonette Serie Mixed colors, zoned in a contrasting shade
G. Mini-star Series Mixed or single zoned colors.
G. Talent Series Mixe or single colors.

‡8in (20cm) ↔ 10in (25cm)

‡8in (20cm) ↔ 10in (25cm)

‡8in (20cm) ↔ 10in (25cm)

‡8in (20cm) ↔ 10in (25cm)

‡8in (20cm) ↔ 10in (25cm)

1 *Gazania* 'Aztec' **2** *G.* 'Cookei' **3** *G.* 'Daybreak Garden Sun'
4 *G.* 'Michael' **5** *G. rigens* var. *uniflora*

nista aetnensis

a Mount Etna broom is an upright,
ost leafless, deciduous shrub that
xcellent on its own or at the back
border in hot, dry situations.
sses of fragrant, pealike, golden
low flowers cover the weeping,
d-green stems during midsummer.

LTIVATION: *Grow in well-drained, light,*
r to moderately fertile soil, in full sun.
p pruning to a minimum; old, straggly
nts are best replaced.

◊ Z7   ↕↔25ft (8m)

nista lydia

is low, deciduous shrub forms
nound of arching, prickle-tipped
nches that are covered with
low, pealike flowers in early
mmer. The small, narrow leaves
e blue-green. Ideal for hot, dry sites
ch as a rock garden or raised bed.

LTIVATION: *Grow in well-drained, light,*
r to moderately fertile soil, in full sun.
ep pruning to a minimum; old, straggly
nts are best replaced.

◊ Z3b   ↕24in (60cm) ↔3ft (1m)

Genista 'Porlock'

The Porlock broom is a semi-evergreen, medium-sized shrub that bears heavy clusters of fragrant bright yellow, pea-like flowers in spring. The mid-green leaves are divided into three leaflets. Shear back after flowering to keep the plant in shape, but do not prune hard. This is a good plant choice for coastal sites.

CULTIVATION: *Grow in well-drained, fertile soil in sun; shelter from hard frosts.*

☼ ◊ Z9   ↔8ft (2.5m)

Gentiana acaulis

The trumpet gentian is a mat-forming, evergreen perennial that bears large, trumpet-shaped, vivid deep blue flowers in spring. The leaves are oval and glossy dark green. Good in a rock garden, raised bed, or trough; thrives in areas with cool, wet summers.

CULTIVATION: *Grow in reliably moist but well-drained, organic soil, in full sun or partial shade. Protect from hot sun in areas with warm, dry summers.*

☼ ☼ ◊ ◊ Z3
↕3in (8cm) ↔to 12in (30cm)

Gentiana asclepiadea

The willow gentian is an arching, clump-forming perennial producing trumpet-shaped, dark blue flowers in late summer and fall; these are often spotted or striped with purple on the insides. The leaves are lance-shaped and fresh green. Suitable for a border or large rock garden.

CULTIVATION: *Grow in moist, fertile, organic soil. Best in light shade, but tolerates sun if the soil is reliably moist.*

❄ ◊ Z4
↕24–36in (60–90cm) ↔18in (45cm)

Gentiana septemfida

This late-summer-flowering gentian is a spreading to upright, clump-forming herbaceous perennial. Clusters of narrowly bell-shaped, bright blue flowers with white throats are borne amid the oval, mid-green leaves. Good for a rock garden or raised bed; thrives in cool, moist summers. The variety var. *lagodechiana*, also recommended, has just one flower per stem.

CULTIVATION: *Grow in moist but well-drained, organic soil, in full sun or partial shade. Protect from hot sun in areas with warm, dry summers.*

☼ ☀ ◊ ◊ Z4
↕6–8in (15–20cm) ↔12in (30cm)

Small Hardy Geraniums

The low-growing members of the genus *Geranium* (not to be confused with pelargoniums; see pp.404–409) are versatile plants, useful not only at the front of borders but also in rock gardens or as a groundcover. These evergreen perennials are long-lived and undemanding, tolerating a wide range of sites and soil types. The lobed and toothed leaves are often variegated or aromatic. In summer, they bear typically saucer-shaped flowers ranging in color from white through soft blues such as 'Johnson's Blue' to the intense pink of *G. cinereum* var. *caulescens*, often with contrasting veins, eyes, or other markings.

CULTIVATION: *Grow in sharply drained, organic soil, in full sun. Feed with a balanced fertilizer every month during the growing season. Remove withered flower stems and old leaves to encourage fresh growth later in the season.*

☼ ◊ Z4

‡to 18in (45cm) ↔3ft (1m) or more

‡to 6in (15cm) ↔to 12in (30cm)

1 *G.* 'Ann Folkard' **2** *Geranium* 'Ballerina'

3
↕to 6in (15cm) ↔ to 12in (30cm)

4
↕to 18in (45cm) ↔ indefinite

5
↕to 6in (15cm) ↔ 20in (50cm)

6
↕12in (30cm) ↔ 24in (60cm)

7
↕to 18in (45cm) ↔ 30in (75cm)

8
↕to 12in (30cm) ↔ 3ft (1m)

9
↕12in (30cm) ↔ 4ft (1.2m)

3 *G. subcaulescens* **4** *G. clarkei* 'Kashmir White' **5** *G. dalmaticum*
6 *G. himalayense* 'Gravetye' **7** *G.* 'Johnson's Blue' **8** *G.* x *riversleaianum* 'Russell Prichard' **9** *G. wallichianum* 'Buxton's Variety'

Large Hardy Geraniums

The taller, clump-forming types of hardy perennial geranium—not to be confused with pelargoniums (see pp.404–409)—make effective, long-lived border plants or fillers among shrubs, requiring a minimum of attention. They are especially suited to cottage garden plantings and between roses. Their lobed, evergreen leaves may be colored or aromatic and give a long season of interest. Throughout summer, this is heightened by an abundance of saucer-shaped flowers in white and shades of blue, pink, and purple. Markings on flowers vary from the dramatic, contrasting dark eyes of *G. psilostemon* to the delicate venation of *G. sanguineum* var. *striatum*.

CULTIVATION: *Best in well-drained, fairly fertile soil, in full sun or partial shade, but tolerant of any soil that is not water-logged. Remove old leaves and withered flower stems to encourage new growth.*

☀ ◐ ◊ ◑ Z4

‡18in (45cm) ↔24in (60cm)

‡↔24in (60cm)

‡20in (50cm) ↔24in (60cm)

1 *G. endressii* **2** *G.* x *magnificum* **3** *G.* ROZANNE ('Gerwat')

24in (60cm)

24in (60cm)

6 ‡↔12in (30cm)

8 ‡24in (60cm) ↔36in (90cm)

9 ‡24in (60cm) ↔36in (90cm)

in (10cm) ↔12in (30cm)

G. pratense 'Mrs Kendall Clark' **5** *G. psilostemon* (syn. *G. armenum*) **6** *G. renardii*
G. sanguineum var. *striatum* **8** *G. sylvaticum* 'Mayflower' **9** *G.* x *oxonianum* 'Wargrave Pink'

Geum 'Lady Stratheden'

A clump-forming perennial bearing double, bright yellow flowers on arching stems over a long period in summer. The mid-green leaves are large and lobed. An easy, long-flowering plant for brightening up a mixed or herbaceous border. The taller 'Fire Opal' (Z4) is closely related, with reddish-orange flowers on purple stems.

CULTIVATION: *Grow in moist but well-drained, fertile soil, in full sun. Avoid sites that become waterlogged in winter.*

☼ ◊ ◖ Z4
‡16–24in (40–60cm) ↔24in (60cm)

Geum montanum

A small, clump-forming perennial grown for its solitary, cup-shaped, deep golden yellow flowers. These are produced in spring and early summer above large, lobed, dark green leaves. Excellent for a rock garden, raised bed, or trough.

CULTIVATION: *Grow in well-drained, preferably gritty, fertile soil, in full sun. Will not tolerate waterlogging in winter.*

☼ ◊ Z3   ‡6in (15cm) ↔12in (30cm)

...illenia trifoliata

...a upright, graceful perennial that
...rms clumps of olive green leaves
...at turn red in autumn. Delicate
...hite flowers with slender petals are
...orne on wiry red stems in summer.
...fective in a shady border or light
...oodland; the cut flowers last well.

...ULTIVATION: *Grow in moist but well-*
...ained, fertile soil. Best in partial shade,
...t tolerates some sun if shaded during
...e hottest part of the day.

∴ ◊ ◊ Z5 ‡3ft (1m) ↔24in (60cm)

...ladiolus communis
...ubsp. *byzantinus*

...n late spring, this upright, cormous
...erennial produces a blaze of
...agenta flowers with purple-
...arked lips. These are arranged
...n spikes above fans of narrow,
...id-green leaves. An elegant subject
...r a mixed or herbaceous border;
...e flowers are good for cutting.

...ULTIVATION: *Grow in fertile soil, in*
...ull sun. Plant corms on a bed of sharp
...and to improve drainage. Benefits from
...light but deep winter mulch where
...arginally hardy.

☼ ◊ Z8 ‡3ft (1m) ↔3in (8cm)

Gladiolus murielae

An upright cormous perennial that bears strongly scented white flowers with purple-red throats. These hang from elegant stems during summer, above fans of narrow, mid-green leaves. Ideal for mixed borders; the flowers are suitable for cutting. Will not survive cold winters. Formerly known as *Acidanthera*.

CULTIVATION: *Grow in fertile soil, in full sun. Plant on a layer of sand to improve drainage. Where not hardy, lift the corms when the leaves turn yellow-brown, remove off the leaves, and store the corms in frost-free conditions.*

☼ ◊ Z8
‡28–39in (70–100cm) ↔2in (5cm)

Gleditsia triacanthos 'Sunburst'

This fast-growing honeylocust is a broadly conical, deciduous tree valued for its beautiful foliage and light canopy. The finely divided leaves are bright gold-yellow when they emerge in spring, maturing to dark green, then yellowing again before they fall. A useful, pollution-tolerant tree for a small garden.

CULTIVATION: *Grow in any well-drained, fertile soil, in full sun. Prune only to remove dead, damaged or diseased wood, from late summer to midwinter.*

☼ ◊ Z4
‡40ft (12m) ↔30ft (10m)

Griselinia littoralis 'Variegata'

A dense and attractive, evergreen shrub that carries glossy leaves variegated with irregular, creamy white margins and grayish streaks. It makes a good evergreen hedge or specimen shrub, particularly for coastal sites, and it establishes quickly. The shrub responds well to trimming in spring and can be cut back hard, if necessary. The flowers are insignificant.

CULTIVATION: *Grow in well-drained soil, in sun.*

※ ◊ Z8   ‡25ft (8m) ↔15ft (5m)

Gunnera manicata

A massive, clump-forming perennial that produces the largest leaves of almost any garden plant, to 6ft (2m) long. These are rounded, lobed, sharply toothed, and dull green, with thick, prickly stalks. Spikes of tiny, greenish-red flowers appear in summer. An imposing plant by water or in a bog garden. Provide protection where marginally hardy.

CULTIVATION: *Best in permanently moist, fertile soil, in full sun or partial shade. Shelter from cold winds. Protect from frost by folding the dead leaves over the dormant crown before winter.*

※ ☼ ◊ ◊ Z6   ‡8ft (2.5m) ↔10–12ft (3–4m) or more

Gymnocarpium dryopteris 'Plumosum'

The oak fern is a delicate woodland plant useful as a deciduous ground-cover for shady spots with reasonab moist soil. Its characteristic triangular fronds arise from long, creeping rhizomes in spring, and darken with age. The rhizomes spread widely but are not invasive. Propagate from rhizomes in spring.

CULTIVATION: *Grow in moist soil, in dappled shade.*

☀ ◊ Z4   ↕8in (20cm) ↔indefini

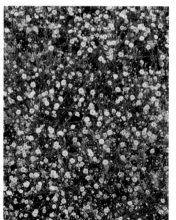

Gypsophila paniculata 'Bristol Fairy'

This herbaceous perennial forms a mound of slightly fleshy, lance-shaped, blue-green leaves on very slender, wiry stems. The profusion of tiny, double white flowers in summer forms a cloudlike display. Very effective cascading over a low wall or as a foil to more upright, sharply defined flowers.

CULTIVATION: *Grow in well-drained, deep, moderately fertile, preferably alkaline soil, in full sun. Resents being disturbed after planting.*

☀ ◊ Z3   ↕↔to 4ft (1.2m

Gypsophila 'Rosenschleier'

A mound-forming perennial, also sold as 'Rosy Veil' or 'Veil of Roses', bearing trailing stems that look great cascading over a low wall. In summer, tiny, double white flowers that age to pale pink are borne in airy sprays, forming a dense cloud or blooms. The slightly fleshy leaves are lance-shaped and blue-green. The flowers dry well for decoration.

CULTIVATION: *Grow in well-drained, deep, moderately fertile, preferably alkaline soil. Choose a position in full sun. Resents root disturbance.*

◑ ◊ Z3   ‡50cm (20in) ↔1m (3ft)

Hakonechloa macra 'Aureola'

This colorful grass is a deciduous perennial that forms a clump of narrow, arching, bright yellow leaves with cream and green stripes. They flush red in fall and persist well into winter. Reddish brown flower spikes appear in late summer. A versatile plant that can be used in a border, rock garden, or containers.

CULTIVATION: *Grow in moist but well-drained, fertile, organic soil. Leaf color is best in partial shade, but it tolerates full sun.*

※ ◑ ◊ ◔ Z5
‡14in (35cm) ↔16in (40cm)

x *Halimiocistus sahucii*

A compact shrub that forms mounds of linear, dark green leaves with downy undersides. Masses of saucer-shaped white flowers are produced throughout summer. Good in a border, at the base of a warm wall, or in a rock garden in the mildest part of Z8.

CULTIVATION: *Best in freely draining, poor to moderately fertile, light, gritty soil in a sunny site. Shelter from excessive winter moisture. Minimum temperature 35°F (2°C).*

☼ ◊ Tender
‡18in (45cm) ↔36in (90cm)

x *Halimiocistus wintonensis* 'Merrist Wood Cream'

A spreading, evergreen shrub bearing creamy yellow flowers with red bands and yellow centers in late spring and early summer. The lance-shaped leaves are gray-green. Good at the front of a mixed border or at the foot of a warm wall. Also suits a raised bed or rock garden.

CULTIVATION: *Grow in freely draining, poor to moderately fertile soil, in full sun. Choose a position protected from excessive winter moisture.*

☼ ◊ Z8   ‡24in (60cm) ↔36in (90cm)

Halimium lasianthum

A spreading bush with clusters of saucer-shaped, golden yellow flowers in late spring and early summer. Each petal normally has a brownish red mark at the base. The foliage is gray-green. Halimiums are suited to a coastal garden and are best grown in a large container for ease of winter protection.

CULTIVATION: *Best in well-drained, moderately fertile sandy soil, in full sun, with shelter from cold, drying winds. Established plants dislike being moved. Trim after flowering to maintain an attractive shape. Minimum temperature 35°F (2°C).*

☼ ◊ Tender   ‡3ft (1m) ↔5ft (1.5m)

Halimium 'Susan'

A small, spreading, evergreen shrub valued for its single or semi-double summer flowers, bright yellow with deep purple markings. The leaves are oval and gray-green. Good for rock gardens in coastal areas. Flowers are best during long, hot summers. *H. ocymoides*, similar but more upright in habit, is also recommended.

CULTIVATION: *Grow in freely draining, fairly fertile, light, sandy soil, in full sun. Provide shelter from cold winds. Trim lightly in spring, as necessary. Minimum temperature 35°F (2°C).*

☼ ◊ Tender
‡18in (45cm) ↔24in (60cm)

Witch Hazels (*Hamamelis*)

These spreading, deciduous shrubs are grown for their large clusters of usually yellow spidery flowers that appear on the branches when the shrubs are bare in winter; those of *H. vernalis* may coincide with the unfurling of the leaves. Each flower has four narrow petals and an enchanting fragrance. Most garden species also display attractive autumn foliage; the broad, bright green leaves turn red and yellow before they fall. Witch hazels bring color and scent to the garden in winter; they are good as specimen plants or grouped in a shrub border or woodland garden.

CULTIVATION: *Grow in moderately fertile, moist but well-drained, acidic to neutral soil, in full sun or partial shade, in an open but not exposed site. Witch hazels also tolerate deep, organic, alkaline soil. Remove wayward or crossing shoots when dormant in late winter or early spring to maintain a healthy, permanent framework.*

☼ ☀ ◊ Z6b (*vernalis* Z5b)

‡↔12ft (4m)

‡↔12ft (4m)

1 *Hamamelis* x *intermedia* 'Arnold Promise' **2** *H.* x *intermedia* 'Barmstedt Gold'

3 ↕↔12ft (4m)

4 ↕↔12ft (4m)

5 ↕↔12ft (4m)

6 ↕↔12ft (4m)

7 ↕↔15ft (5m)

3 *H.* x *intermedia* 'Diane' **4** *H.* x *intermedia* 'Jelena'
5 *H.* x *intermedia* 'Pallida' **6** *H.* x *intermedia* 'Aphrodite' **7** *H. vernalis* 'Sandra'

Hebe albicans

A neat, mound-forming shrub with tightly packed, glaucous gray-green foliage. It bears short, tight clusters of white flowers at the ends of the branches in the first half of summer. A useful evergreen hedging plant in mild coastal areas, but only marginally hardy.

CULTIVATION: *Grow in poor to moderately fertile, moist but well-drained, neutral to slightly alkaline soil, in full sun or partial shade. Shelter from cold, drying winds. It needs little or no pruning.*

☼ ☀ ◊ ◑ Z8
‡24in (60cm) ↔36in (90cm)

Hebe cupressoides 'Boughton Dome'

This dwarf, evergreen shrub is grown for its neat shape and dense foliage that forms a pale green dome. Flowers are infrequent. The congested, slender, grayish green branches carry scalelike, pale green leaves. Excellent in a rock garden; gives a topiary effect without any clipping. Thrives in coastal gardens.

CULTIVATION: *Grow in moist but well-drained, poor to moderately fertile soil, in full sun or partial shade. No regular pruning is necessary.*

☼ ☀ ◊ ◑ Z8
‡12in (30cm) ↔24in (60cm)

Hebe 'Great Orme'

An open, rounded, evergreen shrub that carries slender spikes of small, deep pink flowers that fade to white. These are borne from midsummer to mid-fall amid the lance-shaped, glossy dark green leaves. Good in a mixed or shrub border; unlikely to survive winter without protection.

CULTIVATION: *Grow in moist but well-drained, poor to moderately fertile soil, in sun or light shade. Shelter from cold winds. Pruning is unnecessary, but leggy plants can be cut back in spring. Minimum temperature 35°F (2°C).*

☀ ◊ ◖ Tender   ↕↔4ft (1.2m)

Hebe macrantha

This upright, spreading shrub has leathery green leaves. It bears relatively large flowers for a hebe, produced in clusters of three in early summer. A useful evergreen hedging plant for seaside gardens where it is hardy.

CULTIVATION: *Grow in moist but well-drained, reasonably fertile, neutral to slightly alkaline soil, in full sun or partial shade. Shelter from cold, drying winds. It needs little or no pruning. Minimum temperature 41°F (5°C).*

☀ ◊ ◖ Tender
↕24in (60cm) ↔36in (90cm)

Hebe ochracea 'James Stirling'

A compact shrub that bears its medium-sized white flowers in clusters from late spring to early summer. Like other whipcord hebes it has small, scalelike leaves that lie flat against the stems to give the appearance of a dwarf conifer. An excellent evergreen for a rock garden, the rich ochre-yellow foliage looking very attractive in winter.

CULTIVATION: *Best in moist but well-drained, neutral to slightly alkaline soil. Site in full sun or partial shade. Do not prune unless absolutely necessary.*

☼ ☀ ◊ ◊ Z8   ↕↔24in (60cr

Hebe pinguifolia 'Pagei'

A low-growing, evergreen shrub bearing purple stems with four rank of leathery, oval, blue-green leaves. Abundant clusters of white flowers appear at the tips of the shoots in late spring and early summer. Plant in groups as a groundcover, or in a rock garden.

CULTIVATION: *Grow in moist but well-drained, poor to moderately fertile soil, in sun or partial shade. Best with some shelter from cold, drying winds. Trim to neaten in early spring, if necessary.*

☼ ☀ ◊ ◊ Z7
↕12in (30cm) ↔36in (90cm)

ebe rakaiensis

rounded, evergreen shrub bearing
kes of white flowers from early
midsummer. The leaves are elliptic
d glossy bright green. Ideal either
a small, spreading specimen
rub or as a focal point in a large
ck garden.

LTIVATION: *Grow in moist but well-
ained, poor to moderately fertile soil,
sun or partial shade. Best with some
elter from cold, drying winds. Trim
shape in early spring, if necessary.
nimum temperature 35°F (2°C).*

☀ ◊ ◗ Tender
ft (1m) ↔ 4ft (1.2m)

ebe 'Silver Queen'

dense, rounded, evergreen shrub
earing colourful, oval leaves; these
e mid-green with creamy white
argins. Purple flowers that contrast
ell with the foliage are carried in
ense spikes during summer and
ll. A fine, pollution-tolerant plant
r a mixed border or rock garden.
verwinter in a cool greenhouse.
lue Gem' is a similar plant with
ain leaves.

LTIVATION: *Grow in moist but well-
ained, poor to moderately fertile soil,
sun or light shade. Shelter from cold,
rying winds. No pruning is necessary.
inimum temperature 35°F (2°C).*

❄ ☀ ◊ ◗ Tender   ↕↔ 48in (120cm)

Hedera algeriensis 'Ravensholst'

This vigorous cultivar of Canary Island ivy is a self-clinging, evergreen climber useful as a groundcover or to mask a bare wall. The leaves are shallowly lobed, glossy, and dark green. It will be damaged during an unusually severe winter, but it usually grows back quickly.

CULTIVATION: *Best in fertile, moist but well-drained soil that is rich in organic matter. It tolerates shade and can be pruned or trimmed at any time of year.*

☼ ☀ ◊ ◊ Z8   ‡15ft (5r

Hedera colchica 'Dentata

This Persian ivy is a very vigorous, evergreen, self-clinging climber producing large, heart-shaped, drooping, glossy green leaves. The stems and leaf stalks are flushed purple. A handsome plant for covering an unattractive wall in shade; also effective as a ground-cover. 'Dentata Variegata' has mottled gray-green leaves edged with cream.

CULTIVATION: *Best in moist but well-drained, fertile, ideally alkaline soil, in partial to deep shade. Prune at any time of the year to restrict size.*

☼ ☀ ◊ ◊ Z7   ‡30ft (10m

Hedera colchica 'Sulphur Heart'

This colored-leaf Persian ivy is a very vigorous, self-clinging evergreen climber that can also be grown as groundcover. The large, heart-shaped leaves are dark green suffused with creamy yellow; as they mature, the color becomes more even. Will quickly cover a wall in shade.

CULTIVATION: *Grow in moist but well-drained, fertile, preferably alkaline soil. Tolerates partial shade, but leaf color is more intense in sun. Prune at any time of the year to restrict size.*

☀ ◐ ◊ ◊ Z7   ↕15ft (5m)

Hedera hibernica

Irish ivy is a vigorous, evergreen, self-clinging climber valued for its broadly oval, dark green leaves, which have gray-green veins and five triangular lobes. Useful for covering a wall. Often used as groundcovers under trees or shrubs, but because of rampant growth, be sure to select a site where it can be contained and won't escape into woodlands or parks.

CULTIVATION: *Best in moist but well-drained, fertile, ideally alkaline soil, in partial to full shade. Prune at any time of the year to restrict spread.*

☀ ◐ ◊ ◊ Z5b   ↕to 30ft (10m)

English Ivies (*Hedera helix*)

Hedera helix, the English ivy, is an evergreen, woody-stemmed, self-clinging climber and the parent of an enormous selection of cultivars. Leaf forms vary from heart-shaped to deeply lobed, ranging in color from the bright gold 'Buttercup' to the deep purple 'Atropurpurea'. They are often planted as groundcovers, tolerating even dry shade, but care should be taken to use them only on sites where their rapid growth can be contained. They will also quickly cover featureless walls, but can damage paintwork or invade gutters and windows if not kept in check. Variegated cultivars are especially useful for enlivening dark corners and shaded walls. Small ivies make good houseplants and can be trained over topiary frames.

CULTIVATION: *Best in moist but well-drained, organic, alkaline soil. Choose a position in full sun or shade; ivies with variegated leaves may lose their color in shade. Trim regularly to keep under control.*

☀ ◐ ◊ ◖ Z5b

‡25ft (8m)

‡6ft (2m)

‡6ft (2m)

‡3ft (1m)

‡3ft (1m)

‡12in (30cm)

1 *H. helix* 'Atropurpurea' **2** *H. helix* 'Buttercup' **3** *H. helix* 'Glacier'
4 *H. helix* 'Goldchild' **5** *H. helix* 'Ivalace' **6** *H. helix* 'Little Diamond'

Helenium
'Moerheim Beauty'

This rewarding summer perennial is a garden favorite for its lovely, rich peppery red, daisy-like flowers that appear toward the end of summer when many other flowers are fading. Combined with ornamental grasses and coneflowers, it can bring a late summer garden to life. Deadhead regularly and divide large clumps to maintain vigor.

CULTIVATION: *Grow in moist but well-drained soil in sun.*

☼ ◊ ◊ Z3b
‡36in (90cm) ↔24in (60cm)

Helenium
'Sahin's Early Flowerer'

This sneezeweed was spotted as an accidental seedling and noted for its long flowering season. The reddish-orange to yellow, daisy-like flowers appear earlier than most sneezeweeds, sometimes before midsummer, and the display can continue until fall's end. The color combines well with orange or red dahlias and crocosmias, and most daylilies.

CULTIVATION: *Grow in moist but well-drained soil, in sun.*

☼ ◊ ◊ Z3b   ‡↔24in (60cm)

Helianthemum 'Henfield Brilliant'

This rock rose is a small, spreading, evergreen shrub bearing saucer-shaped, brick-red flowers in late spring and summer. The leaves are narrow and gray-green. Effective in groups on a sunny bank; also good in a rock garden or raised bed or at the front of a border.

CULTIVATION: *Grow in moderately fertile, well-drained, neutral to alkaline soil, in sun. Trim after flowering to keep bushy. Often short-lived, but easily propagated by softwood cuttings in late spring.*

☼ ◊ Z6
‡8–12in (20–30cm) ↔12in (30cm) or more

Helianthemum 'Rhodanthe Carneum'

This long-flowering rock rose, also sold as 'Wisley Pink', is a low and spreading, evergreen shrub. Pale pink, saucer-shaped flowers with yellow-flushed centers appear from late spring to summer amid narrow, gray-green leaves. Good in a rock garden, raised bed, or mixed border.

CULTIVATION: *Best in well-drained, moderately fertile, neutral to alkaline soil, in full sun. Trim after flowering to encourage further blooms.*

☼ ◊ Z6
‡to 12in (30cm) ↔to 18in (45cm) or more

elianthemum 'Visley Primrose'

his primrose yellow rock rose is a fast-
owing, spreading, evergreen shrub.
bears a profusion of saucer-shaped
wers with golden centers over long
riods in late spring and summer.
e leaves are narrowly oblong and
ay-green. Group in a rock garden,
ised bed, or sunny bank. For paler,
eamy flowers, look for 'Wisley White'.

ULTIVATION: *Grow in well-drained,
derately fertile, preferably neutral
alkaline soil, in full sun. Trim after
wering to encourage further blooms.*

◊ Z6

12in (30cm) ↔ to 18in (45cm)
more

Helianthus 'Loddon Gold'

his double-flowered sunflower
a tall, spreading perennial with
arse, oval, mid-green leaves that
e arranged along the upright
ems. Grown for its large, bright
llow flowers, which open during
e summer and last into early fall.
se to extend the season of interest
herbaceous and mixed borders.

ULTIVATION: *Grow in moist to well-
ained, moderately fertile, organic
il. Choose a sheltered site in full
n. Flowers are best during long,
t summers. Stake flower stems.*

◊ ◊ Z5   ‡5ft (1.5m) ↔36in (90cm)

Helianthus 'Monarch'

This semidouble sunflower is a tall, spreading perennial with sturdy, upright stems bearing oval and toothed, mid-green leaves. Large, starlike, bright golden yellow flowers with yellow-brown centers are produced from late summer to fall. A statuesque plant for late-summer interest in a herbaceous or mixed border. 'Capenoch Star' is another recommended perennial sunflower, lemon yellow with golden centers, to 5ft (1.5m) tall.

CULTIVATION: *Grow in any well-drained, moderately fertile soil. Choose a sunny, sheltered site. The stems need support.*

☀ ◊ Z5　　　　‡6ft (2m) ↔4ft (1.2m)

Helichrysum splendidum

A compact, white-woolly, evergreen perennial bearing linear, aromatic, silver-gray foliage. Small, bright yellow flowerheads open at the tips of the upright stems from midsummer to fall and last into winter. Suitable for a mixed border or rock garden; the flowers can be dried for winter decoration.

CULTIVATION: *Grow in well-drained, poor moderately fertile, neutral to alkaline soil, full sun. Remove dead or damaged growth in spring, cutting back leggy shoots into old wood. Minimum temperature 33°F (1°C).*

☀ ◊ Tender　　　　‡↔4ft (1.2m)

Helictotrichon sempervirens

Blue oat grass is a useful plant in a mixed garden border for its hummocks of grayish blue, evergreen leaves. From early summer, tall, oat-like flower spikes emerge above the foliage; these are very graceful with nodding tips and last all summer. Mix in with other blue- or silver-foliaged plants, or grow in clumps as specimen plants. Divide clumps in fall or spring.

CULTIVATION: *Grow in well-drained, neutral to alkaline soil, in full sun or light shade.*

░ ◊ Z4b
‡o 4¹/₂ft (1.4m) ↔24in (60cm)

Heliopsis helianthoides var. *scabra* 'Light of Loddon'

The golden yellow, semidouble flowers of this vigorous perennial appear from midsummer to early fall, making this plant a vivid addition to a sunny border. Unobtrusive support, put into place in spring so that the plant can grow through it, and regular deadheading, improves and lengthens the display. The flowers are good for cutting. Divide large clumps in spring to maintain vigor.

CULTIVATION: *Grow in fertile, moist but well-drained soil, in sun.*

░ ◊ ◊ Z4
‡o 3¹/₂ft (1.1m) ↔24in (60cm)

Helleborus argutifolius

The large Corsican hellebore, sometimes known as *H. corsicus*, is an early-flowering, clump-forming, evergreen perennial bearing large clusters of nodding, pale green flowers. These appear in winter and early spring above the handsome dark green leaves, which are divided into three sharply toothed leaflets. Excellent for early interest in a woodland garden or mixed border.

CULTIVATION: *Grow in moist, fertile, preferably neutral to alkaline soil, in full sun or partial shade. Often short-lived, but self-seeds readily.*

☼ ☀ ◊ Z5b ‡4ft (1.2m) ↔36in (90cm)

Helleborus x hybridus

The evergreen Lenten rose blooms in early spring. Showy sepals range from white and pink to yellow, light purple, and freckled; shapes include double, semidouble, bicolor, and frilled. Buy these variable bloomers in flower. Use as a groundcover or at the base of taller plants.

CULTIVATION: *This adaptable perennial grows best in part shade and moist, well-drained soil rich in organic matter and near neutral pH. Propagate by seed or division.*

☼ ☀ ◊ Z6
‡to 18in (45cm) ↔to 24in (60cm)

...lleborus niger

...ump-forming, usually evergreen
...ennial valued for its nodding
...ters of cup-shaped white flowers
...vinter and early spring. The dark
...en leaves are divided into several
...lets. Effective with snowdrops
...eath winter-flowering shrubs,
...it can be difficult to naturalize.
...ter's Wheel' is a pretty cultivar
...his hellebore, with large flowers.

CULTIVATION: *Grow in deep, fertile, neutral
...lkaline soil that is reliably moist. Site
...appled shade with shelter from cold,
...ing winds.*

... Z4   ↕12in (30cm) ↔18in (45cm)

...lleborus x nigercors

...is hybrid hellebore combines
...orous growth with a long-lasting
...wer display from late winter into
...ly spring. Its large, green-tinged,
...ite flowers are a welcome arrival
...winter. The thick green leaves are
...te profuse and need to be trimmed
...ck in early winter to prevent
...scuring the flowers. Remove old
...wering stems in late spring.

CULTIVATION: *Grow in moist but well
...ained soil, in sun or shade.*

☼ ☀ ◐ ◊ Z5
...in (30cm) ↔36in (90cm)

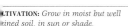

Daylilies (*Hemerocallis*)

Daylilies are clump-forming, herbaceous perennials, so called because each of their showy flowers lasts for only a day; in nocturnal daylilies, the flowers open in late afternoon and last through the night. The blooms are abundant and rapidly replaced, some appearing in late spring while other cultivars flower into late summer. Flower shapes vary from circular to spider-shaped, in shades of yellow, orange, red, and purple. The leaves are straplike and deciduous or evergreen. Taller daylilies make a dramatic contribution to a border; the dwarfer types, such as 'Stella de Oro', and 'Happy Returns', are useful for small gardens or in containers.

CULTIVATION: *Grow in well-drained but moist, fertile soil, in sun; Most tolerate semi-shade. Mulch in spring, and feed with a balanced fertilizer every two week until buds form. Divide and replant every few years, in spring or fall.*

☼ ☀ ◐ ◖ Z3

‡24in (60cm) ↔ 3ft (1m)

‡36in (90cm) ↔ 18in (45cm)

‡20in (50cm) ↔ 3ft (1m)

‡↔ 3ft (1m)

‡24in (60cm) ↔ 3ft (1m)

‡12in (30cm) ↔ 18in (45cm)

1 *H.* 'Buzz Bomb' **2** *H.* 'Golden Chimes' **3** *H.* 'Green Flutter'
4 *H. lilioasphodelus* **5** *H.* 'Oriental Ruby' **6** *H.* 'Stella de Oro'

...patica nobilis

...all, slow-growing, anemone-
...-semi-evergreen perennial
...ng saucer-shaped, purple,
...e, or pink flowers. These appear
...rly spring, usually before the
...ge has emerged. The mid-green,
...etimes mottled leaves are leathery
...divided into three lobes. Good
...shady rock garden. *H. x media*
...ardii' (Z5b) is a very similar plant,
...reliably deep blue flowers.

...TIVATION: *Grow in moist but well-
...ned, fertile, neutral to alkaline soil,
...artial shade. Provide a mulch of leaf
...d in fall or spring.*

◊ ◊ Z5b   ‡4in (10cm) ↔6in (15cm)

...uchera micrantha
r. diversifolia
...lace Purple'

...ump-forming perennial valued
...its glistening, dark purple-red,
...ost metallic foliage, which is
...ped by airy sprays of white flowers
...ummer. The leaves have five
...nted lobes. Plant in groups as a
...undcover for a shady site, but it
...be slow to spread.

...TIVATION: *Grow in moist but well-
...ned, fertile soil, in sun or partial
...de. Tolerates full shade where the
...nd is reliably moist. Lift and divide
...nps every few years, after flowering.*

☀ ◊ ◊ Z4   ‡↔18 (45cm)

Heuchera 'Red Spangles'

This clump-forming, evergreen perennial is valued for its sprays of small, bell-shaped, crimson-scarlet flowers. These are borne in early summer, with a repeat bloom in late summer, on dark red stems above the lobed, heart-shaped, purplish green leaves. Effective as a ground cover when grouped together.

CULTIVATION: *Grow in moist but well-drained, fertile soil, in sun or partial shade. Tolerates full shade where the ground is reliably moist. Lift and divide clumps every three years, after flowering.*

☼ ☀ ◊ ◔ Z3
‡20in (50cm) ↔10in (25cm)

Hibiscus syriacus 'Oiseau Bleu'

Also known as 'Blue Bird', this vigorous, upright, deciduous shrub bears large, mallowlike, lilac-blue flowers with red centers. These are borne from mid- to late summer amid deep green leaves. Ideal for a mixed or shrub border.

CULTIVATION: *Grow in moist but well-drained, fertile, neutral to slightly alkaline soil, in full sun. Prune young plants hard in late spring to encourage branching at the base; keep pruning to a minimum once established.*

☼ ◊ ◔ Z5b   ‡10ft (3m) ↔6ft (2m)

Hibiscus syriacus 'Woodbridge'

Fast-growing, upright, deciduous shrub producing large, deep rose-pink flowers with maroon blotches around the centers. These are borne from late summer to mid-fall amid the lobed, dark green leaves. Valuable for its late season of interest.

CULTIVATION: *Grow in moist but well-drained, fertile, slightly alkaline soil, in full sun. Prune young plants hard to encourage branching; keep pruning to a minimum once established.*

◊ ◊ Z5b   ‡10ft (3m) ↔6ft (2m)

Hippophae rhamnoides

Sea buckthorn is a spiny, deciduous shrub with attractive fruits and foliage. Small yellow flowers in spring are followed by orange berries (on female plants), which persist well into winter. The silvery gray leaves are narrow and claw-like. Good for hedging, especially in coastal areas.

CULTIVATION: *Best in sandy, moist but well-drained soil, in full sun. For good fruiting, plants of both sexes must grow together. Little pruning is required; trim hedges in late summer, as necessary.*

◊ ◊ Z2b   ‡↔20ft (6m)

Hoheria glabrata

This deciduous, spreading tree is grown for its graceful habit and clusters of cup-shaped, fragrant white flowers, which are attractive to butterflies, in midsummer. The broad, dark green leaves turn yellow in fall before they fall. Best in a shrub border in a maritime climate but overwinter indoors.

CULTIVATION: *Grow in moderately fertile, well-drained, neutral to alkaline soil in full sun or partial shade, sheltered from cold, drying winds. Pruning is seldom necessary, but if branches are damaged by cold, cut them back in spring. Minimum temperature 34°F (1°C).*

☼ ☀ ◊ Tender ‡↔22ft (7

Hoheria sexstylosa

Ribbonwood is an evergreen tree or shrub with narrow, glossy, mid-green leaves with toothed margins. It is valued for its graceful shape and abundant clusters of white flowers; attractive to butterflies, they appear in late summer. The cultivar 'Stardust' is recommended.

CULTIVATION: *Best in moderately fertile, well-drained, neutral to alkaline soil in full sun or partial shade, sheltered from cold, drying winds. Pruning is seldom necessary. Minimum temperature 34°F (1°C).*

☼ ☀ ◊ Tender ‡25ft (8m) ↔20ft (6m

Hostas

Hostas are deciduous perennials grown principally for their dense mounds of large, overlapping, lance- to heart-shaped leaves. A wide choice of foliage color is available, from the cloudy blue-green of 'Halcyon' to the bright yellow-green 'Golden Tiara'. Many have leaves marked with yellow or white around the edges; H. 'Fortunei Albopicta' has bold, central splashes of creamy yellow. Upright clusters of funnel-shaped flowers, varying from white through lavender-blue to purple, are borne on tall stems in summer. Hostas are effective at the front of a mixed border, in containers, or as a groundcover under deciduous trees.

CULTIVATION: *Grow in well-drained but reliably moist, fertile soil, in full sun or partial shade. Yellow-leaved hostas color best in full sun with shade at midday. Mulch in spring to conserve moisture throughout the summer.*

☼ ☀ ◐ Z4

‡10in (50cm) ↔3ft (1m)

‡22in (55cm) ↔3ft (1m)

‡22in (55cm) ↔3ft (1m)

‡22in (55cm) ↔3ft (1m)

‡24in (60cm) ↔3ft (1m)

‡12in (30cm) ↔20in (50cm)

Hosta crispula **2** *H.* 'Fortunei Albopicta' **3** *H.* 'Fortunei Aureomarginata'
H. 'Francee' **5** *H.* 'Frances Williams' **6** *H.* 'Golden Tiara'

‡3ft (1m) ↔ 30in (75cm)

‡18in (45cm) ↔ 30in (75cm)

‡18in (45cm) ↔ 3ft (1m)

‡24in (60cm) ↔ 4ft (1.2m)

‡18in (45cm) ↔ 30in (75cm)

‡3ft (1m) ↔ 4ft (1.2m)

7 *Hosta* 'Honeybells' **8** *H. lancifolia* **9** *H.* 'Love Pat' **10** *H.* 'Royal Standard'
11 *H.* 'Shade Fanfare' **12** *H. sieboldiana* var. *elegans*

in (75cm) ↔ 4ft (1.2m)

16in (35–40cm) ↔ 28in (70cm)

15 ‡3ft (1m) ↔ 18in (45cm)

16 ‡18in (45cm) ↔ 28in (70cm)

18 ‡2in (5cm) ↔ 10in (25cm)

in (50cm) ↔ 3ft (1m)

19 ‡30in (75cm) ↔ 3ft (1m)

H. 'Sum and Substance' **14** *H.* Tardiana Group 'Halcyon' **15** *H. undulata* var. *undulata*
H. 'Undulata Univittata' **17** *H. ventricosa* **18** *H. venusta* **19** *H.* 'Wide Brim'

Humulus lupulus 'Aureus'

The golden hops is a twining, perennial climber grown for its attractively lobed, bright golden yellow foliage. Hanging clusters of papery, conelike, greenish-yellow flowers appear in fall. Train over a strong fence or trellis, or up into small tree. The hops dry well.

CULTIVATION: *Grow in moist but well-drained, moderately fertile, organic soil. Tolerates partial shade, but leaf color is best in full sun. Give the twining stems support. Cut back any dead growth to ground level in early spring.*

☼ ◐ ◊ ◊ Z4   ↕20ft (6

Hyacinthoides italica

The Italian bluebell is a smaller pla than the similar-looking English bluebell. The pretty blue and purpl starry flowers appear in spring on upright stems above the narrow leaves. They are carried in clusters up to 30 flowers. This is an attracti plant for a shady or woodland borde Plant bulbs in fall; dig up and divid clumps after flowering.

CULTIVATION: *Grow in moist but well-drained soil, in light shade.*

☼ ◊ ◊ Z5
↕4–8in (10–20cm) ↔2in (5cm)

Hyacinthus orientalis 'Blue Jacket'

This navy blue hyacinth is a bulbous perennial bearing dense, upright spikes of fragrant, bell-shaped flowers with purple veins in early spring. Good for spring bedding; specially prepared bulbs can be planted in pots during fall for an indoor display of early flowers. One of the best true-blue hyacinths. Also try the paler 'Delft Blue'.

CULTIVATION: *Grow in any well-drained, moderately fertile soil or soil mix, in sun or partial shade. Protect container-grown bulbs from extreme cold.*

☀ ◊ Z5
8–12in (20–30cm) ↔ 3in (8cm)

Hyacinthus orientalis 'City of Haarlem'

This primrose yellow hyacinth is a spring-flowering, bulbous perennial bearing upright spikes of fragrant, bell-shaped flowers. The lance-shaped leaves are bright green and emerge from the base of the plant. Good for spring bedding or in containers; specially prepared bulbs can be planted in fall for early flowers indoors.

CULTIVATION: *Grow in well-drained, fairly fertile soil or soil mix, in sun or partial shade. Protect container-grown plants from excessive cold.*

☀ ◊ Z5
8–12in (20–30cm) ↔ 3in (8cm)

Hyacinthus orientalis 'Pink Pearl'

This deep pink hyacinth, bearing dense, upright spikes of fragrant, bell-shaped flowers with paler edges, is a spring-flowering, bulbous perennial. The leaves are narrow and bright green. Excellent in a mixed or herbaceous border; specially prepared bulbs can be planted in pots during fall for an indoor display of early flowers.

CULTIVATION: *Grow in any well-drained, moderately fertile soil or soil mix, in sun or partial shade. Protect container-grown bulbs from extreme cold.*

☼ ☀ ◊ Z5
↕8–12in (20–30cm) ↔3in (8cm)

Hydrangea anomala subsp. *petiolaris*

The climbing hydrangea, often sold simply as *H. petiolaris*, is a woody-stemmed, deciduous, self-clinging climber, usually grown on shady walls for its large, lacecaplike heads of creamy white, summer flowers. The mid-green leaves are oval and coarsely toothed. Often slow to establish, but it then grows quickly.

CULTIVATION: *Grow in any reliably moist fertile soil in sun or deep shade. Little pruning is required, but as the allotted space is filled, cut back overly long shoots after flowering.*

☼ ☀ ◊ Z5
↕50ft (15m)

Hydrangea arborescens 'Annabelle'

upright, deciduous shrub bearing ge, rounded heads of densely cked, creamy white flowers from dsummer to early fall. The leaves broadly oval and pointed. Good its own or in a shrub border; the werheads can be dried for winter coration. 'Grandiflora' has even ger flowerheads.

CULTIVATION: *Grow in moist but well-ained, moderately fertile, organic soil, sun or partial shade. Keep pruning to inimum, or cut back hard each spring a low framework.*

 ◊ ◊ Z2b   ↕5ft (1.5m) ↔8ft (2.5m)

Hydrangea aspera Villosa Group

group of spreading to upright, ciduous shrubs that can become eelike with age. In late summer, ey produce flattened, lacecaplike ads of small, blue-purple or rich ue flowers, surrounded by larger, ac-white or rose-lilac flowers. he leaves are lance-shaped and rk green. Excellent in a woodland wild garden.

CULTIVATION: *Grow in moist but well-ained, moderately fertile, organic soil. e in full sun or semi-shade. Little runing is necessary.*

◊ ◊ ◊ Z6   ↕3–12ft (1–4m)

Hydrangea macrophylla

Cultivars of the common hydrangea, *H. macrophylla*, are rounded shrubs with oval, mid- to dark green, deciduous leaves. Their large, showy flowerheads, borne from mid- to late summer, are available in two distinct forms: lacecaps, such as 'Veitchii', have flat flowerheads, and mophead hydrangeas (Hortensias), such as 'Altona', have round flowerheads. Except in white-flowered cultivars, flower color is influenced by soil pH; acidic soils produce blue flowers, and alkaline soils give rise to pink flowers. All types of hydrangea are useful for a range of garden sites, and the flowerheads dry well for indoor arrangements.

CULTIVATION: *Grow in moist but well-drained, fertile soil, in sun or partial shade with shelter from wind. Prune hard in spring to enhance flowering, cutting stems back to strong pairs of buds.*

☼ ☀ ◐ ◊ ◖ Z6

1 ‡3ft (1m) ↔ 5ft (1.5m)

2 ‡6ft (2m) ↔ 8ft (2.5m)

3 ‡↔ 5ft (1.5m)

4 ‡6ft (2m) ↔ 8ft (2.5m)

5 ‡6ft (2m) ↔ 8ft (2.5m)

1 *H. macrophylla* 'Altona' (Mophead) **2** *H. macrophylla* 'Mariesii Perfecta' (syn. *H. macroph*. 'Blue Wave') (Lacecap) **3** *H. macrophylla* 'Lanarth White' (Lacecap) **4** *H. macrophylla* 'Générale Vicomtesse de Vibraye' (Mophead) **5** *H. macrophylla* 'Veitchii' (Lacecap)

ydrangea paniculata

tivars of *H. paniculata* are
-growing, upright, deciduous
ubs, with oval, mid- to dark green
ves. They are cultivated for their
l clusters of lacy flowers that
ally appear during late summer
early fall; some cultivars,
h as 'Praecox', bloom earlier in
summer. Flowers start greenish
ite and turn mostly creamy white,
h many forms becoming pink-tinged
they age. These versatile shrubs
 suitable for many different garden

uses: as specimen plants, in groups,
or in containers. The flowerheads
are very attractive when dried for
indoor decoration.

CULTIVATION: *Grow in moist but well-
drained, fertile soil. Site in sun or partial
shade with shelter from cold, drying winds.
Pruning is not essential, but plants flower
much better if pruned back annually, in
early spring, to the lowest pair of healthy
buds on a permanent, woody framework.*

☼ ☀ ◊ ◊ Z3b

‡ 10–22ft (3–7m) ↔ 8ft (2.5m)

‡ 10–22ft (3–7m) ↔ 8ft (2.5m)

0–22ft (3–7m) ↔ 8ft (2.5m)

H. paniculata 'Floribunda' **2** *H. paniculata* 'Grandiflora' **3** *H. paniculata* 'Praecox'

Hydrangea quercifolia

The oak-leaved hydrangea is a mou
forming, deciduous shrub bearing
conical heads of white flowers that
fade to pink, from midsummer to f
The deeply lobed, mid-green leaves
turn bronze-purple in fall. Useful i
a variety of garden situations.

CULTIVATION: *Prefers well-drained but
moist, moderately fertile soil, in sun or
partial shade. Leaves may become yello
in shallow, alkaline soil. Keep pruning t
a minimum, in spring.*

☼ ☼ ◊ Z5b   ↕6ft (2m) ↔8ft (2.5

Hydrangea serrata 'Bluebird'

A compact, upright, long-flowering,
deciduous shrub bearing flattened
heads of tiny, rich blue flowers
surrounded by larger, pale blue
flowers from summer to fall.
The narrowly oval, pointed, mid-
green leaves turn red in fall.
'Grayswood' (Z6) is a similar shrub
with mauve flowers.

CULTIVATION: *Grow in moist but well-
drained, moderately fertile, organic soil,
in sun or partial shade. Flowers may
turn pink in alkaline soils. Cut back wea
thin shoots in mid-spring.*

☼ ☼ ◊ Z5b   ↕↔4ft (1.2m

Hydrangea serrata 'Rosalba'

An upright, compact, deciduous shrub valued for its flat flowerheads that appear from summer to fall; these are made up of tiny pink flowers in the center, surrounded by larger white flowers that become red-marked as they age. The leaves are oval, mid-green, and pointed. Ideal as a specimen plant or in a shrub border.

CULTIVATION: *Grow in well-drained but moist, moderately fertile, organic soil, in full sun or partial shade. Flowers may turn blue on acidic soils. Very little pruning is needed.*

✿ ☀ ◐ ◊ Z6　　　　↔4ft (1.2m)

Hypericum 'Hidcote'

This dense, evergreen or semi-evergreen shrub produces abundant clusters of large, cupped, golden yellow flowers that open from mid-summer to early fall. The leaves are dark green and lance-shaped. Suitable for a shrub border; for a taller but narrower shrub, to 6ft (2m) high but otherwise very similar, look for 'Rowallane' (Z8).

CULTIVATION: *Grow in well-drained but moist, moderately fertile soil, in sun or partial shade. Deadhead regularly, and trim annually in spring to increase the flowering potential.*

✿ ☀ ◐ ◊ ◊ Z6b　　‡4ft (1.2m) ↔5ft (1.5m)

Hypericum kouytchense

Sometimes known as *H.* 'Sungold', this species of St. John's wort is a rounded, semi-evergreen bush with arching shoots. It has dark blue-green leaves, but its biggest asset is the large clusters of golden yellow star-shaped flowers borne in profusion during summer and fall, followed by bright bronze-red fruits. Grow in a shrub border or mixed border.

CULTIVATION: *Grow in moderately fertile, moist but well-drained soil, in full sun or partial shade. Prune or trim after flowering, if necessary.*

☼ ☼ ◊ ◊ Z6　　‡3ft (1m) ↔5ft (1.5m)

Iberis sempervirens

A spreading, evergreen subshrub bearing dense, rounded heads of small, unevenly shaped white flowers that are often flushed with pink or lilac. These appear in late spring and early summer, covering the dark green leaves. Best in a rock garden or large wall pocket. The recommended cultivar 'Schneeflocke' can be even more floriferous.

CULTIVATION: *Grow in well-drained, poor to moderately fertile, neutral to alkaline soil, in full sun. Trim lightly after flowering for neatness.*

☼ ◊ Z3
‡to 12in (30cm) ↔ to 16in (40cm)

Ilex x *altaclerensis* 'Golden King' (female)

A compact, evergreen shrub with glossy, dark green leaves edged in gold. The leaf margins may be smooth or toothed. The flowers are insignificant but develop into red berries in fall. Tolerant of pollution and coastal exposure; a good tall windbreak or hedge where winters are not too severe.

CULTIVATION: *Grow in moist but well-drained, moderately fertile soil rich in organic matter. For berries, a male holly must grow nearby. A position in full sun is ideal. Trim or prune in early spring, if necessary.*

☼ ◊ ◊ Z6   ↕20ft (6m) ↔12ft (4m)

Ilex x *altaclerensis* 'Lawsoniana' (female)

This dense and bushy holly forms a compact, evergreen tree or shrub. It bears large, usually spineless, oval, bright green leaves, which are splashed with gold and paler green in the centers. Red-brown berries, ripening to red, develop in fall.

CULTIVATION: *Grow in moist but well-drained soil, in sun for best leaf color. Grow a male holly nearby to ensure a display of berries. Free-standing plants may need some shaping when young. Remove any all-green shoots as seen.*

☼ ◊ Z6   ↕20ft (6m) ↔15ft (5m)

English Hollies (*Ilex aquifolium*)

Ilex aquifolium, the English holly, has many different cultivars, all upright, evergreen trees or large shrubs that are usually grown on their own or as spiny hedges. They have purple stems, gray bark, and dense, glossy foliage. Most cultivars have multicolored, spiny leaves, although those of 'J.C. van Tol' are spineless and dark green. 'Ferox Argentea' has extra-spiny leaves. Male and female flowers are borne on separate plants, so female hollies, such as 'Madame Briot', must be near males, such as 'Golden Milkboy', if they are to bear a good crop of berries. Tall specimens make effective windbreaks.

CULTIVATION: *Grow in moist, well-drained, fertile, organic soil. Choose a site in full sun for good leaf variegation, but tolerates partial shade. Remove any damaged wood and shape young trees in spring; hedges should be trimmed in late summer. Over-enthusiastic pruning will spoil their form.*

☼ ◑ ◊ Z7

‡to 80ft (25m) ↔25ft (8m)

‡to 20ft (6m) ↔ 8ft (2.5m)

‡to 50ft (15m) ↔12ft (4m)

1 *Ilex aquifolium* **2** 'Amber' (female) **3** 'Argentea Marginata' (female)

‡25ft (8m) ↔ 15ft (5m)

o 25ft (8m) ↔ 12ft (4m)

‡20ft (6m) ↔ 12ft (4m)

0ft (6m) ↔ 12ft (4m)

‡20ft (6m) ↔ 15ft (5m)

‡20ft (6m) ↔ 15ft (5m)

20ft (6m) ↔ 12ft (4m)

‡20ft (6m) ↔ 12ft (4m)

‡30ft (10m) ↔ 12ft (4m)

'Ferox Argentea' (male) **5** 'Golden Milkboy' (male) **6** 'Handsworth New Silver' (female) **7** 'J.C. van Tol' (female) **8** 'Madame Briot' (female) **9** 'Pyramidalis' (female) 0 'Pyramidalis Fructo Luteo' (female) **11** 'Silver Milkmaid' (female) **12** 'Silver Queen' (male)

Ilex crenata 'Convexa' (female)

This bushy form of the Japanese holly is a dense, evergreen shrub wi purple-green stems and spineless, oval to elliptic, glossy, mid- to dark green leaves. It bears an abundance of small, black berries in fall. Lends itself for use as hedging or topiary.

CULTIVATION: *Needs moist but well-drained, organic soil, in full sun or partial shade. Grow near a male holly for a good crop of berries. Cut out badly placed growth in early spring, and trim shaped plants in summer.*

☼ ◑ ◊ Z7   ‡8ft (2.5m) ↔6ft (2m

Ilex x meserveae 'Blue Princess' (female)

This blue holly is a vigorous, dense, evergreen shrub with oval, softly spiny, very glossy, greenish-blue leaves. White to pinkish-white, late spring flowers are followed by a profusion of glossy red berries in fall. The dark purplish-green young stems show well when hedging plants are regularly clipped. Dislikes coastal conditions.

CULTIVATION: *Grow in moist but well-drained, moderately fertile soil, in full sun or semi-shade. For berries, a male holly will need to be nearby. Prune in late summer to maintain shape.*

☼ ◑ ◊ Z5   ‡↔10ft (3m

Indigofera amblyantha

...is spreading, deciduous shrub with
...ching stems is grown for its pretty,
...alike flowers and gray-green foliage.
...carries dense, more-or-less upright
...sters of small pink flowers from
...rly summer to fall. In cold climates,
...s best trained against a warm,
...eltered wall. Cut all stems to just
...ove ground level in early spring.

...LTIVATION: *Grow in fertile, moist but
...ell-drained soil, in sun.*

◇ ◊ Z7   ‡6ft (2m) ↔8ft (2.5m)

Indigofera heterantha

...medium-sized, spreading shrub
...own for its pealike flowers and
...egant foliage. The arching stems
...rry gray-green leaves made up of
...any oval to oblong leaflets. Dense,
...pright clusters of small, purple-pink
...owers appear from early summer to
...ll. Train against a warm wall where
...arginally hardy. *I. ambylantha* (see
...ove) is a very similar shrub.

...LTIVATION: *Grow in well-drained but
...oist, moderately fertile soil, in full sun.
...rune in early spring, cutting back to just
...bove ground level.*

❉ ◊ Z8   ‡↔6–10ft (2–3m)

Ipheion uniflorum 'Froyle Mill'

This variety of ipheion is very simil
to 'Wisley Blue' but with dusky viole
mildly fragrant star-like flowers in
spring. Grass-like leaves appear in f
well before the flowers. Plant the
bulbs 3in (8cm) deep, 2in (5cm) apa
in fall in a sunny site. Provide a
protective mulch in winter in areas
where temperatures regularly fall
below 14°F (-10°C).

CULTIVATION: *Grow in well-drained
soil, in full sun. Dig and divide bulbs
after flowering.*

☀ ◊ Z5   ↕↔6–8in (15–20cr

Ipheion uniflorum 'Wisley Blue'

A vigorous, clump-forming, mainly
spring-flowering, bulbous perennial
bearing scented, star-shaped, lilac-
blue flowers; each petal has a pale
base and a dark midrib. Narrow,
straplike, light blue-green leaves
are produced in fall. Useful in
a rock garden or for underplanting
herbaceous plants.

CULTIVATION: *Grow in moist but well-
drained, moderately fertile, organic soil,
in full sun. Where marginally hardy,
provide a mulch in winter.*

☀ ◊ Z5   ↕6–8in (15–20cm

Ipomoea 'Heavenly Blue'

This summer-flowering, twining,
fast-growing form of morning glory
is grown as a climbing annual.
The large, funnel-shaped flowers,
azure-blue with pure white throats,
appear singly or in clusters of two
or three. The heart-shaped, light
to mid-green leaves have slender
tips. Suitable for a summer border,
scrambling among other plants. Seeds
are highly toxic if ingested.

CULTIVATION: *Grow in well-drained,
moderately fertile soil, in sun with shelter
from cold, drying winds. Plant out after
danger of frost has passed.*

☀ ◊ Annual   ↕to 10–12ft (3–4m)

Ipomoea indica

The blue dawn flower is a vigorous,
evergreen climber, perennial in
frost-free conditions. Abundant, rich
purple-blue, funnel-shaped flowers
that often fade to red are borne in
clusters of three to five from late
spring to fall. The mid-green leaves
are heart-shaped or three-lobed. In
mild areas, grow as annuals in a
warm conservatory or summer
border. The seeds are toxic.

CULTIVATION: *Grow in well-drained, faily
fertile soil, in sun with shelter from cold,
drying winds. Plant out after all danger of
frost has passed. Minimum temperature
45°F (7°C).*

☀ ◊ Annual   ↕to 20ft (6m)

Irises for Moist to Wet Soil

Irises that flourish in reliably moist or wet soils produce swollen, horizontal creeping stems known as rhizomes that lie just below the ground. These produce several new offsets each year, so give plants plenty or room, or divide them regularly. They have strap-shaped leaves and flower in blues, purples, white, or yellow in spring and early summer. The true water irises will grow not only in damp ground but also in shallow water; these include *I. laevigata* and *I. pseudacorus*, very vigorous plants that will soon overwhelm a small pond. Where space is limited, try *I. ensata* or, in moist or even in well-drained soil around the water, plant *I. sibirica* or one of its many attractive cultivars.

CULTIVATION: *Grow in deep, acidic soil enriched with well-rotted organic matter, in sun or light shade. Divide existing clumps and replant divisions in early fall or early spring.*

☼ ☀ ◊ ♦ Z3, except as noted

‡36in (90cm) ↔ indefinite

‡36in (90cm) ↔ indefinite

‡32in (80cm) ↔ indefinite

‡32in (80cm) ↔ indefinite

‡3–5ft (0.9–1.5m) ↔ indefinite

‡3–5ft (0.9–1.5m) ↔ indefinite

1 *Iris ensata* 'Flying Tiger' **2** *I. ensata* 'Variegata' (both *ensatas* Z4) **3** *I. laevigata*
4 *I. laevigata* 'Variegata' **5** *I. pseudacorus* **6** *I. pseudacorus* 'Variegata' (both Z4)
7 *I. sibirica* 'Annemarie Troeger' **8** *I. versicolor* **9** *I. sibirica* 'Crème Chantilly'

7 ‡ft (1m) ↔ indefinite

8 ‡8–32in (20–80cm) ↔ indefinite

9 ‡3ft (1m) ↔ indefinite

10 ‡2in (80cm) ↔ indefinite

11 ‡32m (80cm) ↔ indefinite

12 ‡3ft (1m) ↔ indefinite

13 ‡ft (1m) ↔ indefinite

14 ‡32in (80cm) ↔ indefinite

15 ‡3ft (1m) ↔ indefinite

16 ‡32in (80cm) ↔ indefinite

17 ‡ to 3ft (1m) ↔ indefinite

18 ‡ to 3ft (1m) ↔ indefinite

10 *I. sibirica* ‘Dreaming Yellow’ **11** *I. sibirica* ‘Harpswell Happiness’ **12** *I. sibirica* Mikiko’ **13** *I. sibirica* ‘Oban’ **14** *I. sibirica* ‘Perfect Vision’ **15** *I. sibirica* ‘Roisin’ **16** *I. sibirica* ‘Smudger's Gift’ **17** *I. sibirica* ‘Uber den Wolken’ **18** *I. sibirica* 'Zakopane’

Iris bucharica

A fast-growing, spring-flowering, bulbous perennial that carries up to six golden yellow to white flowers on each stem. The glossy, straplike leaves die back after flowering. The most commonly available form of this iris has yellow and white flower

CULTIVATION: *Grow in rich but well-drained, neutral to slightly alkaline soil, in full sun. Water moderately when in growth; after flowering, maintain a period of dry dormancy.*

☼ ◊ Z5
↕8–16in (20–40cm) ↔5in (12cm)

Iris confusa

This freely spreading, rhizomatous perennial with bamboolike foliage produces a succession of up to 30 short-lived flowers on each stem during spring. They are white with yellow crests surrounded by purple or yellow spots. The leaves are arranged in fans at the base of the plant. Suitable for a sheltered, mixed or herbaceous border.

CULTIVATION: *Grow in moist but well-drained, rich soil, in sun or semi-shade. Water moderately when in growth. Keep neat by removing flowered stems.*

☼ ☼ ◊ Z8   ↕3ft (1m) ↔indefinite

Iris delavayi

This rhizomatous, deciduous perennial bears three-branched flower stems in summer, each one topped by two light to dark purple-blue flowers. The rounded fall petals have white and yellow necks. The foliage is gray-green. A handsome perennial with its tall stems, it is easily grown in moist soil.

CULTIVATION: *Grow in moist soil, in full sun or partial shade. Lift and divide congested clumps after flowering.*

 ◊ Z5   ‡5ft (1.5m) ↔indefinite

Iris douglasiana

A robust, rhizomatous perennial with branched flower stems that each bear two or three white, cream, blue, lavender-blue, or red-purple flowers in late spring and early summer. The stiff, glossy, dark green leaves are often red at the bases. A good display plant for a raised bed or trough.

CULTIVATION: *Grow in well-drained, neutral to slightly acidic soil. Site in full sun for the best flowers, or light shade. Does not transplant well, so do not lift and divide unnecessarily.*

☼ ☼ ◊ Z4
6–28in (15–70cm) ↔indefinite

Iris foetidissima 'Variegata'

The stinking iris is not as unpleasant as it sounds, although the evergreen silvery leaves with white stripes, in this cultivar, do have a nasty scent if crushed. A vigorous rhizomatous perennial, it bears yellow-tinged, dull purple flowers in early summer followed by seed capsules that split open in fall to display showy scarlet yellow or, rarely, white seeds. A useful plant for dry shade.

CULTIVATION: *Prefers well-drained, neutral to slightly acidic soil, in shade. Divide congested clumps in fall.*

☼ ☼ ◊ Z7
↕12–36in (30–90cm) ↔indefinite

Iris forrestii

An elegant, early summer-flowering rhizomatous perennial with slender flower stems that each carry one or two scented, pale yellow flowers with brown markings. The very narrow glossy leaves are mid-green above and gray-green below. Easy to grow in an open border.

CULTIVATION: *Grow in moist but well-drained, neutral to slightly acidic soil. Position in full sun or partial shade.*

☼ ☼ ◊ ◊ Z6
↕14–16in (35–40cm) ↔indefinite

Iris graminea

A deciduous, rhizomatous perennial bearing bright green, straplike leaves. From late spring, rich purple-violet flowers, with fall petals tipped white and violet-veined, are borne either singly or in pairs; they are often hidden among the leaves. The flowers have a fruity fragrance.

CULTIVATION: *Grow in moist but well-drained, neutral to slightly acidic soil. Choose a site in full sun or semi-shade. Does not respond well to transplanting.*

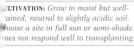 ☀ ◐ ◊ ◊ Z4
‡8–16in (20–40cm) ↔indefinite

Iris 'Katharine Hodgkin'

This very vigorous, tiny but robust, deciduous, bulbous perennial bears delicately patterned, pale blue and yellow flowers, with darker blue and gold markings, in late winter and early spring. The pale to mid-green leaves grow after the flowers have faded. Excellent in a rock garden or at the front of a border, where it will spread slowly to form a clump.

CULTIVATION: *Grow in well-drained, neutral to slightly alkaline soil, in an open site in full sun.*

 ☀ ◊ Z5 ‡5in (12cm) ↔2–3in (5–8cm)

Bearded Irises

These upright, rhizomatous perennials send up fans of sword-shaped, usually broad leaves and simple or branched stems. The flowers are produced in a wide range of colors, with well-developed, often frilly fall and standard petals, and a "beard" of white or colored hairs in the center of each fall petal. These are the most widely cultivated group of irises for garden display, usually producing several flowers per stem from spring into early summer, sometimes again later in the season.

Taller irises suit a mixed border, and smaller ones may be grown in a rock garden, raised bed, or trough.

CULTIVATION: *Grow in well-drained, moderately fertile, neutral to slightly acidic soil in full sun. Plant rhizomes in late summer or early fall, thinly covered with soil. They must not be shaded by other plants. Do not mulch. Divide large or congested clumps in summer.*

☼ ◊ Z3

‡28in (70cm) ↔ 24in (60cm)

‡28in (70cm) ↔ 24in (60cm)

3
‡22in (55m) ↔ 18-24in (45-60cm)

‡28in (70cm) ↔ 24in (60cm)

‡↔ 12in (30cm)

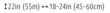

1 *Iris* 'Apricorange' **2** *I.* 'Breakers' **3** *I.* 'Brown Lasso' **4** *I.* 'Early Light' **5** *I.* 'Eyebright'

‡to 28in (70cm) ↔ to 24in (60cm)

‡8–16in (20–40cm) ↔ 12in (30cm)

28in (70cm) ↔ to 24in (60cm)

‡to 28in (70cm) ↔ to 24in (60cm)

28in (70cm) ↔ 24in (60cm)

28in (70cm) ↔ to 24in (60cm)

‡28in (70cm) ↔ 24in (60cm)

28in (70cm) ↔ to 24in (60cm)

‡28in (70cm) ↔ 24in (60cm)

‡33in (85cm) ↔ 24in (60cm)

I. 'Happy Mood' **7** *I.* 'Honington' **8** *I.* 'Katie-Koo' **9** *I.* 'Maui Moonlight'
I. 'Meg's Mantle' **11** *I.* 'Miss Carla' **12** *I.* 'Nicola Jane' **13** *I.* 'Orinoco Flow'
I. 'Paradise' **15** *I.* 'Paradise Bird'

‡28in (70cm) ↔24in (60cm)

‡16-28in (40-70cm) ↔18-24in (45-60cm)

‡28in (70cm) or more ↔24in (60cm)

‡to 28in (70cm) ↔ to 24in (60c

16 *I.* 'Phil Keen' **17** *I.* 'Pink Parchment' **18** *I.* 'Precious Heather' **19** *I.* 'Quark'

n (25cm) ↔ 12in (30cm)

21 ‡to 28in (70cm) ↔ to 24in (60cm)

28in (70cm) ↔ 24in (60cm)

23 ‡to 28in (70cm) ↔ to 24in (60cm)

24 ‡28in (70cm) ↔ 24in (60cm)

MORE CHOICES

'Babbling Brook' Light blue with yellow beard, 38in (96cm) tall.

'Beverly Sills' Ruffled coral pink, 35in (88cm) tall.

'Laced Cotton' Pure white, 36in (90cm) tall.

'Rare Edition' Mulberry and white, early, 24in (60cm) tall.

'Titans Glory' Dark violet, 37in (94cm) tall.

'Victoria Falls' Blue with white beard, 40in (102cm) tall.

25 ‡to 28in (70cm) ↔ to 24in (60cm)

26 ‡36in (90cm) ↔ 24in (60cm)

I. 'Rain Dance' **21** *I.* 'Sherbet Lemon' **22** *I.* 'Sparkling Lemonade'
I. 'Sunny Dawn' **24** *I.* 'Sun Miracle' **25** *I.* 'Templecloud' **26** *I.* 'Vanity'

Iris lacustris

This dwarf, deciduous, rhizomatous perennial bears small flowers in late spring. These are purple-blue to sky blue with gold crests and a white patch on each of the fall peta they arise from basal fans of narro leaves. Suitable for growing in a ro garden or trough.

CULTIVATION: *Grow in reliably moist, acidic soil that is rich in organic matter in sun or partial shade. Water moderat when in growth.*

☼ ◑ ◊ Z4   ↕4in (10cm) ↔indefir

Iris pallida 'Variegata'

This semi-evergreen, rhizomatous perennial is probably the most versatile and attractive variegated iris. The straplike, bright green leaves are clearly striped with golde yellow. (For silver-striped leaves, lo for 'Argentea Variegata'.) The large, scented, soft blue flowers with yello beards are borne in clusters of two t six on branched stems in late spring and early summer. Grow in a mixed or herbaceous border.

CULTIVATION: *Best in well-drained, fertile, slightly alkaline soil, in sun. Water moderately when in growth.*

☼ ◊ Z3b   ↕to 3ft (1m) ↔indefin

Iris setosa

...'s rhizomatous perennial flowers
...ate spring and early summer.
...ch flowering stem bears several
...autiful, blue or blue-purple flowers
...ove the narrow, mid-green leaves.
...sily grown in moist soil.

...LTIVATION: *Grow in moist, neutral to*
...htly acidic soil, in full sun or partial
...de. Lift and divide congested clumps
...er flowering.

☀ ◊ Z3
...-36in (15–90cm) ↔ indefinite

Iris unguicularis

...ast-growing, evergreen, rhizomatous
...rennial, sometimes called *I. stylosa*,
...th short flower stems bearing large,
...grant blooms from late winter
...metimes even earlier) to early
...ring. The pale lavender to deep violet
...tals have contrasting veins and a
...nd of yellow on each fall petal. The
...ves are grasslike and mid-green.
...eal for the base of a sunny wall.

...LTIVATION: *Grow in sharply drained,*
...utral to alkaline soil. Choose a warm,
...eltered site in full sun. Does not like
...be disturbed. Keep neat by removing
...ad leaves in late summer and spring.

◊ Z6b ↕ 12in (30cm) ↔ indefinite

Iris variegata

This slender and robust, deciduous, rhizomatous perennial bears three to six flowers on each branched stem from midsummer. The striking flowers are pale yellow with brown or violet veins on the fall petals; there are many color variations available. The deep green leaves are strongly ribbed.

CULTIVATION: *Grow in well-drained, neutral to alkaline soil, in sun or light shade. Avoid mulching with organic matter, which may encourage rot.*

☼ ◐ ◊ Z4
‡8–18in (20–45cm) ↔ indefinite

Itea ilicifolia

An evergreen shrub bearing upright at first, then spreading, arching shoots. The oval, hollylike leaves are sharply toothed. Tiny, greenish-white flowers are borne in long, catkinlike clusters from midsummer to early fall. Needs a sheltered position in cold areas.

CULTIVATION: *Grow in well-drained but moist, fertile soil, preferably against a warm wall in full sun. Protect with a winter mulch when young.*

☼ ◊ Z7
‡15ft (3–5m) ↔ 10ft (3m)

...sminum mesnyi

...e primrose jasmine is a half hardy,
...ambling, evergreen shrub with
...ge, usually semidouble, bright
...llow flowers. These appear singly
...r in small clusters during spring
...d summer, amid the glossy, dark
...een leaves, which are divided into
...ree oblong to lance-shaped leaflets.
...ll climb if tied to a support.

*...LTIVATION: Grow in any well-drained,
...tile soil, in full sun or partial shade.
...t back flowered shoots in summer to
...courage strong growth from the base.
...nimum temperature 35°F (2°C).*

☀ ◊ Tender
...0 10ft (3m) ↔ 3–6ft (1–2m)

...sminum nudiflorum

...nter jasmine is a lax, mound-
...rming, deciduous shrub with
...nder, arching stems. Small,
...bular yellow flowers are borne
...ngly on the leafless, green shoots
...late winter. The dark green leaves,
...ich develop after the flowers, are
...vided into three leaflets. Tie in a
...amework of stems against a wall,
... let it sprawl unsupported.

*...LTIVATION: Grow in well-drained,
...tile soil. Tolerates semi-shade, but
...wers best in sun. Encourage strong
...owth by cutting back flowered shoots.*

◊ Z7b ↔↔ to 10ft (3m)

Jasminum officinale 'Argenteovariegatum'

This variegated form of the commo[n]
jasmine, *J. officinale*, is a vigorous,
deciduous or semi-deciduous, wood[y]
climber. The gray-green, cream-edg[ed]
leaves are made up of 5–9 sharply
pointed leaflets. Clusters of fragran[t]
white flowers open from summer t[o]
early fall. If tied in initially, it will
twine over supports, such as a trelli[s]
or an arch.

CULTIVATION: *Grow in well-drained,*
fertile soil. Tolerates shade, but flowers
best in full sun. Thin out crowded growt[h]
after flowering.

☼ ◐ ◊ Z8   ‡to 40ft (12[m])

Juglans nigra

Given ideal conditions, black walnut[s]
develop rapidly into impressive shad[e]
tree with furrowed bark and large
leaves divided into many leaflets.
Catkins in late spring are followed
by edible walnuts that mature in
early fall as the foliage turns yellow.
Good nut-bearing varieties include
'Vandersloot' and 'Thomas'. 'Lacinia[ta]'
has attractive foliage. Note: a chemic[al]
secreted by black walnut roots make[s]
it difficult to establish many other
plants under its canopy.

CULTIVATION: *Grow in deep, moist but*
well-drained soil, in full sun.

☼ ◊ ◖ Z3b   ‡100ft (30m) ↔70ft (20[m])

Juniperus communis 'Compressa'

This slow-growing, spindle-shaped, dwarf form of the common juniper bears deep to blue-green, aromatic, evergreen scalelike leaves, borne in whorls of three along the stems. Small, oval or spherical fruits remain on the plant for three years, ripening from green to cloudy blue to black.

CULTIVATION: *Grow in any well-drained soil, preferably in full sun or light dappled shade. No pruning is needed.*

☀ ◊ Z4
↕32in (80cm) ↔18in (45cm)

Juniperus x *pfitzeriana* 'Wilhelm Pfitzer'

This spreading, dense, evergreen shrub has ascending branches of gray-green foliage that droop at the tips; it eventually forms a flat-topped, tiered bush. The flattened, scalelike leaves are borne in whorls of three. Spherical fruits are at first dark purple, becoming paler as they age. Looks nice as a specimen plant or in a large rock garden.

CULTIVATION: *Grow in any well-drained soil, preferably in full sun or light dappled shade. Keep pruning to a minimum, in late fall if necessary.*

☀ ☀ ◊ Z2b ↕4ft (1.2m) ↔10ft (3m)

Juniperus procumbens 'Nana'

A compact, mat-forming conifer that is excellent as a groundcover in a wide range of situations. The needlelike, aromatic, yellow-green or light green leaves are carried in groups of three. Bears berrylike, brown to black, fleshy fruits that take two or three years to ripen.

CULTIVATION: *Grow in any well-drained soil, including sandy, dry, or alkaline conditions. Site in full sun or very light shade. No pruning is required.*

☼ ☀ ◊ Z4
‡6–8in (15–20cm) ↔30in (75cm)

Juniperus squamata 'Blue Star'

This conifer is a low-growing, dense compact, rounded bush with rust-colored, flaky bark. The silvery blue leaves are sharply pointed and grouped in whorls of three. The ripe fruits are oval and black. Useful as a groundcover or in a rock garden.

CULTIVATION: *Grow in any well-drained soil, in full sun or very light shade. Very little pruning is required.*

☼ ☀ ◊ Z3
‡to 16in (40cm) ↔to 3ft (1m)

Kalmia angustifolia

The sheep laurel is a tough, rabbit-proof shrub grown for its spectacular, rounded clusters of small flowers, usually pink to deep red, but occasionally white. They appear in early summer amid the dark green leaves. Useful for a shrub border or rockery; naturally mound-forming, it tolerates trimming to a neat shape.

CULTIVATION: *Choose a partly shaded site in moist, acidic soil, rich in organic matter. Grow in full sun only where the soil remains reliably moist. Mulch in spring with leaf mold or pine needles. Trim or prune hard after flowering.*

⬥ Z3   ↕24in (60cm) ↔5ft (1.5m)

Kalmia latifolia

Mountain laurel is a dense evergreen shrub producing large clusters of flowers from late spring to midsummer. These are cup-shaped, pink or occasionally white, and open from distinctively shaped buds. The oval leaves are glossy and dark green. An excellent specimen shrub for woodland gardens, but flowers best in full sun. 'Ostbo Red' is one of many recommended cultivars.

CULTIVATION: *Grow in moist, organic, acidic soil, in sun or partial shade. Mulch each spring with pine needles or leaf mold. Requires very little pruning, although deadheading is worthwhile.*

❈ ☀ ⬥ Z5b   ↕↔10ft (3m)

Kerria japonica 'Golden Guinea'

This vigorous, suckering, deciduous shrub forms clumps of arching, canelike shoots that arise from ground level each year. Large, single yellow flowers are borne in mid- and late spring along the previous year's growth. ('Flore Pleno' has double flowers.) The bright green leaves are oval and sharply toothed.

CULTIVATION: *Grow in well-drained, fertile soil, in full sun or partial shade. Cut flowered canes back to different levels to obtain flowers at different heights. Chop out unwanted canes and suckers to restrict spread.*

☼ ☀ ◊ Z5b   ‡6ft (2m) ↔8ft (2.5m)

Kirengeshoma palmata

A handsome, upright perennial with broad, lobed, pale green leaves. In late summer and early fall, these are topped by loose clusters of nodding, pale yellow flowers, giving the common name of "yellow wax bells." This plant brings a gentle elegance to a shady border, pondside or woodland garden.

CULTIVATION: *Thrives in moist, acidic soil enriched with leaf mold, in partial shade sheltered from wind. If necessary, divide clumps in spring.*

☀ ◊ Z4
‡24–48in (60–120cm) ↔30in (75cm)

niphofia 'Bees' Sunset'

his red-hot poker is a deciduous
rennial grown for its elegant
ikes of soft yellowish orange
owers. These appear through
mmer above the clumps of
ching, grasslike leaves. Very
tractive to bees.

LTIVATION: *Grow in deep, fertile, moist
t well-drained soil, ideally sandy but
riched with organic matter. Choose a site
full sun or partial shade. Mulch young
ants for their first winter, and divide
ature, crowded clumps in late spring.*

☼ ☀ ◊ ◕ Z6
6in (90cm) ↔24in (60cm)

niphofia caulescens

his stately evergreen perennial bears
ll spikes of flowers from late summer
mid-fall; coral-red, they fade upward
pale yellow with age, giving them
eir common name of red-hot pokers.
hey are carried well above basal
osettes of arching, grasslike,
ue-green leaves. Good for herbaceous
orders; tolerant of coastal exposure.

LTIVATION: *Grow in deep, fertile, moist
t well-drained soil, preferably sandy
nd enriched with organic matter. Position
full sun or partial shade. Mulch young
ants for their first winter. Divide large
umps in late spring.*

☼ ☀ ◊ ◕ Z6
to 4ft (1.2m) ↔24in (60cm)

Kniphofia 'Little Maid'

This clump-forming, deciduous perennial has tall heads of tubular flowers that appear from late summer to early fall. They are pale green in bud, opening to pale buff-yellow, then fading to ivory. The leaves are narrow and grasslike. Good for late displays in a mixed or herbaceous border.

CULTIVATION: *Grow in well-drained, deep, fertile, organic soil, in full sun. Keep moist when in growth. In their first winter and where marginally hardy, provide a light mulch.*

☼ ◊ Z6　‡24in (60cm) ↔18in (45cm)

Kniphofia 'Royal Standard'

A clump-forming, herbaceous perennial of classic red-hot poker appearance that bears tall, conical flowerheads from mid- to late summer. The bright yellow, tubular flowers open from red buds, starting at the base and moving upward. The arching, grasslike leaves make an impressive clump.

CULTIVATION: *Grow in deep, moist but well-drained, organic soil, in sun. Water freely when in growth. Provide a mulch where marginal, especially for young plants in their first winter.*

☼ ◊ Z6　‡3ft (1m) ↔24in (60cm)

oelreuteria paniculata

e golden rain tree is a beautiful,
otic-looking, deciduous tree that
ars large, open clusters of small
llow flowers in midsummer.
ese are followed by unusual
onze-red, inflated pods. The leaf
lor is attractive in its own right,
th reddish leaves emerging in
ring, turning to green, with bright
llow tints in fall. The leaves of
oral Sun' are more intensely
lored. Heat and drought tolerant
d adaptable to a wide range of soils.

ULTIVATION: *Grow in well-drained soil,*
full sun.

: ◊ Z7   ↕↔30ft (10m)

Kolkwitzia amabilis 'Pink Cloud'

he beauty bush is a fast-growing,
uckering, deciduous shrub with
n arching habit. Dense clusters
f bell-shaped pink flowers with
ellow-flushed throats appear in
bundance from late spring to early
ummer. The leaves are dark green
nd broadly oval. Excellent for a
hrub border or as a specimen plant.

ULTIVATION: *Grow in any well-drained,*
ertile soil, in full sun. Let the arching
abit of young plants develop without
runing, then thin out the stems each
ear after flowering, to maintain vigor.

 ◊ Z4b   ↕10ft (3m) ↔12ft (4m)

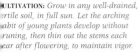

Laburnum x *watereri* 'Vossii'

This spreading, deciduous tree bears long, hanging clusters of golden yellow, pealike flowers in late spring and early summer. The dark green leaves are made up of three oval leaflets. A fine specimen tree for small gardens; it can also be trained on an arch, pergola, or tunnel frame work. All parts are toxic if eaten.

CULTIVATION: *Grow in well-drained, moderately fertile soil, in full sun. Cut back badly placed growth in winter or early spring. Remove any suckers or buds at the base of the trunk.*

☼ ◊ Z6   ↕↔25ft (8r

Lagerstroemia indica 'Hopi'

This large shrub or small deciduous tree produces drooping pink flowers from midsummer into early fall. Its dark green leaves turn red orange to deep red in fall. Ornamental seedheads and pale gray peeling bark add winter interest. Grow it as a shrub in cold climates, and prune to tree shape in warmer regions.

CULTIVATION: *Grow crape myrtle in full sun, and well-drained, fertile, clay or sandy soil. It resists heat, humidity, wind, and browsing animals. Remove spent flowers to encourage rebloom.*

☼ ◊ Z7b   ↕↔to 25ft (8m

amium maculatum 'White Nancy'

his colorful deadnettle is a semi-evergreen perennial that spreads to rm mats; this makes it effective as groundcover between shrubs. Spikes pure white, two-lipped flowers are roduced in summer above triangular oval, silver leaves that are edged th green.

ULTIVATION: *Grow in moist but well-ained soil, in partial or deep shade. an be invasive, so position away from her small plants, and dig up invasive ots or shoots to limit spread.*

☀ ◐ ◊ ◗ Z3

o 6in (15cm) ↔ to 3ft (1m) or more

apageria rosea

he Chilean bellflower is a long-lived, vining, evergreen climber. From ummer to late fall, it produces large, arrowly bell-shaped, waxy red owers borne either singly or in mall clusters. The leaves are oval nd dark green. 'Nash Court' has soft ink flowers. Does well on a wall in cool greenhouse.

ULTIVATION: *Grow in well-drained, oderately fertile soil, preferably in artial shade. Where marginal, shelter om wind and provide a winter mulch. eep pruning to a minimum, removing amaged growth in spring. Minimum emperature 30°F (-1°C).*

◗ ◊ Tender   ↕15ft (5m)

Larix decidua

The European larch is unusual among conifers in that it is deciduous and sheds its soft, pale green needle in fall, once they have faded to a pretty straw yellow. The trees have a roughly conical shape and smooth, scaly gray bark. Small, rounded cone appear in early summer, and usually persist on the branches. This easily grown specimen tree tolerates a wide range of conditions.

CULTIVATION: *Grow in well-drained soil, in sun.*

☼ ◊ Z3b
‡100ft (30m) ↔12–20ft (4–6m)

Lathyrus latifolius

The everlasting or perennial pea is a tendril-climbing, herbaceous perennial with winged stems, ideal for growing through shrubs or over a bank. Clusters of pealike, pink-purple flowers appear during summer and early fall, amid the deciduous, blue-green leaves, which are divided into two oblong leaflets. The seeds are not edible. For white flowers, choose 'Albus' or 'White Pearl'.

CULTIVATION: *Grow in well-drained, fertile, organic soil, in sun or semi-shade. Cut back to ground level in spring and pinch out shoot tips to encourage bushiness. Resents disturbance.*

☼ ◐ ◊ Z4
‡6ft (2m) or more

weet Peas (*Lathyrus odoratus*)

he many cultivars of *Lathyrus odoratus* e annual climbers cultivated for their ng display of beautiful and fragrant owers that cut well and are available most colors except yellow. The owers are arranged in clusters during mmer to early fall. The seeds e not edible. Most look very effective ained on a pyramid of stakes or a ellis, or scrambling amid shrubs and erennials. Compact cultivars such as atio Mixed' suit containers; some of ese are self-supporting. Grow sweet

peas, also, in a vegetable garden, because they attract pollinating bees and other beneficial insects.

CULTIVATION: *Grow in well-drained, fertile soil; for the best flowers, add well-rotted manure the season before planting. Site in full sun or partial shade. Give a balanced fertilizer every other week when in growth. Deadhead or cut flowers regularly. Support the climbing stems.*

☼ ☀ ◊ ◖ Annual

1
6-8ft (2-2.5m)

2 ‡6-8ft (2-2.5m)

3 ‡6-8ft (2-2.5m)

3ft (1m)

5 ‡6-8ft (2-2.5m)

6 ‡6-8ft (2-2.5m)

1 *L.* 'Aunt Jane' **2** *L.* 'Evening Glow' **3** *L.* 'Noel Sutton' **4** *L.* 'Patio Mixed'
5 *L.* 'Teresa Maureen' **6** *L.* 'White Supreme'

Laurus nobilis

Bay, or bay laurel, is a conical, evergreen tree grown for its oval, aromatic, leathery, dark green leave that are used in cooking. Clusters of small, greenish-yellow flowers appear in spring, followed by black berries in fall. Effective when trimmed into formal shapes.

CULTIVATION: *Grow in well-drained but moist, fertile soil, in sun or semi-shade with shelter from cold, drying winds. Grow male and female plants together for a reliable crop of berries. Prune young plants to shape in spring; trim established plants lightly in summer.*

☀ ◐ ◊ Z7 ‡40ft (12m) ↔30ft (10m)

Laurus nobilis 'Aurea'

This golden-leaved bay is a conical tree bearing aromatic, evergreen leaves. These are oval and leathery and can be used in cooking. In spring clusters of small, greenish-yellow flowers appear, followed in fall by black berries on female plants. Good for topiary and in containers, where it makes a much smaller plant.

CULTIVATION: *Grow in well-drained but moist, fertile soil. Position in full sun or partial shade with shelter from cold winds. Prune young plants to shape in spring; once established, trim lightly in summer to encourage a dense habit.*

☀ ◐ ◊ Z7 ‡40ft (12m) ↔30ft (10m)

Lavandula angustifolia 'Hidcote'

This compact lavender with thin, very gray leaves and dark purple flowers is an evergreen shrub useful for edging. Dense spikes of fragrant, tubular flowers, borne at the ends of long, unbranched stalks, appear during mid- to late summer. Like all lavenders, the flowers dry best if cut before they are fully open. 'Munstead' is hardier (Z5).

CULTIVATION: Grow in well-drained, fertile soil, in sun. Cut back flower stems in fall, and trim the foliage lightly with shears at the same time. In colder areas, leave trimming until spring. Do not cut into old wood.

◊ Z6   ↕24in (60cm) ↔30in (75cm)

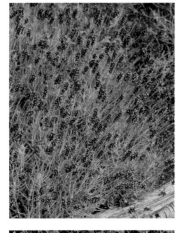

Lavandula angustifolia 'Twickel Purple'

This evergreen shrub is a close relative of 'Hidcote' (above) with a more spreading habit, paler flowers, and greener leaves. Dense spikes of fragrant purple flowers are borne in midsummer above narrowly oblong, gray-green leaves. Good in a shrub border; as with all lavenders, the flowerheads are attractive to bees.

CULTIVATION: Grow in well-drained, fairly fertile soil, in full sun. Trim in fall, or delay until spring in colder areas. Do not cut into old wood.

❋ ◊ Z6   ↕24in (60cm) ↔3ft (1m)

Lavandula x *intermedia* Dutch Group

A tall, robust, bushy lavender, with broad, silvery, aromatic leaves and tall, slender spikes of scented lavender-blue flowers. Suited to a sunny shrub border or large rock or scree garden; makes a good low hedge if regularly trimmed. 'Grappenhall' is very similar but is not as hardy (Z8).

CULTIVATION: *Grow in well-drained, fertile soil, in sun. Cut back flower stem in fall, and trim the foliage lightly with shears at the same time. In colder areas, leave trimming until spring. Do not cut into old wood.*

☼ ◊ Z7   ↕↔4ft (1.2

Lavandula pedunculata subsp. *pedunculata*

French lavender is a compact, evergreen shrub that blooms from late spring to summer. Dense spikes of tiny, fragrant, dark purple flower each spike topped by distinctive, rose-purple bracts, are carried on lo stalks well above the narrow, woolly silvery gray leaves. Effective in a sheltered shrub border or rock garden

CULTIVATION: *Grow in well-drained, fairl fertile soil, in sun. Trim back in spring or, in frost-free climates, after flowering. Avoid cutting into old wood.*

☼ ◊ Z8   ↕↔24in (60cr

rubby Lavateras (*Lavatera*)

ese upright and showy, flowering
ubs with stiff stems and sage-green
ves usually bloom from midsummer
fall in shades of pink and purple.
hough they are short-lived, they
w quickly on any well-drained soil,
luding thin, dry soil, which makes
m a welcome addition to any garden
ere quick results are desired. They
o perform well in coastal areas,
ng able to tolerate salt-laden winds,
the shrubs will need staking if
own in a site exposed to wind.

Where marginally hardy, grow against
a warm, sunny wall.

CULTIVATION: *Grow in any poor to
moderately fertile, well-drained to dry soil,
in full sun. Shelter from cold, drying winds
in frost-prone areas. After cold winters,
cold-damaged plants are best pruned right
down to the base in spring to encourage
new growth and tall, vigorous stems. In
milder areas, trim to shape after flowering.*

☼ ◊ Z5

‡↔ 6ft (2m)   ‡↔ 6ft (2m)

‡↔ 6ft (2m)   ‡↔ 6ft (2m)

↔ 6ft (2m)

L. x *clementii* 'Barnsley' **2** *L.* x *clementii* 'Bredon Springs' **3** *L.* x *clementii* 'Burgundy
ine' **4** *L.* x *clementii* 'Candy Floss' **5** *L.* x *clementii* 'Rosea'

Annual Lavateras (*Lavatera*)

These sturdy, bushy annuals are an excellent choice for planting in groups in a herbaceous border or for summer bedding, flowering continuously from midsummer into autumn. They are softly hairy or downy plants with shallowly lobed, soft green leaves; the open funnel-shaped, pink, reddish-pink, or purple blooms are complemented nicely by the foliage. Although annual lavateras are only a temporary visitor to the garden, with their cottage-garden appearance they seem to look as if they have been arou for years. Excellent for a dry, sunny s and as a source of cut flowers.

CULTIVATION: *Grow in light, moderately fertile, well-drained soil, in full sun. Young plants need a regular supply of water unti they become established; after this, the plants are fairly drought-tolerant. Watch o for aphids, which often attack young grow*

☼ ◊ Annual

1 ‡to 24in (60cm) ↔18in (45cm)   2 ‡to 24in (60cm) ↔18in (45cm)   3 ‡to 24in (60cm) ↔18in (45cm)

4 ‡to 30in (75cm) ↔18in (45cm)   5 ‡to 24in (60cm) ↔18in (45cm)   6 ‡to 30in (75cm) ↔18in (45cm)

1 *Lavatera* 'Beauty Formula Mixture' **2** *L.* 'Pink Beauty' **3** *L.* 'Salmon Beauty'
4 *L.* 'Silver Cup' **5** *L.* 'White Beauty' **6** *L.* 'White Cherub'

...iophyllum buxifolium

...d myrtle is an upright to mat-
...ming, evergreen perennial with
...ssy, dark green foliage and abundant
...r-shaped, pinkish-white flowers
...ate spring and early summer.
...e leaves tint bronze in winter. Good,
...e-flowering underplanting for a
...rub border or woodland garden.

*CULTIVATION: Grow in moist but well-
...ined, acidic soil rich in organic matter.
...oose a site in partial or deep shade with
...tection from cold, drying winds. Trim
...r flowering; it may spread widely if
...unattended.*

☀ ◐ ◊ ◊ Z6

...2–24in (30–60cm) ↔24in (60cm)
...more

...ptospermum rupestre

...is low-growing, evergreen shrub
...th dense foliage bears star-shaped
...ite flowers from late spring to
...mmer. The small, aromatic leaves
...e glossy, elliptic, and dark green.
...tive to coastal areas of Tasmania,
...s useful in seaside gardens
...ovided that the climate is mild.
...ay be sold as *L. humifusum*.

*CULTIVATION: Grow in well-drained,
...tile soil, in full sun or partial shade.
...im young growth in spring to promote
...shiness, but do not cut into old wood.
...nimum temperature 30°F (-1°C).*

☀ ◊ Tender

...–5ft (0.3–1.5m) ↔3–5ft (1–1.5m)

Leptospermum scoparium 'Kiwi'

A compact shrub with arching shoo[ts]
bearing an abundance of small, flat
dark crimson flowers during late
spring and early summer. The smal[l]
aromatic leaves are flushed with
purple when young, maturing to
mid- or dark green. Suitable for a
large rock garden and attractive in
an alpine house display. 'Nicholsii
Nanum' is similarly compact.

CULTIVATION: *Grow in well-drained,*
moderately fertile soil, in full sun or
part shade. Trim new growth in spring
for bushiness; do not cut into old wood.
Minimum temperature 35°F (2°C).

☼ ☀ ◊ Tender   ‡↔3ft (1[

Leucanthemum x *superbum* 'Wirral Supreme'

A robust, clump-forming, daisy-
flowered perennial with, from early
summer to early fall, dense, double
white flowerheads. These are carrie[d]
singly at the end of long stems
above lance-shaped, toothed, dark
green leaves. Good for cut flowers.
'Aglaia' and 'T.E. Killin' are other
recommended cultivars.

CULTIVATION: *Grow in moist but well-*
drained, moderately fertile soil, in full
sun or partial shade. May need staking.

☼ ☀ ◊ ◊ Z4

‡36in (90cm) ↔30in (75cm)

Leucojum aestivum 'Gravetye Giant'

This robust cultivar of summer snowflake is a spring-flowering, bulbous perennial with upright, strap-shaped, dark green leaves, to 16in (40cm) tall. The faintly chocolate-scented, drooping, bell-shaped white flowers with green petal tips are borne in clusters. Good planted near water, or for naturalizing in grass.

CULTIVATION: *Grow in reliably moist, organic soil, preferably near water. Choose a position in partial shade.*

◊ Z4   ‡3ft (1m) ↔3in (8cm)

Leucojum autumnale

A slender, late-summer-flowering, bulbous perennial bearing stems of two to four drooping, bell-shaped white flowers, tinged red at the petal bases. Narrow, upright, grasslike leaves appear at the same time as or just after the flowers. Suitable for a rock garden.

CULTIVATION: *Grow in any moist but well-drained soil. Choose a position in full sun. Divide and replant bulbs once the leaves have died down.*

◊ ◊ Z5b
‡4–6in (10–15cm) ↔2in (5cm)

Lewisia cotyledon

This evergreen perennial produces tight clusters of open funnel-shaped usually pinkish-purple flowers; they may be white, cream, yellow, or apricot. These are borne on long stems from spring to summer. The dark green, fleshy, lance-shaped leaves are arranged in basal rosette Suitable for growing in wall crevice The Sunset Group are recommende garden forms.

CULTIVATION: *Grow in sharply drained, fairly fertile, organic, neutral to acidic s Choose a site in light shade with protect from winter moisture.*

☀ ◊ Z4
‡6–12in (15–30 cm) ↔8–16in (20–40c

Lewisia tweedyi

An evergreen perennial with uprigh to arching stems that bear one to fo open funnel-shaped, white to peach pink flowers in spring and early summer. Lance-shaped, fleshy, deep green leaves flushed with purple ar arranged in rosettes at the base of the plant. Good in a rock garden, or in an alpine house where not hardy.

CULTIVATION: *Grow in sharply drained, organic, fairly fertile, neutral to acidic so in light shade. Protect plants in winter from excessive winter moisture.*

☀ ◊ Z4   ‡8in (20cm) ↔12in (30c

...zularia 'Gregynog Gold'

...rge, robust, clump-forming
...ennial with pyramidal spikes
...aisylike, golden orange, brown-
...tered flowers from late summer
...arly fall. These are carried
...upright stems above the large,
...nded, mid-green leaves. Excellent
...water; it naturalizes readily in
...st soils. Dark-leaved 'Desdemona',
...y 3ft (1m) tall, and 'The Rocket'
...other recommended ligularias.

...TIVATION: *Grow in reliably moist, deep,*
...derately fertile soil. Position in full sun
...n some midday shade, and shelter from
...ng winds.

☀ ◊ Z4   ↕6ft (2m) ↔3ft (1m)

...gustrum lucidum

...e Chinese privet is a vigorous,
...nical, evergreen shrub with
...ssy dark green, oval leaves. Loose
...sters of small white flowers
... produced in late summer and
...ly fall, followed by oval, blue-
...ck fruits. Good as hedging but
...o makes a useful, well-shaped
...nt for a shrub border.

...LTIVATION: *Best in well-drained soil,*
...full sun or partial shade. Cut out any
...wanted growth in winter.

☀ ◊ Z8   ↕↔30ft (10m)

Ligustrum lucidum 'Excelsum Superbum'

This variegated Chinese privet, wit
yellow-margined, bright green leav
is a fast-growing, conical, evergreer
shrub. Loose clusters of small,
creamy white flowers appear in lat
summer and early fall, followed by
oval, blue-black fruits.

CULTIVATION: *Grow in any well-drained
soil, in full sun for the best leaf color.
Remove unwanted growth in winter. Rem
any shoots that have plain green leaves a
soon as seen.*

☼ ◊ Z8   ↕↔30ft (10

Lilium candidum

The Madonna lily is an upright,
bulbous perennial, bearing sprays
of up to 20 highly fragrant, trumpet-
shaped flowers on each stiff stem
in midsummer. The flowers have
pure white petals with tinted yellow
bases, and yellow anthers. The
lance-shaped, glossy bright green
leaves that appear after the flowers
usually last over winter.

CULTIVATION: *Grow in well-drained,
neutral to alkaline soil that is rich in we
rotted organic matter. Tolerates drier soi
than most lilies. Position in full sun with
the base in shade.*

☼ ◊ Z6   ↕3–6ft (1–2

Lilium formosanum var. *pricei*

An elegant, clump-forming perennial bearing very fragrant, slender, trumpet-shaped flowers. These are borne singly or in clusters of up to three during summer. The flowers have curved petal tips, white insides, and strongly purple-flushed outsides. Most of the oblong, dark green leaves grow at the base of the stem. Lovely for an unheated greenhouse or conservatory.

CULTIVATION: *Grow in moist, neutral to acidic, organic soil or soil mix, in sun with the base in shade. Protect from excessively hot sun.*

◊ Z8   ‡2–5ft (0.6–1.5m)

Lilium henryi

A fast-growing, clump-forming perennial that bears a profusion of slightly scented, "turkscap" flowers with reflexed, or backward-bending petals) in late summer. These are deep orange with brown spots and red anthers, carried on purple-marked green stems above lance-shaped leaves. Excellent for a wild garden or woodland planting.

CULTIVATION: *Grow in well-drained, neutral to alkaline soil with added leaf mold or well-rotted organic matter. Choose a position in partial shade.*

◊ Z3b   ‡3–10ft (1–3m)

Lilium longiflorum

The Easter lily is a fast-growing perennial carrying short clusters of one to six pure white, strongly fragrant, trumpet-shaped flowers with yellow anthers. They appear during midsummer above scattered lance-shaped, deep green leaves. One of the smaller, less hardy lilies it grows well in containers and under glass.

CULTIVATION: *Best in well-drained soil or soil mix with added organic matter, in partial shade. Tolerates alkaline soil.*

☀ ◊ Z8   ↕16–39in (40–100c

Lilium martagon var. *album*

A clump-forming, vigorous perenni bearing sprays of up to 50 small, nodding, glossy white, "turkscap" flowers with strongly curled petals. The leaves are elliptic to lance-shaped, mostly borne in dense whorls. Unlike most lilies, it has an unpleasant odor and is better sited in a border or wild garden, for whic it is well suited. Looks good planted with var. *cattaniae*, with its deep maroon flowers.

CULTIVATION: *Best in almost any well-drained soil, in full sun or partial shade Water freely when in growth.*

☀ ☀ ◊ Z3   ↕3–6ft (1–2

...ium monadelphum

...s stout, clump-forming perennial,
... known as *L. szovitsianum*, bears
...o 30 large, fragrant, trumpet-
...ped flowers on each stiff stem in
...y summer. The blooms are pale
...ow, flushed brown-purple on the
...sides and flecked purple-maroon
...he insides. The scattered, bright
...en leaves are narrowly oval. Good
...containers: it tolerates drier
...ditions than most lilies.

...TIVATION: *Grow in any well-drained*
... in full sun. Tolerates fairly heavy,
...line soils.

◊ Z6   ‡3–5ft (1–1.5m)

...ium Pink
...rfection Group

...ese thick-stemmed lilies bear
...sters of large, scented, trumpet-
...ped flowers with curled petals
...midsummer. Flower colors range
...m deep purplish-red to purple-
...k, all with bright orange anthers.
...e mid-green leaves are straplike.
...cellent for cutting.

...LTIVATION: *Grow in well-drained soil*
...t is enriched with leaf mold or well-
...ted organic matter. Choose a position
... full sun with the base in shade.

◊ Z3b   ‡5–6ft (1.5–2m)

Lilium pyrenaicum

A relatively short, bulbous lily that produces up to 12 nodding, green-yellow or yellow, purple-flecked flowers per stem, in early to mid summer. Their petals are strongly curved back. The green stems are sometimes spotted with purple, and the lance-shaped, bright green leaves often have silver edges. Not a good lily for patio planting, since its scent is unpleasant.

CULTIVATION: *Grow in well-drained, neutral to alkaline soil with added leaf mold or well-rotted organic matter. Position in full sun or partial shade.*

☼ ◑ ◊ Z4   ‡12–39in (30–100c

Lilium regale

The regal lily is a robust, bulbous perennial with very fragrant, trumpet-shaped flowers opening during midsummer. They can be borne in clusters of up to 25 and are white, flushed with purple or purple brown on the outsides. The narrow leaves are numerous and glossy dark green. A bold statement in a mixed border. Suitable for growing in pots

CULTIVATION: *Grow in well-drained soil enriched with organic matter. Dislikes very alkaline conditions. Position in full sun or partial shade.*

☼ ◑ ◊ Z4   ‡2–6ft (0.6m–2

...nnanthes douglasii

...poached egg plant is an upright
...preading annual that produces
...ofusion of white-edged, yellow
...ers from summer to fall. The
...ly toothed, glossy, bright
...ow-green leaves are carried on
...der stems. Good for brightening
... rock garden or path edging.
...active to hoverflies, which help
...trol aphids.

TIVATION: *Grow in moist but well-*
...ned, fertile soil, in full sun. Sow seed
...oors during spring or fall. After
...ering, it self-seeds freely.

◊ Annual   ↕↔to 6in (15cm)

...monium sinuatum
...rever Gold'

...upright perennial bearing tightly
...ked clusters of bright yellow
...vers from summer to early fall.
...e stiff stems have narrow wings.
...st of the dark green leaves are
...anged in rosettes around the base
...he plant. Suitable for a sunny border
...n a gravel garden. The flowers dry
...l for indoor arrangements. Like
...ny other statice, this is usually
...wn as an annual.

TIVATION: *Grow in well-drained,*
...ferably sandy soil, in full sun.
...erates dry and stony conditions.

◊ Z8   ↕24in (60cm) ↔12in (30cm)

Liquidambar styraciflu[a] 'Worplesdon'

Sweetgum trees are often mistaken for maples because of their similar foliage and wonderful fall colors, which range from yellow to orange, purple, and crimson. 'Worplesdon' is one of the most reliable forms for its intense red, orange and yellow, deeply lobed fall leaves. These narrowly conical, deciduous trees also have attractive bark. Spiky globular seedpods are attractive on the tree but a maintenance issue when they drop in winter.

CULTIVATION: *Thrives in moist soil but adaptable to drier sites. Full sun.*

☀ ◊ ◑ Z6   ‡80ft (25m) ↔40ft (12

Liriodendron tulipifera

The stately tulip tree has a broadly columnar habit, spreading with age. The deciduous, squarish, lobed leaves are dark green, turning butter yellow in fall. Tulip-shaped, pale green flowers, tinged orange at the base, appear in summer and are followed by conelike fruits in fall. An excellent specimen tree for a large garden.

CULTIVATION: *Grow in moist but well-drained, moderately fertile, preferably slightly acidic soil. Choose a site in full sun or partial shade. Keep pruning of established specimens to a minimum.*

☀ ☼ ◊ ◑ Z5b
‡100ft (30m) ↔50ft (15m)

...riope muscari

...s stout, evergreen perennial
...ms dense clumps of dark green,
...aplike leaves. Spikes of small,
...et-purple flowers open in fall
...id the foliage and may be followed
...black berries. Good in a woodland
...der, or use as a drought-tolerant
...undcover for shady areas.

...TIVATION: *Grow in light, moist but
...-drained, moderately fertile soil.
...fers slightly acidic conditions. Position
...artial or full shade with shelter from
...d. Tolerates drought.*

☀ ◊ ◔ Z6
...in (30cm) ↔18in (45cm)

...thodora diffusa
'eavenly Blue'

...preading, evergreen shrub,
...netimes sold as *Lithospermum*
...avenly Blue', that grows flat
...ng the ground. Deep azure blue,
...nnel-shaped flowers are borne in
...ofusion over long periods from
...e spring into summer. The leaves
...e elliptic, dark green, and hairy.
...ow in an open position in a rock
...den or raised bed.

...TIVATION: *Grow in well-drained,
...anic, acidic soil, in full sun. Trim
...tly after flowering.*

◊ Z6
...n (15cm) ↔24in (60cm) or more

Lobelia cardinalis 'Queen Victoria'

This short-lived, clump-forming perennial bears almost luminous spikes of vivid red, two-lipped flowers from late summer to mid-fall. Both the leaves and stems are deep purple-red. Effective in a mixed border or waterside planting 'Bee's Flame' is a very similar plant enjoying the same conditions. Both are irresistible to hummingbirds.

CULTIVATION: *Grow in deep, reliably mo fertile soil, in full sun. Short-lived but cc be easily propagated by division in sprin*

☀ ◖ Z4　　　‡3ft (1m) ↔12in (30c

Lobelia 'Crystal Palace'

A compact, bushy perennial that is almost always grown as an annual, with vibrant clusters of two-lipped, dark blue flowers during summer to fall. The tiny leaves are dark green and bronzed. Useful for edging and for spilling over the edges of containers.

CULTIVATION: *Grow in deep, fertile soil c soil mix that is reliably moist, in full sur or partial shade. Plant out, after the risk of frost has passed, in spring.*

☀ ◐ ◖ Annual
‡to 4in (10cm) ↔4–6in (10–15cm)

Lonicera x *italica*

This vigorous, deciduous, woody-stemmed honeysuckle is a free-flowering, twining or scrambling climber. In summer and early fall, bears large whorls of tubular, very fragrant, soft flesh pink flowers, flushed red-purple with yellow insides; red berries follow later in the season. The leaves are oval and dark green. Train onto a wall or up into a small tree.

CULTIVATION: *Grow in moist but well-drained, fertile, organic soil, in full sun or partial shade. Once established, cut back shoots by up to one-third after they have flowered.*

☼ ◐ ◌ ◊ Z7　　　‡22ft (7m)

Lonicera nitida 'Baggesen's Gold'

This dense, evergreen shrub bearing tiny, oval, bright yellow leaves on arching stems. Inconspicuous yellow-green flowers are produced in spring, occasionally followed by small, blue-purple berries. Excellent for hedging or topiary in urban gardens, since it is pollution-tolerant.

CULTIVATION: *Grow in any well drained soil, in full sun or partial shade. Trim hedges at least 3 times a year, between spring and fall. Plants that become bare at the base will put out renewed growth if cut back hard.*

☼ ◊ Z7　　　↔5ft (1.5m)

Lonicera periclymenum 'Graham Thomas'

This long-flowering form of English honeysuckle is a woody, deciduous, twining climber bearing abundant, very fragrant, tubular white flower These mature to yellow over a long period in summer, without the red flecking seen on *L. periclymenum* 'Belgica'. The leaves are mid-green and oval in shape.

CULTIVATION: *Grow in moist but well-drained, fertile, organic soil. Thrives in full sun but prefers shade at the base. Once established, cut back shoots by up to one-third after flowering.*

☼ ◐ ◊ ◊ Z5 ‡22ft (7

Lonicera periclymenum 'Serotina'

The late Dutch honeysuckle is a fast-growing, deciduous, twining climber with very fragrant, rich red-purple flowers that appear in abundance during mid- and late summer. These may be followed by red berries. The leaves are oval and mid-green. If given plenty of space, it scrambles naturally with little pruning needed.

CULTIVATION: *Grow in well-drained but moist, organic, fertile soil, in sun with shade at the base. To keep trained specimens within bounds, prune shoots back by one-third after flowering.*

☼ ◐ ◊ ◊ Z5 ‡22ft (7

nicera sempervirens

is twining eastern North American
ive is semi-evergreen in warm
nates. Tubular flowers in coral,
, orange, or yellow attract
mmingbirds. Orange winter berries
ract songbirds. Drought tolerant.
table for a large container with
ellis, or cascading over an arbor
fence. 'Sulphurea' is a yellow-
wered variety.

LTIVATION: *Grow in full sun, average to
r soil, and do not fertilize. Prune in late
ter to promote flowering.*

☼ ◊ ◊ Z5　　　　　‹→to 15ft (5m)

nicera x *tellmanniana*

wining, deciduous, woody-stemmed
mber that bears clusters of coppery-
ange, tubular flowers that open
m late spring to midsummer.
e deep green, elliptic leaves have
e-white undersides. Train onto a
ll or fence or up into a large shrub.
mmer-flowering *L. tragophylla*
6-9) is one of its parents.

LTIVATION: *Grow in moist but well-
ained, fertile, organic soil. Will tolerate
l sun, but it produces better flowers in
nore shaded position. After flowering,
m shoots by one-third.*

☼ ◊ ◊ Z6　　　　　↕15ft (5m)

Lotus hirsutus

This is a silvery shrub with grayish green, very downy leaves. In summer and early fall, clusters of pink-flushed creamy white, pea-like flowers appear. These mature into reddish-brown seed pods. Good for a sheltered rock garden or Mediterranean-style border, where the shrub can be trimmed lightly in spring if required.

CULTIVATION: *Needs well-drained soil, in sun as it dislikes winter wet.*

☼ ◊ Z7   ↕to 24in (60cm) ↔to 3ft (1...

Lupinus arboreus

The tree lupine is a fast-growing, sprawling, semi-evergreen shrub grown for its spikes of fragrant, clear yellow flowers that open through the summer. The divided leaves are bright and gray-green. Native to scrub of coastal California, it is tolerant of seaside conditions.

CULTIVATION: *Grow in light or sandy, well drained, fairly fertile, slightly acidic soil, in full sun. Cut off seedheads to prevent self-seeding, and trim after flowering to keep compact.*

☼ ◊ Z8   ↕↔6ft (2...

ychnis chalcedonica

ltese cross is a clump-forming
rennial that produces slightly
ned, brilliant red flowerheads
early to midsummer. These are
rne on upright stems above the
al, mid-green, basal leaves. The
wers are small and cross-shaped.
od for a sunny border or wild
rden, but it needs some support.
self-seeds freely.

LTIVATION: *Grow in moist but well-
ined, fertile, organic soil, in full sun
ight dappled shade.*

☀ ◊ ◑ Z3b
–4ft (1–1.2m) ↔12in (30cm)

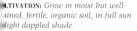

ycoris radiata

d spider lily, an Amaryllis family
ember, sends up leafless stalks
pped with red, spidery flowers
early fall. In mild climates,
rappy leaves follow and last till
ring, when it goes dormant. Grow
der trees, as fillers in borders.
cold climates, grow in pots and
nter in a frost-free area. Cut
wers last several days.

LTIVATION: *Grow in full sun to part
ade in average soil. Drought tolerant.
g and divide every three years.*

☀ ◊ ◑ Z8
8–24in (46–61cm) ↔6–12in(15–30cm)

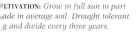

Lysichiton americanus

Yellow skunk cabbage is a striking, colorful perennial that flowers in early spring and is ideal for a waterside planting. Each dense spike of tiny, greenish-yellow flowers is hooded by a bright yellow spathe and has an unpleasant, slightly musky scent. The large, dark green leaves, 20–48in (50–120cm) long, emerge from the base of the plant.

CULTIVATION: *Grow in moist, fertile, organic soil. Position in full sun or partial shade, allowing plenty of room for the large leaves to develop.*

☀ ◑ ◊ Z6   ↕3ft (1m) ↔4ft (1.2

Lysichiton camtschatcensis

White skunk cabbage is a bold waterside perennial with a slightly musky scent. In early spring, dense spikes of tiny green flowers emerge, cloaked by pointed white spathes. The large, dark green leaves, up to 3ft (1m) long, grow from the base. Ideal beside a stream or a pond.

CULTIVATION: *Grow in moist, waterside conditions, in fertile, organic soil. Positio in full sun or partial shade, allowing roo for the leaves to develop.*

☀ ◑ ◊ Z4   ↕↔to 3ft (1r

ysimachia clethroides

is spreading, clump-forming,
rbaceous perennial is grown for
tapering spikes of tiny, star-shaped
ite flowers. These droop when in
d, straightening up as the flowers
en in mid- to late summer. The
rrow leaves are yellow-green
en young, maturing to mid-green
th pale undersides. Suitable for
turalizing in a wild woodland
bog garden.

LTIVATION: *Grow in reliably moist soil
at is rich in organic matter, in full sun
partial shade. May need staking.*

☼ ◐ Z3b   ‡3ft (1m) ↔24in (60cm)

ysimachia nummularia
urea'

olden creeping Jenny is a rampant,
rawling, evergreen perennial that
akes an excellent groundcover
ant. Its golden yellow leaves
e broadly oval in shape, with
eart-shaped bases. The bright
ellow, cup-shaped, summer flowers
rther enhance the foliage color.

ULTIVATION: *Grow in reliably moist soil
at is enriched with well-rotted organic
atter. Site in full sun or partial shade.*

☼ ◐ Z4   ‡2in (5cm) ↔indefinite

Macleaya x *kewensis* 'Kelway's Coral Plume'

A clump-forming perennial grown for its foliage and large, graceful plumes of tiny, coral-pink to deep buff flowers. These open from pink buds from early summer, appearing float above large, olive green leaves. Grow among shrubs, or group to form a hazy screen. *M. cordata*, with paler flowers, can be used similarly.

CULTIVATION: *Best in moist but well-drained, moderately fertile soil, in sun or light shade. Shelter from cold winds. May be invasive; chop away roots at the margins of the clump to confine.*

☼ ☀ ◊ ◊ Z4
‡7ft (2.2m) ↔3ft (1m) or more

Magnolia grandiflora 'Exmouth'

This hardy cultivar of the bull bay is a dense, evergreen tree bearing glossy dark green leaves with russet-haired undersides. *M. grandiflora* is quite distinct from other magnolias, since it blooms sporadically from late summer to fall, producing flowers that are large, very fragrant, cup-shaped and creamy white.

CULTIVATION: *Best in well-drained but moist, organic, acidic soil, in full sun or light shade. Tolerates dry, alkaline conditions. Mulch with leaf mold in spring. Keep pruning to a minimum.*

☼ ☀ ◊ ◊ Z8
‡20–60ft (6–18m) ↔to 50ft (15m)

Magnolia grandiflora 'Goliath'

This cultivar of bull bay is slightly less hardy than 'Exmouth' (see facing page, below) but has noticeably larger flowers, to 12in (30cm) across. It is a dense, conical, evergreen tree with slightly twisted, dark green leaves. The cup-shaped, very fragrant, creamy white flowers appear from late summer to fall.

CULTIVATION: *Best in well-drained but moist, organic, acidic soil, in full sun or light shade. Tolerates dry, alkaline conditions. Mulch with leaf mold in spring. Keep pruning to a minimum.*

☀ ◊ ◊ Z8
‡50–60ft (6–18m) ↔ to 50ft (15m)

Magnolia liliiflora 'Nigra'

A dense, summer-flowering shrub bearing goblet-shaped, deep purplered flowers. The deciduous leaves are elliptic and dark green. Plant as a specimen or among other shrubs and trees. Unlike many magnolias, it begins to flower when quite young.

CULTIVATION: *Grow in moist but well-drained, rich, acidic soil, in sun or semi-shade. Mulch in early spring. Prune young shrubs in midsummer to encourage a good shape; once mature, very little other pruning is needed.*

☀ ◊ ◊ Z5
‡10ft (3m) ↔8ft (2.5m)

Spring-flowering Magnolias

Spring-flowering magnolias are handsome deciduous trees and shrubs valued for their elegant habit and beautiful, often fragrant blooms which emerge just before the leaves. Flowers range from the tough but delicate-looking, star-shaped blooms of *M. stellata*, to the exotic, gobletlike blooms of hybrids such as 'Ricki'. Attractive red fruits form in fall. The architectural branch framework of the bare branches makes an interesting display for a winter garden, especially when grown as free-standing specimens. *M.* x *soulangeana* 'Rustica Rubra' can be trained against a wall.

CULTIVATION: *Best in deep, moist but well-drained, organic, neutral to acidic soil.* M. wilsonii *tolerates alkaline conditions. Choose a position in full sun or partial shade. After formative pruning when young, restrict pruning to the removal of dead or diseased branches after flowering.*

☀ ☀ ◊ ◖ Zones vary

‡30ft (10m) ↔25ft (8m)

‡50ft (15m) ↔30ft (10m)

‡↔30ft (10m)

‡30ft (10m) ↔20ft (6m)

1 *M.* x *loebneri* 'Merrill' (Z5) **2** *M. campbellii* 'Charles Raffill' (Z7)
3 *M. denudata* (Z5b) **4** *M.* 'Elizabeth' (Z6b)

‡12ft (4m)

6 ‡25ft (8m) ↔20ft (6m)

7 ‡30ft (10m) ↔15ft (5m)

9 ‡28ft (9m) ↔20ft (6m)

8 ‡20ft (6m)

10 ‡25ft (8m) ↔20ft (6m)

11 ‡10ft (3m) ↔12ft (4m)

M. 'Ricki' (Z5b) **6** M. x *loebneri* 'Leonard Messel' (Z5) **7** M. *salicifolia* 'Wada's Memory' (Z6) **8** M. x *soulangeana* 'Rustica Rubra' (Z5b) **9** M. x *kewensis* 'Wada's Memory' (Z6) **10** M. *wilsonii* (Z8) **11** M. *stellata* (Z5)

Mahonia aquifolium 'Apollo'

Oregon grape is a low-growing evergreen shrub with dark green leaves; these are divided into several spiny leaflets and turn brownish purple in winter. Dense clusters of deep golden flowers open in spring, followed by small, blue-black fruits. Can be grown as a groundcover.

CULTIVATION: *Grow in moist but well-drained, rich, fertile soil in semi-shade; tolerates sun if the soil remains moist. Every 2 years after flowering, shear groundcover plants close to the ground.*

☼ ◐ ◊ ◑ Z4b
↕24in (60cm) ↔4ft (1.2m)

Mahonia japonica

A dense, upright, winter-flowering, evergreen shrub bearing large, glossy dark green leaves divided into many spiny leaflets. Long, slender spikes of fragrant, soft yellow flower are borne from late fall into spring, followed by purple-blue fruits. Good i a shady border or woodland garden.

CULTIVATION: *Grow in well-drained but moist, moderately fertile, organic soil. Prefers shade but will tolerate sun if soil remains moist. Limit pruning to removal of dead wood, after flowering.*

☼ ◐ ◊ ◑ Z7   ↕6ft (2m) ↔10ft (3m

Mahonia x media 'Buckland'

A vigorous, upright, evergreen shrub bearing dense and sharply spiny, dark green foliage. Small, fragrant, bright yellow flowers are produced in arching spikes from late fall to early spring. A good vandal-resistant shrub for a boundary or front garden.

CULTIVATION: *Best in moist but well-drained, fairly fertile, organic soil. Thrives in semi-shade, but will become leggy in deep shade. Little pruning is needed, but overly long stems can be cut back to a framework after flowering. Minimum temperature 35°F (2°C).*

※ ◊ ◑ Tender ↕15ft (5m) ↔12ft (4m)

Mahonia x media 'Charity'

A fast-growing, evergreen shrub, very similar to 'Buckland' (above), but it has more upright, densely packed flower spikes. The dark green leaves are spiny, making it useful for barrier or vandalproof planting. Fragrant yellow flowers are borne from late fall to spring.

CULTIVATION: *Grow in moist but well-drained, moderately fertile, rich soil. Prefers partial shade, and will become leggy in deep shade. After flowering, bare, leggy stems can be pruned hard to promote strong growth from lower down. Minimum temperature 35°F (2°C).*

※ ◊ ◑ Tender ↕15ft (5m) ↔12ft (4m)

Malus floribunda

The Japanese crabapple is a dense, deciduous tree with a long season of interest. Graceful, arching branches bearing dark green foliage, flower during mid- to late spring to give a fine display of pale pink blossoms. The flowers are followed by small yellow crabapples; these often persist providing a valuable source of winter food for garden wildlife.

CULTIVATION: *Grow in moist but well-drained, moderately fertile soil, in sun or light shade. Prune to shape in the winter months when young; older specimens require little pruning.*

☼ ☀ ◊ ◖ Z5b   ↕↔30ft (10m)

Malus 'John Downie'

This vigorous, deciduous tree is upright when young, becoming conical with age. Large, cup-shaped white flowers, which open from pale pink buds in late spring, are followed by egg-shaped, orange and red crabapples. The oval leaves are bright green when young, maturing to dark green. An ideal small garden tree.

CULTIVATION: *Grow in well-drained but moist, fairly fertile soil. Flowers and fruits are best in full sun, but it tolerates some shade. Remove damaged or crossing shoots when dormant to form a well-spaced crown. Avoid hard pruning of established branches.*

☼ ☀ ◊ ◖ Z3   ↕30ft (10m) ↔20ft (6m)

alus tschonoskii

is upright, deciduous tree with
wept branches produces
k-flushed white blossoms in late
ing, followed in fall by red-flushed
low crabapples. The leaves turn
m green to a vibrant gold, then
-purple in fall. It is taller than
ny crabapples, but is still a
utiful specimen tree that can be
commodated in smaller gardens.

LTIVATION: *Grow in well-drained,
derately fertile soil. Best in full sun,
tolerates some shade. Forms a good
pe with little or no pruning; it does
respond well to hard pruning.*

☀ ◊ Z6   ↕40ft (12m) ↔22ft (7m)

alus x zumi
olden Hornet'

broadly pyramidal, deciduous tree
aring a profusion of large, cup-shaped,
nk-flushed white flowers that open
m deep pink buds in late spring. Small
llow crabapples follow and persist well
to winter. The display of golden fruit is
rther enhanced when the dark green
liage turns yellow in fall.

LTIVATION: *Grow in any but water-
gged soil, in full sun for best flowers
d fruit. To produce a well-spaced
own, remove damaged or crossing
oots on young plants when dormant.
not prune older specimens.*

☀ ◊ ◊ Z4b   ↕30ft (10m) ↔25ft (8m)

Malva moschata f. *alba*

This white to very light pink-flower musk mallow is a bushy, upright perennial suitable for wildflower gardens or borders. The very attractive and showy flowers are borne in clusters from early to late summer amid the slightly musk-scented, mid-green foliage.

CULTIVATION: *Grow in moist but well-drained, moderately fertile soil, in full sun. Taller plants may need staking. Often short-lived, but self-seeds readily.*

☼ ◊ Z4　‡3ft (1m) ↔24in (60cm)

Matteuccia struthiopteris

The ostrich fern forms clumps of upright or gently arching, pale green deciduous fronds. In summer, smaller dark brown fronds form at the center of each clump, which persist until late winter. An excellent foliage perennial for a damp, shady border and for woodland or waterside plantings.

CULTIVATION: *Grow in moist but well-drained, organic, neutral to acidic soil. Choose a site in light dappled shade.*

☼ ◊ ◊ Z3　‡3–5ft (1–1.5m) ↔18–30in (45–75cm)

Meconopsis betonicifolia

The Tibetan blue poppy is a clump-forming perennial bearing upright stems of large, saucer-shaped flowers that are clear blue or often purple-blue or white. These appear in early summer, above the oval and bluish-green leaves. Naturalizes well in a woodland garden.

CULTIVATION: *Best in moist but well-drained, rich, acid soil. Site in partial shade with shelter from cold winds. May be short-lived, especially in hot and dry conditions. Divide clumps after flowering to maintain vigor.*

◊ ◊ Z3   ‡4ft (1.2m) ↔18in (45cm)

Meconopsis grandis

The Himalayan blue poppy is an upright, clump-forming perennial, similar to *M. betonicifolia* (above), but with larger, less clustered, rich blue or purplish-red flowers. These are carried above the mid- to dark green foliage in early summer. Appealing when grown in large groups in a woodland setting.

CULTIVATION: *Grow in moist, leafy, acid soil. Position in partial shade with shelter from wind. Mulch generously and water in dry spells; may fail to flower if soil becomes too dry.*

◊ ◊ Z3   ‡4ft (1.2m) ↔24in (60cm)

Melianthus major

The honey bush is an excellent folia[ge]
shrub of upright to spreading habit.
From late spring to midsummer,
spikes of blood red flowers may
appear above the gray-green to brig[ht]
blue-green, divided leaves. In milde[r]
climates it is ideal for a coastal gard[en]
but will need winter protection.

CULTIVATION: *Grow in moist but well-
drained, fertile soil. Choose a sunny site
protected from wind and excessive winte[r]
moisture. Makes an attractive pot plant
if given a large enough container.
Minimum temperature 30°F (-1°C).*

☼ ◊ Tender
↕6–10ft (2–3m) ↔3–10ft (1–3m)

Metasequoia glyptostroboides

The dawn redwood is an elegant
deciduous conifer with a neat,
narrowly conical outline. The soft,
fern-like leaves, which are emerald
green when young, are set off
by the shaggy, cinnamon-brown
bark. The leaves turn a warm
russet gold before dropping in fall.
Wonderful large specimen tree,
particularly in a waterside site.
'Gold Rush' is a selection with
golden leaves.

CULTIVATION: *Thrives in full sun and
deep, moist soil; tolerates wet sites.*

☼ ☼ ◊ ● Z5b
↕70–130ft (20–40m) ↔15ft (5m)

Mimulus cardinalis

The scarlet monkey flower is a creeping perennial with tubular, scarlet, sometimes yellow-marked flowers. They appear throughout summer amid the oval, light green leaves, on hairy stems. Good for adding color to a warm border.

CULTIVATION: *Grow in any well-drained, fertile, organic soil; tolerates quite dry conditions. Position in sun or light dappled shade. May be short-lived, but easily propagated by division in spring.*

☀ ◊ Z7 ‡3ft (1m) ↔24in (60cm)

Miscanthus sinensis 'Flamingo'

This variety is one of the best of the miscanthus grasses, notable for its soft pink flowerheads that droop over the gracefully arching foliage from late summer. Miscanthus make good garden plants for sunny positions, either in large containers or in a border, where they will give structural interest well into winter. Cut back plants in early spring. May self sow in fertile soil.

CULTIVATION: *Best in moist but well-drained soil, in full sun.*

☀ ◊◊ Z4 ‡to 6ft (2m) ↔5ft (1.5m)

Molinia caerulea 'Variegata'

The purple moor grass is a tufted perennial forming clumps of cream-striped, narrow, dark green leaves. Dense, purple flowering spikes are produced over a long period from spring to fall on tall, ochre-tinted stems. A good structural plant for a border or a woodland garden.

CULTIVATION: *Grow in any moist but we drained, preferably acidic to neutral soil in full sun or partial shade.*

☼ ☀ ◊ Z4
↕to 24in (60cm) ↔16in (40cm)

Monarda 'Cambridge Scarlet'

This bee balm is a clump-forming perennial bearing shaggy heads of rich scarlet-red, tubular flowers fro midsummer to early fall. They appe in profusion above the aromatic leaves and are very attractive to bee hence the common name. A colorfu addition to any mixed or herbaceou border. 'Gardenview Scarlet' is equally bright and less mildew pron

CULTIVATION: *Prefers moist but well-drained, moderately fertile, organic soil, in full sun or light dappled shade. Keep moist in summer, but protect from excessive moisture in winter.*

☼ ☀ ◊ ◊ Z3b ↕3ft (1m) ↔18in (45cm)

onarda 'Croftway Pink'

lump-forming, herbaceous
ennial with shaggy heads of
ular pink flowers carried above
small, aromatic, light green
ves from midsummer to early fall.
ts mixed or herbaceous borders;
flowers attract bees. 'Beauty of
bham' (Z4-9) is similar, but with
uve outer bracts surrounding the
k flowers.

LTIVATION: *Grow in well-drained,*
ly fertile, organic soil that is reliably
ist in summer. Site in full sun or light
de, with protection from excessive
ter moisture.

☼ ◊ Z3b   ↕3ft (1m) ↔18in (45cm)

uscari armeniacum

vigorous, bulbous perennial that
ars dense spikes of tubular, rich
e flowers in early spring. The
d-green leaves are straplike and
gin to appear in fall. Plant massed
gether in borders or allow to spread
d naturalize in grass, although it
n be invasive.

LTIVATION: *Grow in moist but well-*
ained, fairly fertile soil, in full sun.
vide clumps of bulbs in summer.

◊ Z3   ↕8in (20cm) ↔2in (5cm)

Muscari aucheri

This bulbous perennial, less invasi
than *M. armeniacum* (see previous
page, bottom), bears dense spikes
of small, bright blue spring flowers
The flower spikes, often topped wi
paler blue flowers, are carried abov
the basal clumps of strap-shaped,
mid-green leaves. Suitable for a
rock garden. Sometimes known
as *M. tubergenianum*.

CULTIVATION: *Grow in moist but well-
drained, moderately fertile soil. Choose
a position in full sun.*

☼ ◊ Z4   ‡6in (15cm) ↔2in (5c

Myrtus communis

The common myrtle is a rounded
shrub with dense, evergreen foliage
From midsummer to early fall,
amid the small, glossy dark green,
aromatic leaves, it bears great
numbers of fragrant white flowers
with prominent tufts of stamens.
Purple-black berries appear later
in the season. Can be grown as
an informal hedge or a specimen
shrub. Where marginally hardy,
grow against a warm, sunny wall.

CULTIVATION: *Best in well-drained but
moist, fertile soil, in full sun. Protect
from cold, drying winds. Trim in spring,
tolerates close clipping.*

☼ ◊ Z8   ‡↔10ft (3r

...yrtus communis bsp. *tarentina*

...s dense, evergreen shrub is
...re compact and rounded than
... species (see facing page, below),
...h smaller leaves and pink-tinted
...am flowers. These appear during
...l-spring to early fall and are
...owed by white berries. Grow
...a border or as an informal hedge.

...TIVATION: *Grow in moist but well-
...ined, moderately fertile soil. Choose
...te in full sun with shelter from cold,
...ng winds. Trim back in spring;
...rates close clipping.*

◊ Z8   ↕↔5ft (1.5m)

...andina domestica

...avenly bamboo is an upright,
...ergreen or semi-evergreen shrub
...h fine spring and fall color.
...e divided leaves are red when
...ung, maturing to green, then
...shing red again in late fall.
...nical clusters of small white
...wers with yellow centers appear
... midsummer, followed by long-
...ting, bright red fruits.

...LTIVATION: *Grow in moist but well-
...ined soil, in full sun. Cut back on
...inting, then prune in mid-spring to
...ep the plant neat.*

◊ Z7   ↕6ft (2m) ↔5ft (1.5m)

Small Daffodils (*Narcissus*)

Small and miniature daffodils make good spring-flowering, bulbous perennials for both indoor and outdoor displays. They are cultivated for their elegant, mostly yellow or white flowers, of which there is great variety in shape. The blooms are carried either singly or in clusters above basal clumps of long, strap-shaped leaves on upright, leafless stems. All small daffodils are suitable for a rock garden, and they can look effective when massed together to form drifts. Because of their manageable size, these daffodil are useful for indoor displays. Some, such as *N. bulbocodium*, will naturali in short, fine grass.

CULTIVATION: *Best in well-drained, fertile soil that is moist during growth, preferab in sun. Feed with a balanced fertilizer aft flowering to encourage good flowers the following year. Deadhead as flowers fade, and allow the leaves to die down naturall do not tie them into bunches.*

☼ ◊ Z4

‡14in (35cm) ↔ 3in (8cm)

‡4–6in (10–15cm) ↔ 2–3in (5–8cm)

‡12in (30cm) ↔ 3in (8cm)

‡6–8in (15–20cm) ↔ 2–3in (5–8cm)

‡12in (30cm) ↔ 3in (8cm)

‡12in (30cm) ↔ 3in (8cm)

1 *N.* 'Avalanche' **2** *N. bulbocodium* **3** *N.* 'Charity May'
4 *N. cyclamineus* **5** *N.* 'Dove Wings' **6** *N.* 'February Gold'

(17cm) ↔ 2–3in (5–8cm)

8
↕ 8in (20cm) ↔ 3in (8cm)

(20cm) ↔ 3in (8cm)

10
↕ 7in (17cm) ↔ 2–3in (5–8cm)

11
↕ 4–6in (10–15cm) ↔ 2–3in (5–8cm)

in (15cm) ↔ 2–3in (5–8cm)

13
↕ 4–10in (10–25cm) ↔ 2–3in (5–8cm)

N. 'Hawera' **8** N. 'Jack Snipe' **9** N. 'Jetfire' **10** N. 'Jumblie'
N. minor **12** N. 'Tête-à-tête' **13** N. triandrus

Large Daffodils (*Narcissus*)

Large daffodils are tall, bulbous perennials, easily cultivated for their showy, mostly white or yellow flowers in spring. These are borne singly or in clusters on upright, leafless stems above long, strap-shaped, mid-green foliage arising from the bulb. A great diversity of elegant flower shapes is available, those illustrated all are excellent for cutting; 'Sweetness' has blooms that last particularly well when cut. Most look very effective flowering in large groups between shrubs or in a border. Some naturalize easily in gra or under deciduous trees and shrubs a woodland garden.

CULTIVATION: *Best in well-drained, fertile soil, preferably in full sun. Keep soil relia moist during the growing season, and fee with a balanced fertilizer after flowering to ensure good blooms the following year. Deadhead as flowers fade, and allow lea to die down naturally.*

☼ ◊ Z4

‡18in (45cm) ↔ 6in (15cm)

‡16in (40cm) ↔ 5in (12cm)

‡16in (40cm) ↔ 5in (12cm)

‡16in (40cm) ↔ 6in (15cm)

1 *N.* 'Actaea' **2** *N.* 'Empress of Ireland' **3** *N.* 'Ceylon' **4** *N.* 'Cheerfulness'

‡18in (40cm) ↔ 6in (15cm)

6
‡18in (45cm) ↔ 6in (15cm)

7
‡14in (35cm) ↔ 6in (15cm)

‡18in (45cm) ↔ 6in (15cm)

9
‡16in (40cm) ↔ 6in (15cm)

10
‡16in (40cm) ↔ 3in (8cm)

13
‡16in (40cm) ↔ 3in (8cm)

‡18in (45cm) ↔ 6in (15cm)

12
‡18in (45cm) ↔ 6in (15cm)

14
‡18in (45cm) ↔ 6in (15cm)

N. 'Ice Follies' **6** *N.* 'Kingscourt' **7** *N.* 'Merlin' **8** *N.* 'Mount Hood'
N. 'Passionale' **10** *N.* 'Suzy' **11** *N.* 'Saint Keverne' **12** *N.* 'Tahiti'
N. 'Sweetness' **14** *N.* 'Yellow Cheerfulness'

Nepeta racemosa

This catmint is a fairly low, spread
perennial with strongly aromatic,
grayish green foliage and spires of
vivid blue flowers through summe
It is a good, drought-tolerant plant
for the edge or middle of a sunny
border, or spilling over a low wall.
Cats, bees, and butterflies find the
plant irresistible. Shear in fall whe
the foliage is looking tired. 'Walker
Low' is a good compact variety.

CULTIVATION: *Grow in well-drained soi*
sun or partial shade.

☼ ◑ ◊ Z4
‡to 12in (30cm) ↔20in (50cm) or m

Nerine bowdenii

This robust perennial is one of the
best late-flowering bulbs. In fall, it
bears open sprays of five to ten
trumpet-shaped, faintly scented,
bright pink flowers with curled,
wavy-edged petals. The straplike,
fresh green leaves appear after the
flowers, at the base of the plant.
The flowers are good for cutting.

CULTIVATION: *Grow in well-drained soil,*
in a sunny, sheltered position. Provide
a deep, dry mulch in winter.

☼ ◊ Z8
‡18in (45cm) ↔5–6in (12–15cm)

...cotiana 'Lime Green'

...s striking flowering tobacco is
...pright, free-flowering, bushy
...ual, ideal for a summer border. It
...s loose clusters of night-scented,
...ow-green flowers, with long
...ats and flattened faces, from
... to late summer. The leaves are
...-green and oblong. Also good
...r patios, where the evening scent
... be appreciated. For mixed colors
...include lime green, the Domino
...es is recommended.

...TIVATION: *Grow in moist but well-
...ned, fertile soil. Choose a position
...ll sun or partial shade.*

❋ ◊ Annual
...in (60cm) ↔ 10in (25cm)

...gella 'Miss Jekyll'

...s tall, slender annual bears
...tty, sky blue flowers during
...mmer that are surrounded by
...athery "ruff" of bright green
...age. These are followed later
... the season by attractive, inflated
...d pods. The blooms last well
...en cut, and the seed pods can be
...ed for indoor flower arrangements.
...ere is a white version, also
...ommended: 'Miss Jekyll Alba'.

...TIVATION: *Grow in well-drained soil,
...ll sun. Like all love-in-a-mists, it self-
...ds freely, although seedlings may differ
... the parent.*

◊ Annual
... 18in (45cm) ↔ to 9in (23cm)

Waterlilies (*Nymphaea*)

These aquatic perennials are cultivated for their showy, sometimes fragrant summer flowers and rounded, floating leaves. The shade cast by the leaves is useful in reducing growth of pond algae. Flowers are mostly white, yellow, pink, or red with yellow stamens in the centers. Spread varies greatly, so choose carefully to match the size of your water feature. Planting depths may be between 18–30in (45cm–75cm), though 'Pygmaea Helvola' can grow in water no deeper than 6in (15cm).

Using aquatic planting containers makes lifting and dividing much eas

CULTIVATION: *Grow in still water in full s Plant in aquatic soil mix with rhizomes j below the surface, anchored with a layer gravel. Stand young plants on bricks so t shoot tips reach the water surface; lower plants as stems lengthen. Remove yellow leaves regularly. Divide in spring. Use ar aquatic fertilizer.*

☼ Z3 (hardy), Tender (tropical)

1 ↔ 4–5ft (1.2–1.5m) hardy
2 ↔ 5–8ft (1.5–2.5m) tropical
3 ↔ 3–4ft (1–1.2m) hardy
4 ↔ 3–4ft (1–1.2m) tropical
5 ↔ 4–5ft (1.2–1.5m) hardy
6 ↔ 10–16in (25–40cm) hardy

1 *Nymphaea* 'Escarboucle' **2** *N.* 'Gladstoniana' **3** *N.* 'Gonnère'
4 *N.* 'James Brydon' **5** *N.* 'Chromatella' **6** *N. tetragona* 'Helvola'

ssa sinensis

e Chinese tupelo is a deciduous
e, conical in form, grown for its
ely foliage. The elegant leaves are
nze when young, maturing to dark
en, then becoming brilliant shades
orange, red, and yellow in fall. The
wers are inconspicuous. Ideal as a
cimen tree near water.

TIVATION: *Grow in fertile, reliably
st but well-drained, neutral to acidic*
in sun or partial shade, with shelter
n cold, drying winds. Thin out
ded branches in late winter.

☼ ◐ ◊ Z8   ↕↔30ft (10m)

ssa sylvatica

aller tree than *N. sinensis* (above),
e black gum is similar in form,
h drooping lower branches. Its
rk green leaves change to a glorious
play of orange, yellow, or (usually)
in fall. A brilliant tree for fall
lor, with brownish-gray bark that
eaks up into large pieces on mature
ecimens. It tolerates acidic soil.

TIVATION: *Grow in moist but well-*
ined, fertile, neutral to acidic soil,
sun or partial shade. Shelter from
d, drying winds, and prune in late
nter, if necessary.

☼ ◐ ◊ Z5b
ft (20m) ↔30ft (10m)

Oenothera fruticosa 'Fyrverkeri'

An upright, clump-forming perenni
carrying clusters of short-lived, cup-
shaped, bright yellow flowers that
open in succession from late spring
to late summer. The lance-shaped
leaves are flushed red-purple when
young, contrasting beautifully with
the red stems. Nice with bronze- or
copper-leaved plants. *O. macrocarpa*
subsp. *glauca* (Z6) is quite similar,
with slightly paler flowers.

CULTIVATION: *Grow in sandy, well-
drained, fertile soil. Choose a site
in full sun.*

☼ ◊ Z3b
↕12–39in (30–100cm) ↔12in (30cm)

Oenothera macrocarpa

This vigorous perennial has flowers
similar to *O. fruticosa* 'Fyrverkeri'
(above), but its trailing habit makes
this plant more suitable for border
edging. The golden yellow blooms
appear from late spring to early
fall amid the lance-shaped, mid-
green leaves. Can also be used in
a scree bed or rock garden. Also
known as *O. missouriensis*.

CULTIVATION: *Grow in well-drained, poor
to moderately fertile soil. Position in full
sun in a site that is not prone to excessive
winter moisture.*

☼ ◊ Z4   ↕6in (15cm) ↔20in (50cr

earia macrodonta

ummer-flowering, evergreen
ub or small tree that forms an
right, broadly columnar habit.
ge clusters of fragrant, daisylike
ite flowers with reddish-brown
nters are borne amid the sharply
thed, glossy dark green leaves.
ood hedging plant or windbreak
coastal areas in mild climates.

LTIVATION: *Grow in well-drained, fertile
, in full sun with shelter from cold,
ing winds. Prune unwanted or cold-
naged growth in late spring. Minimum
perature 41°F (5°C).*

◊ Tender   ↕20ft (6m) ↔15ft (5m)

mphalodes cappadocica

is clump-forming, shade-loving,
ergreen perennial bears sprays
small, azure-blue, forget-me-not-
e flowers with white centers.
ese appear in early spring above
e pointed, mid-green leaves.
ective planted in groups through
woodland garden.

LTIVATION: *Grow in moist, organic,
derately fertile soil. Choose a site in
rtial shade.*

◊ Z6

o 10in (25cm) ↔to 16in (40cm)

Omphalodes cappadoci 'Cherry Ingram'

This clump-forming, evergreen perennial is very similar to the species (see previous page, bottom) but with larger, deep blue flowers that have white centers. These appear in early spring, above the pointed, finely hairy, mid-green leaves. Nice in a woodland garden.

CULTIVATION: *Best in reliably moist, moderately fertile, organic soil. Choose a site in partial shade.*

☀ ◊ Z6
↕to 10in (25cm) ↔to 16in (40cm)

Onoclea sensibilis

The sensitive fern forms a beautifully textured mass of arching, finely divided, broadly lance-shaped, deciduous fronds. The foliage is pinkish bronze in spring, maturing to pale green. Thrives at the edge of water or in a damp, shady border.

CULTIVATION: *Grow in moist, organic, preferably acidic soil. Site in partial shade, since fronds will scorch in sun.*

☀ ◊ ◊ Z3b   ↕24in (60cm) ↔indefini

hiopogon planiscapus grescens'

evergreen, spreading perennial
s clumps of grasslike, curving,
ost black leaves. It looks very
sual and effective when planted
ravel-covered soil. Spikes of
ll, tubular, white to lilac flowers
ear in summer, followed by round,
-black fruits in fall.

TIVATION: *Grow in moist but well-
ned, fertile, organic, slightly acidic
in full sun or partial shade. Top-dress
leaf mold in fall, where practical.*

❋ ◊ ◊ Z6
 (20cm) ↔12in (30cm)

iganum laevigatum

oody-based, bushy perennial
ring open clusters of small,
ular, purplish-pink flowers from
spring to fall. The oval, dark
en leaves are aromatic, powerfully
when crushed. Good in a rock
den or scree bed. The flowers are
active to bees.

TIVATION: *Grow in well-drained,
r to moderately fertile, preferably
aline soil. Position in full sun. Trim
k flowered stems in early spring.*

◊ Z6
‡24in (60cm) ↔18in (45cm)

Origanum laevigatum 'Herrenhausen'

A low-growing perennial that is hardier than the species (see prev page, bottom), with purple-flushed young leaves and denser whorls of pink flowers in summer. The mat foliage is dark green and aromatic Attractive in a Mediterranean-styl planting or rock garden.

CULTIVATION: *Grow in very well-draine poor to fairly fertile, preferably alkalin soil, in full sun. Trim back flowered st in early spring.*

☼ ◊ Z6   ↕↔18in (45

Origanum vulgare 'Aureum'

Golden marjoram is a colorful, bus perennial with tiny, golden yellow leaves that age to greenish yellow. Short spikes of tiny, pretty pink flowers are occasionally produced summer. The highly aromatic leave can be used in cooking. Good as a groundcover on a sunny bank or in an herb garden, although it tends to spread quickly.

CULTIVATION: *Grow in well-drained, po to moderately fertile, alkaline soil. Positi in full sun. Trim back after flowering t maintain a compact form.*

☼ ◊ Z5   ↕↔12in (30c

...manthus x *burkwoodii*

...nse and rounded, evergreen
...b, sometimes known as
...marea burkwoodii, carrying
..., slightly toothed, leathery, dark
...n leaves. Profuse clusters of
...ll, very fragrant white flowers,
...a long throats and flat faces, are
...e in spring. Ideal for a shrub
...er or as a hedge.

...TIVATION: *Grow in well-drained,*
...le soil, in sun or partial shade with
...er from cold, drying winds. Prune
...ape after flowering, giving hedges
...m in summer.

☼ ◊ Z7 ↔10ft (3m)

...manthus *heterophyllus*
...oshiki'

...s small, rounded shrub has much
...offer. The multicolored, holly-like
...ves are speckled in pink, coral,
...am, and yellow. Fragrant white
...vers bloom in fall. Grow as a low
...lge, specimen, or container plant.
...l excellent for hedging.

...TIVATION: *Tolerates sun or part shade,*
... does best with afternoon shade in
...rmer regions. Site in moist or dry,
...rage soil, with slightly acid to neutral
... Pest resistant.

☼ ◊ Z7 ↔4ft (1.2m)

Osmunda regalis

The royal fern is a stately, clump-forming perennial with bright gree finely divided foliage. Distinctive, rust-colored fronds are produced a the center of each clump in summe Excellent in a damp border or at th margins of a pond or stream. Ther an attractive version of this fern w crested fronds, 'Cristata', growing slightly less tall, to 4ft (1.2m).

CULTIVATION: *Grow in very moist, ferti organic soil, in semi-shade. Tolerates fu sun if soil is wet enough.*

☼ ☼ ◊ ◑ Z4   ‡6ft (2m) ↔12ft (4

Osteospermum jucundu

A neat, clump-forming, woody-base perennial bearing large, daisylike, mauve-pink flowers that are flushe bronze-purple on the undersides. The blooms open in succession fror late spring until fall. Ideal for wall crevices or at the front of a border. Also known as *O. barberae*. 'Blackthorn Seedling', with dark purple flowers, is a striking cultiva

CULTIVATION: *Best in light, well-drained, fairly fertile soil. Choose a site in full su Deadhead to prolong flowering. Minimu temperature 45°F (7°C).*

☼ ◊ Tender
‡4–20in (10–50cm) ↔20–39in (50–100cm)

teospermum Hybrids

se evergreen subshrubs are grown
marily for their daisylike, bright,
cheerful flowerheads, sometimes
n pinched petals or centers in
trasting colors. They are borne
gly or in open clusters over a long
son, which begins in late spring
ends in fall. Numerous cultivars
e been named, varying from deep
genta through to white, pink, or
ow. Osteospermums are ideal for
nny border, although the flowers
se in dull conditions. These are

grown as annuals in colder areas,
or in containers so that they can
easily be moved into a greenhouse
or conservatory during winter.

CULTIVATION: *Grow in light, moderately
fertile, well-drained soil in a warm,
sheltered site in full sun. Overwinter in
frost-free conditions. Regular deadheading
will encourage more flowers. Minimum
temperature 45°F (7°C).*

☼ ◊ Tender

‡24in (60cm)

2 ‡12in (30cm) ↔18in (45cm)

3 ‡↔24in (60cm)

‡18in (45cm)

5 ‡14in (35cm) ↔18in (45cm)

6 ‡↔24in (60cm)

Osteospermum 'Buttermilk' **2** *O.* 'Hopleys' **3** *O.* 'Pink Whirls'
O. 'Stardust' **5** *O.* 'Weetwood' **6** *O.* 'Whirligig'

Oxalis adenophylla

A bulbous perennial forming clum
of pretty, gray-green leaves that ar
divided into many heart-shaped
leaflets. In late spring, widely fun
shaped, purple-pink flowers contr
beautifully with the foliage. Native
to the Andes, it suits a well-draine
rock garden, trough, or raised bed.
Pink-flowered *O. enneaphylla* and
blue-flowered *O.* 'Ione Hecker' (Z9
are very similar, though they grow
from rhizomatous roots rather
than bulbs.

CULTIVATION: *Grow in any moderately
fertile soil with good drainage. Choose
a position in full sun.*

☼ ◊ Z5   ‡4in (10cm) ↔6in (15c

Pachysandra terminalis

This freely spreading, bushy,
evergreen foliage perennial makes
a very useful groundcover plant
for a shrub border or woodland
garden. The oval, glossy, dark gree
leaves are clustered at the tips of th
stems. Spikes of small white flower
are produced in early summer.
There is a less vigorous version
with white-edged leaves, 'Variegata
and a few selections, including
'Green Sheen', with glossier foliage.

CULTIVATION: *Grow in any but very
dry soil that is rich in organic matter,
in partial or full shade.*

☼ ◑ ◊ Z3   ‡8in (20cm) ↔indefin

eonia delavayi

upright, sparsely branched,
.duous shrub bearing nodding,
l-shaped, rich dark red flowers in
y summer. The dark green leaves
deeply cut into pointed lobes and
e blue-green undersides. A tall
peony, good in a shrub border.

TIVATION: *Grow in deep, moist*
well-drained, fertile, organic soil.
tion in full sun or partial shade
shelter from cold, drying winds.
occasionally cut an old, leggy
back to ground level in fall,
avoid regular or hard pruning.

☼ ◊ ◊ Z6   ‡6ft (2m) ↔4ft (1.2m)

eonia lactiflora
owl of Beauty'

erbaceous, clump-forming
rennial bearing very large, bowl-
ped flowers in late spring. These
ve carmine-pink, red-tinted petals
anged around a dense cluster of
amy white stamens. The leaves
mid-green and divided into
ny leaflets. Ideal for a mixed
herbaceous border.

TIVATION: *Grow in deep, moist but*
l-drained, fertile, organic soil, in full
or partial shade. Provide support.
sents being disturbed.

☼ ◊ ◊ Z2   ‡↔3ft (1m)

Paeonia lactiflora 'Sarah Bernhardt'

With its large, fragrant, fully doub[le] flowers, this peony is indispensab[le] in a herbaceous border. The flowe[rs] are light pink with ruffled, silver-margined inner petals and appear in early summer above the clumps of mid-green, deeply divided leave[s]

CULTIVATION: *Grow in moist but well-drained, deep, fertile, organic soil, in fu[ll] sun or semi-shade. Flowers may need support. Does not like to be disturbed once established.*

☀ ☀ ◊ ◊ Z2 ↔3ft (1[

Paeonia ludlowii

This vigorous, deciduous shrub has an upright and open form. In late spring, large, bright yellow, noddin[g] flowers open amid the bright green foliage. The leaves are deeply divid[ed] into several pointed leaflets. Good i[n] a shrub border or planted on its ow[n]

CULTIVATION: *Best in deep, well-drained but moist, fertile, organic soil. Site in sun or semi-shade with shelter from cold, drying winds. Avoid hard pruning, but occasionally cut old, leggy stems to ground level in fall.*

☀ ☀ ◊ ◊ Z6 ↔5ft (1.5[

Paeonia officinalis 'Rubra Plena'

This long-lived, clump-forming herbaceous peony makes a fine late-spring-flowering addition to any border display. The large, fully double, vivid crimson flowers, with ruffled, satiny petals, contrast well with the deep green, divided leaves. 'Rosea Plena', very similar, is also recommended.

CULTIVATION: Grow in well-drained but moist, deep, fertile, organic soil. Choose a site in full sun or partial shade. Support the flowering stems.

☼ ◐ ◊ ◊ Z2   ↕↔30in (75cm))

Panicum virgatum 'Shenandoah'

Native to prairie regions from Canada to Central America, switchgrass forms vase-shaped clumps. Its upright foliage is green in summer, turning red in late summer to fall, when it is topped by airy pink flowerheads. Plant in masses or as specimens in mixed borders.

CULTIVATION: Grows best in full sun and is adaptable to a wide range of soils, from dry to wet; it is drought tolerant and untroubled by pests and diseases. Cut back in late winter and divide as needed. May self sow in fertile soil..

☀ ☼ ◊ ◊ Z4   ↕↔3ft (1m)

Papaver orientale 'Beauty of Livermere'

This tall Oriental poppy with crimson-scarlet flowers is an upright, clump-forming perennial. The flowers open during late spring and develop into large seed pods. Each petal has a bold, black mark at the base. The mid-green, divided leaves are borne on upright, bristly stems. Looks spectacular in a border.

CULTIVATION: *Grow in well-drained, poor to moderately fertile soil. Choose a position in full sun.*

☼ ◊ Z3 ‡3–4ft (1–1.2m) ↔36in (90cm)

Papaver orientale 'Black and White'

This Oriental poppy, white-flowered with crimson-black markings at the petal bases, is a clump-forming perennial. The flowers are borne above the mid-green foliage at the tips of white-bristly, upright stems during late spring; they are followed by distinctive seed pods. Makes a good border perennial.

CULTIVATION: *Best in deep, moderately fertile soil with good drainage. Choose a position in full sun.*

☼ ◊ Z3
‡18–36in (45–90cm) ↔24–36in (60–90cm)

Papaver orientale 'Cedric Morris'

This Oriental poppy has very large, soft pink flowers with black-marked bases that are set off well against the gray-hairy foliage. It forms upright clumps that are well suited to a herbaceous or mixed border. Distinctive seed pods develop after the flowers have faded.

CULTIVATION: *Grow in deep, moderately fertile soil with good drainage. Choose a position in full sun.*

✷ ◊ Z3
‡18–36in (45–90cm) ↔24–36in (60–90cm)

Papaver rhoeas 'Shirley Mixed'

These field poppies are summer-flowering annuals with single, semi-double or double, bowl-shaped flowers in shades of yellow, orange, pink, and red. These appear on upright stems above the finely divided, bright green leaves. Can be naturalized in a wildflower meadow.

CULTIVATION: *Best in well-drained, poor to moderately fertile soil, in full sun. Divide and replant clumps in spring.*

✷ ◊ Annual ‡3ft (1m) ↔12in (30cm)

Parahebe perfoliata

Digger's speedwell is a spreading, evergreen perennial bearing short spikes of blue, saucer-shaped flowers in late summer. The blue- or gray-green, overlapping leaves are oval and slightly leathery. Suitable for gaps in walls or a rock garden with winter protection.

CULTIVATION: *Grow in poor to fairly fertile soil with good drainage, in full sun. Provide shelter from cold, drying winds. Minimum temperature 41°F (5°C).*

☼ ◊ Tender
↕24–30in (60–75cm) ↔18in (45cm)

Parrotia persica

Persian ironwood is a slow-growing, deciduous, often multitrunked tree with four-season interest. Small red flowers appear in spring before reddish purple leaves emerge and turn green, then yellow, orange, or crimson in fall. Peeling bark sparks winter interest. Excellent specimen or street tree. 'Horizontalis' is semi-weeping; 'Vanessa' is upright.

CULTIVATION: *Grow in full sun or dappled shade, in well-drained, slightly acidic soil. Drought tolerant once established and rarely troubled by pests.*

☼ ☼ ◊ Z6   ↕↔20–40ft (6–12m

Parthenocissus henryana

Chinese Virginia creeper is a woody, twining, deciduous climber with colorful foliage in fall. The insignificant summer flowers are usually followed by blue-black berries. The conspicuously white-veined leaves, made up of three to five leaflets, turn bright red late in the season. Train over a wall or a strongly built fence.

CULTIVATION: *Grow in well-drained but moist, fertile soil. Tolerates sun, but leaf color is best in deep or partial shade. Young plants may need some support. Prune back unwanted growth in fall.*

☀ ◊ ◊ Z8 ‡30ft (10m)

Parthenocissus tricuspidata

Even more vigorous than Virginia creeper (*P. quinquefolia* Z2b), Boston ivy is a woody, deciduous climber with foliage that turns a beautiful color in fall. The variably lobed, bright green leaves flush a brilliant red, fading to purple before they fall. It creates a strong textural effect on featureless walls.

CULTIVATION: *Best in moist but well-drained, fertile, organic soil. Position in partial or full shade. Young plants may need some support before they are established. Remove any unwanted growth in fall.*

☀ ◊ ◊ Z5b ‡70ft (20m)

Passiflora caerulea

The blue passionflower is a fast-growing, evergreen climber valued for its large, exotic flowers, crowned with prominent blue- and purple-banded filaments. These are borne from summer to fall amid the dark green, divided leaves. Where not hardy, grow in a cool greenhouse.

CULTIVATION: *Best in moist but well-drained, moderately fertile soil, in a sunny, sheltered site. Remove crowded growth in spring, cutting back flowered shoots at the end of the season.*

☼ ◊ ◑ Z7　　　‡30ft (10m) or mo

Passiflora caerulea 'Constance Elliott'

A fast-growing, evergreen climber, resembling the species (above), but with white flowers, borne from summer to fall. The leaves are dark green and deeply divided into three to nine lobes. Good for a pergola where dependably hardy, but it need the shelter of a cool greenhouse in colder areas.

CULTIVATION: *Grow in moist but well-drained, moderately fertile soil. Choose a sheltered site in full sun. Remove weak growth in spring, cutting back flowered shoots at the end of the season.*

☼ ◊ ◑ Z7　　　‡30ft (10m) or mo

...ssiflora racemosa

...e red passionflower is a vigorous
...mber noted for its large, bright
...d flowers borne in hanging clusters
... summer and fall. They are followed
... deep green fruits. The leathery
...ves are glossy and midgreen.
...ry eye-catching in a greenhouse
...conservatory.

...LTIVATION: *Grow in a greenhouse bed or
...ge container in soil-based potting mix.
...vide full light, with shade from hot sun.
...ter sparingly in winter. Prune in early
...ing. Minimum temperature 61°F (16°C)*

☀ ◊ ◊ Tender   ↕15ft (5m)

...atrinia scabiosifolia

...lden lace forms tidy mounds of
...ractive foliage. Its airy clusters
... tiny yellow flowers bloom on
...l stems above the foliage from
...e summer into fall. The slender
...wer stems may need support.

...LTIVATION: *Although it prefers full sun
...d well-drained, moist, humus-rich soil,
...s cold-hardy perennial tolerates dry
...l, as well as heat and humidity. It has
... serious insect or disease problems.*

◊ Z5   ↕to 3ft (1m) ↔to 1.5ft (50cm)

Scented-Leaved Geraniums

These geraniums, not to be confused with hardy geraniums (see pp.258–261), are tender, evergreen perennials. Many are grown specifically for their pretty, scented foliage. Their flowers, generally in pinks and mauves, are less showy and more delicate in form than those of the zonal and regal pelargoniums, bred more specifically for floral display. Leaf fragrance varies from sweet or spicy through to the citrus of *P. crispum* 'Variegatum' or the peppermint-like *P. tomentosum*.

They will perfume a greenhouse or conservatory, or use as summer edging along a path or in pots on a patio, where they will be brushed against and release their scent.

CULTIVATION: *Grow in well-drained, fertile, neutral to alkaline soil or soil mix. In cold areas, overwinter in frost-free conditions, cutting back topgrowth by one-third. Repot as growth resumes. Minimum temperature 35°F (2°C).*

☼ ◊ Tender

‡20in (50cm) ↔ 10–12in (25–30cm)

‡↔24in (60cm)

‡24–36in (60–90cm) ↔ 24in (60c

‡to 4ft (1.2m) ↔ 12in (30cm)

‡18in (45cm) ↔ 8–10in (20–25cm)

‡30–36in (35–45cm) ↔ 6in (15c

1 *Pelargonium* 'Attar of Roses' **2** *P.* 'Bolero' **3** *P.* 'Charity' **4** *P.* 'Citriodorum'
5 *P.* 'Copthorne' **6** *P. crispum* 'Variegatum'

7
4in (60cm) ↔ 12in (30cm)

8
↕↔ 24in (60cm)

9
↕ 12–16in (30–40cm) ↔ 8in (20cm)

0
↔ 24in (60cm)

11
↕ 12–14in (30–35cm) ↔ 6in (15cm)

12
↕ 36in (90cm) ↔ 12in (30cm)

13
↕ 12–14in (30–35cm) ↔ 10in (25cm)

14
↕ 24in (60cm) ↔ 12in (30cm)

5
↕ 2–16in (30–40cm) ↔ 12in (30cm)

16
↕ 18–20in (45–50cm) ↔ 10in (25cm)

17
↕ 30–36in (75–90cm) ↔ to 30in (75cm)

P. 'Gemstone' **8** *P.* 'Grace Thomas' **9** *P.* 'Lady Plymouth' **10** *P.* 'Lara Starshine'
5 *P.* 'Mabel Grey' **12** *P.* 'Nervous Mabel' **13** *P.* 'Orsett' **14** *P.* 'Peter's Luck'
5 *P.* 'Royal Oak' **16** *P.* 'Sweet Mimosa' **17** *P. tomentosum*

Flowering Geraniums

Geraniums grown for their bold flowers are tender, evergreen perennials: most cultivars are bushy, but there are also trailing types for windowboxes and hanging baskets. Flower forms vary from the tightly frilled 'Apple Blossom Rosebud' to the delicate, narrow-petaled 'Bird Dancer'; colors range from shades of orange through pink and red to rich purple, and some have colored foliage. A popular choice as bedding plants, flowering from spring into summer, although many will flower throughout the year if kept above 45°F (7°C), making them excellent for a conservatory and as houseplants.

CULTIVATION: *Grow in well-drained, fertile, neutral to alkaline soil or soil mix, in sun or partial shade. Deadhead regularly to prolong flowering. In cold areas, overwinter in frost-free conditions, cutting back by one third. Repot in late winter as new growth resumes. Minimum temperature 35°F (2°C).*

☼ ☀ ◊ Tender

1
‡10–12in (25–30cm) ↔ to 10in (25cm)

2
‡to 12in (30cm) ↔ 10in (25cm)

3
‡12–16in (30–40cm) ↔ 8–10in (20–25cm)

1 *Pelargonium* 'Alice Crousse' **2** *P.* AMETHYST 'Fisdel' **3** *P.* 'Apple Blossom Rosebud'

–8in (15–20cm) ↔ 6in (15cm)

‡10–12in (25–30cm) ↔ 6in (15cm)

‡18–24in (45–60cm) ↔ to 10in (25cm)

4–5in (10–12cm) ↔ 3–4in (7–10cm)

‡16–18in (40–45cm) ↔ 10in (25cm)

P. 'Bird Dancer' **5** *P.* 'Dolly Varden' **6** *P.* 'Flower of Spring'
P. 'Francis Parrett' **8** *P.* 'Happy Thought'

‡16–18in (40–45cm) ↔ to 12in (30cm)

‡10–12in (25–30cm) ↔ 5in (12cm)

‡to 12in (30cm) ↔ 12in (30cm)

‡16–18in (40–45cm) ↔ 8in (20cm)

‡to 24in (60cm) ↔ to 10in (25cm)

‡to 24in (60cm) ↔ 10in (25cm)

‡8in (20cm) ↔ 7in (18cm)

9 *Pelargonium* 'Irene' **10** *P.* 'Mr Henry Cox' **11** *P.* Multibloom Series
12 *P.* 'Paton's Unique' **13** *P.* 'The Boar' **14** *P.* 'Voodoo' **15** *P.* Video Series

egal (Martha Washington) Geraniums

ese bushy, half-hardy perennials and
rubs have gloriously showy, blowsy
wers, earning them the sobriquet
e queen of geraniums." Their main
wering period is from spring to early
mmer, with blooms carried in clusters
reds, pinks, purples, orange, white,
d reddish black; colors are combined
some cultivars. Often grown as
ntainer plants in cold-winter areas
th for indoor and outdoor display,
hough they may also be used in
mmer bedding designs.

CULTIVATION: *Best in good-quality, moist but
well-drained potting mix, in full light with
shade from strong sun. Water moderately
during growth, feeding every two weeks
with a liquid fertilizer. Water sparingly if
overwintering in a frost-free greenhouse. Cut
back by one-third and repot in late winter.
Outdoors, grow in fertile, neutral to alkaline,
well-drained soil in full sun. Deadhead
regularly. Minimum temperature 45°F (7°C).*

☼ ◊ ◐ Tender

 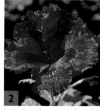 

3in (45cm) ↔ to 10in (25cm)   ‡18in (45cm) ↔ to 10in (25cm)   ‡18in (45cm) ↔ to 10in (25cm)

MORE CHOICES

Chew Magna' Pink
etals with a red blaze.
Leslie Judd' Salmon-
pink and wine-red.
'Lord Bute' Dark
reddish black flowers.
'Spellbound'
Pink with wine-red
petal markings.

‡12–16in (30–40cm) ↔ to 8in (20cm)   ‡12–16in (30–40cm) ↔ to 8in (20cm)

Pelargonium 'Ann Hoystead' **2** *P.* 'Bredon'
P. 'Carisbrooke' **4** *P.* 'Lavender Grand Slam' **5** *P.* 'Sefton'

Penstemons

Penstemons are elegant, semi-evergreen perennials valued for their spires of tubular, foxglovelike flowers, in white and shades of pink, red, and purple, held above lance-shaped leaves. Smaller penstemons, such as *P. newberryi*, are at home in a rock garden or as edging plants, while larger cultivars make reliable border perennials that flower throughout summer and into fall. 'Andenken an Friedrich Hahn' and 'Schoenholzeri' are among the hardiest cultivars, although most types benefit from a dry winter mulch where marginally hardy. Penstemons tend to be short-lived and are best replaced after a few seasons.

CULTIVATION: *Grow border plants in well-drained, organic soil, and dwarf cultivars in sharply drained, gritty, poor to moderately fertile soil. Choose a site in full sun or partial shade. Deadhead regularly to prolong the flowering season.*

☼ ☀ ◊ Zones vary

1 ‡4ft (1.2m) ↔18in (45cm) **2** ‡↔18–24in (45–60cm) **3** ‡30in (75cm) ↔24in (60cm)

1 *P.* 'Alice Hindley' (Z8) **2** *P.* 'Apple Blossom' (Z6) **3** *P.* 'Andenken an Friedrich Hahn' (syn. *P.* 'Garnet') (Z8)

1 ↕in (90cm) ↔ 30in (75cm)

5 ↕ 18–24in (45–60cm) ↔ 12in (30cm)

6 ↕in (25cm) ↔ 12in (30cm)

7 ↕ 36in (90cm) ↔ 24in (60cm)

8 ↕ 24in (60cm) ↔ 18in (45cm)

P. 'Chester Scarlet' (Z7) **5** *P.* 'Evelyn' (Z7) **6** *P. newberryi* (Z6) **7** *P.* 'Schoenholzeri'
(syn. *P.* 'Firebird', *P.* 'Ruby') (Z5) **8** *P.* 'White Bedder' (syn. *P.* 'Snowstorm') (Z7)

Perilla frutescens var. *crispa*

An upright, bushy annual grown for its frilly, pointed, deep purple to broze, almost iridescent foliage. Spikes of tiny white flowers appear in summer. The dark foliage makes a contrasting background to the bright flowers of summer bedding plants. Abundantly self-seeds.

CULTIVATION: *Grow in moist but well-drained, fertile soil. Position in sun or partial shade. Plant in spring after all danger of frost has passed.*

☼ ☀ ◊ ◊ Annual
‡to 3ft (1m) ↔to 12in (30cm)

Perovskia 'Blue Spire'

This upright, deciduous subshrub, grown for its foliage and flowers, suits a mixed or herbaceous border. Branching, airy spikes of tubular, violet-blue flowers are borne in profusion during late summer and early fall, above the silvery gray, divided leaves. Tolerates coastal conditions.

CULTIVATION: *Best in poor to moderately fertile soil that is well-drained. Tolerates alkaline soil. For vigorous, bushy growth prune back hard each spring to a low framework. Position in full sun.*

☼ ◊ Z5   ‡4ft (1.2m) ↔3ft (1r

rsicaria affinis
1perba'

igorous, evergreen perennial,
merly in the genus *Polygonum*,
: forms mats of lance-shaped,
p green leaves that turn rich
wn in fall. Dense spikes of
g-lasting, pale pink flowers,
ng to dark pink, are borne from
1summer to mid-fall. Plant in
ups at the front of a border or use
a groundcover. 'Darjeeling Red' is
iilar and equally good.

TIVATION: *Grow in any moist soil, in
sun or partial shade. Dig out invasive
s in spring or fall.*

☼ ◑ ◊ Z3
10in (25cm) ↔24in (60cm)

rsicaria amplexicaulis
iretail'

mp forming red bistort is a
uable border perennial, producing
wers from midsummer until the
t frosts in fall. The bright red
wers are individually, quite
all, but their effect is enhanced
ause they are densely clustered
apering spikes on tall stems
ve the mounded foliage. 'Alba'
s white flowers.

LTIVATION: *Best in moist soil, in full sun
partial shade.*

☼ ◑ ◊ Z4   ↕↔4ft (1.2m)

Persicaria bistorta 'Superba'

A fast-growing semi-evergreen perennial, formerly in the genus *Polygonum*, that makes a good groundcover. Dense, cylindrical, soft pink flowerheads are produced over long periods from early summer to mid-fall, above the clumps of mid-green foliage.

CULTIVATION: *Best in any well-drained, reliably moist soil, in full sun or partial shade. Tolerates dry soil.*

☼ ☀ ◊ ◊ Z3b
↕30in (75cm) ↔36in (90cm)

Persicaria vacciniifolia

This creeping, evergreen perennial, formerly in the genus *Polygonum*, bears glossy mid-green leaves that flush red in fall. In late summer and fall, spikes of deep pink flowers appear on branching, red-tinted stems. Suits a rock garden by water, or at the front of a border. Good as a groundcover.

CULTIVATION: *Grow in any moist soil, in full sun or semi-shade. Control spread by digging up invasive roots in spring or fall.*

☼ ☀ ◊ Z6
↕8in (20cm) ↔20in (50cm) or more

rorhagia saxifraga

creeping, wiry stems of the
c flower root to form mats of
s-like, rich green leaves that
studded throughout summer
many tiny, white or pink
ers. The plant thrives in
r soils and makes a good
nd cover or neat edging to
ny borders and rock gardens.

'IVATION: *Grow in any poor to*
erately fertile, well-drained soil, in sun.

Z5　　‡4in (10cm) ↔8in (20cm)

alaris arundinacea
cta'

deners' garters is an evergreen,
np-forming perennial grass
n narrow, white-striped leaves.
plumes of pale green flowers,
oming buff when mature, are
ne on upright stems during early to
-summer. Good as a groundcover,
t can be very invasive.

'IVATION: *Grow in any soil, in full*
or partial shade. Cut down all but
new young shoots in early summer to
urage fresh growth. To control spread,
nd divide regularly.

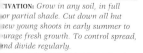

◖ ◖ Z3b　　‡3ft (1m) ↔indefinite

Philadelphus 'Beauclerk'

A slightly arching, deciduous shrub
valued for its clusters of fragrant,
large white flowers with slightly
pink-flushed centers. These are
borne in early and midsummer,
amid the broadly oval, dark green
leaves. Grow in a shrub border,
on its own, or as a screen.

CULTIVATION: *Grow in any well-drained,
moderately fertile soil. Tolerates shallow
alkaline soil and light shade, but flowers
are best in full sun. Cut back 1 in 4 stems
to the ground after flowering to stimulate
strong growth.*

☼ ☀ ◊ Z3   ↕↔8ft (2...)

Philadelphus 'Belle Etoile'

This arching, deciduous shrub is
similar to, but more compact than
'Beauclerk' (above). An abundance
of very fragrant, large white flowers
with bright yellow centers appears
during late spring to early summer.
The leaves are tapered and dark
green. Good in a mixed border.

CULTIVATION: *Grow in any moderately
fertile soil with good drainage. Flowers
best in full sun, but tolerates partial shade.
After flowering, cut 1 in 4 stems back to
the ground to stimulate strong new growth.*

☼ ☀ ◊ Z5   ↕4ft (1.2m) ↔8ft (2.5...)

Philadelphus coronarius 'Variegatus'

This upright, deciduous shrub has attractive, mid-green leaves that are heavily marked with white around the edges. Short clusters of very fragrant white flowers open in early summer. Use to brighten up the back of a mixed border or woodland garden, or on its own.

CULTIVATION: Grow in any fairly fertile soil with good drainage, in sun or semi-shade. For the best foliage, grow in light shade and prune in late spring. For the best flowers, grow in sun, cutting some stems to the ground after flowering.

☀ ◊ Z4　↕8ft (2.5m) ↔6ft (2m)

Philadelphus 'Manteau d'Hermine'

This deciduous shrub is low and spreading in habit, with long-lasting, double, very fragrant, creamy white flowers. These appear from early to midsummer amid the pale to mid-green, elliptic leaves. Good in a mixed border.

CULTIVATION: Grow in any well-drained, fairly fertile soil. Tolerates partial shade, but flowers are best in full sun. Cut back main stems to the ground after flowering, for strong new growth.

☀ ◊ Z4　↕3ft (1m) ↔5ft (1.5m)

Phlomis fruticosa

Jerusalem sage is a mound-forming spreading, evergreen shrub, carryir sagelike and aromatic, gray-green leaves with woolly undersides. Short spikes of hooded, dark golden yellow flowers appear from early to midsummer. Effective when massed in a border.

CULTIVATION: *Best in light, well-drained, poor to fairly fertile soil, in sun. Prune out any weak or leggy stems in spring.*

☼ ◊ Z8　　‡3ft (1m) ↔5ft (1.5r

Phlomis russeliana

An upright, evergreen border perennial, sometimes known as either *P. samia* or *P. viscosa*, bearing pointed, hairy, mid-green leaves. Spherical clusters of hooded, pale yellow flowers appear along the stems from late spring to fall.

CULTIVATION: *Grow in any well-drained, moderately fertile soil, in full sun or light shade. May self-seed.*

☼ ☀ ◊ Z5　　‡3ft (1m) ↔30in (75cm

Phlox divaricata 'Chattahoochee'

Short-lived, semi-evergreen border perennial bearing many flat-faced, long-throated, lavender-blue flowers with red eyes. These are produced over a long period from summer to early fall amid the lance-shaped leaves that are carried on purple-tinted stems.

CULTIVATION: *Grow in moist but well-drained, organic, fertile soil. Choose site in partial shade.*

◊ ◊ Z5　　‡6in (15cm) ↔12in (30cm)

Phlox douglasii 'Boothman's Variety'

Low and creeping, evergreen perennial that forms mounds of narrow, dark green leaves. Dark-eyed, violet-pink flowers with long throats and flat faces appear in late spring or early summer. Good in a rock garden or wall or as edging for raised beds.

CULTIVATION: *Grow in well-drained, fertile soil, in full sun. In areas with low rainfall, position in dappled shade.*

☀ ◊ Z5　　‡8in (20cm) ↔12in (30cm)

Phlox drummondii cultivars

The Greek name *Phlox* means "a flame," referring to the very bright colors of the blooms. *P. drummondii*, the annual phlox, is the parent of many named cultivars used primarily for bold summer bedding. They are upright to spreading, bushy annuals that bear bunched clusters of hairy purple, pink, red, lavender-blue, or white flowers in late spring. The flowers are often paler at the centers, with contrasting marks at the bases of the petal lobes. The stem-clasping leaves are mid-green.

Useful in rock gardens, herbaceous borders, flower beds, or in containers if raised in a greenhouse, they may come into bloom earlier.

CULTIVATION: *Grow in reliably moist but well-drained, sandy soil, in full sun. Enrich the soil with plenty of organic matter before planting and feed once a week with a dilute liquid fertilizer. Slugs and snails are attracted to young plants.*

☼ ◐ ◊ ◊ Annual

1 ‡4–18in (10–45cm) ↔10in (25cm)   2 ‡4–18in (10–45cm) ↔10in (25cm)   3 ‡4–18in (10–45cm) ↔10in (25cm)

4 ‡4–18in (10–45cm) ↔10in (25cm)   5 ‡4–18in (10–45cm) ↔10in (25cm)   6 ‡4–18in (10–45cm) ↔10in (25cm)

1 *Phlox drummondii* 'Beauty Mauve' **2** 'Beauty Pink' **3** 'Brilliancy Mixed'
4 'Brilliant' **5** 'Buttons Salmon with Eye' **6** 'Phlox of Sheep'

lox 'Kelly's Eye'

gorous, evergreen, mound-
ning perennial producing a
rful display of long-throated,
faced, pale pink flowers with
purple centers in late spring
early summer. The leaves are
green and narrow. Suitable
a rock garden or wall crevices.

TIVATION: *Grow in fertile soil that good drainage, in full sun. In low-fall areas, site in partial shade.*

☀ ◇ Z5b ↕↔8in (20cm)

lox maculata 'Alpha'

ultivar of meadow phlox with
, fat clusters of lilac-pink flowers
t appear above the foliage in the
t half of summer. It is an upright
baceous perennial with wiry
ms. Ideal in a moist border and a
d source of fragrant cut flowers.

TIVATION: *Grow in fertile, moist soil ull sun or partial shade. Remove spent vers to prolong flowering, and cut back he ground in fall. May need staking.*

☀ ◆ Z3b
36in (90cm) ↔18in (45cm)

Phlox paniculata **cultivars**

Cultivars of the so-called garden phlox, *P. paniculata*, are herbaceous plants bearing dome-shaped or conical clusters of flowers above lance-shaped, toothed, mid-green leaves. Appearing throughout summer and into fall, the flat-faced, long-throated, delicately fragranced flowers are white, pink, red, purple, or blue, often with contrasting centers; they are long-lasting when cut. Larger flowers can be encouraged by removing the weakest shoots in spring when the plant is still quite young.

All types are well suited to a herbaceous border; most cultivars ne staking, but others, such as 'Fujiyam have particularly sturdy stems.

CULTIVATION: *Grow in any reliably moist fertile soil. Choose a position in full sun partial shade. Feed with a balanced liqu fertilizer in spring and deadhead regular to prolong flowering. After flowering, cu back all foliage to ground level.*

☼ ☀ ◐ ◊ Z3

1 ‡4ft (1.2m) ↔ 24in (60cm) **2** ‡36in (90cm) ↔ 18in (45cm) **3** ‡4ft (1.2m) ↔ 24in (60cm)

4 ‡3¹/₂ft (1.1m) ↔ to 3ft (1m) **5** ‡3ft (1m) ↔ 18in (45cm) **6** ‡4ft (1.2m) ↔ 24–39in (60–100cm)

1 *Phlox paniculata* 'Brigadier' **2** 'Eventide' **3** *P. paniculata* 'Mount Fuji' (syn *P.* 'Fujiyama') **4** 'Le Mahdi' **5** 'Mother of Pearl' **6** 'Windsor'

lox stolonifera 'ue Ridge'

eping phlox, a perennial native
astern North America, creates
rresting swath of lavender-
flowers in spring. It spreads
ckly without becoming invasive.
as a bed edging or grow in a
dland garden. 'Bruce's White'
white flowers with a yellow eye.

TIVATION: *Grows best with part
appled shade in moist, acid, well-
ned soil.*

↕ Z4
10in (15–25cm) ↔ to 2ft (64cm)

lox subulata 'arjorie'

ss pink is a ground-hugging,
ni-evergreen perennial that
omes woody over time.
rjorie' has unusual hairy,
dlelike leaves and deep pink
ly spring flowers with darker
k lines radiating out from the
ters. Ideal for borders, along
edge of walls, and rock gardens.
ere are many other named forms.

TIVATION: *Grow in full sun in moist,
l-drained, and neutral to slightly
aline soil. Shear after flowering to
mote rebloom.*

↕ Z3 ↕6in (15cm) ↔ to 24in (60cm)

Phormium cookianum subsp. *hookeri* 'Cream Delight'

This mountain flax forms a clump of broad, arching leaves, to 5ft (1.5) long, each with broad vertical band of creamy yellow. Tall, upright clusters of tubular, yellow-green flowers appear in summer. An unusual plant, often used as a foca point. Good in a large container, and tolerant of coastal exposure.

CULTIVATION: *Grow in fertile, moist but well-drained soil, in full sun. Where marginal, provide a deep, dry winter mulch. Divide crowded clumps in sprin.*

☼ ◐ ◊ ◖ Z8   ↕6ft (2m) ↔10ft (3

Phormium cookianum subsp. *hookeri* 'Tricolor

This striking perennial, very usefu as a focal point in a border, forms arching clumps of broad, light gree leaves, to 5ft (1.5m) long; they are boldly margined with creamy yello and red stripes. Tall spikes of tubul yellow-green flowers are borne in summer. Where not hardy, grow in a container during the summer, and overwinter under glass.

CULTIVATION: *Grow in moist but well-drained soil, in sun. Provide a deep, dry winter mulch where marginal.*

☼ ◊ ◖ Z8
↕2–6ft (0.6–2m) ↔1–10ft (0.3–3m)

...ormium 'Sundowner'

...ump-forming, evergreen
...ennial valued for its form and
...iant coloring. It has broad,
...nze-green leaves, to 5ft (1.5m)
..., with creamy rose-pink
...rgins. In summer, tall, upright
...sters of tubular, yellow-green
...vers are borne, followed by
...orative seedheads that persist
...ough winter. A good choice for
...stal gardens.

...TIVATION: *Grow in any deep soil that
...s not dry out, but best in a warm, wet,
...tered site in full sun. Provide a deep
...ch in winter, and divide overcrowded
...mps in spring.*

 ◊ ◊ Z8   ↕↔to 6ft (2m)

...ormium tenax

...e New Zealand flax is an evergreen
...ennial that forms clumps of very
...g, tough leaves, to 10ft (3m) in
...gth in ideal conditions. They are
...k green above and blue-green
...neath. Dusky red flowers appear
...summer on very tall, thick, and
...right spikes. One of the largest
...ormiums—a striking plant with
...corative seedheads in winter.

...TIVATION: *Best in deep, reliably moist
...well-drained soil in a warm, sheltered
... in full sun. Mulch deeply for winter
...d divide overcrowded clumps in spring.*

 ◊ ◊ Z8   ↕12ft (4m) ↔6ft (2m)

Phormium tenax Purpureum Group

An evergreen perennial that forms clumps of long, stiff, sword-shaped deep copper to purple-red leaves. Large spikes of dark red, tubular flowers on blue-purple stems appear in summer. Ideal for coastal gardens. Can be container-grown, or choose the similar but much smaller 'Nanum Purpureum'.

CULTIVATION: *Grow in deep, fertile, organic soil that is reliably moist. Position in full sun with shelter from cold winds. Where marginal, provide a deep, dry mulch in winter.*

☼ ◊ Z8   ‡8ft (2.5m) ↔3ft (

Phormium 'Yellow Wave

An evergreen perennial forming clumps of broad, arching, yellow-green leaves with mid-green vertic stripes; they take on chartreuse tones in fall. Spikes of tubular red flowers emerge from the center of each leaf clump in summer. Especially good for seaside gardens it will add a point of interest to any border, especially in winter when it remains bold and attractive.

CULTIVATION: *Best in fertile, moist but well-drained soil, in full sun. Provide a deep, dry mulch for winter where marginal. Divide clumps in spring.*

☼ ◊ ◐ Z8   ‡10ft (3m) ↔6ft (2

Photinia x fraseri 'Red Robin'

upright, compact, evergreen
ub often grown as a formal or
mi-formal hedge for its bright
young foliage, the effect of
ich is prolonged by clipping.
e mature leaves are leathery,
ce-shaped, and dark green.
sters of small white flowers
ear in mid-spring. 'Robusta'
nother recommended cultivar.

TIVATION: *Grow in moist but well-*
ned, fertile soil, in full sun or semi-
de. Clip hedges 2 or 3 times a year
erpetuate the colorful foliage.

☀ ◐ ◑ Z8   ↕↔15ft (5m)

Photinia villosa

preading, shrubby tree grown
its foliage, flowers, and fruits.
t clusters of small white flowers
ear in late spring and develop
o attractive red fruits. The dark
en leaves are bronze when
ng, turning orange and red
fall before they fall. Attractive
year round, and tolerant of
rmanently damp soil.

TIVATION: *Grow in fertile, moist*
well-drained, neutral to acidic soil,
full sun or partial shade. Remove any
gested, damaged, or diseased growth
ate winter.

☀ ◐ ◑ Z5b   ↕↔15ft (5m)

Phygelius aequalis 'Yellow Trumpet'

An upright, evergreen shrub formi
loose spikes of hanging, tubular, pa
cream-yellow flowers during summ
The leaves are oval and pale green.
Good in a herbaceous or mixed
border; where margnally hardy,
provide protection against a warm,
sunny wall.

CULTIVATION: *Best in moist but well-
drained soil, in sun. Provide shelter fro.
wind and cut cold-damaged stems back
to the base in spring. Deadhead to prol
flowering. Dig up unwanted shoots to
contain spread.*

☀ ◊ ◖ Z8   ↕↔3ft (1

Phygelius capensis

The Cape figwort is an evergreen
shrub valued for its summer displa
of upright spikes of orange flowers.
The foliage is dark green, and the
plant may be mistaken for a novel-
colored fuchsia. Grow near the back
of a herbaceous border, against a
warm, sunny wall for protection.
Hummingbirds are attracted to this

CULTIVATION: *Grow in fertile, moist
but well-drained soil, in full sun with
shelter from cold, drying winds. Remove
spent flower clusters to encourage more
blooms, and provide a dry winter mulch
where marginally hardy. Cut back to the
ground in spring.*

☀ ◊ ◖ Z8   ↕4ft (1.2m) ↔5ft (1.5

Phygelius x *rectus* 'African Queen'

An upright, evergreen border shrub that bears long spikes of hanging, tubular, pale red flowers with orange to yellow mouths. These appear in summer above the oval, dark green leaves. Best against a warm wall where marginally hardy.

CULTIVATION: *Grow in moist but well-drained, fertile soil, in sun with shelter from cold, drying winds. Cut cold-damaged stems back to the base in spring. Deadhead to prolong flowering.*

✶ ◊ ◊ Z8   ↕3ft (1m) ↔4ft (1.2m)

Phygelius x *rectus* 'Devil's Tears'

An upright, evergreen shrub with dark green foliage. In summer, it carries spikes of hanging, red-pink flowers with yellow throats. A reasonably compact shrub with abundant flowers, ideal for a herbaceous or mixed border.

CULTIVATION: *Best in moist but well-drained, reasonably fertile soil, in full sun. Remove spent flower clusters to encourage further blooming, and cut the plant back to ground level in spring, if damaged over winter; otherwise, trim to shape.*

✶ ◊ ◊ Z8   ↕↔5ft (1.5 m)

Phygelius x rectus 'Salmon Leap'

This upright shrub is very similar to 'Devil's Tears' (see previous page), but with orange flowers that turn slightly back toward the stems. They appear in large sprays above the dark green foliage. Good in a mixed or herbaceous border.

CULTIVATION: *Grow in moist but well-drained, fertile soil, in full sun. Remove spent flower clusters to encourage more blooms. Cut the plant back to ground level in spring if damaged by winter weather; otherwise, trim to shape.*

☀ ◊ ◊ Z8   ‡4ft (1.2m) ↔5ft (1.5m)

Phyllostachys nigra

Black bamboo is an arching, clump-forming, evergreen shrub. The gentle, lance-shaped, dark green leaves are produced on slender green canes that turn black in their second or third year. Use as a screen or as a large feature plant.

CULTIVATION: *Grow in moist but well-drained soil, in sun or partial shade with shelter from cold winds. Mulch over winter. Cut out damaged and overcrowded canes in spring or early summer. Confine spread by burying a barrier around the roots.*

☀ ◐ ◊ ◊ Z7   ‡10–15ft (3–5m) ↔6–10ft (2–3m)

Phyllostachys nigra f. henonis

This clump-forming, evergreen bamboo is similar to the black bamboo in habit (see facing page, below), but it has bright green canes that mature to yellow-green in the second or third year. The lance-shaped, dark green leaves are downy and rough when young.

CULTIVATION: *Grow in well-drained but moist soil, in sun or semi-shade. Shelter from cold winds and mulch over winter. Thin crowded clumps in late spring. Bury a barrier around the roots to confine spread.*

☀ ◐ ◊ ◔ Z7
‡ 10–15ft (3–5m) ↔ 6–10ft (2–3m)

Physocarpus opulifolius 'Diabolo'

Eastern ninebark, so named for its peeling, multi-hued bark, is most famous for its deep purple, maplelike foliage, which turns bronze in fall. Clusters of white or pink flowers bloom in midsummer. Best as a specimen or as a contrast to pale flowered and silver-leaved plants in a border.

CULTIVATION: *It is cold hardy, adaptable, and drought tolerant, preferring well-drained, acidic soil, in full sun. It tolerates clay soil and part shade. Remove some of the oldest stems each year to promote vigorous new growth.*

☀ ◐ ◊ Z2b   ‡ ↔ 10ft (3m)

Physostegia virginiana 'Vivid'

An upright, densely clump-forming border perennial bearing spikes of bright purple-pink, hooded flowers from midsummer to early fall above the narrow, mid-green leaves. The flowers are good for cutting and will remain in a new position if they are moved on the stalks; because of this, it is known as the obedient plant. Looks good mixed with the white cultivar, 'Summer Snow'.

CULTIVATION: *Grow in reliably moist, fertile organic soil. Position in full sun or partial shade.*

☀ ◑ ◊ Z3b

↕12–24in (30–60cm) ↔12in (30cm)

Picea glauca var. *albertiana* 'Conica'

A conical, slow-growing, evergreen conifer with dense, blue-green foliage. The short, slender needles are borne on buff-white to ash-gray stems. Oval cones appear during summer, green at first, then maturing to brown. Makes an excellent neat specimen tree for a small garden.

CULTIVATION: *Grow in deep, moist but well-drained, preferably neutral to acidic soil, in full sun. Prune in winter if necessary, but keep to a minimum.*

☀ ◊ ◊ Z3

↕6–20ft (2–6m) ↔3–8ft (1–2.5m)

Picea mariana 'Nana'

...is dwarf, low-growing form of
...ck spruce is a mound-forming
...nifer with scaly, gray-brown
...k. The evergreen, bluish gray
...edles are short, soft, and slender.
...eful in a rock garden or conifer
...d or as an edging plant.

CULTIVATION: *Best in deep, moist but well-*
...ained, fertile, organic soil, in partial
...ade. Completely remove any shoots that
...ow vigorous upright growth as soon as
...y are seen.

◊ Z2b   ‡↔20in (50cm)

Picea pungens 'Koster'

...is conical evergreen conifer,
...th attractive horizontal branches,
...comes more columnar with age,
...d the young growth is clothed in
...very blue foliage. The long, sharp-
...inted needles turn greener as they
...ature. Cylindrical green cones are
...orne during the summer, aging to
...le brown. Good in large gardens as
...prominent specimen tree. 'Hoopsii'
...very similar with blue-white foliage
...d a more conical form.

CULTIVATION: *Grow in well-drained, fertile,*
...utral to acidic soil, in full sun. Prune
...late fall or winter if necessary, but keep
...a minimum.

◊ Z2   ‡50ft (15m) ↔15ft (5m)

Pieris 'Forest Flame'

An upright, evergreen shrub valued
for its slender, glossy, lance-shaped
leaves that are bright red when
young; they mature through pink
and creamy white to dark green.
Upright clusters of white flowers
enhance the effect in early to mid-
spring. Ideal for a shrub border or
a peaty, acidic soil; it will not thrive
in alkaline soil.

CULTIVATION: *Grow in moist but well-
drained, fertile, organic, acidic soil, in
full sun or partial shade. Shelter from
cold, drying winds. It can be trimmed
lightly after flowering.*

☼ ☀ ◊ ◊ Z5b   ‡12ft (4m) ↔6ft (2:

Pieris formosa var. *forrestii* 'Wakehurst'

This upright, evergreen, acidic-soil-
loving shrub has brilliant red young
foliage that matures to dark green.
The large, slightly drooping clusters
of small, fragrant white flowers from
mid-spring are also attractive. Grow
in a woodland garden or shrub borde
'Jermyns' is very similar, with darke
red young leaves.

CULTIVATION: *Best in well-drained but
moist, fertile, organic, acidic soil. Site
in full sun or partial shade with shelter
from cold winds. It can be trimmed
lightly after flowering.*

☼ ☀ ◊ ◊ Z8   ‡15ft (5m) ↔12ft (4m

...eris japonica 'Blush'

...ounded, evergreen shrub that
...rs small, pink-flushed white
...wers in late winter and early
...ing. These are carried in long,
...ooping clusters amid the glossy
...k green foliage. A good early-
...wering border shrub.

...LTIVATION: *Grow in well-drained but
...ist, fertile, organic, acidic soil. Site
...full sun or partial shade. Trim lightly
...er flowering, removing any dead,
...maged or diseased shoots.*

☀ ◑ ◊ ◊ Z5b ‡12ft (4m) ↔10ft (3m)

...leostegia viburnoides

...slow-growing, woody, evergreen
...mber that is dusted with feathery
...sters of tiny, creamy white flowers
...late summer and fall. The glossy
...rk green, leathery leaves look very
...ractive against a large tree trunk
...shady wall.

...LTIVATION: *Grow in well-drained, fertile
...l, in full sun or shade. Shorten stems
...er flowering as the plant begins to
...tgrow the allotted space.*

☀ ◊ Z7 ‡20ft (6m)

Pinus mugo 'Mops'

This dwarf pine is an almost spheric
conifer with scaly, gray bark and thi
upright branches. The shoots are
covered with long, well-spaced, dark
bright green needles. The dark brow
oval cones take a few years to ripen.
Effective in a large rock garden or,
where space allows, planted in group

CULTIVATION: *Grow in any well-drained*
soil, in full sun. Very little pruning is
required since growth is slow.

☀ ◊ Z2b   ‡to 3ft (1m) ↔to 6ft (2

Pinus sylvestris
Aurea Group

Unlike most Scotch pine trees, pine
in this group grow slowly, making
them suited to smaller gardens,
particularly when winter turns the
blue-green, evergreen pine needles
golden yellow in response to cold
weather. Pine trees tolerate a range
conditions, including coastal sites a
drought. Resist pruning and allow th
tree to develop its shape naturally.

CULTIVATION: *Grow in well-drained soil,*
in sun.

☀ ◊ ◊ Z2   ‡30ft (10m) ↔15ft (5

Pittosporum tenuifolium

columnar, evergreen shrub, much
[va]lued for its glossy green leaves with
[w]avy edges. Fast growing at first, it
[th]en broadens out into a tree. Tiny,
[h]oney-scented, purple-black, bell-
[s]haped flowers open from late spring.
[M]akes a good hedge. There is a gold-
[le]aved version, 'Warnham Gold'.

CULTIVATION: *Grow in well-drained but
[m]oist, fertile soil, in full sun or partial
[s]hade. Provide shelter from cold winds.
[T]rim to shape in spring; avoid pruning
[af]ter midsummer.*

☼ ☀ ◊ ◗ Z8
12–30ft (4–10m) ↔ 6–15ft (2–5m)

Pittosporum tenuifolium
'Tom Thumb'

[A] compact, rounded, evergreen
[f]oliage shrub that would suit a mixed
[b]order designed for year-round
[i]nterest. The glossy bronze-purple
[le]aves are elliptic and wavy-edged.
[T]iny, honey-scented, purple flowers
[a]re borne in late spring and early
[s]ummer. Shelter against a warm wall
[w]here marginally hardy.

CULTIVATION: *Grow in well-drained but
[m]oist, fertile soil, in full sun for best color.
[P]rovide shelter from cold winds. Trim to
[s]hape in spring; established plants need
[li]ttle pruning.*

☼ ☀ ◊ ◗ Z8   ↕ 3ft (1m) ↔ 24in (60cm)

Platycodon grandiflorus

The balloon flower is a clump-forming perennial producing cluster of large purple to violet-blue flowers that open from balloon-shaped buds in late summer, above bluish green, oval leaves. For a rock garden or herbaceous border. 'Apoyama', with deep-colored flowers, and 'Mariesii' are recommended cultivars.

CULTIVATION: *Best in deep, well-drained, fertile soil that does not dry out, in full sun or partial shade. Flower stems may need staking. Established plants dislike root disturbance.*

☼ ◑ ◊ Z3b
‡to 24in (60cm) ↔12in (30cm)

Pleioblastus variegatus

This upright, evergreen bamboo is much shorter than *P. viridistriatus* (see facing page, above), with cream- and green-striped foliage. The lance-shaped leaves, borne on hollow, pale green canes, are covered in fine white hairs. Suits a sunny border backed by shrubs, and where it has space to spread; it will swamp less vigorous neighbors unless confined.

CULTIVATION: *Grow in moist but well-drained, fertile, organic soil, in sun with shelter from cold winds. Thin out clumps in late spring. Bury a barrier around the roots to confine spread.*

☼ ◊ ◑ Z8   ‡30in (75cm) ↔4ft (1.2m

Pleioblastus viridistriatus

This upright bamboo is an evergreen shrub grown for its brilliant green, yellow-striped foliage. The bristly-edged, lance-shaped leaves are carried on purple-green canes. Effective in an open glade in a woodland garden. Good in sun, backed by trees or tall shrubs.

CULTIVATION: *Grow in moist but well-drained, fertile, organic soil, in full sun for best leaf color. Provide shelter from cold, drying winds. Thin over-crowded clumps in late spring or early summer. Confine spread by burying a barrier around the roots.*

☼ ◊ ◊ Z8   ↕↔to 5ft (1.5m)

Plumbago auriculata

Cape leadwort is a scrambling, semi-evergreen, frost-tender shrub often trained as a climber. It bears dense trusses of long-throated, sky blue flowers from summer to late fall, amid the oval leaves. Plants overwintered under glass can be moved outside in summer. Often sold as *P. capensis*.

CULTIVATION: *Grow in well-drained, fertile soil or soil mix, in full sun or light shade. Pinch out the tips of young plants to promote bushiness, and tie climbing stems to a support. Cut back to a permanent framework in early spring. Minimum temperature 36°F (2°C).*

☼ ◊ ◊ Tender
10–20ft (3–6m) ↔3–10ft (1–3m)

Polemonium **'Lambrook Mauve'**

This clump-forming perennial, a garden variety of Jacob's ladder, forms rounded mounds of neat, divided, mid-green leaves. An abundance of funnel-shaped, sky blue flowers cover the foliage from late spring to early summer. Good in any border or in a wild garden.

CULTIVATION: *Grow in well-drained but moist, moderately fertile soil, in full sun or partial shade. Deadhead regularly.*

☼ ◑ ◊ ◊ Z3b   ↕↔18in (45cm)

Polygonatum x *hybridum*

Solomon's seal is a perennial for a shady border, bearing hanging clusters of tubular, small white flowers with green mouths, along slightly arching stems. These appear in late spring among elliptic, bright green leaves. Round blue-black fruits develop after the flowers. For a woodland garden. *P.* x *odoratum* 'Flore Pleno' is a very similar but smaller plant.

CULTIVATION: *Grow in moist but well-drained, fertile organic soil. Position in partial or full shade.*

☼ ◑ ◊ ◊ Z4
↕to 5ft (1.5m) ↔12in (30cm)

Polystichum acrostichoides

This attractive, glossy fern, native to eastern North America, earned the common name Christmas fern because its fronds stay green through the winter holidays. In spring, silvery fiddleheads emerge. Use this clump-former as a groundcover or edging, or naturalize in a woodland setting.

CULTIVATION: *Plant in full to part shade, in cool, moist, humus-rich, well-drained soil. The fronds lie flat on the ground in winter. It spreads by rhizomes. Propagate by root division.*

☀ ◗ Z4   ↕↔1–3ft (0.3–1m)

Polystichum aculeatum

The prickly shield fern is an elegant, evergreen perennial producing a shuttlecock of finely divided, dark green fronds. An excellent foliage plant for shady areas in a rock garden or well-drained border.

CULTIVATION: *Grow in fertile soil that has good drainage, in partial or deep shade. Choose a site sheltered from excessive winter moisture. Remove the previous year's dead fronds before the new growth unfurls in spring.*

☀ ◗ Z3b   ↕24in (60cm) ↔3ft (1m)

Potentilla fruticosa

Cultivars of *P. fruticosa* are compact and rounded, deciduous shrubs that produce an abundance of flowers over a long period from late spring to midfall. The leaves are dark green and composed of several oblong leaflets. Flowers are saucer-shaped and wildroselike, sometimes borne singly, but often in clusters of three. Most cultivars are yellow-flowered, but blooms may also be white, as with 'Abbotswood', or flushed with pink, as in 'Daydawn'. These are undemanding shrubs that make invaluable additions to mixed or shrub borders; they can also be grown as attractive low hedges.

CULTIVATION: *Grow in well-drained, poor to moderately fertile soil. Best in full sun, but many tolerate partial shade. Trim lightly after flowering, cutting older wood to the base and removing weak, twiggy growth. Old shrubs sometimes respond well to renovation, but may be better replaced.*

☼ ◊ Z2b

‡30in (75cm) ↔ 4ft (1.2m)

‡3ft (1m) ↔ 5ft (1.5m)

‡3ft (1m) ↔ 4ft (1.2m)

‡3ft (1m) ↔ 5ft (1.5m)

1 *P. fruticosa* 'Abbotswood' **2** *P. fruticosa* 'Elizabeth'
3 *P. fruticosa* 'Daydawn' **4** *P. fruticosa* 'Primrose Beauty'

Potentilla 'Gibson's Scarlet'

A dense, clump-forming herbaceous perennial grown for its very bright scarlet flowers, borne in succession throughout summer. The soft green leaves are divided into five leaflets. Good for a rock garden or for a bold summer color in a mixed herbaceous border. 'William Rollisson' is a similar plant, with more orange-red, semidouble flowers.

CULTIVATION: *Grow in well-drained, poor to moderately fertile soil. Choose a position in full sun.*

◊ Z3b   ↕18in (45cm) ↔24in (60cm)

Potentilla megalantha

A compact, clump-forming perennial bearing a profusion of upright, cup-shaped, rich yellow flowers during mid- to late summer. The slightly hairy, mid-green leaves are divided into three coarsely scalloped leaflets. Good for the front of a border.

CULTIVATION: *Grow in poor to fairly fertile soil that has good drainage. Choose a position in full sun.*

◊ Z4   ↕6–12in (15–30cm) ↔6in (15cm)

Potentilla nepalensis 'Miss Wilmott'

A summer-flowering perennial that forms clumps of mid-green, divided leaves on wiry, red-tinged stems. The small pink flowers, with cherry red centers, are borne in loose clusters. Good for the front of a border or in cottage-style plantings.

CULTIVATION: *Grow in any well-drained, poor to moderately fertile soil. Position in full sun or light dappled shade.*

☼ ☼ ◊ Z5
‡12–18in (30–45cm) ↔24in (60cm)

Primula denticulata

The drumstick primrose is a robust, clump-forming perennial bearing spherical clusters of small purple flowers with yellow centers. They are carried on thick, upright stalks from spring to summer, above the basal rosettes of oblong to spoon-shaped, mid-green leaves. Thrives in damp, but not waterlogged, soil; ideal for a waterside planting.

CULTIVATION: *Best in moist, organic, neutral to acidic or peaty soil. Choose a site in partial shade, but tolerates full sun where soil is reliably damp.*

☼ ☼ ◊ Z2   ‡↔18in (45cm

imula elatior

e oxlip is a semi-evergreen
ennial wildflower that can
y in appearance. Clusters
ubular yellow flowers emerge
m the basal rosettes of scalloped,
l-green leaves on stiff, upright
ns in spring and summer.
nt in groups to naturalize
moist meadow.

TIVATION: *Grow in moderately fertile,*
?, moist but well-drained soil. Site in
ial shade, but full sun is tolerated as
g as the soil remains moist at all times.

☼ ◊ ◊ Z4　　　　　$\leftrightarrow$12in (30cm)

imula flaccida

osette-forming, deciduous
ennial for an open woodland
den or alpine house. In summer,
. flowering stems bear conical
sters of funnel-shaped and
wnward-pointing, floury,
ender-blue flowers, carried
ve the pale to mid-green leaves.

TIVATION: *Grow in deep or partial*
de in peaty, gritty, moist but sharply
ined, acidic soil. Protect from excessive
ter moisture.

☼ ◊ ◊ Z5
in (50cm) $\leftrightarrow$12in (30cm)

Primula florindae

The giant cowslip is a deciduous, summer-flowering perennial that grows naturally by pools and strea It forms clumps of oval, toothed, mid-green leaves that are arranged in rosettes at the base of the plant. Drooping clusters of up to 40 funnel-shaped, sweetly scented yellow flowers are borne well abov the foliage on upright stems. Good in a bog garden or waterside settin

CULTIVATION: *Grow in deep, reliably mo organic soil, in partial shade. Tolerates full sun if soil remains moist.*

☼ ☀ ◊ Z3   ↕4ft (1.2m) ↔3ft (

Primula frondosa

This deciduous border perennial, with its rosettes of spoon-shaped, mid-green leaves, carries yellow-eyed, pink to purple flowers in late spring or early summer. They are carried in loose clusters of up to 30 at the top of upright stems, and eac has a pale yellow eye at its center.

CULTIVATION: *Best in deep, moist, neutr to acidic loam or peaty soil enriched wi organic matter. Site ideally in partial shade, but it tolerates full sun if the soil is reliably moist.*

☼ ☀ ◊ Z3b
↕6in (15cm) ↔10in (25cm)

...mula
...d-Laced Group

...oup of semi-evergreen
...mroses grown for their showy
...ng flowers in the border or in
...ainers. Clusters of golden-eyed,
... dark mahogany-red or black
...ers, with a thin gold margin
...nd each petal, are carried atop
...ght flowering stems above the
...etimes reddish foliage.

...IVATION: *Grow in moist, deep,*
...ral to acidic loam or peaty soil
...s rich in organic matter. Choose
... in partial shade, or in full sun
... soil is reliably moist.*

☼ ◊ Z6   ↕↔12in (30cm)

...mula 'Guinevere'

...st-growing, evergreen, clump-
...ning perennial, sometimes called
...ryarde Guinevere', that bears
...ters of pale purplish-pink flowers.
...y have yellow centers, flat faces,
... long throats and are carried
...e the deep bronze, oval leaves
...pring. Suits damp, shady places.

...IVATION: *Grow in moist, neutral to*
...c soil that is well-drained, in partial
...e. Tolerates full sun, but only if the
...emains always damp.*

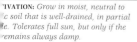

... ◊ Z5   ↕5in (12cm) ↔10in (25cm)

Polyanthus Primroses (*Primula*)

Garden polyanthus are rosette-forming, evergreen perennials with a complex parentage, which probably includes *P. veris* (see p.451) and *P. elatior* (see p.445). The plants form sturdy, basal rosettes of oval, heavily veined leaves, overshadowed by the colorful clusters of flat-faced flowers from late winter to early spring. A splendid array of primary and pastel colors is available, mostly red, blue-violet, orange, yellow, white, or pink, with yellow centers. Groups such as the Crescendo and Rainbow series are among the most easily grown bedding and container plants, brightening up gardens, patios, and windowsills in winter.

CULTIVATION: *Grow in moderately fertile, moist but well-drained, organic soil or soil-based mix in a cool site in full sun or partial shade. Sow seed in summer, and plant out in fall in well-prepared soil. Divide large clumps in fall.*

☼ ☀ ◐ ◊ ◑ Z4

‡6in (15cm) ↔12in (30cm)

‡6in (15cm) ↔12in (30cm)

‡6in (15cm) ↔12in (30cm)

‡6in (15cm) ↔12in (30cm)

1 *Primula* 'Crescendo Bright Red' **2** *P.* 'Crescendo Pink and Rose Shades'
3 *P.* 'Rainbow Blue Shades' **4** *P.* 'Rainbow Cream Shades'

Primula kewensis

...rimrose for a windowsill,
...enhouse, or conservatory, this
...n evergreen perennial that
...ms rosettes of noticeably toothed,
...htly floury, mid-green leaves.
...ives an early spring display of
...grant yellow flowers in whorls
...g upright flowering stems.

...TIVATION: *In a container, grow in
...-based potting mix with added grit or
...t. As a houseplant, choose a site with
...ght filtered light. Minimum temperature
...F (2°C).*

☀ ◊ ◖ Tender
‡18in (45cm) ↔8in (20cm)

Primula obconica
...ibre Magenta'

...cold climates, the many obconicas
...ke colorful display plants for
...ool greenhouse. This one has
...nched heads of magenta flowers
...t darken with age, on dark, hairy
...ms emerging from among coarse,
...d-green leaves. Also makes a good
...use- or cool conservatory plant;
...ntact with foliage may cause a rash.

...LTIVATION: *Grow in a soil-based potting
...x with added grit or peat. Choose a
...ot with bright filtered light. Water freely
...en in growth and feed weekly with a
...f-strength liquid fertilizer. Minimum
...mperature 36°F (2°C).*

☀ ◊ Tender
↕↔12in (30cm)

Candelabra Primroses (*Primula*)

Candelabra primroses are robust, herbaceous perennials, so called because their flowers are borne in tiered clusters that rise above the basal rosettes of broadly oval leaves in late spring or summer. Depending on the species, the foliage may be semievergreen, evergreen, or deciduous. The flowers have flat faces and long throats; as with most cultivated primroses, there is a wide choice of colors, from the brilliant red 'Inverewe' to the golden yellow *P. prolifera*. Some flowers change colo[r] as they mature; those of *P. bulleyana* fade from crimson to orange. All look most effective when grouped togethe[r] in a bog garden or waterside setting.

CULTIVATION: *Grow in deep, moist, neutr[al] to acidic, organic soil. Site in partial sha[de] although full sun is tolerated if the soil remains moist at all times. Divide and replant clumps in early spring.*

☼ ◐ ◊ Z3

1 ↕↔24in (60cm)

2 ↕↔24in (60cm)

3 ↕30in (75cm) ↔24in (60cm)

4 ↕ to 3ft (1m) ↔24in (60cm)

5 ↕ to 3ft (1m) ↔24in (60cm)

1 *P. bulleyana* **2** *P. prolifera* (syn. *P. helodoxa*) **3** *P.* 'Inverewe' **4** *P. pulverulenta*
5 *P. pulverulenta* Bartley Hybrids

rimula rosea

eciduous perennial that bears
nded clusters of glowing pink,
g-throated flowers on upright
lks in spring. Clumps of oval,
thed, mid-green leaves emerge
er the flowers; these are tinted
-bronze when young. Good for
og garden or waterside planting.

LTIVATION: *Grow in deep, reliably moist,
tral to acidic, organic soil. Prefers
tial shade, but tolerates full sun if
soil is moist at all times.*

◊ Z3b   ↕↔8in (20cm)

rimula veris

e cowslip is a semi-evergreen,
ring-flowering perennial with
ariable appearance. Thick flower
ms carry dense clusters of small,
nnel-shaped, sweetly scented,
dding yellow flowers above the
mps of lance-shaped, crinkled
ves. Lovely naturalized in damp
assy areas.

LTIVATION: *Best in deep, moist but well-
ained, fertile, organic soil, in semi-shade
full sun, if soil remains reliably damp.*

☼ ◊ Z4   ↕↔10in (25cm)

Primula 'Wanda'

A very vigorous, semi-evergreen perennial that bears clusters of flat-faced, claret red flowers with yellow centers over a long period in spring. The oval, toothed, purplish green leaves are arranged in clumps at the base of the plant. Good in a waterside setting.

CULTIVATION: *Best in deep, moist but well-drained, fertile, organic soil. Prefers partial shade but tolerates full sun if soil remains damp.*

☼ ☀ ◊ ◊ Z3
‡4–6in (10–15cm) ↔12–16in (30–40cm)

Prunella grandiflora 'Loveliness'

This vigorous, spreading perennial bears dense, upright spikes of light purple, tubular flowers in summer. The lance-shaped, deep-green leaves are arranged in clumps at ground level. Versatile groundcover when planted in groups; the flowers are attractive to beneficial insects.

CULTIVATION: *Grow in any soil, in sun or partial shade. May swamp smaller plants, so allow room to expand. Divide clumps in spring or fall to maintain vigor. Deadhead to prevent self-seeding.*

☼ ☀ ◊ ◊ Z3b
‡6in (15cm) ↔to 3ft (1m) or more

Prunus x cistena

...upright, slow-growing, deciduous ...ub valued in particular for its ...age, which is red when young, ...turing to red-purple. Bowl-...ped, pinkish-white flowers ...n from mid- to late spring, ...metimes followed by small, ...rrylike, purple-black fruits. ...d as a windbreak hedge.

...TIVATION: *Grow in any but water-...ed soil, in full sun. Prune back ...rcrowded shoots after flowering. ...grow as a hedge, prune the shoot ...of young plants then trim in ...summer to encourage branching.*

○ ◑ Z3 ↕↔5ft (1.5)

Prunus glandulosa 'Alba Plena'

...is small cherry is a neat, rounded, ...ciduous shrub producing dense ...sters of pure white, bowl-shaped, ...ble flowers during late spring. ...e narrowly oval leaves are pale to ...d-green. Brings beautiful spring ...ssoms to a mixed or shrub border. ...e cultivar 'Sinensis' (Z5) has double ...k flowers.

...LTIVATION: *Grow in any moist but ...ll-drained, moderately fertile soil, in ...n. Can be pruned to a low framework ...ch year after flowering to enhance the ...wering performance.*

◑ ◑ Z5 ↕↔5ft (1.5m)

Prunus 'Kiku-Shidare-Zakura'

Also known as 'Cheal's Weeping', this small deciduous cherry tree is grown for its weeping branches an clear pink blossoms. Dense cluster of large, double flowers are borne in mid- to late spring, with or befor the lance-shaped, mid-green leaves which are flushed bronze when young. Excellent in a small garden.

CULTIVATION: *Best in any moist but wel drained, moderately fertile soil, in full s Tolerates alkalinity. After flowering, prune out only dead, diseased or dama wood; remove any shoots growing from the trunk as they appear.*

☼ ◊ ◊ Z6   ↕↔10ft (3

Prunus laurocerasus 'Otto Luyken'

This compact cherry laurel is an evergreen shrub with dense, glossy dark green foliage. Abundant spike of white flowers are borne in mid- to late spring and often again in fall followed by conical red fruits that ripen to black. Plant in groups as a low hedge or to cover bare ground.

CULTIVATION: *Grow in any moist but we drained, moderately fertile soil, in full sr Prune in late spring or early summer to restrict size.*

☼ ◊ ◊ Z7   ↕3ft (1m) ↔5ft (1.5

runus lusitanica bsp. *azorica*

s Portugal laurel is a slow-
wing, evergreen shrub bearing
nder spikes of small, fragrant
ite flowers in early summer.
e oval, glossy, dark green leaves
ve red stalks. Purple berries appear
er in the season. Attractive year-
nd as a dense screen or hedge.

LTIVATION: *Grow in any moist but well-
ined, fairly fertile soil, in sun with
lter from cold, drying winds. In late
ing, prune to restrict size, or to remove
or overcrowded shoots.*

○ ◊ Z8 ↔ to 70ft (20m)

runus serrula

rounded, deciduous tree that is
lued for its striking, glossy, copper-
own to mahogany-red bark that
els with age. Small, bowl-shaped
ite flowers in spring are followed
cherrylike fruits in fall. The leaves
e lance-shaped and dark green,
rning yellow in fall. Best used as
specimen tree.

LTIVATION: *Best in moist but well-
ained, moderately fertile soil, in full
n. Remove dead or damaged wood
er flowering, and remove any shoots
owing from the trunk as they appear.*

○ ◊ Z7 ↕ 30ft (10m)

Flowering Cherries (*Prunus*)

Ornamental cherries are cultivated primarily for their white, pink, or red flowers that create a mass of bloom, usually on bare branches, from late winter to late spring; cultivars of *P. x subhirtella* flower from late fall. Most popular cultivars not only bear dense clusters of showy, double flowers but have other ornamental characteristics to extend their interest beyond the flowering season: *P. sargentii*, for example, has brilliant fall foliage color, some have shiny, colored bark. All of these features ma flowering cherries superb specimen trees for small as well as large garden

CULTIVATION: *Grow in any moist but well-drained, fairly fertile soil, in sun. Keep all pruning to an absolute minimum; restrict formative pruning to shape to young plan only. Remove any damaged or diseased growth in midsummer, and keep trunks clear of sprouting shoots.*

☼ ◐ ◊ ◑ Zones vary

1 ‡70ft (20m) ↔30ft (10m)

2 ‡↔40ft (12m)

3 ‡30ft (10m) ↔25ft (8m)

4 ‡30ft (10m) ↔25ft (8m)

5 ‡50ft (15m) ↔30ft (10m)

6 ‡30ft (10m) ↔25ft (8m)

1 *P. avium* (Z4b) **2** *P. avium* 'Plena' (Z4b) **3** *P.* 'Kanzan' (Z6) **4** *P.* 'Okame' (Z8)
5 *P. padus* 'Colorata' (Z2) **6** *P.* 'Pandora' (Z7)

‡↔25ft (8m)

9 ‡to 70ft (20m) ↔50ft (15m)

ft (15m) ↔30ft (10m)

10 ‡25ft (8m) ↔30ft (10m)

11 ‡15ft (5m) ↔25ft (8m)

13 ‡30ft (10m) ↔20ft (6m)

14 ‡25ft (8m) ↔30ft (10m)

2 ‡25ft (8m)

15 ‡25ft (8m) ↔30ft (10m)

16 ‡to 50ft (15m) ↔30ft (10m)

P. padus 'Watereri' (Z2) **8** *P.* 'Pink Perfection' (Z6) **9** *P. sargentii* (Z5b)
P. 'Shirofugen' (Z6) **11** *P.* 'Shogetsu' (Z6) **12** *P. x subhirtella* 'Autumnalis Rosea' (Z7)
P. 'Spire' (Z7) **14** *P.* 'Taihaku' (Z6) **15** *P.* 'Ukon' (Z6) **16** *P. x yedoensis* (Z7)

Pseudopanax lessonii 'Gold Splash'

This evergreen, upright to spreading shrub or tree bears yellow-splashed deep green foliage. In summer, less conspicuous clusters of yellow-green flowers are carried amid toothed leaves that are divided into teardrop-shaped leaflets. Purple-black fruits appear later in the season. Grow in a container as a foliage plant for a conservatory.

CULTIVATION: *Best in well-drained, fertile soil or soil mix, in sun or partial shade. Prune to restrict spread in early spring. Minimum temperature 35°F (2°C).*

☼ ◐ ◊ Tender
‡10–20ft (3–6m) ↔6–12ft (2–4m)

Pterostyrax hispida

The fragrant epaulette tree is a small deciduous tree or large shrub valued for its very pretty, hanging clusters of perfumed white flowers that appear in the early part of summer among broad, bright green leaves. The peeling gray bark is aromatic. Remove wayward or crossing shoots in winter.

CULTIVATION: *Grow in deep, fertile, well-drained, and neutral to acid soil, in sun or partial shade.*

☼ ◐ ◊ Z6   ‡50ft (15m) ↔40ft (12m)

Pulmonaria 'Lewis Palmer'

This lungwort, sometimes called 'Highdown', is a deciduous perennial that forms clumps of upright, flowering stems. These are topped by open clusters of pink then blue, funnel-shaped flowers in early spring. The coarse, softly hairy leaves, dark green with white spots, are arranged along the stems. Grow in a wild or woodland garden.

CULTIVATION: *Best in moist but not water-logged, fertile, organic soil, in deep or light shade. Divide and replant clumps after flowering every few years.*

☀ ◑ Z4　　　↕↔18in (45cm)

Pulmonaria rubra

This lovely clump-forming, evergreen perennial is a good groundcover plant for a shady position. It has attractive, bright green foliage and brings early color with its funnel-shaped, bright brick-to salmon-colored flowers from late winter to mid-spring. They are attractive to bees and other beneficial insects.

CULTIVATION: *Grow in organic, fertile, moist but not waterlogged soil, in full to partial shade. Remove old leaves after flowering. Divide large or crowded clumps after flowering or in fall.*

☀ ◑ Z4
to 16in (40cm) ↔36in (90cm)

Pulmonaria saccharata Argentea Group

This group of evergreen perennials has almost completely silver leaves A striking color contrast occurs fro late winter to early spring, when funnel-shaped red flowers appear; these age to a dark violet. They mal good clumps at the front of a shady mixed border.

CULTIVATION: *Best in fertile, moist but n waterlogged, organic soil sited in full or partial shade. After flowering, remove old leaves and divide congested clumps.*

☼ ☀ ◊ Z4 ‡2in (30cm) ↔24in (60c

Pulmonaria 'Sissinghurst White'

A neat, clump-forming, evergreen perennial valued for its pure white spring flowers and white-spotted foliage. The elliptic, hairy, mid- to dark green leaves are carried on upright stems below funnel-shaped flowers that open from pale pink bu in early spring. Plant in groups as a groundcover in a shady position.

CULTIVATION: *Grow in moist but not waterlogged, organic soil. Best in deep or light shade, but tolerates full sun. Divide and replant clumps every 2 or 3 years, after flowering.*

☼ ☀ ◊ Z4 ‡to 12in (30cm) ↔18in (45cm)

...ulsatilla halleri

...is silky-textured herbaceous
...rennial, ideal for a rock garden,
...densely covered in long, silver
...irs. It bears upright, bell-shaped,
...e violet-purple flowers in late
...ring above finely divided, light
...een leaves. The first flowers often
...en before the new spring leaves
...ve fully unfurled.

...LTIVATION: *Grow in fertile, very
...ell-drained gritty soil in full sun. May
...sent disturbance, so leave established
...ants undisturbed.*

...◊ Z3   ‡8in (20cm) ↔6in (15cm)

...ulsatilla vulgaris

...he pasque flower is a compact
...rennial forming tufts of finely
...vided, light green foliage. Its bell-
...aped, nodding, silky-hairy flowers
...e carried above the leaves in
...ring; they are deep to pale purple
...occasionally white, with golden
...nters. Good in a rock garden, scree
...d, or trough, or between paving.

...LTIVATION: *Best in fertile soil with very
...od drainage. Site in full sun and away
...om excessive winter moisture. Do not
...sturb once planted.*

...◊ Z3
...4–8in (10–20cm) ↔8in (20cm)

Pulsatilla vulgaris 'Alba'

This clump-forming perennial, a white form of the pasque flower, bears nodding, bell-shaped, silky-hairy white flowers with bold yellow centers in spring. These are carried above the finely divided, light green foliage, which is hairy when young. Very pretty in a rock garden or scree bed.

CULTIVATION: *Best in fertile soil with very good drainage. Position in full sun with protection from excessive winter moisture. Resents disturbance.*

☼ ◊ Z3　　　　↔8in (20cm)

Pyracantha 'Orange Glow'

An upright to spreading, spiny, evergreen shrub bearing profuse clusters of tiny white flowers in late spring. Orange-red to dark orange berries follow in fall and persist well into winter. The leaves are oval and glossy, dark green. Excellent as a vandal-resistant barrier hedge, which may also attract nesting birds.

CULTIVATION: *Grow in well-drained, fertile soil, in full sun to deep shade. Shelter from cold, drying winds. Prune in mid-spring, and trim new leafy growth again in summer to expose the berries.*

☼ ◐ ◊ Z7　　　　↔10ft (3m)

Pyracantha 'Watereri'

A vigorous, upright, spiny shrub that forms a dense screen of evergreen foliage, ornamented by its abundance of white spring flowers and bright red berries in fall. The leaves are elliptic and dark green. Good as a barrier hedge or in a shrub border; can also be trained against a shady wall. Attractive to birds. For yellow berries, look for 'Soleil d'Or' (Z7) or *P. rogersiana* 'Flava' (Z8).

CULTIVATION: *Grow in well-drained, fertile soil, in sun or shade with shelter from cold winds. Cut back unwanted growth in mid-spring, and trim leafy growth in summer to expose the berries.*

☀ ◊ Z7   ↕↔8ft (2.5m)

Pyrus calleryana 'Chanticleer'

This very thorny ornamental pear has a narrowly conical shape and makes a good specimen tree for a small garden. Attractive sprays of small white flowers in mid-spring are followed by spherical brown fruits in fall. The oval, finely scalloped leaves are glossy, dark green and deciduous; they turn red before they fall. Tolerates urban pollution.

CULTIVATION: *Grow in any well-drained, fertile soil, in full sun. Prune in winter to maintain a well-spaced crown.*

☼ ◊ Z5b   ↕50ft (15m) ↔20ft (6m)

Pyrus salicifolia 'Pendul[a]

This weeping pear is a deciduous tree with silvery-gray, willowlike leaves that are downy when young. Dense clusters of small, creamy white flowers appear during spring, followed by pear-shaped green fruit[s] in fall. A fine, pollution-tolerant tree for an urban garden.

CULTIVATION: *Grow in fertile soil with go[od] drainage, in sun. Prune young trees in winter to create a well-spaced, balanced framework of branches.*

☼ ◊ Z5　　　　‡25ft (8m) ↔20ft (6[m])

Quercus palustris

The pin oak is a North American native tree with an attractive pyramidal shape and straight trunk. In fall, its leaves are ablaze in orange and bronze, with some lingering into winter. Use this pollution- and drought-resistant tree as a shade or street tree.

CULTIVATION: *Pin oak thrives in full sun and moist, neutral to slightly acid, clay soil. It tolerates compacted and wet soil, pollution, and even drought, but develops chlorosis in alkaline soils.*

☼ ◊ ◊ Z4
‡50–75ft (15–23m) ↔35–40ft (11–12m)

amonda myconi

tiny, neat evergreen perennial
th basal rosettes of dark green,
ghtly crinkled, broadly oval leaves.
late spring and early summer,
ep violet-blue flowers are borne
ove the foliage on short stems.
nk- and white-flowered variants also
cur. Grow in a rock garden or on a
y wall. *R. nathaliae* (Z6) is similar
th paler leaves.

LTIVATION: *Plant in moist but well-*
rained, moderately fertile, organic soil,
partial shade. Set plants at an angle to
oid water pooling and rot. Leaves wither
too dry, but recover with watering.

❋ ◊ ◊ Z3   ‡4in (10cm) ↔8in (20cm)

anunculus aconitifolius 'Flore Pleno'

hite bachelor's buttons is a clump-
orming, herbaceous perennial
earing small, almost spherical,
lly double white flowers that last
r a long time during late spring
nd early summer. The toothed leaves
re deeply lobed and glossy dark
reen. Good for a woodland garden.

LTIVATION: *Grow in moist but well-*
rained, organic soil. Site in deep or
artial shade.

❋ ❋ ◊ ◊ Z5
24in (60cm) ↔18in (45cm)

Ranunculus calandrinioides

This clump-forming perennial produces clusters of up to three cup-shaped, white or pink-flushed flowers from late winter to early spring. The lance-shaped, blue-green leaves emerge from the base in spring and die down in summer. Grow in a rock garden, scree bed, or alpine house.

CULTIVATION: *Best in gritty, sharply drained, organic soil, in sun. Water sparingly when dormant in summer.*

☼ ◊ Z8   ‡8in (20cm) ↔6in (15cr

Rhamnus alaternus 'Argenteovariegata'

This Italian buckthorn is a fast-growing, upright to spreading, evergreen shrub bearing oval, leathery, gray-green leaves with creamy white margins. Clusters of tiny, yellow-green flowers are borne in spring, followed by spherical red fruits that ripen to black.

CULTIVATION: *Grow in any well-drained soil, in full sun. Prune out unwanted growth in early spring; remove any shoots with all-green leaves as seen.*

☼ ◊ Z8   ‡15ft (5m) ↔12ft (4m

…heum palmatum …trosanguineum'

…r architectural value in the garden,
…w plants top ornamental rhubarb,
…tatuesque perennial with large,
…unded, toothed, dark green leaves
…36in (90cm) across. Tall, feathery,
…erry pink flowerheads rise above
…e foliage in early summer. Ideal
… a moist border, particularly near
…ter. The leaves of 'Atrosanguineum'
…ve a purplish tint when young.

…ULTIVATION: *Best in deep, moist soil,*
…riched with plenty of organic matter,
full sun or partial shade.

☀ ◐ ◊ ◑ Z4   ↕8ft (2.5m) ↔6ft (2m)

…hodanthemum …osmariense

… spreading subshrub valued for its
…rofusion of daisylike flowerheads
…ith white petals and yellow eyes.
…ese are borne from early spring to
…ll, covering the silver, softly hairy,
…nely divided leaves. Grown in a cool
…reenhouse or an alpine house, it will
…ower year-round if deadheaded.

…ULTIVATION: *Grow in very well-drained*
…oil, in a sunny position. Deadhead
…egularly to prolong flowering. Minimum
…mperature 37°F (3°C).

☀ ◊ Tender
…4–12in (10–30cm) ↔12in (30cm)

Evergreen Azaleas (*Rhododendron*)

Azaleas can be distinguished from true rhododendrons by their smaller dark green leaves and more tubular flowers. They also tend to make smaller, more spreading, twiggy shrubs. Botanically, rhododendrons have at least ten stamens per flower, and azaleas just five. Evergreen azaleas make beautiful, spring-flowering shrubs, blooming in almost every color, and good for a variety of uses: dwarf or compact types are excellent in containers on shaded patios, and larger varieties will brighten up areas in permanent light shade. They do well in sun provided that the soil is not allowed to dry out.

CULTIVATION: *Ideal in moist but well-drained, organic, acidic soil in part-day shade. Shallow planting is essential. Little formative pruning is necessary. If older plants become congested, thin in early summer. Maintain a mulch of leaf mold, but do not cultivate around the root area.*

☼ ◐ ◊ Zones vary

1 ↕↔4ft (1.2m) 2 ↕↔3½ft (1.3m) 3 ↕↔24in (60cm)

4 ↕↔24in (60cm) 5 ↕↔24in (60cm) 6 ↕↔24in (60cm)

1 *Rhododendron* 'Azuma-kagami' (Z7) 2 *R.* 'Beethoven' (Z8) 3 *R.* 'Hatsugiri' (Z7)
4 *R.* 'Hinodegiri' (Z7) 5 *R.* (Obtusum Group) 'Hinomayo' (Z7) 6 *R.* 'Irohayama' (Z7)

▸5ft (1.5m)

▸5ft (1.5m)

MORE CHOICES

'Addy Wery' Vermilion-red flowers. Z7

'Elsie Lee' Light reddish mauve flowers. Z8

'Hexe' Crimson. Z7

'Hino-crimson' Brilliant red flowers. Z7

'Kure-no-yuki' White, also called 'Snowflake'. Z7

'Louise Dowdle' Vivid red-purple flowers. Z8

'Vida Brown' Rose-red. Z8

'Wombat' Pink flowers. Z8

9
↕↔4ft (1.2m)

10
↕↔24–36in (60–90cm)

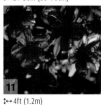

11
↕↔4ft (1.2m)

12
↕↔4ft (1.2m)

R. 'John Cairns' (Z8) **8** *R.* 'Kirin' (Z7) **9** *R.* 'Palestrina' (Z8) **10** *R.* 'Rosebud' (Z7)
11 *R.* 'Vuyk's Scarlet' (Z8) **12** *R.* 'Vuyk's Rosyred' (Z8)

Deciduous Azaleas (*Rhododendron*)

A group of very hardy flowering shrubs, the only rhododendrons whose dark green leaves are deciduous, often coloring brilliantly before they fall. Deciduous azaleas are perhaps the most beautiful types of rhododendron, with large clusters of sometimes fragrant, white to yellow, orange, pink, or red flowers in spring and early summer. There is quite a variety in size, shape, and growth habit, but they suit most garden uses well, especially in light shade. *R. luteum* thrives in sun where the soil is reliably moist. Grow them in containers if your soil is unsuitable.

CULTIVATION: *Grow in moist but well-drained, acidic soil enriched with plenty of organic matter, ideally in partial shade. Shallow planting is essential; maintain a thick mulch of leaf mold, which will nourish the plant. Little or no pruning is necessary. Do not cultivate around the base of the plant; this will damage the roots*

☼ ☀ ◊ ◗ Zones vary

1 ↕↔8ft (2.5m) **2** ↕↔10ft (3m) **3** ↕↔7ft (2.2m)

4 ↕↔5–8ft (1.5–2.5m) **5** ↕↔5ft (1.5m)

1 *Rhododendron albrechtii* (Z6) **2** *R. austrinum* (Z7) **3** *R.* 'Cecile' (Z5)
4 *R.* 'Corneille' (Z5b) **5** *R.* 'Homebush' (Z5b)

MORE CHOICES

'Coccineum Speciosum' Orange-red flowers. Z5

'Daviesii' White.

'Gibraltar' Crimson buds opening to orange with a yellow flash. Z5

'Golden Lights' Yellow to gold, fragrant. Z4

'Klondyke' Red buds opening to orange-gold. Z6

'Orchid Lights' Pink to lilac, compact plant. Z4

'Rosy Lights' Rose pink with darker shading, spreading form. Z4

6
‡↔ 6ft (2m)

8
‡↔ 5–8ft (1.5–2.5m)

↘12ft (4m)

↘6ft (2m)

↘8ft (2.5m)

11
‡↔ 6ft (2m)

R. 'Irene Koster' (Z6) **7** *R. luteum* (Z4) **8** *R.* 'Narcissiflorum' (Z5)
R. 'Persil' (Z6) **10** *R.* 'Spek's Orange' (Z6) **11** *R.* 'Strawberry Ice' (Z5)

Large Rhododendrons

Large, woodland-type rhododendrons, which can reach treelike proportions, are grown primarily for their bright, sometimes fragrant, mostly spring flowers which are available in a wide spectrum of shapes and colors. They are ideal for adding color to shaded areas or woodland gardens. Most leaves are oval and dark green, although the attractive young foliage of *R. bureaui* is light brown. Some cultivars, like 'Cynthia' or 'Purple Splendour', are tolerant of direct sun (in reliably moist soil), making them more versatile than others; they make glorious, spring-flowering screens or hedges for a large garden.

CULTIVATION: *Grow in moist but well-drained, organic, acidic soil. Most prefer dappled shade in sheltered woodland. Shallow planting is essential. Little formative pruning is necessary, although most can be renovated after flowering to leave a balanced framework of old wood.*

☼ ☀ ◊ ◐ Zones vary

↕↔10ft (3m)

↕↔10ft (3m)

↕↔11ft (3.5m)

1 *R.* 'Blue Peter' (Z5) **2** *R. bureaui* (Z6) **3** *R.* 'Crest' (Z7)

20ft (6m)

5 ‡to 40ft (12m) ↔15ft (5m)

12ft (4m)

10ft (3m)

8 ‡↔12ft (4m)

10ft (3m)

10 ‡↔10ft (3m)

11 ‡↔10ft (3m)

R. 'Cynthia' (Z6) **5** *R. falconeri* (Z9) **6** *R.* 'Fastuosum Flore Pleno' (Z5b)
R. 'Furnivalls Daughter' (Z6) **8** *R.* 'Loderi King George' (Z7) **9** *R.* 'Purple
lendour' (Z7) **10** *R.* 'Sappho' (Z7) **11** *R.* 'Susan' J.C. Williams (Z7)

Medium-sized Rhododendrons

These evergreen rhododendrons, between 5–10ft (1.5–3m) tall, are much valued for their attractive, often scented blooms; the flowers are carried amid dark green foliage throughout spring. 'Yellow Hammer' will often produce an early show of flowers in fall, and the foliage of 'Winsome' is unusual for its bronze tints when young. A vast number of different medium-sized rhododendrons are available, all suitable for shrub borders or grouped together in mass plantings. Some sun-tolerant varieties especially low-growing forms like 'Ma Day', are suitable for informal hedgin

CULTIVATION: *Grow in moist but well-drained, organic, acidic soil. Most prefer light dappled shade. Shallow planting is essential. 'Fragrantissimum' requires extra care in colder areas; provide a thick winter mulch and avoid siting in a frost pocket. Trim after flowering, if necessary.*

☼ ☀ ◊ ◗ Zones vary

↕↔ 6ft (2m)   ↕↔ 5ft (1.5m)

1 *R.* 'Fabia' (Z8) **2** *R.* 'Golden Torch' (Z7)

3

6ft (2m)

4

‡↔ 5ft (1.5m)

5

‡↔ 5ft (1.5m)

6

6ft (2m)

7

6ft (2m)

8

‡↔ 5ft (1.5m)

R. 'Fragrantissimum' (Min. temp. 41°F [5°C]) **4** *R.* 'Hydon Dawn' (Z8) **5** *R.* 'May Day' (Z8) **6** *R.* 'Titian Beauty' (Z8) **7** *R.* 'Yellow Hammer' (Z8) **8** *R.* 'Winsome' (Z6)

Dwarf Rhododendrons

Dwarf rhododendrons are low-growing, evergreen shrubs with mid- to dark green, lance-shaped leaves. They flower throughout spring in a wide variety of showy colors and flower forms. If soil conditions are too alkaline for growing rhododendrons in the open garden, these compact shrubs are ideal in containers on shaded patios; 'Ptarmigan' is particularly suited to this kind of planting since it is able to tolerate periods without water. Dwarf rhododendrons are also effective in rock gardens. In areas with cold winters, the earliest spring flowers may be vulnerable to frost.

CULTIVATION: *Grow in moist but well-drained, leafy, acidic, organic soil. Site in sun or partial shade, but avoid the deep shade directly beneath a tree canopy. Best planted in spring or fall; shallow planting is essential. No pruning is necessary.*

☼ ☀ ◊ ◖ Zones vary

‡↔3¹/₂ft (1.1m)

2
‡↔4ft (1.2m)

3
‡↔24in (60cm)

4
‡↔18–36in (45–90cm)

1 *R.* 'Cilpinense' (Z8) **2** *R.* 'Doc' (Z5b) **3** *R.* 'Dora Amateis' (Z5)
4 *R.* 'Ptarmigan' (Z7)

...us typhina 'Dissecta'

...us typhina, staghorn sumac
...so seen as *R. hirta*), is an upright,
...ciduous shrub with velvety red
...oots that resemble antlers. This
...m has long leaves, divided into
...ny finely cut leaflets, which
...n a brilliant orange-red in fall.
...right clusters of less significant,
...low-green flowers are produced
...summer, followed by velvety
...sters of deep crimson-red fruits.

...TIVATION: *Grow in moist but well-
...ined, fairly fertile soil, in full sun
...btain best fall color. Remove any
...kering shoots arising from the
...und around the base of the plant.*

◊ ◊ Z3　　　　　↕6ft (2m) ↔10ft (3m)

...bes sanguineum
'...rocklebankii'

...is slow-growing flowering currant
...n upright, deciduous shrub with
...nded, aromatic, yellow leaves,
...ght when young and fading in
...mmer. The tubular, pale pink
...wers, borne in hanging clusters
...spring, are followed by small,
...e-black fruits. 'Tydeman's White'
...a very similar shrub, sometimes a
...le taller, with pure white flowers.

...TIVATION: *Grow in well-drained, fairly
...ile soil. Site in sun, with shade during
...hottest part of the day. Prune out some
...er stems after flowering. Cut back
...rgrown specimens in winter.*

☼ ◊ Z6b　　　　　↕↔4ft (1.2m)

Ribes sanguineum 'Pulborough Scarlet'

This vigorous flowering currant, larg[er] than 'Brocklebankii', (see previous page, bottom) is an upright, deciduo[us] shrub, bearing hanging clusters of tubular, dark red flowers with white centers in spring. The aromatic, dar[k] green leaves are rounded with tooth[ed] lobes. Small, berrylike, blue-black fruits develop during the summer.

CULTIVATION: *Grow in well-drained, moderately fertile soil, in full sun. Cut out some older stems after flowering; overgrown specimens can be pruned hard in winter or early spring.*

☼ ◊ ◑ Z6b ‡6ft (2m) ↔8ft (2.5[m])

Robinia hispida

The bristly locust is an upright and arching, deciduous shrub with spiny shoots, useful for shrub borders on poor, dry soils. Deep rose-pink, pealike flowers appear in hanging spikes during late spring and early summer; these are followed by brow[n] seed pods. The large, dark green lea[ves] are divided into many oval leaflets.

CULTIVATION: *Grow in any but water-logged soil, in sun. Provide shelter from wind to avoid damage to the brittle branches. No pruning is necessary.*

☼ ◊ Z5 ‡8ft (2.5m) ↔10ft (3[m])

binia pseudoacacia *risia'*

 black locust, *R. pseudoacacia*,
 fast-growing, broadly columnar,
iduous tree, in this cultivar
ring gentle, yellow-green foliage
 is golden yellow when young,
ning orange-yellow in fall. Usually
rse, hanging clusters of fragrant,
like, small white flowers appear
early summer. The stems are
mally spiny.

TIVATION: *Grow in moist but well-
ned, fertile soil, in full sun. When
ng, maintain a single trunk by
oving competing stems as soon as
sible. Do not prune once established.*

◑ ◊ Z4   ‡50ft (15m) ↔25ft (8m)

dgersia pinnata *iperba'*

lump-forming perennial that bears
ight clusters of star-shaped, bright
k flowers. These are borne in mid- to
 summer above bold, heavily veined,
k green foliage. The divided leaves,
o 36in (90cm) long, are purplish
nze when young. Good near water,
 bog garden, or for naturalizing at
oodland margin. For creamy white
wers, look for *R. podophylla* (Z3b).

TIVATION: *Best in moist, organic
, in full sun or semi-shade. Provide
ter from cold, drying winds. Will
tolerate drought.*

☼ ◊ Z4   ‡4ft (1.2m) ↔30in (75cm)

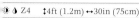

Hybrid Tea Roses (*Rosa*)

These deciduous shrubs are often grown in formal bedding displays, laid out with neat paths and edging. They are distinguished from other roses in that they carry their large flowers either singly or in clusters of two or three. The first blooms appear in early summer, and repeat flushes continue well into fall. In a formal bed, group five or six of the same cultivar together, and interplant with some standard roses to add some variation in height. These roses also combine well with herbaceous perennials and other shrubs in mixed borders.

CULTIVATION: *Grow in moist but well-drained, fertile soil, in full sun. Cut spent flower stems back to the first leaf for repeat blooms. Prune main stems to about 10in (25cm) above ground level in early spring, and remove any dead or diseased wood as necessary at the base.*

☼ ◊ ◑ Z6

1 ↕↔24in (60cm)

2 ↕to 6ft (2m) ↔32in (80cm)

3 ↕3½ft (1.1m) ↔30in (75cm)

4 ↕3½ft (1.1m) ↔30in (75cm)

5 ↕30in (75cm) ↔24in (60cm)

1 *Rosa* ABBEYFIELD ROSE 'Cocbrose' **2** *R.* Alexander 'Harlex'
3 *R.* 'Blessings' **4** *R.* ELINA 'Dicjana' **5** *R.* FREEDOM 'Dicjem'

‡32in (80cm) ↔ 26in (65cm)

‡30in (75cm) ↔ 28in (70cm)

‡3ft (1m) ↔ 30in (75cm)

‡4ft (1.2m) ↔ 3ft (1m)

‡3ft (1m) ↔ 24in (60cm)

‡3ft (1m) ↔ 30in (75cm)

‡3½ft (1.1m) ↔ 24in (60cm)

‡3ft (1m) ↔ 30in (75cm)

R. 'Indian Summer' **7** R. 'Ingrid Bergman' **8** R. JUST JOEY **9** R. LOVELY LADY 'Dicjubell' **10** R.
SHIRVILLE 'Harqueterwife' **11** R. PEACE 'Madame A. Meilland' **12** R. REMEMBER ME 'Cocdestin'
ROYAL WILLIAM 'Korzaun' **14** R. SAVOY HOTEL 'Harvintage' **15** R. SILVER JUBILEE **16** R. 'Troika'

Floribunda Roses (*Rosa*)

These very free-flowering roses come in a very wide range of flower colors. They are set apart from hybrid tea roses by their large, many-flowered clusters of relatively small blooms. Nearly all are fragrant, some being much more so than others. They lend themselves well to informal or cottage garden designs, mixing well with herbaceous perennials as well as other shrubs. Remember to consider the color of the flowers when choosing all neighboring plants, since blooms will continue to appear from late spring to well into fall.

CULTIVATION: Best in moist but well-drain fairly fertile soil, in full sun. Deadhead fo repeat blooms. Prune main stems to abou 12in (30cm) above ground level in early spring, and remove any dead or diseased wood as necessary.

☼ ◊ ◑ Z6

1 ‡20in (50cm) ↔24in (60cm) **2** ‡3ft (1m) ↔30in (75cm) **3** ‡30in (75cm) ↔24in (60cm) **4** ‡3ft (1m) ↔24in (60cm) **5** ‡4ft (1.2m) ↔3ft (1m) **6** ‡32in (80cm) ↔30in (75cm)

1 *Rosa* AMBER QUEEN 'Harroony' **2** *R.* ANISLEY DICKSON 'Dickimono' **3** *R.* ANNA LIVIA 'Kormetter' **4** *R.* 'Arthur Bell' **5** *R.* CHINATOWN **6** *R.* CITY OF LONDON 'Harukfore'

in (75cm) ↔ 24in (60cm)   ‡3ft (1m) ↔ 30in (75cm)   ‡32in (80cm) ↔ 26in (65cm)

30in (75cm)   ‡32in (80cm) ↔ 24in (60cm)   ‡4ft (1.2m) ↔ 3ft (1m)

8in (70cm) ↔ 24in (60cm)   ‡30in (75cm) ↔ 24in (60cm)   ‡to 8ft (2.2m) ↔ 3ft (1m)

R. ESCAPADE 'Harpade' **8** *R.* Fragrant Delight' **9** *R.* ICEBERG 'Korbin' **10** *R.* MANY HAPPY TURNS 'Harwanted' **11** *R.* MARGARET MERRIL 'Harkuly' **12** *R.* MOUNTBATTEN 'Harmantelle' *R.* SEXY REXY 'Macrexy' **14** *R.* TANGO 'Macfirwal' **15** *R.* 'The Queen Elizabeth'

Climbing Roses (*Rosa*)

Climbing roses are often vigorous plants that will reach varying heights depending on the cultivar. All types have stiff, arching stems, usually with dense, glossy leaves divided into small leaflets. The frequently scented flowers are borne in summer, some in one exuberant flush, others having a lesser repeat flowering. They can be trained against walls or fences as decorative features in their own right, planted as a complement to other climbers, such as clematis, or allowed to scramble up into other wall-trained shrubs or ever old trees. They are invaluable for disguising unsightly garden building or as a backdrop to a summer border.

CULTIVATION: *Best in moist but well-drain fairly fertile soil, in sun. Deadhead unless hips are wanted. As plants mature, prune back to within the allowed area after flowering. Occasionally cut an old main stem back to the base to renew growth. Do not prune in the first two years.*

☼ ◊ ◦ Z6, unless noted

1 ↕↔to 20ft (6m)

2 ↕10ft (3m)↔8ft (2.5m)

3 ↕↔7ft (2.2m)

4 ↕to 30ft (10m) ↔20ft (6m)

5 ↕to 15ft (5m) ↔12ft (4m)

1 *Rosa banksiae* 'Lutea' (Z7) **2** R. COMPASSION **3** R. DUBLIN BAY 'Macdub'
4 R. *filipes* 'Kiftsgate' (Z7) **5** R. 'Gloire de Dijon' (Z7)

10ft (3m) ↔ 6ft (2m)

7 ‡10ft (3m) ↔ 7ft (2.2m)

8 ‡↔ 8ft (2.5m)

ft (5m) ↔ 10ft (3m)

‡ft (3m) ↔ 8ft (2.5m)

11 ‡to 20ft (6m) ↔ 12ft (4m)

12 ‡to 10ft (3m) ↔ 6ft (2m)

R. GOLDEN SHOWERS **7** R. HANDEL 'Macha' **8** R. 'Maigold' **9** R. 'Madame Alfred Carrière'
R. 'New Dawn' **11** R. 'Madame Grégoire Staechelin' **12** R. 'Zéphirine Drouhin'

Rambling Roses (*Rosa*)

Rambling roses are very similar to climbers (see p.484) but have more lax, flexible stems. These are easier to train onto complex structures such as arches, tunnels, and pergolas, or ropes and chains suspended between rigid uprights, provided they are solidly built; most ramblers are vigorous. Unlike climbers, they can succumb to mildew if trained flat against walls. Ramblers have divided, glossy green leaves, borne on thorny or prickly stems. Flowers are often scented, arranged singly or in cluster and are borne during summer. Some bloom only once, others having a less repeat flowering later on.

CULTIVATION: *Best in moist but well-drain fertile soil, in full sun. Train stems of you plants on to a support, to establish a permanent framework; prune back to this each year after flowering has finished, an remove any damaged wood as necessary.*

☼ ◊ ◖ Z6

‡ to 15ft (5m) ↔ 10ft (3m)

‡ to 15ft (5m) ↔ 12ft (4m)

1 *Rosa* 'Albéric Barbier' **2** *R.* 'Albertine'

30ft (10m) ↔ 20ft (6m)

to 15ft (5m) ↔ to 12ft (4m)

5 ↕↔ 20ft (6m)

7 ↕↔ to 12ft (4m)

6 to 20ft (6m) ↔ 12ft (4m)

8 ↕↔ 12ft (4m)

R. 'Bobbie James' **4** R. 'Félicité Perpétue' **5** R. 'Rambling Rector' **6** R. 'Seagull'
R. 'Sanders' White Rambler' **8** R. 'Veilchenblau'

Patio and Miniature Roses (*Rosa*)

These small or miniature shrub roses, bred especially for their compact habit and small flower size, greatly extend the range of garden situations in which roses can be grown. They produce flowers in a wide range of colors, blooming over long periods from summer to fall amid deciduous, glossy, green leaves. With the exception of 'Ballerina', which can grow to a height of about 5ft (1.5m), most are under 3ft (1m) tall, making them invaluable for confined, sunny spaces. Planted in large containers or raised beds, they are also excellent for decorating patios.

CULTIVATION: *Grow in well-drained but moist, moderately fertile soil that is rich in well-rotted organic matter. Choose an open, sunny site. Remove all but the strongest shoots in late winter, then reduce these by about one-third of their height. Cut out any dead or damaged wood as necessary.*

☼ ◊ ◊ Z6

‡18in (45cm) ↔16in (40cm)

‡to 5ft (1.5m) ↔4ft (1.2m)

‡30in (75cm) ↔24in (60cm)

‡18in (45cm) ↔12in (30cm)

‡20in (50cm) ↔16in (40cm)

‡30in (75cm) ↔30in (60cm)

1 *Rosa* ANNA FORD 'Harpiccolo' **2** *R.* 'Ballerina' **3** *R.* 'Cecile Brunner'
4 *R.* CIDER CUP 'Dicladida' **5** *R.* GENTLE TOUCH 'Diclulu' **6** *R.* 'Mevrouw Nathalie Nypels'

‡4ft (1.2m) ↔3ft (1m)

‡16in (40cm) ↔24in (60cm)

↕0in (25cm) ↔12in (30cm)

‡16in (40cm) ↔14in (35cm)

↔14in (35cm)

↔24–30in (60–90cm)

‡↔3–5ft (1–1.5m)

R. 'Perle d'Or' **8** *R.* QUEEN MOTHER 'Korquemu' **9** *R.* 'Stacey Sue' **10** *R.* SWEET DREAM 'Fryminicot' **11** *R.* SWEET MAGIC 'Dicmagic' **12** *R.* 'The Fairy' **13** *R.* 'Yesterday'

Groundcover Roses (*Rosa*)

Groundcover roses are low-growing, spreading, deciduous shrubs, ideal for the front of a border, in both formal and informal situations. They produce beautiful, fragrant flowers over long periods from summer into fall, amid divided, glossy green leaves, on thorny or prickly, sometimes trailing stems. Only those of really dense habit, such as SWANY 'Meiburenac', will provide weed-smothering cover, and even these are effective only if the ground is weed-free to begin with. Most give their best cascading over a low wall or when used to clothe a steep bank that is otherwise difficult to plant.

CULTIVATION: *Best in moist but well-drained reasonably fertile, organic soil, in full sun. Prune shoots back after flowering each year to well within the intended area of spread, removing any dead or damaged wood. Annual pruning will enhance flowering performance.*

☼ ◐ ◊ ◗ Z6

1 ‡34in (85cm) ↔ 3½ft (1.1m) 2 ‡18in (45cm) ↔ 4ft (1.2m)

3 ‡30in (75cm) ↔ 4ft (1.2m) 4 ‡3ft (1m) ↔ 4ft (1.2m)

1 *Rosa* BONICA 'Meidomonac' **2** *R.* 'Nozomi' **3** *R.* RED BLANKET 'Intercell'
4 *R.* ROSY CUSHION 'Interall'

n (15cm) ↔ 18in (45cm)

0in (50cm) ↔ 5ft (1.5m)

‡32in (80cm) ↔ 4ft (1.2m)

to 30in (75cm) ↔ 5½ft (1.7m)

‡30in (75cm) ↔ 4ft (1.2m)

R. SNOW CARPET 'Maccarpe' **6** *R.* SUMA 'Harsuma' **7** *R.* SURREY 'Korlanum'
R. SWANY 'Meiburenac' **9** *R.* TALL STORY 'Dickooky'

Old Garden Roses (*Rosa*)

The history of old garden roses extends back to Roman times, demonstrating their lasting appeal in garden design. They are deciduous shrubs, composed of a very large number of cultivars categorized into many groups, such as the gallica, damask, and moss roses. Because almost all old garden roses flower in a single flush in early summer, they should be mixed with other flowering plants to maintain a lasting display. Try underplanting non-climbing types with spring bulbs, and climbing cultivars can be interwoven with a late-flowering clematis.

CULTIVATION: *Best in moist but well-drained, fertile soil, in full sun. Little pruning is necessary; occasionally remove an old stem at the base to alleviate congested growth and to promote new shoots. Trim to shape in spring as necessary. Unless hips are wanted, remove spent flowers as they fade.*

☀ ◊ ◊ Z5, unless noted

1 ↕7ft (2.2m) ↔ 5ft (1.5m)

2 ↕4ft (1.2m) ↔ 3ft (1m)

3 ↕3ft (1m) ↔ 4ft (1.2m)

4 ↕5ft (1.5m) ↔ 4ft (1.2m)

5 ↕5ft (1.5m) ↔ 4ft (1.2m)

6 ↕5ft (1.5m) ↔ 4ft (1.2m)

1 *Rosa* 'Alba Maxima' **2** *R.* 'Belle de Crècy' **3** *R.* 'Cardinal de Richelieu' **4** *R.* 'Céleste'
5 *R.* x *centifolia* 'Cristata' *(syn.* 'Chapeau de Napoléon') **6** *R.* x *centifolia* 'Muscosa'

↕↔4ft (1.2m) or more

↕↔to 6ft (2m)

↕↔4ft (1.2m)

ft (1.5m) ↔4ft (1.2m)

↕4½ft (1.3m) ↔4ft (1.2m)

↕5ft (1.5m) ↔4ft (1.2m)

o 6ft (2m) ↔4ft (1.2m)

↕5ft (1.5m) ↔4ft (1.2m)

↕5ft (1.5m) ↔4ft (1.2m)

5ft (1.5m) ↔4ft (1.2m)

↕↔4ft (1.2m)

↕↔3ft (1m)

R. 'Charles de Mills' **8** *R.* 'De Rescht' **9** *R.* 'Duc de Guiche' **10** *R.* 'Fantin-Latour' **11** *R.* 'Félicité armentier' **12** *R.* 'Ferdinand Pichard' **13** *R.* 'Henri Martin' **14** *R.* 'Ispahan' **15** *R.* 'Königin on Dänemark' **16** *R.* 'Madame Hardy' **17** *R.* 'Président de Sèze' **18** *R.* 'Tuscany Superb'

Modern Shrub Roses (*Rosa*)

These roses are slightly larger and more spreading than most others, combining the stature of old garden roses with some of the benefits of modern types. Their general good health and vigor makes them easy to grow, and they repeat-flower over a long period, making ideal summer-flowering, deciduous shrubs for the back of a low-maintenance shrub border in a large garden. Like other roses, there is a wide choice in flower shape and color, and several have a superb fragrance. Flowering begins in early summer, with repeat flushes well into fall.

CULTIVATION: *Grow in well-drained but moist, moderately fertile, organic soil. Choose an open, sunny site. To keep them at a manageable size, prune every year in early spring. It is often better to let them grow naturally, however; their form is easily spoiled by severe or careless pruning*

☼ ◊ ◐ Z6, unless noted

1 ↕5ft (1.5m) ↔3½ft (1.1m)
2 ↕↔4ft (1.2m)
3 ↕↔ to 11ft (3.5m)
4 ↕6ft (2m) ↔5ft (1.5m)
5 ↕↔5ft (1.5m)
6 ↕5ft (1.5m) ↔4ft (1.2m)

1 *Rosa* 'Blanche Double de Coubert' (Z2b) **2** *R.* 'Buff Beauty' **3** *R.* 'Cerise Bouquet' (Z4) **4** *R.* CONSTANCE SPRY (Z3) **5** *R.* 'Cornelia' **6** *R.* 'Felicia'

‡ft (2m) ↔3ft (1m) **8** ‡5ft (1.5m) ↔3ft (1m) **9** ‡4ft (1.2m) ↔5ft (1.5m)

‡ft (1.5m) ↔4ft (1.2m) **11** ‡↔7ft (2.2m) **12** ‡↔7ft (2.2m)

13 ‡↔3½ft (1.1m) **14** ‡7ft (2.2m) ↔6ft (2m)

15 6ft (2m) ↔3ft (1m) **16** ‡↔3½ ft (1.1m) **17** ‡6ft (2m) ↔4ft (1.2m)

R. 'Fred Loads' (Z4) **8** *R.* GERTRUDE JEKYLL 'Ausbord' **9** *R.* GRAHAM THOMAS 'Ausmas' *(Z5)* **10** *R.* Jacqueline du Pré' (Z3) **11** *R.* 'Marguerite Hilling' **12** *R.* 'Nevada' (Z2) **13** *R.* 'Penelope' **14** *R.* Roseraie de l'Häy' (Z2) **15** *R.* 'Sally Holmes' **16** *R.* 'The Lady' **17** *R.* WESTERLAND 'Korwest' (Z3)

Roses for Wild Areas (*Rosa*)

The best types of rose for wild gardens are the species or wild roses; many naturalize easily. Either shrubs or climbers, most have a natural-looking, scrambling or arching growth habit with single, five-petaled, often fragrant flowers that appear in early summer on the previous year's growth. Although the main flowering season is fleeting, in many the flowers develop into beautiful rosehips, just as attractive as the flowers. Hips vary in color from orange to red or black and often persist into winter, providing valuable food for hungry wildlife.

CULTIVATION: *Best in moist but well-drained, reasonably fertile, organic soil. In a wild garden, little pruning is needed; to control hedges, trim after flowering each year, removing any dead or damaged wood. The flowers are borne on the previous summer's stems, so do not remove too many older branches.*

☼ ◊ ◖ Zones as noted

1 ‡7ft (2.2m) ↔ 8ft (2.5m)

2 ‡32in (80cm) ↔ 3ft (1m)

3 ‡3ft (1m) ↔ 4ft (1.2m)

4 ‡32in (80cm) ↔ 3ft (1m)

5 ‡6ft (2m) ↔ 5ft (1.5m)

1 *R.* 'Complicata' (Z4) **2** *R.* 'Fru Dagmar Hastrup' (Z2b) **3** *R. gallica* var. *officinalis* (Z4) **4** *R. gallica* 'Versicolor' (Z4) **5** *R. glauca* (Z2b)

‡½ft (1.1m) ↔ 4½ft (1.3m)

‡5–8ft (1.5–2.5m) ↔ 4–6ft (1.2–2m)

8 ‡to 10ft (3m) ↔ 6ft (2m)

9 ‡4ft (1.2m) ↔ 3ft (1m)

10 ‡6ft (2m) ↔ 3ft (1m)

11 ↔ 3–8ft (1–2.5m)

12 ‡6ft (2m) ↔ 3ft (1m)

13 ‡8ft (2.5m) ↔ 3ft (1m)

R. 'Golden Wings' (Z3) **7** *R. mulliganii* (Z6) **8** *R. nutkana* 'Plena' (Z3) **9** *R. x odorata* 'Mutabilis' (Z6) **10** *R. primula* (Z6) **11** *R. rugosa* 'Rubra' (Z2) **12** *R. xanthina* 'Canary Bird' (Z4b) **13** *R. xanthina* var. *hugonis* (Z5)

Rosmarinus officinalis 'Miss Jessopp's Upright'

This vigorous, upright rosemary is an evergreen shrub with aromatic foliage that can be used in cooking. From mid-spring to early summer, whorls of small, purple-blue to white flowers are produced amid the narrow, dark green, white-felted leaves, often with a repeat show in fall. A good hedging plant for a kitchen garden. For white flowers, try 'Sissinghurst White'.

CULTIVATION: *Grow in well-drained, poor to moderately fertile soil. After flowering, trim any shoots that spoil the symmetry.*

☼ ◊ Z7   ‡↔6ft (2n

Rosmarinus officinalis Prostratus Group

These low-growing types of rosemary are aromatic, evergreen shrubs ideal for a rock garden or the top of a dry wall. Whorls of small, two-lipped, purple-blue to white flowers are produced in late spring, and often again in fall. The dark green leaves have white-felted undersides and can be cut in sprigs for culinary use. Plant in a sheltered position where marginally hardy.

CULTIVATION: *Grow in well-drained, poor to moderately fertile soil, in full sun. Trim or lightly cut back shoots that spoil the symmetry, after flowering.*

☼ ◊ Z7   ‡6in (15cm) ↔5ft (1.5m

Rubus 'Benenden'

This flowering raspberry is an ornamental, deciduous shrub with spreading, arching, thornless branches and peeling bark. It is valued for its abundance of large, saucer-shaped, roselike flowers with glistening, pure white petals in late spring and early summer. The lobed leaves are dark green. Suitable for a shrub border.

CULTIVATION: *Grow in any rich, fertile soil, in full sun or partial shade. After flowering, occasionally remove some old stems to the base to relieve overcrowding and to promote new growth.*

☼ ◑ ◊ Z8   ↕↔10ft (3m)

Rubus thibetanus

The ghost bramble is an upright, summer-flowering, deciduous shrub named for its conspicuously white-coated, prickly stems in winter. The small, saucer-shaped, red-purple flowers are carried amid fernlike, white-hairy, dark green leaves, followed by spherical black fruits, also with a whitish coating. *R. cockburnianus* (Z7) is also valued for its white winter stems.

CULTIVATION: *Grow in any fertile soil, in sun or partial shade. Each spring, cut all flowered stems back to the ground, leaving the previous season's new, unflowered shoots unpruned.*

☼ ◑ ◊ Z4b   ↕↔8ft (2.5m)

Rudbeckia fulgida var. *sullivantii* 'Goldsturm'

This black-eyed Susan is a clump-forming perennial valued for its strongly upright form and large, daisylike, golden yellow flowerheads with cone-shaped, blackish-brown centers. These appear above the substantial clumps of lance-shaped, mid-green leaves during late summer and fall. It is a bold addition to a late summer border, and the cut flowers last reasonably well in water.

CULTIVATION: *Grow in any moist but well-drained soil that does not dry out, in full sun or light shade.*

☼ ☀ ◊ ◊ Z3b
‡to 24in (60cm) ↔18in (45cm)

Rudbeckia laciniata 'Goldquelle'

A tall but compact perennial that bears large, fully double, bright lemon yellow flowers from midsummer to mid-fall. These are carried above loose clumps of deeply divided, mid-green leaves. The flowers are good for cutting.

CULTIVATION: *Grow in any moist but well-drained soil, in full sun or light dappled shade.*

☼ ☀ ◊ ◊ Z3
‡to 36in (90cm) ↔18in (45cm)

alix babylonica var. *ekinensis* 'Tortuosa'

he dragon's claw willow is a fast-
rowing, upright, deciduous tree
ith curiously twisted shoots that
e striking in winter. In spring,
llow-green catkins appear with
e contorted, bright green leaves
ith gray-green undersides. Plant
vay from drains, since roots are
vasive and water-seeking. Also
ld as *S. matsudana* 'Tortuosa'.

CULTIVATION: *Grow in any but very dry*
shallow, alkaline soil. Choose a sunny
te. Thin occasionally in late winter
stimulate new growth, which best
hibits the twisted growth pattern.

❁ ◊ Z5   ‡50ft (15m) ↔25ft (8m)

alix 'Boydii'

his tiny, very slow-growing,
pright, deciduous shrub with
narled branches is suitable for
anting in a rock garden or trough.
he small, almost rounded leaves
re rough-textured, prominently
eined, and grayish green. Catkins
re only produced occasionally,
early spring.

CULTIVATION: *Grow in any deep, moist*
ut well-drained soil, in full sun;
illows dislike shallow, alkaline soil.
Vhen necessary, prune in late winter
maintain a healthy framework.

❁ ◊ Z5b
2in (30cm) ↔8in (20cm)

Salix caprea 'Kilmarnock'

The Kilmarnock willow is a small, weeping, deciduous tree ideal for a small garden. It forms a dense, umbrella-like crown of yellow-brown shoots studded with silvery catkins in mid- and late spring, before the foliage appears. The broad, toothed leaves are dark green on top and gray-green beneath.

CULTIVATION: *Grow in any deep, moist but well-drained soil, in full sun. Prune annually in late winter to prevent the crown from becoming congested. Remove shoots on the clear trunk.*

☼ ◑ ◊ Z5 ↕6ft (2m) ↔6ft (2m)

Salix hastata 'Wehrhahnii'

This small, slow-growing, upright, deciduous shrub, with dark purple-brown stems and contrasting silvery gray, early spring catkins, makes a beautiful specimen for winter color displays. The leaves are oval and bright green.

CULTIVATION: *Grow in any moist soil, in sun; does not tolerate shallow, alkaline soils. Prune in spring to maintain a balance between young stems, which usually have the best winter color, and older wood with catkins.*

☼ ◊ Z7 ↔3ft (1m)

alix lanata

e woolly willow is a rounded,
w-growing, deciduous shrub with
ck shoots that have an attractive
ite-woolly texture when young.
rge, upright, golden to gray-yellow
kins emerge on older wood in late
ring among the dark green, broadly
al, silvery-gray-woolly leaves.

LTIVATION: *Grow in moist but well-*
ained soil, in sun. Tolerates semi-shade,
t dislikes shallow, alkaline soil. Prune
casionally in late winter or early spring
maintain a balance between old and
ung stems.

☀ ◐ ◊ ◊ Z4   ↕3ft (1m) ↔5ft (1.5m)

alix reticulata

his little willow shrub has trailing
anches that bear rounded, deeply
ined, dark green leaves, which
e white-hairy beneath. In spring,
produces upright, pink-tipped
tkins, and these are a useful source
pollen for emerging bumblebees.
he plant makes a good groundcover
r the front of a border.

LTIVATION: *Grow in any poor to fertile,*
ell-drained soil, in sun.

☀ ◊ Z3
–4in (8–10cm) ↔12in (30cm)

Salvia argentea

This short-lived perennial forms large clumps of soft, felty gray leaves around the base of the plant. Spikes of hooded, two-lipped, white or pinkish-white flowers are borne in mid- and late summer, on strong, upright stems. Removing the spike before it blooms may prolong the life of the plant.

CULTIVATION: *Grow in light, very well-drained to gravelly soil. Use a cloche or glass panel to protect from excessive winter moisture.*

☀ ◊ Z4 ‡36in (90cm) ↔24in (60cm)

Salvia cacaliifolia

Usually grown as an annual in cool climates, this upright and hairy, herbaceous perennial bears spikes of deep blue flowers in early summer, held above mid-green foliage. A distinctive sage with a brilliant flower color, for bedding, filling gaps in borders, or containers.

CULTIVATION: *Grow in light, moderately fertile, moist but well-drained soil enriched with organic matter. Choose a site in full sun to light dappled shade. Minimum temperature 36°F (2°C).*

☀ ☀ ◊ ◊ Tender
‡36in (90cm) ↔12in (30cm)

Salvia coccinea 'Pseudococcinea'

Bushy, short-lived perennial
when grown as an annual in colder
climates, with toothed, dark green,
hairy leaves and loose, slender
spikes of soft cherry red flowers
from summer to fall. An exotic-
looking addition to a summer
display, and good in containers.

CULTIVATION: *Grow in light, moderately
fertile well-drained soil, rich in organic
matter. Site in full sun. Minimum
temperature 41°F (5°C).*

◊ Tender
‡24in (60cm) ↔12in (30cm)

Salvia discolor

This upright, herbaceous perennial,
which is normally treated as a
summer annual in colder climates,
is valued for both its flowers and
foliage. Its green leaves have a
densely white-woolly surface,
forming an unusual display in
themselves until the long spikes
of deep purplish-black flowers
extend above them in late summer
and early fall.

CULTIVATION: *Thrives in light, moderately
fertile, moist but well-drained, organic soil.
A position in full sun or light shade is best.
Minimum temperature 36°F (2°C).*

 ☀ ◊ ◑ Tender
‡18in (45cm) ↔12in (30cm)

Salvia fulgens

An upright, evergreen, summer-flowering subshrub bearing spikes of tubular, two-lipped red flowers. The oval, toothed or notched leaves are rich green above and densely white-woolly beneath. Provides brilliant color for bedding or containers.

CULTIVATION: *Grow in light, moist but well-drained, moderately fertile, organic soil, in full sun or semi-shade. Minimum temperature 36°F (2°C).*

☼ ☀ ◊ Tender
‡6in (15cm) ↔8in (20cm)

Salvia guaranitica 'Blue Enigma'

A subshrubby perennial that grows well as a summer annual for bedding displays in cool climates. It is admired for its deep blue flowers, more fragrant than those of the species, that tower above the mid-green foliage from the end of summer until late fall.

CULTIVATION: *Grow in light, moderately fertile, moist but well-drained soil enrich with organic matter. Choose a site in full sun to light dappled shade.*

☼ ☀ ◊ ◊ Z9
‡5ft (1.5m) ↔36in (90cm)

Salvia x jamensis 'Hot Lips'

This eye-catching salvia has very striking red and white flowers that appear throughout summer. Except in very sheltered west-coast gardens, it will not be hardy but can be overwintered indoors as a houseplant. Cuttings, rooted in late summer, will survive on a sunny windowsill for planting out the following spring when danger of frost is past. The aromatic leaves smell of mint when crushed.

CULTIVATION: *Grow in well-drained soil in full sun. Minimum temperature 41°F (5°C).*

❍ ◊ Tender
‡30in (75cm) ↔30in (75cm)

Salvia leucantha

The Mexican bush sage is a small evergreen shrub. The leaves are mid-green, white-downy beneath, and long spikes of white flowers with purple to lavender-blue calyces appear in fall. Also beautiful year-round in a greenhouse bed or large container.

CULTIVATION: *Grow in moist but well-drained, fertile soil, in sun or partial shade. Under glass, grow in well-drained potting soil mix in full light with shade from hot sun, and water moderately while in flower. Minimum temperature 41°F (5°C).*

☼ ❍ ◊ Tender
‡3ft (1m) or more ↔16–36in (40–90cm)

Salvia microphylla 'Pink Blush'

An unusual flower color for this shrubby perennial, with mid-green leaves and tall, slender spires of intense fuchsia-pink flowers. 'Kew Red' and 'Newby Hall' are also recommended, both with red flower

CULTIVATION: *Grow in light, moist but well-drained, moderately fertile soil that is rich in organic matter, in full sun. Minimum temperature 36°F (2°C).*

☼ ◊ Tender
‡3ft (90cm) ↔2ft (60cm)

Salvia officinalis 'Icterina'

A very attractive, yellow and green variegated form of culinary sage that has a mound-forming, subshrubby habit and aromatic, evergreen, velvety leaves. Less significant spike of small, lilac-blue flowers appear in early summer. Ideal for an herb or kitchen garden. 'Kew Gold' (Z5b) is a very similar plant, although its leaves are often completely yellow.

CULTIVATION: *Grow in moist but well-drained, fairly fertile, organic soil. Site in full sun or partial shade.*

☼ ◊ Z6
‡32in (80cm) ↔3ft (1m)

alvia officinalis urpurascens Group

rple culinary sage is an upright, ergreen subshrub suitable for unny border. Its red-purple, omatic young leaves and spikes of ac-blue flowers produce an ractive combination, the latter pearing during the first half of mmer. A useful plant to add color an herb garden.

LTIVATION: *Grow in light, moderately tile, organic, moist but well-drained l, in full sun or light shade. Trim to pe each year after flowering.*

☀ ◊ ◊ Z6
32in (80cm) ↔3ft (1m)

alvia officinalis 'ricolor'

is variegated sage is an upright, ergreen perennial with gray-green olly, aromatic leaves with cream d pink to beet purple marking. early to midsummer, it produces ikes of lilac-blue flowers, attractive butterflies.

LTIVATION: *Grow in moist but well-ained, reasonably fertile soil enriched th organic matter, in full sun or light ppled shade. Trim back ungainly wth each year after flowering.*

☀ ◊ ◊ Z5b
↕↔3ft (1m)

Salvia patens 'Cambridge Blue'

This lovely cultivar of *S. patens* is an upright perennial with tall, loose spikes of pale blue flowers. It is a striking addition to a herbaceous or mixed border or to bedding and patio containers. The flowers are borne during midsummer to mid-fall above the oval, hairy, mid-green leaves. When marginally hardy, provide shelter at the base of a warm wall.

CULTIVATION: *Grow in well-drained soil, in full sun. Overwinter young plants in frost-free conditions.*

☼ ◊ Z8
↕18–24in (45–60cm) ↔18in (45cm)

Salvia pratensis Haematodes Group

A short-lived perennial, sometimes sold as *S. haematodes*, forming basal clumps of large, dark green leaves. In early and midsummer, spreading spikes of massed blue-violet flowers with paler throats emerge from the center of the clump. Provides color for bedding, filling gaps in beds and borders, or containers. 'Indigo' is another attractive recommended cultivar.

CULTIVATION: *Grow in moist but well-drained, moderately fertile, organic soil. Site in full sun or light shade.*

☼ ◊ Z4
↕36in (90cm) ↔12in (30cr

Salvia x *sylvestris* 'Mainacht'

neat, clump-forming, pleasantly omatic perennial bearing tall, nse, upright spikes of indigo-blue wers during early and midsummer. e narrow, softly hairy, mid-green aves are scalloped at the edges. ovides strong contrast for ver-leaved plants in a herbaceous der. 'Blauhugel' and 'Tänzerin' e other recommended cultivars.

ULTIVATION: *Grow in well-drained, tile soil, in sun. Tolerates drought. t back after the first flush of flowers encourage a later set of blooms.*

◊ Z4   ‡28in (70cm) ↔18in (45cm)

Salvia uliginosa

e bog sage is a graceful, upright rennial bearing spikes of clear ue flowers from late summer to d-fall. These are carried above nce-shaped, toothed, mid-green aves, on branched stems. Good r moist borders; where not rdy, it can be container-grown a cool conservatory.

ULTIVATION: *Needs moist but well-ained, fertile soil or soil mix. Choose sunny, sheltered position. Taller plants ll need support.*

◊ ◊ Z6b   ‡6ft (2m) ↔36in (90cm)

Sanguisorba canadensis

Canadian burnet is a deciduous perennial with compound, serrated leaves and showy spikes of densely packed, small creamy flowers that have an appealing fuzzy look. This long bloomer produces flowers from early summer to early fall. Ideal for wetland, bog, and rain gardens.

CULTIVATION: *Thrives in full sun but tolerates part sun, and requires fertile, moist soil. Water regularly during droughts during the growing season, but allow to dry out when dormant. May spread rapidly in moist, fertile sites.*

☼ ☀ ◊ ♦ Z4
‡4–5ft (1–1.5m) ↔2–4ft (0.5–1.2m)

Sambucus nigra 'Guincho Purple'

This popular cultivar of the common elder is an upright shrub with dark green, divided leaves; these turn black-purple then red in fall. In early summer, musk-scented, pink-tinged white flowers are borne in large, flattened clusters, followed by small black fruits. Elders are ideal in new gardens, because they establish themselves in a short space of time.

CULTIVATION: *Grow in any fertile soil, in sun or partial shade. For the best foliage effect, either cut all stems to the ground in winter or prune out old stems and reduce length of young shoots by half.*

☼ ☀ ◊ Z4
‡↔20ft (6m)

Santolina chamaecyparissus

Lavender cotton is a rounded, evergreen shrub grown for its foliage. The slender, white-woolly stems are densely covered with narrow, gray-white, finely cut leaves. The small yellow flowerheads in summer can be removed to enhance the foliage effect. Suitable for a mixed border or as low, informal hedging. For a dwarf version, look for var. *nana*.

CULTIVATION: *Grow in well drained, poor to moderately fertile soil, in full sun. Remove old flowerheads, and trim long shoots in fall. Cut old, straggly plants back hard each spring.*

❀ ◊ Z7   ‡20in (50cm) ↔3ft (1m)

Santolina rosmarinifolia 'Primrose Gem'

A dense, rounded, evergreen shrub, similar to *S. chamaecyparissus* (see above), but with bright green leaves and paler flowers. These are borne at the tips of slender stems in midsummer, above the finely cut aromatic leaves. Useful for filling gaps in a sunny border.

CULTIVATION: *Grow in well drained, poor to moderately fertile soil, in full sun. In fall, remove old flowerheads and prune long shoots. Cut old, straggly plants back hard each spring.*

❀ ◊ Z8   ‡24in (60cm) ↔3ft (1m)

Saponaria ocymoides

Tumbling Ted is a sprawling, mat-forming perennial that carries a profusion of tiny pink flowers in summer. The hairy, bright green leaves are small and oval. Excellent as part of a dry bank, scree, or rock garden, although it may swamp smaller plants. 'Rubra Compacta' is a neater version of this plant, with dark red flowers.

CULTIVATION: *Grow in gritty, sharply drained soil, in full sun. Cut back hard after flowering to keep compact.*

☀ ◊ Z3
↕3in (8cm) ↔18in (45cm) or more

Sarcococca confusa

Christmas box is a dense, evergreen shrub, giving an unparalleled winter fragrance. Clusters of small white flowers appear in midwinter, followed by small, glossy black fruits. The tiny, oval leaves are glossy and dark green. Excellent as a low hedge near a door or entrance. Tolerates atmospheric pollution, dry shade, and neglect.

CULTIVATION: *Grow in moist but well-drained, fertile, organic soil. Site in deep or semi-shade with protection from wind. Remove dead and damaged growth each year in spring.*

☼ ◑ ● Z8
↕6ft (2m) ↔3ft (1m

arcococca hookeriana ar. digyna

his perfumed, evergreen shrub is
ry similar to *S. confusa* (see facing
ge, below), but with a more compact
d spreading habit. The tiny, fragrant
hite flowers, which are followed by
nall, black or blue-black fruits, have
nk anthers; they are borne amid
ossy leaves, more slender and pointed
an those of *S. hookeriana*, in winter.
e flowers are good for cutting.

LTIVATION: *Grow in moist but well-
ained, fertile, organic soil, in shade.
g up spreading roots in spring to
nfine to its allotted space.*

☀ ◐ Z6　　　↕5ft (1.5m) ↔6ft (2m)

atureja montana

inter savory is an attractive herb
ot often seen in gardens. It forms
small semi-evergreen subshrub
vered in small, dark green,
ightly grayish leaves. Lavender-
nk to purple flowers adorn the low
ounded foliage throughout summer
d cater to a variety of insects. The
romatic foliage has a spicy scent and
n be used as a culinary herb.

LTIVATION: *Grow in reliably well-
ained, neutral to slightly alkaline soil,
full sun.*

◐ ◊ Z4b　　　↕16in (40cm) ↔8in (20cm)

Saxifraga 'Jenkinsiae'

This neat and slow-growing, evergreen perennial forms very dense cushions of gray-green foliage. It produces an abundance of solitary, cup-shaped, pale pink flowers with dark centers in early spring, on short, slender red stems. Good for rock gardens or troughs.

CULTIVATION: *Best in moist but sharply drained, moderately fertile, neutral to alkaline soil, in full sun. Provide shade from the hottest summer sun.*

☼ ◊ Z7   ↕2in (5cm) ↔8in (20cm)

Saxifraga Southside Seedling Group

A mat-forming, evergreen perennial that is suitable for a rock garden. Open sprays of small, cup-shaped white flowers, spotted heavily with red, are borne in late spring and early summer. The oblong to spoon-shaped, pale green leaves form large rosettes close to the soil level.

CULTIVATION: *Grow in very sharply drained, moderately fertile, alkaline soil. Choose a position in full sun.*

☼ ◊ Z5b   ↕12in (30cm) ↔8in (20cm)

cabiosa caucasica live Greaves'

is delicate, perennial scabious,
th solitary, lavender-blue flower-
ads, is ideal for a cottage garden.
e blooms have pincushion-like
nters and are borne above the
imps of gray-green leaves during
d- to late summer. The flowerheads
t well for indoor arrangements.

*LTIVATION: Grow in well-drained,
oderately fertile, neutral to slightly
kaline soil, in full sun. Deadhead
prolong flowering.*

◊ Z4   ‡↔24in (60cm)

cabiosa caucasica Miss Willmott'

clump-forming perennial that
very similar to 'Clive Greaves'
bove), but with white flowerheads.
hese are borne in mid- to late
mmer and are good for cutting.
e lance-shaped leaves are
ay-green and arranged around
e base of the plant. Appropriate
r a cottage garden.

*LTIVATION: Grow in well-drained,
oderately fertile, neutral to slightly
kaline soil, in full sun. Deadhead
prolong flowering.*

◊ Z3b   ‡36in (90cm) ↔24in (60cm)

Schizostylis coccinea '**Sunrise**'

This clump-forming, vigorous perennial bears upright spikes of salmon-pink flowers which open in fall. The long leaves are sword-shaped and ribbed. Good in sheltered spots, for a border front, or above water level in a waterside planting. When cut, the flowers last well in water.

CULTIVATION: *Best in moist but well-drained, fertile soil, in sun. Naturally forms congested clumps, but these are easily lifted and divided in spring.*

☀ ◗ Z8   ↕24in (60cm) ↔12in (30cm)

Sciadopitys verticillata

Japanese umbrella pine is a slow-growing, broad needled evergreen that has a pyramidal or spiral growth habit when young. As it ages, it develops a loose habit with drooping, spreading branches. Interesting texture of needles makes it ideal as an accent tree or in groupings of mixed evergreens.

CULTIVATION: *Full to part sun, normal to moist sand, clay, or loam, rarely bothered by pests or diseases.*

☀ ☀ ◗ Z6
↕30–70 (10–20m) ↔20–30ft (6–10m)

Scilla bifolia

A small, bulbous perennial bearing early-spring flowers, this naturalizes well under trees and shrubs or in grass. The slightly one-sided spikes of several star-shaped, blue to purple-blue flowers are carried above the clumps of narrow, basal leaves.

CULTIVATION: *Grow in well-drained, moderately fertile, organic soil, in full sun or partial shade.*

◊ Z3 ‡6in (15cm) ↔2in (5cm)

Scilla mischtschenkoana 'Tubergeniana'

This dwarf, bulbous perennial has slightly earlier flowers than *S. bifolia* (above) that are silvery blue with darker stripes. They are grouped together in elongating spikes, appearing at the same time as the semi-upright, narrow, mid-green leaves. Naturalizes in open grass. Also known as *S. tubergeniana*.

CULTIVATION: *Grow in well-drained, moderately fertile soil that is rich in well-rotted organic matter, in full sun.*

◊ Z3 ‡6in (15cm) ↔2in (5cm)

Sedum kamtschaticum '**Variegatum**'

This clump-forming, semi-evergreen perennial has eye-catching, fleshy leaves, mid-green with pink tints and cream margins. During late summer, these contrast nicely with flat-topped clusters of small, star-shaped, yellow flowers that age to crimson later in the season. Suitable for rock gardens and border

CULTIVATION: *Grow in well-drained, gritt fertile soil. Choose a site in full sun, but will tolerate light shade.*

☼ ◊ Z3b   ‡4in (10cm) ↔10in (25cr

Sedum '**Ruby Glow**'

This low-growing perennial is an ideal choice for softening the front of a mixed border. It bears masses of small, star-shaped, ruby red flowers from midsummer to early fall above clumps of fleshy, green-purple leaves. The nectar-rich flowers attract bees, butterflies, and other beneficial insects.

CULTIVATION: *Grow in well-drained, fertile soil that has adequate moisture in summer. Position in full sun.*

☼ ◊ Z3b   ‡10in (25cm) ↔18in (45cm

Sedum spathulifolium '*Cape Blanco*'

A vigorous, evergreen perennial that forms a mat of silvery green foliage, often tinted bronze-purple, with a heavy bloom of white powder over the innermost leaves. Small clusters of star-shaped, bright yellow flowers are borne just above the leaves in summer. A very attractive addition to a trough or raised bed.

CULTIVATION: *Grow in well-drained, moderately fertile, gritty soil. Position in full sun, but tolerates light shade.*

☼ ◊ Z6   ‡4in (10cm) ↔24in (60cm)

Sedum spathulifolium '*Purpureum*'

This fast-growing, summer-flowering perennial forms tight, evergreen mats of purple-leaved rosettes; the central leaves are covered with a thick, silvery bloom. Flat clusters of small, star-shaped, bright yellow flowers appear throughout summer. Suitable for a rock garden or the front of a sunny, well-drained border.

CULTIVATION: *Grow in gritty, moderately fertile soil with good drainage, in sun or partial shade. Trim occasionally to prevent encroachment on other plants.*

❋ ☼ ◊ Z6   ‡4in (10cm) ↔24in (60cm)

Sedum spectabile 'Brilliant'

This cultivar of *S. spectabile*, the ice plant, is a clump-forming, deciduous perennial with brilliant pink flowerheads, excellent for the front of a border. The small, star-shaped flowers, packed into dense, flat clusters on fleshy stems, appear in late summer above the succulent, gray-green leaves. The flowerheads are attractive to bees and butterflies and dry well on or off the plant.

CULTIVATION: *Grow in well-drained, fertile soil with adequate moisture during summer, in full sun.*

☼ ◊ Z3b   ↕↔18in (45cm)

Sedum spurium 'Schorbuser Blut'

This vigorous, evergreen perennial forms mats of succulent, mid-green leaves that become purple-tinted when mature. Rounded clusters of star-shaped, deep pink flowers are borne during late summer. Suitable for a rock garden.

CULTIVATION: *Grow in well-drained, moderately fertile, neutral to slightly alkaline soil, in full sun. Tolerates light shade. To improve flowering, divide the clumps or mats every 3 or 4 years.*

☼ ☀ ◊ Z3b
↕4in (10cm) ↔24in (60cm)

edum telephium *tropurpureum* Group

his clump-forming, deciduous
erennial is valued for its very dark
urple foliage that contrasts well
ith other plants. During summer
d early fall, attractive pink
owers with orange-red centers are
ustered above the oval, slightly
alloped leaves.

ULTIVATION: Grow in well-drained,
oderately fertile, neutral to slightly
kaline soil, in full sun. Divide clumps
ery 3 or 4 years to improve flowering.

❄ ◊ Z3
8–24in (45–60cm) ↔12in (30cm)

emiarundinaria *astuosa*

arihira bamboo has tall, straight
d thick canes that are shiny and
id-green with purplish stripes,
rticularly when young. Its narrow,
rap-like leaves are glossy and green.
eal for screening, as a windbreak,
r as a specimen; it can form large
umps, but keep the roots confined
sing an impermeable root barrier
prevent the clump from spreading.

ULTIVATION: Grow in moist but well-
rained soil, in sun or partial shade.

❄ ❉ ◊ ◖ Z7
o 22ft (7m) ↔6ft (2m) or more

Sempervivum arachnoideum

The cobweb houseleek is a mat-forming, evergreen succulent, so named because the foliage is webbed with white hairs. The small, fleshy, mid-green to red leaves are arranged in tight rosettes. In summer, flat clusters of star-shaped, reddish-pink flowers appear on leafy stems. Suitable for growing in a scree bed, wall crevice, or trough.

CULTIVATION: *Grow in gritty, sharply drained, poor to moderately fertile soil. Choose a position in full sun.*

☼ ◊ Z4   ‡3in (8cm) ↔12in (30cm)

Sempervivum ciliosum

A mat-forming, evergreen succulent carrying very hairy, dense rosettes of incurved, lance-shaped, gray-green leaves. It bears flat, compact heads of star-shaped, greenish-yellow flowers throughout summer. The rosettes of leaves die after flowering but are rapidly replaced. Best in an alpine house in areas prone to very wet winters.

CULTIVATION: *Grow in gritty, sharply drained, poor to moderately fertile soil, in sun. Tolerates drought conditions, but dislikes excessive winter moisture or climates that are warm and humid.*

☼ ◊ Z8   ‡3in (8cm) ↔12in (30cm)

empervivum tectorum

he common hen and chicks is a
igorous, mat-forming, evergreen
ucculent with large, open rosettes
f thick, oval, bristle-tipped, blue-
reen leaves, often suffused red-
urple. In summer, dense clusters
f star-shaped, red-purple flowers
ppear on upright, hairy stems.
ery attractive growing on old roof
les or among terracotta fragments.

ULTIVATION: *Grow in gritty, sharply
rained, poor to moderately fertile soil.
Choose a site in full sun.*

☼ ◊ Z4 ‡6in (15cm) ↔20in (50cm)

Sidalcea 'Elsie Heugh'

he prairie mallow bears spires
f satiny, purple-pink flowers with
rettily fringed petals over long
eriods from midsummer. These
ppear over a mound of lobed, glossy
right green leaves. Grow in a mixed
r herbaceous border. The flowers
re good for cutting; deadhead after
lowering to encourage more blooms.
Plants may need staking.

CULTIVATION: *Best in well-drained soil,
n sun.*

☼ ☀ ◊ Z5 ‡36in (90cm) ↔18in (45cm)

Silene schafta

A clump-forming, spreading, semi-evergreen perennial with floppy stems bearing small, bright green leaves. Profuse sprays of long-tubed, deep magenta flowers with notched petals are borne from late summer to fall. Suitable for a raised bed or rock garden.

CULTIVATION: *Grow in well-drained, neutral to slightly alkaline soil, in full sun or light dappled shade.*

☼ ◐ ◊ Z3b ↕↔12in (30cm

Silphium perfoliatum

A sunflower relative native to eastern North America, the cup plant forms an imposing clump of aromatic dark green foliage above which branching heads of bright yellow daisylike flowers bloom from midsummer to fall. These attract a variety of pollinating insects, which makes this plant ideal for wildlife and meadow gardens. It tolerates both drought and poorly drained sites.

CULTIVATION: *Grow in sun or light shade, in normal to moist soil.*

☼ ◐ ◊ Z6 ↕8ft (2.5m) ↔3ft (1m)

Skimmia x *confusa* 'Kew Green' (male)

A compact, dome-shaped, evergreen shrub carrying aromatic, pointed, mid-green leaves. Conical spikes of fragrant, creamy white flowers open in spring. There are no berries, but it will pollinate female skimmias if they are planted nearby. Good in a shrub border or woodland garden.

CULTIVATION: *Grow in moist but well-drained, moderately fertile, organic soil. Tolerates full sun to deep shade, atmospheric pollution, and neglect. Requires little or no pruning.*

☀ ◐ ● ◊ Z7
↕1½–10ft (0.5–3m) ↔5ft (1.5m)

Skimmia japonica 'Rubella' (male)

This tough, dome-shaped, evergreen shrub bears dark red flower buds in fall and winter, opening in spring as fragrant heads of white flowers. The oval leaves have red rims. No berries are produced, but it will pollinate female skimmias nearby. (Where space permits only one plant, 'Robert Fortune' produces both flowers and berries.) Tolerates pollution and coastal conditions.

CULTIVATION: *Grow in moist, fertile, neutral to slightly acidic soil, in partial or full shade. Cut back any shoots that spoil the shape.*

☀ ◐ ● ◊ Z7
↕↔to 20ft (6m)

Solanum crispum 'Glasnevin'

This long-flowering Chilean potato tree is a fast-growing, scrambling, woody-stemmed, evergreen climber. Fragrant, deep purple-blue flowers, borne in clusters at the tips of the stems during summer and fall, are followed by small, yellow-white fruits. The leaves are oval and dark green. Grow on a warm, sunny wall.

CULTIVATION: *Grow in any moist but well-drained, moderately fertile soil, in full sun or semi-shade. Cut back weak and badly placed growth in spring. Tie to a support as growth proceeds. Minimum temperature 41°F (5°C).*

☀ ◐ ◌ ◑ Tender   ↕20ft (6m)

Solanum laxum 'Album'

This white-flowered potato vine is a scrambling, woody-stemmed, semi-evergreen climber. It produces broad clusters of fragrant, star-shaped, milk-white flowers, with prominent, lemon-yellow anthers, from summer into fall. They are followed by black fruits. The leaves are mid- to dark green and oval. Use as an annual for baskets and planters where not hardy.

CULTIVATION: *Grow in any moist but well-drained, fertile soil, in full sun or semi-shade. Thin out shoots in spring. The climbing stems need support. Minimum temperature 35°F (2°C).*

☀ ◐ ◌ ◑ Tender   ↕20ft (6m)

Solidago 'Goldenmosa'

This compact, vigorous goldenrod is a bushy perennial topped with bright golden yellow flowerheads in late summer and early fall. The leaves are wrinkled and mid-green. Valuable in a wild garden or for late summer color; the flowers are good for cutting. Note: goldenrods do not cause hayfever. Other plants blooming at the same time, notably ragweeds, are the culprits.

CULTIVATION: *Grow in well-drained, poor to moderately fertile, preferably sandy soil, in full sun. Remove flowered stems to prevent self-seeding.*

※ ◊ Z4 ‡30in (75cm) ↔18in (45cm)

Sophora SUN KING ('Hilsop')

This shrubby, evergreen relative of the Japanese pagoda tree has dark green leaves divided into many small leaflets. It is valued for its clusters of deep yellow flowers that bloom on spikes over a long period from late winter into early spring, when few other plants are in flower. The display is particularly good after a long, hot summer. Grow as a specimen shrub or in a mixed border.

CULTIVATION: *Best in well-drained soil, in sun.*

※ ◊ Z8 ‡↔10ft (3m)

Sorbus aria 'Lutescens'

This compact whitebeam is a broadly columnar, deciduous tree, bearing oval and toothed, silvery-gray foliage that turns russet and gold in fall. Clusters of white flowers appear in late spring, followed by brown-speckled, dark red berries. It makes a beautiful specimen tree, tolerating a wide range of conditions. 'Majestic' is similar but taller, with larger leaves.

CULTIVATION: *Grow in moist but well-drained, fertile soil, in sun. Tolerates heavy clay soils, semi-shade, urban pollution, and exposed conditions. Remove any dead wood in summer.*

☼ ☀ ◊ ◊ Z4   ‡30ft (10m) ↔25ft (8m)

Sorbus hupehensis var. *obtusa*

This variety of the Hubei mountain ash is an open and spreading tree that gives a fine display of fall color. Broad clusters of white flowers in late spring are followed by round white berries; these ripen to dark pink late in the season. The blue-green leaves, divided into many leaflets, turn scarlet before they fall.

CULTIVATION: *Grow in any moist but well-drained soil, preferably in full sun, but tolerates light shade. Remove any dead or diseased wood in summer.*

☼ ☀ ◊ ◊ Z6   ‡↔25ft (8m)

Sorbus 'Joseph Rock'

[Th]is broadly columnar, upright,
[de]ciduous tree has bright green
[le]aves that are divided into many
[sh]arply toothed leaflets. These color
[at]tractively to orange, red, and purple
[in] fall. In late spring, white flowers
[ap]pear in broad clusters, followed
[by] round, pale yellow berries that
[rip]en to orange-yellow.

[CU]LTIVATION: *Grow in moist but well-
[dr]ained, fertile soil, in sun. Very prone
[to] fireblight, the main sign of which is
[bl]ackened leaves; affected growth must
[be] pruned back in summer to at least
[24]in (60cm) below the diseased area.*

◊ ◖ Z4 ‡30ft (10m) ↔22ft (7m)

Sorbus reducta

[A] deciduous shrub that forms a
[lo]w thicket of upright branches.
[M]uch-valued for its ornamental,
[da]rk green foliage that turns a rich
[re]d in fall. Small, open clusters
[of] white flowers appear in late
[sp]ring, followed by white, crimson-
[fl]ushed berries. Tolerates pollution.

[CU]LTIVATION: *Grow in well-drained,
[m]oderately fertile soil, in an open,
[su]nny site. To thin congested plants,
[re]move shoots that arise from the base
[wh]ile they are still young and soft.*

◖ ◊ Z4b ‡5ft (1.5m) ↔6ft (2m)

Sorbus vilmorinii

A spreading shrub or small tree with elegant, arching branches bearing dark green leaves divided into many leaflets. The deciduous foliage gives a lovely display in fall, turning orange- or bronze-red. Clusters of white flowers appear in late spring and early summer, followed later in the season by dark red berries that age to pink then white.

CULTIVATION: *Grow in well-drained, moderately fertile, organic soil, in full sun or dappled shade. Remove any dead or diseased wood in summer.*

☼ ☼ ◊ Z3   ↕↔15ft (5m)

Spigelia marilandica

Indian pink is a pretty wildflower that ranges from the American Midwest to the Deep South. In early summer, its red tubular flowers with yellow centers bloom just above the foliage. Clumps spread slowly; ideal for shaded borders or woodland gardens. Attracts hummingbirds and butterflies.

CULTIVATION: *Thrives in part shade and moist, well drained, organic-rich soil. Cut back after flowering to encourage a second flush in fall; few pests or diseases; divide in fall or spring. Toxic: keep away from children.*

☼ ☼ ◊ Z7b
↕12–24in (30–60cm) ↔24in (60cm)

Spiraea japonica 'Anthony Waterer'

A compact, deciduous shrub that makes a good informal flowering hedge. The lance-shaped, dark green leaves, usually margined with creamy white, are red when young. Dense heads of tiny pink flowers are borne amid the foliage in mid- to late summer.

CULTIVATION: *Grow in any well-drained, fairly fertile soil that does not dry out, in full sun. On planting, cut back stems to leave a framework 6in (15cm) high; prune back close to this every year in spring. Deadhead after flowering.*

✤ ◊ Z2b   ↕↔ to 5ft (1.5m)

Spiraea japonica 'Goldflame'

This compact, deciduous, flowering shrub bears pretty, bright yellow leaves that are bronze-red when young. Dense, flattened heads of tiny, dark pink flowers appear at the tips of slightly arching stems during mid- and late summer. Ideal for a rock garden. 'Nana' (Z3b) is even smaller, to 18in (45cm) tall.

CULTIVATION: *Grow in well-drained soil that does not dry out completely, in full sun. On planting, cut back stems to a framework 6in (15cm) high; prune back close to this each year in spring. Deadhead after flowering.*

✤ ◊ Z2b   ↕↔ 30in (75cm)

Spiraea nipponica 'Snowmound'

This fast-growing and spreading, deciduous shrub has arching, reddish green stems. The dense clusters of small white flowers in midsummer make an invaluable contribution to any shrub border. The rounded leaves are bright green when young, darkening as they age.

CULTIVATION: *Grow in any moderately fertile soil that does not dry out too much during the growing season, in full sun. Cut back flowered stems in fall, and remove any weak growth.*

☼ ◊ Z3   ↕↔4ft (1.2m

Spiraea x *vanhouttei*

Bridal wreath is a fast-growing, deciduous shrub, more compact in habit than *S. nipponica* 'Snowmound' (above), but with similar mounds of white flowers during early summer. The diamond-shaped leaves are dark green above with blue-green undersides. Grow as an informal hedge or in a mixed border.

CULTIVATION: *Grow in any well-drained, fertile soil that does not dry out, in sun. In fall, cut back flowered stems, removing any weak or damaged growth.*

☼ ◊ Z3   ↕6ft (2m) ↔5ft (1.5m

tachyurus praecox

his spreading, deciduous shrub
ears oval, mid-green leaves on
rching, red-purple shoots. Hanging
pikes of tiny, bell-shaped, pale
ellow-green flowers appear on the
are stems in late winter and early
pring. Suitable for a shrub border,
nd lovely in a woodland garden.

ULTIVATION: *Grow in moist but well-
rained, organic, fertile, neutral to
cidic soil. Prefers partial shade but
lerates full sun if soil is kept reliably
oist. Regular pruning is unnecessary.*

☼ ☀ ◊ ◑ Z7
3–12ft (1–4m) ↔10ft (3m)

tipa gigantea

olden oats is a fluffy, evergreen,
erennial grass forming dense tufts
f narrow, mid-green leaves. In
ummer, these are topped by silvery
o purplish-green flowerheads that
urn gold when mature and persist
vell into winter. Makes an imposing
eature at the back of a border.

ULTIVATION: *Grow in well-drained, fertile
oil, in full sun. Remove dead leaves and
lowerheads in early spring.*

☼ ◊ Z7
↕8ft (2.5m) ↔4ft (1.2m)

Styrax japonicus

Japanese snowbell is a gracefully spreading, deciduous tree bearing hanging clusters of fragrant, bell-shaped, dainty white flowers that are often tinged with pink. These appear during mid- to late spring amid oval, rich green leaves that turn yellow or red in fall. Ideal for a woodland garden.

CULTIVATION: *Grow in moist but well-drained, neutral to acidic soil, in full sun with shelter from cold, drying winds. Tolerates dappled shade. Allow to develop naturally without pruning.*

☼ ☀ ◊ ◊ Z5b ‡30ft (10m) ↔25ft (8m)

Styrax obassia

The fragrant snowbell is a broadly columnar, deciduous tree bearing beautifully rounded, dark green leaves that turn yellow in fall. Fragrant, bell-shaped white flowers are produced in long, spreading clusters in mid- and late spring.

CULTIVATION: *Grow in moist but well-drained, fertile, organic, neutral to acid soil, in full sun or partial shade. Shelter from cold, drying winds. Dislikes pruning leave to develop naturally.*

☼ ☀ ◊ ◊ Z6 ‡40ft (12m) ↔22ft (7m)

ymphytum x plandicum 'Variegatum'

his upright, clump-forming, bristly
rennial has large, lance-shaped,
id-green leaves with broad cream
argins. Drooping clusters of pink-
ue buds open to blue-purple flowers
om late spring to late summer. Best
a wild garden or shady border.
ss invasive than green-leaved types.

ULTIVATION: *Grow in any moist soil, in
n or partial shade. For the best foliage
ect, remove flowering stems before they
oom. Liable to form plain green leaves
grown in poor or infertile soil.*

☼ ◐ ◊ Z3
6in (90cm) ↔24in (60cm)

yringa meyeri 'Palibin'

his compact, slow-growing,
eciduous shrub with a rounded
ape is much valued for its
oundant clusters of fragrant,
avender-pink flowers in spring.
he leaves are dark green and
val. Makes a bold contribution
any shrub border. Sometimes
en as *S. palibiniana.*

ULTIVATION: *Grow in deep, moist but
ell-drained, fertile, preferably alkaline
il, in full sun. Deadhead for the first
w years until established. Prune out
eak and damaged growth in winter.*

☼ ◊ ◊ Z2b
‡6ft (2m) ↔5ft (1.5m)

Syringa pubescens subsp *microphylla* 'Superba'

This upright to spreading, conical, deciduous shrub bears spikes of fragrant, rose-pink flowers at the tips of slender branches. First appearing in spring, they continue to open at irregular intervals until fall. The oval, mid-green leaves are red-green when young. Makes a good screen or informal hedge. 'Miss Kim' is a smaller, more compact cultivar (Z2).

CULTIVATION: *Grow in moist but well-drained, fertile, organic, neutral to alkaline soil, in full sun. Prune out any weak or damaged growth in winter.*

☼ ◊ ◊ Z3　　　　　↕↔to 20ft (6m)

Syringa vulgaris 'Charles Joly'

This dark-purple-flowered form of common lilac is a spreading shrub or small tree. Very fragrant, double flowers appear during spring in dense, conical clusters. The deciduous leaves are heart-shaped to oval and dark green. Use as a backdrop in a shrub or mixed border.

CULTIVATION: *Grow in moist but well-drained, fertile, organic, neutral to alkaline soil, in full sun. Young shrubs require minimal pruning; old, lanky stems can be cut back hard in winter.*

☼ ◊ ◊ Z2　　　　　↕↔22ft (7m)

Syringa vulgaris 'Katherine Havemeyer'

A spreading lilac, forming a large shrub or small tree, producing dense clusters of very fragrant, double, lavender-blue flowers. These open from purple buds in spring. The deciduous, mid-green leaves are heart-shaped. 'Madame Antoine Buchner' is a very similar recommended lilac with slightly pinker flowers.

CULTIVATION: *Grow in moist but well-drained, fertile, neutral to alkaline, organic soil in sun. Mulch regularly. Little pruning is necessary, but it tolerates hard pruning to renovate it.*

◊ ◊ Z2  ↔22ft (7m)

Syringa vulgaris 'Madame Lemoine'

This lilac is very similar in form to 'Katherine Havemeyer' (above) but has compact spikes of large, very fragrant, double white flowers. These are borne in late spring and early summer amid the deciduous, heart-shaped to oval, mid-green leaves. 'Vestale' is another recommended white lilac, with single flowers.

CULTIVATION: *Grow in deep, moist but well-drained, fertile, neutral to alkaline, organic soil, in sun. Do not prune young plants, but older shrubs can be cut back hard in winter to renovate.*

☼ ◊ ◊ Z2 ↔22ft (7m)

Tamarix tetrandra

This large, arching shrub, with feathery foliage on purple-brown shoots, bears plumes of light pink flowers in mid- to late spring. The leaves are reduced to tiny, needle-like scales. Particularly useful on light, sandy soils; in mild coastal gardens, it makes a good windbreak or hedge. For a similar shrub that flowers in late summer, look for *T. ramossissima* 'Rubra' (Z3).

CULTIVATION: *Grow in well-drained soil, in full sun. Cut back young plants by almost half after planting. Prune each year after flowering, or the shrub may become top-heavy and unstable.*

☼ ◊ Z6   ↕↔10ft (3n

Tanacetum coccineum 'Brenda'

A bushy, herbaceous perennial, grown for its daisylike, magenta-pink, yellow-centered flowerheads in early summer borne on upright stems above aromatic, finely divided, gray-green foliage. The cut flowers last well in water. 'James Kelway' is very similar, while 'Eileen May Robinson' has pale pink flowers.

CULTIVATION: *Grow in well-drained, fertile, neutral to slightly acidic soil, in an open, sunny site. Cut back after the first flush of flowers to encourage a second flowering later in the season.*

☼ ◊ Z3b
↕28–32in (70–80cm) ↔18in (45cm)

Taxus baccata

English yew is a slow-growing, broadly conical, evergreen conifer. The needlelike, dark green leaves are arranged in two ranks along the shoots. Male plants bear yellow cones in spring, and female plants produce cup-shaped, fleshy, bright red fruits in fall. Excellent as a dense hedge and as a backdrop to colorful plants. All parts are toxic.

CULTIVATION: *Grow in any well-drained, fertile soil, in sun to deep shade. Tolerates alkaline or acidic soils. Plant both sexes together, for berries. Trim or cut back to renovate in summer or early fall.*

☀ ◐ ◊ Z6   ↕70ft (20m) ↔30ft (10m)

Taxus baccata
'Dovastonii Aurea' (female)

This slow-growing, evergreen conifer has wide-spreading, horizontally tiered branches that weep at the tips. It is smaller than the English yew (above) and has yellow-margined to golden yellow foliage. Fleshy, bright red fruits appear in fall. All parts of this plant are poisonous if eaten.

CULTIVATION: *Grow in any well-drained, fertile soil, in sun or deep shade. Tolerates alkaline or acidic conditions. Plant close to male yews for a reliable display of fall berries. Trim or cut back to renovate in summer or early fall.*

☀ ◐ ◊ Z6   ↕15ft (5m) ↔6ft (2m)

Taxus baccata 'Fastigiata' (female)

Irish yew is a dense, strongly uprig[ht] evergreen conifer that becomes columnar with age. The dark green leaves are not two-ranked like othe[r] yews but stand out all around the shoots. All are female, bearing fles[hy] berrylike, bright red fruits in late summer. All parts are toxic if eaten.

CULTIVATION: *Grow in any reliably moist soil but tolerates most conditions includin[g] very dry, alkaline soils, in full sun or deep shade. Plant with male yews for a reliable crop of berries. Trim or cut back to renova[te] in summer or early fall, if necessary.*

☀ ☀ ◊ ◊ Z6 ↕30ft (10m) ↔12ft (4[m])

Thalictrum delavayi 'Hewitt's Double'

An upright, clump-forming perenni[al] more floriferous than *T. delavayi*, that produces upright sprays of long-lasting, pomponlike, rich mauv[e] flowers from midsummer to early fall. Finely divided, mid-green leave[s] are carried on slender stems shaded dark purple. An excellent foil in a herbaceous border to plants with bolder leaves and flowers.

CULTIVATION: *Grow in moist but well-drained, organic soil, in sun or light shade. Divide clumps and replant every few years to maintain vigor.*

☀ ☀ ◊ ◊ Z5 ↕4ft (1.2m) ↔24in (60cm)

alictrum flavum *bsp. glaucum*

s subspecies of yellow meadow
is a summer-flowering, clump-
ng perennial that bears large,
ight heads of fragrant, sulfur-
ow flowers. These appear above
-green, divided leaves. Good at
margins of a woodland.

TIVATION: *Best in moist, organic soil,
artial shade. Tolerates sun and dry
Flower stems may need staking.*

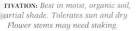☀ ◊ ♦ Z6   ‡3ft (1m) ↔24in (60cm)

uja occidentalis *olmstrup'*

s shrublike form of eastern
orvitae is a slow-growing conifer
h a conical shape. The dense,
1-green leaves are apple-scented
l arranged in vertical sprays.
all oval cones appear amid the
age. Plant alone as specimen tree
se as a hedge.

TIVATION: *Grow in deep, moist but
l-drained soil, in full sun. Shelter from
1, drying winds. Trim as necessary
pring and late summer.*

◊ ♦ Z3
12ft (4m) ↔10–15ft (3–5m)

Thuja occidentalis 'Rheingold'

This bushy, spreading, slow-growing conifer is valued for its golden yellow foliage that is pink-tinted when young and turns bronze in winter. Small, oval cones are carried amid the billowing sprays of apple-scented, scalelike leaves. Good as a specimen tree.

CULTIVATION: *Grow in deep, moist but well-drained soil, in a sheltered, sunny site. Trim in spring and late summer, but be careful not to spoil the form.*

☼ ◊ ◑ Z3
↕3–6ft (1–2m) ↔10–15ft (3–5m)

Thuja orientalis 'Aurea Nana'

This dwarf Oriental arborvitae is an oval-shaped conifer with fibrous red-brown bark. The yellow-green foliage, which fades to bronze over winter, is arranged in flat, vertical sprays. Flask-shaped cones are borne amid the foliage. Good in a rock garden.

CULTIVATION: *Grow in deep, moist but well-drained soil, in sun with shelter from cold, drying winds. Trim in spring and again in late summer as necessary.*

☼ ◊ ◑ Z7
↕↔ to 24in (60c

Thuja plicata '*Stoneham Gold*'

This slow-growing, dwarf form of western red cedar is a conical conifer with fissured, red-brown bark and flattened, irregularly arranged sprays of bright gold, aromatic foliage; the tiny, scalelike leaves are very dark green within the bush. The cones are small and elliptic. Ideal for a rock garden.

CULTIVATION: *Grow in deep, moist but well-drained soil, in full sun with shelter from cold, drying winds. Trim in spring and again in late summer.*

☀ ◊ ◑ Z6 ↔ to 6ft (2m)

Thunbergia grandiflora

The blue trumpet vine is a vigorous, woody-stemmed, evergreen climber that can be grown as an annual in cold climates. Lavender- to violet-blue, sometimes white, trumpet-shaped flowers with yellow throats appear in hanging clusters during summer. The oval to heart-shaped, dark green leaves are softly hairy.

CULTIVATION: *Grow in moist but well-drained, fertile soil or soil mix, in sun. Provide shade during the hottest part of the day. Give the climbing stems support. Minimum temperature 50°F (10°C).*

☀ ◊ Tender ↕ 15–30ft (5–10m)

Thymus pulegioides 'Bertram Anderson'

A low-growing, rounded, evergreen shrub carrying small, narrow, gray-green leaves strongly suffused with yellow. They are aromatic and can be used in cooking. Heads of pale lavender-pink flowers are borne above the foliage in summer. Lovely in an herb garden. Sometimes sold as 'Anderson's Gold'.

CULTIVATION: *Best in well-drained, neutral to alkaline soil, in full sun. Trim after flowering, and remove sprigs for cooking as they are needed.*

☼ ◊ Z5
↕to 12in (30cm) ↔to 10in (25cm)

Thymus serpyllum var. *coccineus*

A mat-forming, evergreen subshrub with finely hairy, trailing stems bearing tiny, aromatic, mid-green leaves. Crimson-pink flowers are borne in congested whorls during summer. Suitable for planting in paving crevices, where the foliage will release its fragrance when stepped on. May also be seen as *T. praecox* 'Coccineus'.

CULTIVATION: *Grow in well-drained, neutral to alkaline, gritty soil. Choose a position in full sun. Trim lightly after flowering to keep the plant neat.*

☼ ◊ Z4
↕10in (25cm) ↔18in (45cm)

Thymus 'Silver Queen'

This rounded, evergreen shrub is similar to 'Bertram Anderson' (see facing page, above), but with silver-white foliage. Masses of oblong, lavender-pink flowerheads are borne throughout summer. Plant in an herb garden; the aromatic leaves can be used in cooking.

CULTIVATION: *Grow in well-drained, neutral to alkaline soil, in full sun. Trim after flowering, and remove sprigs for cooking as needed.*

☼ ◊ Z5
‡to 12in (30cm) ↔ to 10in (25cm)

Tiarella cordifolia

This vigorous, summer-flowering, evergreen perennial is commonly known as foam flower and gets its name from the tiny, star-shaped, creamy white flowers. These are borne in a profusion of upright sprays above lobed, pale green leaves that turn bronze-red in fall. Ideal as a groundcover in a woodland garden, as is the similar *T. wherryi* (Z4b).

CULTIVATION: *Best in cool, moist, organic soil, in deep or light shade. Tolerates a wide range of soil types.*

✱ ☼ ◊ Z4
‡4–12in (10–30cm) ↔ to 12in (30cm)

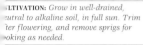

Tilia 'Petiolaris'

This linden is a broad deciduous tree with graceful, drooping branches, best suited for a large garden. The heart-shaped leaves mature from fresh green in spring to a deeper green in summer, then golden yellow in fall. Although bees and other pollinators appreciate the dangling clusters of richly scented summer flowers, they are too inconspicuous to be of great ornamental interest.

CULTIVATION: *Grow in moist but well-drained soil, in sun or light shade.*

☼ ☼ ◊ ◊ Z4b
‡100ft (30m) ↔70ft (20m)

Tolmiea menziesii 'Taff's Gold'

A spreading, clump-forming, semi-evergreen perennial carrying ivy-like, long-stalked, pale lime green leaves mottled with cream and pale yellow. An abundance of tiny, nodding, slightly scented, green and chocolate brown flowers appear in slender, upright spikes during late spring and early summer. Plant in groups to cover the ground in a woodland garden.

CULTIVATION: *Grow in moist but well-drained, organic soil, in partial or deep shade. Sun will scorch the leaves.*

☼ ☼ ◊ ◊ Z7
‡12–24in (30–60cm) ↔3ft (1m)

rachelospermum sminoides

r jasmine is an evergreen, woody-
mmed climber with attractive,
l, glossy, dark green leaves. The
y fragrant flowers, creamy white
ng to yellow, have five twisted
al lobes. They are borne during
d- to late summer, followed by
g seed pods. Grow in a cool
enhouse or conservatory. The
iegated-leaved form, 'Variegatum',
also recommended.

LTIVATION: *Grow in any well-drained,
derately fertile soil, in full sun or
tial shade. Tie in young growth.
nimum temperature 35°F (2°C).*

☀ ◊ Tender   ‡28ft (9m)

rachycarpus fortunei

e Chusan palm is one of the
rdiest palm trees. It has a single,
right trunk with a head of
n-shaped, many-fingered, dark
en leaves. Small yellow flowers
pear in hanging clusters in early
mmer, followed by small, round
ck fruits on female plants. It makes
good container tree for a warm,
eltered patio, but is also suitable
r the open garden, where hardy.

LTIVATION: *Best in a sheltered spot
well-drained soil, in sun.*

☀ ◊ Z7b
70ft (20m) ↔8ft (2.5m)

Tradescantia x andersoniana 'J.C.Weguelin'

This tufted, clump-forming perenn
bears large, pale blue flowers with
three wide-open, triangular petals.
These appear from early summer
to early fall in paired clusters
at the tips of branching stems. The
slightly fleshy, mid-green leaves are
long, pointed, and arching. Effectiv
in a mixed or herbaceous border bu
self-seeds regularly.

CULTIVATION: *Grow in moist, fertile soil,
in sun or partial shade. Deadhead to
encourage repeat flowering.*

☼ ☀ ◊ Z3b
‡24in (60cm) ↔18in (45cm)

Tradescantia x andersoniana 'Osprey'

This clump-forming perennial bear
clusters of large white flowers on
the tips of the upright stems from
early summer to early fall. Each
flower has three triangular petals
surrounded by two leaflike bracts.
The mid-green leaves are narrow
and often purple-tinted. A long-
flowering plant for a mixed or
herbaceous border. Lovely mixed
with dark blue-flowered 'Isis'.

CULTIVATION: *Grow in moist but well-
drained, fertile soil, in sun or partial
shade. Deadhead to prevent self-seeding.*

☼ ☀ ◊ ◊ Z3b
‡24in (60cm) ↔18in (45cm)

ricyrtis formosana

upright, herbaceous perennial
own for its white, purple-spotted.
r-shaped flowers on zig-zagging,
tly hairy stems. These appear in
rly fall above lance-shaped, dark
een leaves that clasp the stems. An
usual plant for a shady border or
en woodland garden.

LTIVATION: *Grow in moist, organic*
l. Choose a sheltered site in deep or
rtial shade. Provide a deep winter
lch where there is unlikely to be
ep snow cover.

☀ ◊ Z4
) 32in (80cm) ↔18in (45cm)

rillium grandiflorum

ake robin is a vigorous, clump-
rming perennial grown for its
rge, three-petaled, pure white
owers that often fade to pink.
nese are carried during spring
nd summer on slender stems above
whorl of three large, dark green,
most circular leaves. Effective in
e company of hostas. The cultivar
lore Pleno' has double flowers.

LTIVATION: *Grow in moist but well-*
ained, leafy, neutral to acidic soil, in
ep or light shade. Provide an annual
lch of leaf mold in fall.

☀ ☀ ◊ ◊ Z4
6in (40cm) ↔12in (30cm)

Trollius x *cultorum* 'Orange Princess'

This globeflower is a robust, clump-forming perennial with orange-gold flowers. These are held above the mid-green foliage in late spring. The leaves are deeply cut with five rounded lobes. Good for bright color beside a pond or stream or in a damp border. For bright yellow flowers, choose the otherwise similar 'Goldquelle'.

CULTIVATION: *Best in heavy, moist, fertile soil, in full sun or partial shade. Cut stems back hard after the first flush of flowers to encourage further blooms.*

☼ ☀ ◐ Z3b
‡to 36in (90cm) ↔18in (45cm)

Tropaeolum majus 'Hermine Grashoff'

This double-flowered nasturtium is a strong-growing, often scrambling annual climber. Long-spurred, bright red flowers appear during summer and fall above the light green, wavy-margined leaves. Excellent for hanging baskets and other container

CULTIVATION: *Grow in moist but well-drained, fairly poor soil, in full sun. The climbing stems need support. Minimum temperature 35˚F (2˚C).*

☼ ◊ Tender
‡3–10ft (1–3m) ↔5–15ft (1.5–5m)

Tropaeolum speciosum

The flame nasturtium is a slender, herbaceous climber that produces long-spurred, bright vermilion flowers throughout summer and fall. These are followed by small, bright blue fruits. The mid-green leaves are divided into several leaflets. Effective growing through dark-leaved hedging plants that contrast with its flowers.

CULTIVATION: *Grow in moist, organic, neutral to acidic soil, in full sun or partial shade. Provide shade at the roots, and support the climbing stems.*

☀ ◊ ◊ Z8 ‡to 10ft (3m)

Tsuga canadensis 'Jeddeloh'

This dwarf form of Canada hemlock is a small, vase-shaped conifer with deeply furrowed, purplish-gray bark. The bright green foliage is made up of needlelike leaves that are arranged in two ranks along the stems. An excellent small specimen tree for shady places; also popular for bonsai training.

CULTIVATION: *Grow in moist but well-drained, organic soil, in full sun or partial shade. Trim during summer.*

☀ ◊ ◊ Z4 ‡5ft (1.5m) ↔6ft (2m)

Tulipa clusiana var. *chrysantha*

This yellow-flowered lady tulip is a bulbous perennial that flowers in early- to mid-spring. The bowl- to star-shaped flowers, tinged red or brownish purple on the outsides, are produced in clusters of up to three per stem above the linear, gray-green leaves. Suitable for a raised bed or rock garden.

CULTIVATION: *Grow in well-drained, fertile soil, in full sun with shelter from strong winds. Deadhead and remove any fallen petals after flowering.*

☼ ◊ Z4   ↕12in (30cr

Tulipa linifolia

This slender, variable, bulbous perennial bears bowl-shaped red flowers in early and mid-spring. These are carried above the linear, gray-green leaves with wavy red margins. The petals have yellow margins and black-purple marks at the base. Good for a rock garden.

CULTIVATION: *Grow in sharply drained, fertile soil, in full sun with shelter from strong winds. Deadhead and remove any fallen petals after flowering.*

☼ ◊ Z4   ↕8in (20cn

ulipa linifolia
atalinii Group

nder, bulbous perennials, often
d as *T. batalinii,* bearing solitary,
wl-shaped, pale yellow flowers
th dark yellow or bronze marks
the insides. These appear from
rly to mid-spring above linear,
ay-green leaves with wavy red
argins. Use in spring bedding;
e flowers are good for cutting.

LTIVATION: *Grow in sharply drained,
tile soil, in full sun with shelter from
rong winds. Deadhead and remove
y fallen petals after flowering.*

◊ Z4 ‡14in (35cm)

ulipa turkestanica

his bulbous perennial produces
to 12 star-shaped white flowers
er stem in early and mid-spring.
hey are flushed with greenish gray
the outsides and have yellow or
ange centers. The linear, gray-
een leaves are arranged beneath
e flowers. Grow in a rock garden
sunny border, away from paths
seating areas, because the flowers
ave an unpleasant scent.

LTIVATION: *Grow in well-drained,
rtile soil, in full sun with shelter from
rong winds. Deadhead and remove
y fallen petals after flowering.*

◊ Z4 ‡12in (30cm)

Tulipa cultivars

These cultivated varieties of tulip are spring-flowering, bulbous perennials with a much wider range of flower color than any other spring bulbs, from the buttercup yellow 'Hamilton' through to the violet-purple 'Blue Heron' and the multicolored, red, white, and blue 'Union Jack'. This diversity makes them invaluable for bringing variety into the garden, either massed together in large containers or beds, or planted in a mixed border. Flower shape is also varied; as well as the familiar cup-shaped blooms, as in 'Dreamland', the are also conical, goblet-, and starshape forms. All are good for cutting.

CULTIVATION: *Grow in well-drained, fertile soil, in sun with shelter from strong winds and excessive moisture. Remove spent flowers. Plant the bulbs in fall.*

☀ ◊ Z4

1 ‡6in (15cm)

2 ‡24in (60cm)

3 ‡20in (50cm)

4 ‡16in (40cm)

5 ‡20in (50cm)

6 ‡12in (30cm)

1 *T.* 'Ancilla' **2** *T.* 'Blue Heron' **3** *T.* 'China Pink'
4 *T.* 'Don Quichotte' **5** *T.* 'Hamilton' **6** *T.* 'Oriental Splendour'

7 24in (60cm)

8 ‡12in (30cm)

9 14in (35cm)

10 ‡24in (60cm)

11 ‡8in (20cm)

12 ‡16in (40cm)

13 ‡24in (60cm)

14 ‡20in (50cm)

7 *T.* 'Dreamland' **8** *T.* 'Keizerskroon' **9** *T.* 'Prinses Irene' **10** *T.* 'Queen of Sheba'
11 *T.* 'Red Riding Hood' **12** *T.* 'Spring Green' **13** *T.* 'Union Jack' **14** *T.* 'West Point'

Uvularia grandiflora

Large merrybells is a slow-spreading, clump-forming perennial bearing solitary or paired, narrowly bell-shaped, sometimes green-tinted yellow flowers. They hang gracefully from slender, upright stems during mid- to late spring above the downward-pointing, lance-shaped, mid-green leaves. Excellent for a shady border or woodland garden.

CULTIVATION: *Grow in moist but well-drained, fertile, organic soil, in deep or partial shade.*

☀ ☀ ◐ ◊ ◊ Z3
‡to 30in (75cm) ↔12in (30cm)

Vaccinium corymbosum 'Top Hat'

Highbush blueberry is a deciduous, acid-soil-loving shrub. 'Top Hat' is a compact selection that bears dangling white flowers in spring, followed by flavorful ½-inch blue berries in mid- to late summer, and red leaves in fall. It is excellent for containers and small gardens, and its berries are enjoyed by birds and wildlife.

CULTIVATION: *Grow in sun or open shade and moist, acidic soil. Plant two or three bushes to optimize pollination and fruit set.*

☀ ☀ ◊ Z4
‡36in (90cm) ↔23in (60cm)

Vaccinium glaucoalbum

A mound-forming, dense, evergreen shrub bearing elliptic, leathery, dark green leaves with bright bluish-white undersides. Very small, pink-tinged white flowers appear in hanging clusters during late spring and early summer, followed by edible, white-bloomed, blue-black berries. Good in an open woodland garden.

CULTIVATION: *Grow in open, moist but well-drained, peaty or sandy, acidic soil, in sun or part shade. Trim in spring. Minimum temperature 41˚F (5˚C).*

☼ ☀ ◊ ◖ Tender

‡20–48in (50–120cm) ↔3ft (1m)

Vaccinium vitis-idaea Koralle Group

These heavy-fruiting cowberries are creeping, evergreen shrubs with oval, glossy dark green leaves, shallowly notched at the tips. In late spring and early summer, small, bell-shaped, white to deep pink flowers appear in dense, nodding clusters. These are followed by a profusion of round, bright red berries that are edible but taste acidic. Makes a good groundcover for an open woodland garden.

CULTIVATION: *Best in peaty or sandy, moist but well-drained, acidic soil, in full sun or part shade. Trim in spring.*

☼ ☀ ◊ ◖ Z1

‡10in (25cm) ↔indefinite

Veltheimia bracteata

A bulbous perennial with basal rosette. of thick, waxy, straplike, glossy, dark green leaves, from which upright flowering stems grow in spring, to be topped by a dense cluster of tubular, pink-purple flowers with yellow spots. An unusual house or conservatory plant where winter protection is needed.

CULTIVATION: *Plant bulbs in fall with the neck just above soil level, in soil-based potting mix with added sharp sand. Site in full sun, reducing watering as the leaves fade. Keep the soil just moist during dormancy. Minimum temperature 35–41°F (2–5°C).*

☼ ◊ Tender ‡18in (45cm) ↔12in (30cm)

Veratrum nigrum

An imposing, rhizomatous perennial that produces a tall and upright, branching spike of many reddish-brown to black flowers from the center of a basal rosette of pleated, mid-green leaves. The small, star-shaped flowers that open in late summer have an unpleasant scent, so choose a moist, shady site not too close to paths or patios.

CULTIVATION: *Grow in deep, fertile, moist but well-drained soil with added organic matter. If in full sun, make sure the soil remains moist. Shelter from cold, drying winds. Divide congested clumps in fall or early spring.*

☼ ☀ ◊ ◊ Z6 ‡48in (120cm) ↔24in (60cm)

Verbascum bombyciferum

This mullein is a very tall perennial that forms basal rosettes of densely packed leaves covered in silky silver hairs. Short-lived, it dies back in summer after the magnificent display of its tall, upright flower spike that is covered in silver hairs and sulfuryellow flowers. For a large border, or it may naturalize by self-seeding in a wild garden.

CULTIVATION: *Grow in alkaline, poor, well-drained soil, in full sun. Support may be needed in fertile soil because of the resultant more vigorous growth. Divide plants in spring, if necessary.*

☼ ◊ Z4   ‡6ft (1.8m) ↔24in (60cm)

Verbascum 'Cotswold Beauty'

A tall, evergreen, short-lived perennial that makes a bold addition to any large border. It bears upright spikes of saucer-shaped, peachy pink flowers, with darker centers, over a long period from early to late summer. These spikes tower over the wrinkled, gray-green foliage, most of which is clumped near the base of the plant. It may naturalize in a wild or lightly wooded garden.

CULTIVATION: *Best in well-drained, poor, alkaline soil, in full sun. In fertile soil, it grows taller and will need support. Divide in spring, if necessary.*

☼ ◊ Z5   ‡4ft (1.2m) ↔18in (45cm)

Verbascum dumulosum

This evergreen subshrub forms small, spreading domes of densely felted, gray or gray-green leaves on white-downy stems. In late spring and early summer, clusters of small, saucer-shaped yellow flowers with red-purple eyes appear amid the foliage. Where marginal, grow in crevices of a warm, sunny wall.

CULTIVATION: *Best in gritty, sharply drained, moderately fertile, preferably alkaline soil, in full sun. Shelter from excessive winter moisture.*

☼ ◊ **Z6**
‡to 10in (25cm) ↔to 16in (40cm)

Verbascum 'Gainsborough'

This short-lived, semi-evergreen perennial is valued for its spires of saucer-shaped, soft yellow flowers, borne throughout summer. Most of the oval and gray-green leaves are arranged in rosettes around the base of the stems. A very beautiful, long-flowering plant for a herbaceous or mixed border.

CULTIVATION: *Grow in well-drained, fertile soil, in an open, sunny site. Often short-lived, but it is easily propagated by root cuttings taken in winter.*

☼ ◊ **Z6**
‡4ft (1.2m) ↔12in (30cm)

Verbascum 'Letitia'

This dense, rounded, evergreen subshrub produces a continuous abundance of small, clear yellow flowers with reddish-purple centers throughout summer. The lance-shaped, irregularly toothed, gray-green leaves are carried beneath the clustered flowers. Suitable for a raised bed or rock garden. Where marginally hardy, grow in crevices of a protected drystone wall.

CULTIVATION: *Best in sharply drained, fairly fertile, alkaline soil, in sun. Avoid sites with excessive winter moisture.*

☼ ◊ Z6
‡to 10in (25cm) ↔to 12in (30cm)

Verbena bonariensis

This is a very useful and easy border plant that can effortlessly add stature to a garden. Its tall, wiry stems rise above most other perennials in midsummer, without obscuring them, and bear small, rounded heads of vibrant purple-violet flowers. These bloom well into fall and are attractive to bees and butterflies. A great "see-through" plant for mixed borders. Self sows in fertile soils. Grow as an annual where not hardy.

CULTIVATION: *Grow in moist but well-drained soil in sun.*

☼ ◊ ◑ Z7b
‡5ft (1.5m) ↔20in (50cm)

Verbena 'Sissinghurst'

A mat-forming perennial bearing rounded heads of small, brilliant magenta-pink flowers that appear from late spring to fall—most prolifically in summer. The dark green leaves are cut and toothed. Excellent for edging a path or growing in a container. In cold areas, overwinter in a greenhouse.

CULTIVATION: *Grow in moist but welldrained, moderately fertile soil or soil mix. Choose a site in full sun.*

☀ ◊ Z8 ‡to 8in (20cm) ↔to 3ft (1m

Veronica gentianoides

This early-summer-flowering, mat-forming perennial bears shallowly cup-shaped, pale blue or white flowers. These are carried in upright spikes that arise from rosettes of glossy, broadly lance-shaped, dark green leaves at the base of the plant. Excellent for the edge of a border.

CULTIVATION: *Grow in moist but well-drained, moderately fertile soil, in full sun or light shade.*

☀ ☀ ◊ Z3b ‡↔18in (45cm)

Veronica prostrata

The prostrate speedwell is a dense, mat-forming perennial. In early summer, it produces upright spikes of saucer-shaped, pale to deep blue flowers at the tips of sprawling stems. The small, bright to mid-green leaves are narrow and toothed. Grow in a rock garden. The cultivar 'Spode Blue' is also recommended.

CULTIVATION: *Best in moist but well-drained, poor to moderately fertile soil. Choose a position in full sun.*

☼ ◊ Z4
‡to 6in (15cm) ↔ to 16in (40cm)

Veronica spicata subsp. *incana*

The silver speedwell is an entirely silver-hairy, mat-forming perennial with upright flowering stems. These are tall spikes of star-shaped, purple-blue flowers, borne from early to late summer. The narrow leaves are silver-hairy and toothed. Ideal for a rock garden. The cultivar 'Wendy', with bright blue flowers, is also recommended.

CULTIVATION: *Grow in well-drained, poor to moderately fertile soil, in full sun. Avoid excessive winter moisture.*

☼ ◊ Z3
‡↔12in (30cm)

Viburnum x *bodnantense* 'Dawn'

A strongly upright, deciduous shrub carrying toothed, dark green leaves, bronze when young. From late fall to spring, when branches are bare, small, tubular, heavily scented, dark pink flowers that age to white are borne in clustered heads, followed by small, blue-black fruits. 'Charles Lamont' is another lovely cultivar of this shrub, as is 'Deben', with almost white flowers.

CULTIVATION: *Grow in any deep, moist but well-drained, fertile soil, in full sun. On old crowded plants, cut the oldest stems back to the base after flowering.*

☼ ◊ ◑ Z7　　　‡10ft (3m) ↔6ft (2m)

Viburnum x *carlcephalum*

This vigorous, rounded, deciduous shrub has broadly heart-shaped, irregularly toothed, dark green leaves that turn red in fall. Rounded heads of small, fragrant white flowers appear amid the foliage during late spring. Suits a shrub border or a woodland garden.

CULTIVATION: *Grow in deep, moisture-retentive, fertile soil. Tolerates sun or semi-shade. Little pruning is necesary.*

☼ ☼ ◑ Z6　　　‡↔10ft (3m)

Viburnum davidii

A compact, evergreen shrub that forms a dome of dark green foliage consisting of oval leaves with three distinct veins. In late spring, tiny, tubular white flowers appear in flattened heads; female plants bear tiny but decorative, oval, metallic blue fruits, later in the season. Looks good planted in groups.

CULTIVATION: *Best in deep, moist but well-drained, fertile soil, in sun or semi-shade. Grow male and female shrubs together for reliable fruiting. Keep neat, if desired, by cutting wayward stems back to strong shoots, or to the base of the plant, in spring.*

☀ ◐ ◌ ◖ Z8　　　↕↔3–5ft (1–1.5m)

Viburnum farreri

This strongly upright, deciduous shrub has oval, toothed, dark green leaves which are bronze when young and turn red-purple in fall. During mild periods in winter and early spring, small, fragrant, white or pink-tinged flowers are borne in dense clusters on the bare stems. These are occasionally followed by tiny, bright red fruits.

CULTIVATION: *Grow in any reliably moist but well-drained, fertile soil, in full sun or partial shade. Thin out old shoots after flowering.*

☀ ◐ ◌ ◖ Z5b　　　↕10ft (3m) ↔8ft (2.5m)

Viburnum opulus '*Xanthocarpum*'

A vigorous, deciduous shrub bearing maplelike, lobed, mid-green leaves that turn yellow in fall. Flat heads of showy white flowers are produced in late spring and early summer, followed by large bunches of spherical, bright yellow berries. 'Notcutt's Variety' and 'Compactum' are recommended red-berried cultivars, the latter much smaller, to only 5ft (1.5m) tall.

CULTIVATION: *Grow in any moist but well-drained soil, in sun or semi-shade. Cut out older stems after flowering to relieve overcrowding.*

☼ ☀ ◊ ◑ Z2b　　　‡15ft (5m) ↔12ft (4m)

Viburnum plicatum '*Mariesii*'

A spreading, deciduous shrub bearing distinctly tiered branches. These are clothed in heart-shaped, toothed, dark green leaves that turn red-purple in fall. In late spring, saucer-shaped white flowers appear in spherical, lacecaplike heads. Few berries are produced; for a heavily fruiting cultivar, look for 'Rowallane'.

CULTIVATION: *Grow in any well-drained, fairly fertile soil, in sun or semi-shade. Requires little pruning other than to remove damaged wood after flowering; be careful not to spoil the form.*

☼ ☀ ◊ Z5b　　　‡10ft (3m) ↔12ft (4m)

Viburnum tinus 'Eve Price'

This very compact, evergreen shrub has dense, dark green foliage. Over a long period from late winter to spring, pink flower buds open to tiny, star-shaped white flowers carried in flattened heads; they are followed by small, dark blue-black fruits. Can be grown as an informal hedge.

CULTIVATION: *Grow in any moist but well-drained, moderately fertile soil, in sun or partial shade. Train or clip after flowering to maintain desired shape.*

☼ ☀ ◊ ◊ Z8　　　　↕↔10ft (3m)

Vinca major 'Variegata'

This variegated form of the greater periwinkle, also known as 'Elegantissima', is an evergreen subshrub with long, slender shoots bearing oval, dark green leaves that have creamy white margins. Dark violet flowers are produced over a long period from mid-spring to fall. Useful as a groundcover for a shady bank, but it may become invasive.

CULTIVATION: *Grow in any moist but well-drained soil. Tolerates deep shade but flowers best with part-day sun.*

☼ ☀ ◊ ◊ Z7　↕18in (45cm) ↔indefinite

Vinca minor '**Atropurpurea**'

This dark-flowered lesser periwinkle is a mat-forming, groundcover shrub with long trailing shoots. Dark plum-purple flowers are produced over a long period from mid-spring to fall, amid the oval, dark green leaves. For light blue flowers, choose 'Gertrude Jekyll'.

CULTIVATION: *Grow in any but very dry soil, in full sun for best flowering, but tolerates partial shade. Restrict growth by cutting back hard in early spring.*

☼ ☀ ◊ ◊ Z4
‡4–8in (10–20cm) ↔ indefinite

Viola cornuta

The horned violet is a spreading, evergreen perennial that produces an abundance of slightly scented, spurred, violet to lilac-blue flowers; the petals are widely separated, with white markings on the lower ones. The flowers are borne amid the mid-green, oval leaves from spring to summer. Suitable for a rock garden. The Alba Group has white flowers.

CULTIVATION: *Grow in moist but well-drained, poor to moderately fertile soil, in sun or partial shade. Cut back after flowering to keep compact.*

☼ ☀ ◊ ◊ Z4
‡to 6in (15cm) ↔ to 16in (40cm)

Viola 'Jackanapes'

A robust, clump-forming, evergreen perennial bearing spreading stems with oval and toothed, bright green leaves. Spurred, golden yellow flowers with purple streaks appear in late spring and summer; the upper petals are deep brownish purple. Good for containers or summer bedding.

CULTIVATION: *Grow in moist but well-drained, fairly fertile soil, in full sun or semi-shade. Often short-lived but is easily grown from seed sown in spring.*

☼ ☼ ◊ ◊ Z4
‡to 5in (12cm) ↔to 12in (30cm)

Viola 'Nellie Britton'

This clump-forming, evergreen perennial with spreading stems produces an abundance of spurred, pinkish-mauve flowers over a long period in summer. The oval, midgreen leaves are toothed and glossy. Suitable for the front of a border.

CULTIVATION: *Best in well-drained but moist, moderately fertile soil, in full sun or partial shade. Deadhead frequently to prolong flowering.*

☼ ☼ ◊ ◊ Z6
‡to 6in (15cm) ↔to 12in (30cm)

Vitis coignetiae

The crimson glory vine is a fast-growing, deciduous climber with large, heart-shaped, shallowly lobed, dark green leaves that turn bright red in fall. Small, blue-black grapes appear in fall. Train against a wall or over a trellis.

CULTIVATION: *Grow in well-drained, neutral to alkaline soil, in sun or semi-shade. Fall color is best on poorer soils. Pinch out the growing tips after planting and allow the strongest shoots to form a permanent framework. Prune back to this each year in midwinter.*

☼ ☀ ◊ Z5   ‡50ft (15m)

Vitis vinifera 'Purpurea'

This purple-leaved grape is a woody, deciduous climber bearing rounded, lobed, toothed leaves; these are white-hairy when young, turning plum-purple, then dark purple, before they fall. Tiny, pale green summer flowers are followed by small purple grapes in fall. Grow over a sturdy fence or pergola, or through a large shrub or tree.

CULTIVATION: *Grow in well-drained, slightly alkaline soil, in sun or semi-shade. Fall color is best on poorer soils. Prune back to an established framework each year in midwinter.*

☼ ☀ ◊ Z6   ‡22ft (7m)

Weigela florida 'Foliis Purpureis'

A compact, deciduous shrub with arching shoots that produces clusters of funnel-shaped, dark pink flowers with pale insides in late spring and early summer. The bronze-green foliage is made up of oval, tapered leaves. Pollution-tolerant, so it is ideal for urban gardens.

CULTIVATION: *Best in well-drained, fertile, organic soil, in full sun. Prune out some older branches at ground level each year after flowering.*

◊ ◊ Z4b   ‡3ft (1m) ↔5ft (1.5m)

Weigela florida 'Variegata'

A dense, deciduous shrub that produces abundant clusters of funnel-shaped, dark pink flowers with pale insides. These are borne in late spring and early summer amid attractive, gray-green leaves with white margins. Suitable for a mixed border or open woodland. Tolerates urban pollution. 'Praecox Variegata' (Z4b) is another attractive variegated weigela.

CULTIVATION: *Grow in any well-drained, fertile, organic soil, in full sun. Prune out some of the oldest branches each year after flowering.*

◊ ◊ Z4b   ‡6–8ft (2–2.5m)

Wisteria floribunda 'Alb[...]*

This white-flowered Japanese wisteria is a fast-growing, woody climber with bright green, divided leaves. The fragrant, pealike flowers appear during spring in very long, drooping spikes; beanlike, velvety green seed pods usually follow. Train against a wall, up into a tree, or over a sturdy framework.

CULTIVATION: *Grow in moist but well-drained, fertile soil, in sun or partial shade. Prune back new growth in summer and in late winter to control spread and promote flowering.*

☼ ☀ ◊ ◊ Z6   ‡28ft (9m) or mo[...]

Wisteria frutescens 'Amethyst Falls'

This American native wisteria is a deciduous woody climber that grows much less rampantly than Asian wisterias, making it better suited to small gardens. The dangling clusters of fragrant lilac flowers bloom in late spring and sometimes again in summer. It is ideal for a larg[...] container as well as along fences or on an arbor. Provide strong support.

CULTIVATION: *Grow in full to part sun and moist, fertile soil. Water regularly until established. Prune in late winter, as needed.*

☼ ☀ ◊ ◊ Z7
‡10–20ft (3–6m) ↔2–5ft (0.5–1.5m)

isteria sinensis

inese wisteria is a vigorous,
ciduous climber that produces
ng, hanging spikes of fragrant,
alike, lilac-blue or white flowers.
ese appear amid the bright green,
vided leaves in late spring and
rly summer, usually followed by
anlike, velvety green seed pods.
ba' is a white-flowered form.

LTIVATION: *Grow in moist but well-
ained, fertile soil. Provide a sheltered
e in sun or partial shade. Cut back
g shoots to 2 or 3 buds, in late winter.*

☼ ◊ ◊ Z6   ‡28ft (9m) or more

ucca filamentosa
'Bright Edge'

n almost stemless, clump-forming
rub with basal rosettes of rigid,
nce-shaped, dark green leaves, to
in (75cm) long, with broad yellow
argins. Tall spikes, to 6ft (2m) or
ore, of nodding, bell-shaped white
owers, tinged with green or cream,
e borne in summer. A striking,
rchitectural specimen for a border
courtyard. The leaves of 'Variegata'
e edged white.

LTIVATION: *Grow in any well-drained
il, in full sun. Remove old flowers at
e end of the season. Where marginally
ardy, mulch over winter.*

☼ ◊ Z4   ‡30in (75cm) ↔5ft (1.5m)

Yucca flaccida 'Ivory'

An almost stemless, evergreen shrub that forms a dense, basal clump of swordlike leaves. Tall spikes, to 5ft (1.5m) or more, of nodding, bell-shaped white flowers are borne in mid- and late summer. The lance-shaped, dark blue-green leaves, fringed with curly or straight thread are arranged in basal rosettes. Thrives in coastal gardens and on sandy soils.

CULTIVATION: *Grow in any well-drained soil but needs a hot, dry position in full sun to flower well. Where marginally hardy, mulch over winter.*

☀ ◊ Z4   ↕↔5ft (1.5r

Zantedeschia aethiopica

This relatively small-flowered calla lily is a clump-forming perennial. Almost upright, cream-yellow flowe are borne in succession from late spring to midsummer, followed by long, arrow-shaped leaves, evergreen in mild areas. May be used as a waterside plant in shallow water.

CULTIVATION: *Best in moist but well-drained, fertile, organic soil. Choose a site in full sun or partial shade. Mulch deeply for winter where marginally hardy Minimum temperature 35°F (2°C).*

☀ ☼ ◊ ◗ Tender
↕36in (90cm) ↔24in (60cm)

antedeschia aethiopica 'Green Goddess'

This green-flowered calla lily is a clump-forming, robust perennial that is evergreen in mild climates. Upright and white-centered flowers appear from late spring to midsummer above the dull green, arrow-shaped leaves. Good in shallow water.

CULTIVATION: *Grow in moist, organic, fertile soil. Choose a site in full sun or partial shade. Mulch deeply over winter where marginally hardy. Minimum temperature 35°F (2°C).*

❄ ☀ ◊ ◆ Tender
‡36in (90cm) ↔24in (60cm)

Zauschneria californica 'Dublin'

This deciduous California fuchsia, sometimes called 'Glasnevin', is a clump-forming perennial bearing a profusion of tubular, bright red flowers during late summer and early fall. The gray-green leaves are lance-shaped and hairy. Provides spectacular, late-season color for a drystone wall or border. Grow at the base of a warm wall.

CULTIVATION: *Best in well-drained, moderately fertile soil, in full sun. Provide shelter from cold, drying winds. Minimum temperature 35°F (2°C).*

☀ ◊ Tender
‡to 10in (25cm) ↔to 12in (30cm)

THE PLANTING GUIDE

Container Plants for Spring

A pot of evergreens and bright spring flowers and bulbs brings cheer to a front door or patio on a chilly early spring day. Tailor the soil to suit the plants: camellias and rhododendrons can be grown in acidic soil mix, for example. Because soil freezes more completely in containers above ground, only plants from two zones warmer will survive reliably in areas with very cold winters.

Ajuga reptans 'Catlin's Giant'
Perennial Z4 Clumps of green leaves and spikes of blue flowers.
↕8in (20cm) ↔24–36in (60–90cm)

Arabis caucasica 'Variegata'
Perennial Z3 Trailing plant with white flowers and yellow margined leaves.
↕6in (15cm) ↔20in (50cm)

Aubrieta x *cultorum* Hybrids
Perennial Z4 Mat-forming plants with bright flowers in pink, red, and purple shades.
↕2in (5cm) ↔24in (60cm)

Aurinia saxatilis
Perennial   page 110

Bergenia 'Ballawley'
Perennial   page 120

Camellia japonica cultivars
Evergreen shrubs   pages 132–133

Camellia x *williamsii* 'Donation'
Evergreen shrub   page 136

Chaenomeles speciosa 'Geisha Girl'
Shrub Z5 Soft apricot, semidouble flowers in abundance.
↕3ft (1m) ↔4ft (1.2m)

Chamaecyparis lawsoniana 'Minima Glauca'
Evergreen shrub Z6 A small neat conifer with blue-green leaves.
↕24in (60cm)

Chionodoxa forbesii 'Pink Giant'
Bulb Z4 Star-shaped, white-centered pink flowers.
↕4–8in (10–20cm) ↔1¼in (3cm)

Crocus chrysanthus 'Ladykiller'
Bulb Z4 White, scented flowers with purple stripes on buds.
↕3in (7cm) ↔2in (5cm)

Euphorbia myrsinites
Perennial   page 23

Erica carnea 'Myretoun Ruby'
Evergreen shrub Z4 Spreading habit, with pink flowers that deepen as they age.
↕6in (15cm) ↔18in (45cm)

Hedera helix 'Kolibri'
Evergreen shrub Z5b Trailing stems; leaves variegated white and green.
↕18in (45cm)

Helleborus niger
Perennial   page 288

Hyacinthus orientalis 'City of Haarlem'
Bulb   page 295

Hyacinthus orientalis 'Gipsy Queen'
Bulb Z4 Orange-pink, scented flowers.
↕10in (25cm)

Hyacinthus orientalis 'Hollyhock'
Bulb Z4 Double red flowers.
↕8in (20cm)

Hyacinthus orientalis 'Violet Pearl'
Bulb Z4 Spikes of scented, amethyst violet flowers with paler petal edges.
‡10in (25cm)

Ilex x altaclerensis 'Golden King'
Evergreen shrub   page 303

Myosotis sylvatica 'Blue Ball'
Biennial   page 47

Narcissus 'Ceylon'
Bulb   page 380

Narcissus 'Cheerfulness'
Bulb   page 380

Narcissus small daffodils
Bulbs   pages 378–379

Phlox subulata 'Candy Stripe'
Perennial Z3 Evergreen perennial with bright pink and white striped flowers.
‡4in (10cm) ↔20in (50cm)

Pieris 'Forest Flame'
Evergreen shrub   page 434

Pieris japonica 'Purity'
Evergreen shrub Z5 Compact, with white flowers and pale young growth.
‡↔3ft (1m)

Primula Gold-laced Group
Perennial   page 447

Primula 'Guinevere'
Perennial   page 447

Pulsatilla vulgaris
Perennial   page 461

Rhododendron 'Curlew'
Evergreen shrub Z7 Small clusters of bright yellow flowers.
‡↔24in (60cm)

Rhododendron 'Doc'
Evergreen shrub   page 476

Rhododendron 'Homebush'
Shrub   page 470

Rhododendron 'Mother's Day'
Evergreen shrub Z7 Bright red-flowered evergreen azalea.
↔5ft (1.5m)

Tulipa 'Apricot Beauty'
Bulb Z4 Pastel, salmon-pink flowers of great beauty.
‡14in (35cm)

Tulipa 'Cape Cod'
Bulb Z4 Yellow flowers striped with red above prettily marked leaves.
‡8in (20cm)

Tulipa 'Carnaval de Nice'
Bulb Z4 Red and white-striped blooms like double peonies.
‡16in (40cm)

Tulipa clusiana var. *chrysantha*
Bulb   page 554

Tulipa cultivars
Bulbs   pages 556–557

Tulipa praestans 'Unicum'
Bulb Z4 Cream-edged leaves and one to four scarlet flowers per stem.
‡12in (30cm)

Tulipa 'Toronto'
Bulb Z4 Multiflowered tulips with three to five flowers of deep coral-pink.
‡10in (25cm)

Viburnum farreri
Shrub   page 567

Viola Universal Series
Biennial Z6 Wide range of colors with flowers throughout spring.
‡6in (15cm) ↔to 12in (30cm)

Viola 'Velour Blue'
Biennial Z6 Compact plants with masses of small light blue flowers.
‡6in (15cm) ↔8in (20cm)

Container Plants for Summer

Containers can bring color to areas that have no soil; they can be filled with permanent plants, or used to add extra color when filled with annuals and tender perennials. In a large pot, combine the two with a shrub augmented by lower, temporary plants. There is a huge choice, but every container will need regular water and fertilizer if it is to look its best.

Abutilon megapotamicum
Shrub page **61**

Agapanthus caudatus subsp. *patens*
Perennial page **79**

Amaranthus caudatus
Annual page **29**

Argyranthemum 'Vancouver'
Perennial page **99**

Bidens ferulifolia
Perennial page **90**

Brugmansia x *candida*
'Grand Mariner'
Tender shrub Min. temp. 45°F (7°C).
Large pendulous trumpet-shaped apricot flowers are fragrant at night.
‡10ft (3m) ↔ to 5ft (1.5m)

Calendula 'Fiesta Gitana'
Annual page **33**

Campanula carpatica 'Blue Clips'
Perennial Z4 Mound-shaped plant with a long flowering period.
‡9in (23cm) ↔ 12in (30cm)

Catharanthus roseus 'Pacific Punch'
Tender perennial page **34**

Clematis 'Doctor Ruppel'
Climber page **161**

Crocosmia 'Lucifer'
Perennial page **184**

Dianthus 'La Bourboule'
Perennial page **205**

Diascia barberae
'Blackthorn Apricot'
Perennial page **206**

Fuchsia hybrids
Shrubs pages **245–247**

Gazanias
Perennials page **254**

Hosta 'Francee'
Perennial page **291**

Hydrangea macrophylla 'Ayesha'
Shrub Z7 Unusual because the blooms are cupped, resembling Syringa (lilac) flowers.
‡5ft (1.5m) ↔ 6ft (2m)

Lavatera 'Silver Cup'
Annual page **340**

Lilium formosanum var. *pricei*
Perennial page **347**

Lilium longiflorum
Perennial page **348**

Lilium monadelphum
Perennial page **349**

Lobularia maritima 'Carpet of Snow'
Annual page **45**

Lonicera x *brownii*
'Dropmore Scarlet'
Shrub Z2b Deciduous climber with bright red trumpet-shaped blooms.
‡12ft (4m) ↔ 6ft (2m)

Lotus maculatus
Tender perennial Narrow, silvery leaves contrast with orange, clawlike flowers on trailing shoots.
‡8in (20cm) ↔indefinite

Nicotiana langsdorfii
Annual Spikes of small, green, tubular flowers with flaring trumpets.
‡to 5ft (1.5m) ↔ 14in (35cm)

Osteospermum cultivars
Perennials   page **393**

Pelargonium 'Attar of Roses'
Perennial   page **404**

Pelargoniums, flowering
Perennials   pages **406–408**

Penstemon 'Andenken an Friedrich Hahn'
Perennial   page **410**

Perovskia 'Blue Spire'
Perennial   page **412**

Petunia 'Lavender Storm'
Annual Compact, ground-covering plants with large blooms.
‡12in (30cm) ↔16in (40cm)

Petunia 'Million Bells Blue'
Annual Masses of small flowers on bushy, compact plants.
‡10in (25cm)

Plumbago auriculata
Scrambling shrub   page **439**

Rosa Patio Hybrids
                              pages **488–489**

Salvia patens 'Cambridge Blue'
Perennial   page **510**

Scaevola aemula
Tender perennial   page **53**

Thunbergia alata Susie Hybrids
Tender vine   page **56**

Tropaeolum majus 'Hermine Grashoff'
Climber   page **552**

Verbena 'Lawrence Johnston'
Perennial Z8 Bright green foliage with intense, fiery red flowers.
‡18in (45cm) ↔24in (60cm)

Verbena 'Sissinghurst'
Annual Spreading plant with fine leaves and magenta-pink flowers.
‡to 8in (20cm) ↔ to 3ft (1m)

Container Plants for Fall

Fall is a season of great change as the leaves of deciduous plants become brilliant before they fall. Most annuals have finished their display, but some plants, especially fuchsias, asters, salvias, dwarf chrysanthemums, and dahlias, continue to provide splashes of colorful flowers. Evergreens form a strong and solid background to all garden displays.

Acer tataricum ssp. *ginnala*
Shrub   page 70

Argyranthemum 'Jamaica Primrose'
Tender perennial   page 99

Aster 'Little Carlow'
Perennial   page 106

Canna 'Lucifer'
Tender perennial Dwarf, with green leaves and red, yellow-edged flowers.
↕24in (60cm) ↔20in (50cm)

Chamaecyparis lawsoniana 'Ellwood's Gold'
Conifer   page 149

Euonymus europaeus 'Red Cascade'
Shrub   page 231

Gaultheria mucronata 'Crimsonia'
Evergreen shrub Z7 Acidic-soil-loving, fine-leaved shrub with showy, deep pink berries.
↕↔4ft (1.2m)

Hibiscus syriacus 'Woodbridge'
Shrub   page 289

Hydrangea paniculata 'Grandiflora'
Shrub   page 299

Hypericum x *moserianum* 'Tricolor'
Shrub Z5b Variegated narrow, flushed pink leaves, and yellow flowers.
↕12in (30cm) ↔24in (60cm)

Juniperus communis 'Compressa'
Conifer   page 325

Nandina domestica 'Firepower'
Shrub Z7 Compact plant with red fall color and berries.
↕18in (45cm) ↔24in (60cm)

Osmanthus heterophyllus 'Variegatus'
Evergreen shrub Z7 Hollylike cream-edged leaves and fragrant, white flowers in fall.
↕↔15ft (5m)

Rudbeckia hirta 'Toto'
Annual Z3 Orange flowers with black centers on very compact plants.
↕↔8in (20cm)

Rudbeckia fulgida var. *sullivantii* 'Goldsturm'
Perennial   page 500

Sedum spectabile 'Brilliant'
Perennial   page 522

Solidago 'Goldenmosa'
Perennial   page 529

Thuja orientalis 'Aurea Nana'
Conifer   page 544

Viburnum dilatatum 'Erie'
Shrub Z5 Free flowering with bright red fruit that persist well. Good fall color.
↕6ft (2m) ↔10ft (3m)

Container Plants for Winter

Few plants flower during cold winter months; use those that do in containers by doors and windows, where they can be seen from the comfort of the home. Many evergreens, especially variegated ones, look cheery when other plants are bare. Plant shrubs out in the garden after a few years in pots. To give a little protection against freezing, wrap pots with bubble plastic.

Calamagrostis x *aciflora* 'Karl Foerster'
Perennial Z4 Ornamental grass with showy seed plumes that stand up to winter weather and last well.
‡6ft (2m) ↔24in (60cm)

Corylus avellana 'Contorta'
Shrub page 175

Cyclamen coum
Bulb Z5 Deep green heart-shaped leaves and pink flowers.
‡2–3in (5–8cm) ↔4in (10cm)

Erica carnea 'Springwood White'
Evergreen shrub page 219

Erica x *darleyensis* 'Arthur Johnson'
Evergreen shrub Z5 The upright stems have deep green leaves and bear pink flowers in winter.
‡30in (75cm) ↔42in (60cm)

Euonymus alatus
Shrub page 230

Euonymus fortunei 'Harlequin'
Evergreen shrub Z5 Compact shrub, young leaves heavily splashed with white.
‡↔16in (40cm)

Festuca glauca 'Blaufuchs'
Ornamental grass page 238

Hedera helix 'Eva'
Evergreen climber Z5b Small gray-green leaves edged with white.
‡4ft (1.2m)

Ilex aquifolium 'Ferox Argentea'
Evergreen shrub page 305

Lamium maculatum 'Beacon Silver'
Perennial Z3 Bright silver-gray foliage and magenta-pink flowers.
‡8in (20cm) ↔3ft (1m)

Laurus nobilis
Evergreen shrub or small tree page 336

Liriope muscari 'John Burch'
Perennial Z6 Grassy plant with gold-striped leaves and violet flowers.
‡12in (30cm) ↔18in (45cm)

Salix babylonica var. *pekinensis* 'Tortulosa'
Shrub page 501

Skimmia japonica 'Rubella'
Evergreen shrub page 527

Viburnum trilobum 'Wentworth'
Shrub Z2 Upright shrub with good fall color and persistent bright red fruits.
‡15ft (5m) ↔12ft (4m)

Viola 'Floral Dance'
Biennial Z6 Winter pansies in mixed colors.
‡6in (15cm) ↔to 12in (30cm)

Viola 'Mello 21'
Biennial Z6 Pansy mixture of 21 colors.
‡6in (15cm) ↔to 12in (30cm)

Yucca gloriosa 'Variegata'
Evergreen shrub Z7 Erect shrub with sharp, pointed leaves edged with yellow.
‡↔6ft (2m)

Containers in Sunny Sites

A sunny position where pots can be placed allows the cultivation of a huge range of plants. Apart from most bedding, many tender plants that must spend cold winters under cover should thrive in a sheltered sunny position and bring a touch of the exotic. Specimen plants are best grown in their own containers; simply group them together to create masterful associations.

Aloe vera
Succulent   page **85**

Artemesia schmidtiana
Perennial Z3b Mounded plant with silver foliage often sold as "Silver Mound." Can be cut back hard in mid-summer if growth becomes straggly.
‡12in (30cm) ↔18in (45cm)

Brachyscome 'Strawberry Mist'
Tender perennial Low, spreading plant with feathery foliage and pink daisylike flowers. Sometimes sold as Brachycome.
‡10in (25cm) ↔18in (45cm)

Correa backhouseana
Evergreen shrub   page **172**

Erica erigena 'Irish Dusk'
Evergreen shrub Z5 Deep pink flowers are produced from fall to spring on plants with grayish-green leaves.
‡24in (60cm) ↔18in (45cm)

Festuca glauca 'Blaufuchs'
Perennial   page **238**

Fuchsia 'Madame Cornéllissen'
Tender Upright, with masses of red and white single flowers.
‡↔24in (60cm)

Gazania 'Daybreak Red Stripe'
Perennial Z8 Raise from seed for showy yellow blooms striped with red.
‡to 8in (20cm) ↔to 10in (25cm)

Geranium 'Ann Folkard'
Perennial   page **258**

Geranium subcaulescens
Perennial   page **259**

Geranium palmatum
Perennial Z8 Bold clumps of foliage with large mauve flowers in summer.
‡↔to 4ft (1.2m)

Hebe albicans
Evergreen shrub   page **272**

Helianthemum 'Wisley Primrose'
Perennial   page **281**

Heliotropum arborescens 'Marine'
Tender shrub (usually grown as an annual) Sweetly scented mauve-blue flowers on a compact plant.
‡↔18in (45cm)

Hosta 'Krossa Regal'
Perennial Z3 A magnificent cultivar with upright gray leaves and tall spikes of lilac flowers.
‡28in (70cm) ↔30in (75cm)

Ipomoea 'Heavenly Blue'
Annual climber   page **309**

Jasminum mesnyi
Climber   page **323**

Lathyrus odoratus 'Patio Mixed'
Annual climber   page **335**

Lobelia erinus Cascade Series Mixed
Annual   page **44**

Mimulus aurantiacus
Evergreen shrub   page **46**

Myrtus communis subsp. *tarentina*
Evergreen shrub   page **377**

Nepeta x *faassenii* 'Dropmore'
Perennial Z3 Lax plant with gray foliage and blue flowers freely produced.
↕24in (60cm) ↔18in (45cm)

Osteospermum 'Whirligig'
Tender   page 49

Passiflora 'Amethyst'
Climber Fast-growing frost-tender climber that produces beautiful lavender flowers all summer.
↕12ft (4m)

Pelargonium 'Deacon Moonlight'
Tender Pale lilac double flowers above neat foliage on compact plants.
↕8in (20cm) ↔10in (25cm)

Pelargonium 'Dolly Varden'
Perennial   page 417

Pelargonium 'Vista Deep Rose'
Tender perennial Single color in this seed-raised F2 series.
↕↔12in (30cm)

Penstemon 'Apple Blossom'
Perennial   page 410

Penstemon 'Osprey'
Perennial Z6 Spikes of white flowers edged with pink.
↕↔18in (45cm)

Petunia 'Duo Peppermint'
Annual Double, pink flowers, quite weather-resistant in wet summers.
↕8in (20cm) ↔12in (30cm)

Phormium 'Sundowner'
Perennial   page 425

Rehmannia glutinosa
Tender Slightly sticky leaves on tall stems that carry dusky pink, foxglovelike flowers.
↕6–12in (15–30cm) ↔to 12in (30cm)

Rosa Patio and Miniature Hybrids
Shrub   page 488–489

Sempervivum arachnoideum
Succulent   page 524

Solenopsis axillaris
Tender Dome-shaped, feathery, with delicate but showy star-shaped, blue flowers.
↕↔12in (30cm)

Tagetes 'Naughty Marietta'
Annual   page 55

Thymus x *citriodorus* 'Aureus'
Evergreen shrub Z5 Low-growing bush, scented of lemon, with gold leaves and pink flowers.
↕12in (30cm) ↔to 10in (25cm)

Tropaeolum majus
'Alaska Salmon Orange'
Annual   page 56

Tropaeolum peregrinum
Annual A climber with light green foliage and bright yellow flowers resembling small birds in flight.
↕12ft (4m) ↔12in (30cm)

Containers in Shade

A shady site can be a difficult place to grow plants—the soil is often dry—but a wide range of interesting plants can be grown in containers. Remember that rain may not reach plants under trees; regular watering is needed all year, plus fertilizing in summer. Add bulbs for spring color and flowering plants in summer. Combine plants for form and texture as well as color.

Acer palmatum var. *dissectum* **'Crimson Queen'**
Shrub Z6 Arching shoots with finely toothed purple leaves.
‡10ft (3m) ↔12ft (4m)

Ageratum **'Southern Cross'**
Annual Neat, bushy plants with white and blue fluffy flowers.
‡↔10in (25cm)

Ajuga reptans **'Rainbow'**
Perennial Z3 Mats of bronze leaves spotted with pink and yellow; blue flowers.
‡6in (15cm) ↔18in (45cm)

Alchemilla mollis
Perennial   page 81

Astilbe x *arendsii* **'Erica'**
Perennial Z3 Sprays of pale pink flowers over bronzy foliage.
‡36in (90cm) ↔24in (60cm)

Begonia **Nonstop Series**
Tender Compact plants with double flowers in many colors.
‡↔12in (30cm)

Camellia japonica **'Lavinia Maggi'**
Evergreen shrub   page 133

Dryopteris erythrosora
Fern Z4 Colorful fern with copper-red young fronds.
‡24in (60cm) ↔15in (38cm)

Dryopteris wallichiana
Fern   page 212

Fuchsia **'Dollar Princess'**
Tender A robust plant with small, red and purple, double flowers.
‡12–18in (30–45cm) ↔18–24in (45–60cm)

Hakonechloa macra **'Aureola'**
Ornamental grass   page 267

Hedera helix **'Ivalace'**
Evergreen climber   page 278

Heuchera **'Pewter Moon'**
Perennial Z4 Purple leaves overlaid with a silver sheen and spikes of pink flowers.
‡16in (40cm) ↔12in (30cm)

Hosta **'Royal Standard'**
Perennial   page 292

Ilex crenata **'Convexa'**
Evergreen shrub   page 306

Impatiens **'Blackberry Ice'**
Annual Double purple flowers and white variegated foliage.
‡to 28in (70cm)

Pieris japonica **'Little Heath'**
Evergreen shrub Compact, acidic-soil-loving, with white-edged leaves flushed pink in spring.
‡↔24in (60cm)

Rhododendron **'Vuyk's Scarlet'**
Evergreen shrub   page 469

Viola **'Imperial Antique Shades'**
Biennial Z7 Large flowers in pink, cream, and parchment colors.
‡6in (15cm) ↔8in (25cm)

Foliage for Hanging Baskets

Although flowering plants are the most popular choice for hanging baskets, they can often be enhanced with attractive foliage plants. Silver-leaved plants are the most widely grown foil for flowers, but there are trailing plants that have gold, green, and red foliage, and it is not difficult to plant a beautiful basket using plants chosen solely for their colorful and contrasting leaves.

Begonias, Foliage
Perennials pages **112–113**

Chlorophytum comosum '**Vittatum**'
Tender perennial Variegated narrow leaves; arching stems bearing plantlets.
‡6–8in (15–20cm) ↔ 6–12in (15–30cm)

Glechoma hederacea '**Variegata**'
Perennial Z4 Long, pendent stems with gray-green leaves edged with white.
↔ trailing to 6ft (2m)

Hedera helix '**Goldchild**'
Evergreen climber page **278**

Helichrysum petiolare '**Limelight**'
Tender shrub Arching stems with felted pale green leaves, yellow in sun.
‡3ft (1m) ↔ indefinite

Helichrysum petiolare '**Variegatum**'
Evergreen shrub page **41**

Lamium maculatum '**Aureum**'
Perennial Z3 Creeping, with bright yellow leaves marked white, and pink flowers.
‡8in (20cm) ↔ 3ft (1m)

Lysimachia congestiflora
'**Outback Sunset**'
Perennial Z7 Semi-trailing, with green, cream, and bronze leaves and clusters of yellow flowers.
‡6in (15cm) ↔ 12in (30cm)

Lysimachia nummularia '**Aurea**'
Perennial page **361**

Pelargonium '**Swanland Lace**'
Tender perennial Trailing plant with pink flowers and leaves veined with yellow.
↕12in (30cm)

Plectranthus forsteri '**Marginatus**'
Tender perennial Scented foliage, edged with white. New growth arches strongly.
‡10in (25cm) ↔ 3ft (1m)

Saxifraga stolonifera '**Tricolor**'
Perennial Z7 Round leaves edged with white and flushed pink; plantlets form on long runners.
↔ to 12in (30cm)

Tropaeolum majus **Alaska Series**
Annual Easily raised, bushy nasturtiums with white-splashed leaves.
‡to 12in (30cm) ↔ to 18in (45cm)

Flowers for Hanging Baskets

Most gardens, and houses or apartments without gardens, can be brightened by a few hanging baskets. They are easy to plant, and there are lots of cheerful plants to choose from, all with a long flowering season and a low or trailing habit. Baskets require regular watering and fertilizing to grow and flower well all summer. Automatic irrigation systems take the worry out of vacation watering.

Abutilon megapotamicum
Shrub   page **61**

Acalypha reptans
Tender perennial Spreading plant with short red-hot cats'-tail flowers.
↕6in (15cm) ↔24in (60cm)

Anagallis monellii
Perennial Z8 Spreading plant with small leaves and bright, intense, deep blue flowers.
↕4–8in (10–20cm) ↔16in (40cm)

Antirrhinum 'Candelabra Lemon Blush'
Perennial Z8 Bushy habit with trailing flower stems carrying pale yellow flowers, flushed with pink.
↕↔15in (38cm)

Begonia fuchsioides
Tender perennial Arching stems set with tiny, glossy leaves bear pendent pink or red flowers.
↕30in (75cm) ↔18in (45cm)

Begonia 'Illumination Orange'
Perennial   page **114**

Begonia 'Irene Nuss'
Perennial   page **115**

Begonia sutherlandii
Perennial   page **115**

Convolvulus sabatius
Perennial   page **168**

Diascia 'Lilac Belle'
Perennial Z8 Loose spikes of mauve-pink flowers.
↕8in (20cm) ↔12in (30cm)

Fuchsia 'Golden Marinka'
Shrub   page **248**

Fuchsia 'Jack Shahan'
Shrub   page **248**

Fuchsia 'La Campanella'
Shrub   page **248**

Fuchsia 'Lena'
Shrub   page **248**

Lobelia erinus 'Colour Cascade'
Annual Trailing stems with flowers in shades of blue, pink, and white.
↕6in (15cm) ↔18in (45cm)

Lobelia richardsonii
Perennial Z5 Bushy but rather sparse, trailing stems with small leaves and blue flowers.
↕6in (15cm) ↔12in (30cm)

Mimulus aurantiacus
Evergreen shrub   page **46**

Parochetus communis
Perennial Min. temp. 35°F (2°C). A fast-growing trailer with cloverlike leaves and pale blue, pealike flowers.
↕4in (10cm) ↔12in (30cm)

Pelargonium Amethyst 'Fisdel'
Perennial   page **406**

Pelargonium 'Lila Mini Cascade'
Tender perennial Single, pink flowers on a compact but vigorous plant.
↕18–20in (45–50cm) ↔6–8in (15–20cm)

Pelargonium 'Madame Crousse'
Tender perennial Trailing plant with
semidouble pink flowers.
‡20–24in (50–60cm) ↔6–8in (15–20cm)

Pelargonium 'Oldbury Cascade'
Tender perennial Rich red flowers
on a compact plant with cream variegated
leaves.
‡18in (45cm) ↔12in (30cm)

Pelargonium 'Rouletta'
Tender perennial Double white flowers,
heavily margined with red.
‡20–24in (50–60cm) ↔6–8in (15–20cm)

Pelargonium 'The Boar'
Perennial   page 408

Pelargonium 'Ville de Paris'
Tender perennial Single, pink
flowers produced in profusion on
a pendulous plant.
‡24in (60cm) ↔18in (45cm)

Pelargonium 'Yale'
Tender perennial The trailing stems
carry clusters of semidouble bright
red flowers.
‡8–10in (20–25cm) ↔6–8in (15–20cm)

Petunia Daddy Series
Annual Large flowers, heavily veined
with darker shades.
‡14in (35cm) ↔12–36in (30–90cm)

Petunia 'Marco Polo Adventurer'
Annual Large, double flowers of bright
rose pink on trailing plants.
‡15in (38cm)

Petunia 'Surfinia Pastel Pink'
Annual Large flowers of mid-pink on a
strong plant that trails well.
‡9–16in (23–40cm) ↔12–36in (30–90cm)

Scaevola aemula 'Blue Fan'
Tender perennial Blue, fan-like flowers
freely produced on a spreading plant.
‡6in (15cm) ↔4ft (1.2m)

Schizanthus pinnatus 'Hit Parade'
Annual   page 54

Sutera cordata 'Knysna Hills'
Tender perennial Bushy plant with
massed heads of tiny, pale pink flowers.
‡8in (20cm) ↔24in (60cm)

Sutera cordata 'Snowflake'
Tender perennial Spreading, small-
leafed plant with tiny, five-petaled white
flowers for months.
‡4in (10cm) ↔24in (60cm)

Tropaeolum majus
'Whirlybird Scarlet'
Annual Bushy, trailing plants with single
and semi-double flowers.
‡10in (25cm) ↔14in (35cm)

Verbena 'Imagination'
Tender perennial Seed-raised,
loosely-branched plants with small, deep
violet flowers.
‡↔15in (38cm)

Verbena 'Tapien Pink'
Tender perennial Trailing stems with
clusters of small pink flowers.
‡↔15in (38cm)

Viola 'Sunbeam'
Biennial Z4-5 Semi-trailing plant with
small yellow flowers.
‡↔12in (30cm)

Spring-Flowering Bulbs

The first signs that winter is giving way to spring are usually the flowers of spring bulbs. From tiny winter aconites that open as the leaves push through the soil to majestic crown imperials, there are bulbs for every situation. Most are tolerant of a wide range of soils, and many can be grown in the shade of trees. Grown in pots, they can be brought into the home to be enjoyed.

Allium cristophii

page **83**

Anemone blanda 'White Splendour'

page **90**

Bulbocodium vernum
Z5 Bright pink, crocus-like flowers in early spring before the leaves.
↕↔4in (10cm)

Camassia cuisickii
Z5 Sheaves of narrow leaves and tall racemes of blue starlike blooms.
↕24–32in (60–80cm) ↔4in (10cm)

Chionodoxa luciliae

page **152**

Chionodoxa sardensis
Z4 Deep blue starry flowers on slender stems.
↕4–8in (10–20cm) ↔1¼in (3cm)

Corydalis flexuosa
Z5 Clumps of delicate foliage and nodding bright blue flowers.
↕6–12in (15–30cm) ↔8in (20cm)

Corydalis solida 'George Baker'

page **174**

Crocus angustifolius
Z4 Clusters of orange-yellow flowers in spring.
↕↔2in (5cm)

Crocus chrysanthus 'Blue Pearl'
Z4 Lilac-blue flowers with white and yellow centers.
↕3in (8cm) ↔1½in (4cm)

Crocus chrysanthus 'E.A. Bowles'

page **185**

Crocus sieberi 'Hubert Edelstein'

page **185**

Crocus sieberi 'Tricolor'

page **185**

Crocus tommasinianus
Z4 An early-flowering crocus with slender, silvery lilac flowers.
↕3–4in (8–10cm) ↔1in (2.5cm)

Eranthis hyemalis

page **217**

Erythronium californicum 'White Beauty'
Z4 The recurved white flowers are held above mottled leaves.
↕6–14in (15–35cm) ↔4in (10cm)

Erythronium 'Pagoda'

page **226**

Fritillaria imperialis 'Aureomarginata'
Z5 Tall stems carrying heads of orange flowers, with yellow-margined leaves.
↕5ft (1.5m) ↔10–12in (25–30cm)

Fritillaria pallidiflora

page **243**

Galanthus nivalis
Z3 The common but easily grown snowdrop, best planted while in leaf.
↕↔4in (10cm)

Hyacinthoides hispanica
Z3 Bluebell-like spikes of flowers in blue, pink, or white.
‡20in (50cm) ↔12in (30cm)

Hyacinthus orientalis 'Blue Jacket'

Hyacinthus orientalis 'Anna Marie'
Z5 Spikes of scented, pale pink flowers.
‡8in (20cm) ↔3in (8cm)

Ipheion uniflorum 'Froyle Mill'

Iris bucharica

Iris danfordiae
Z5 Lemon yellow blooms appear in early spring before the narrow foliage.
‡6in (15cm) ↔4in (10cm)

Iris reticulata 'Cantab'
Z5 Pale blue flowers with deeper falls. Long leaves develop after flowering.
‡4–6in (10–15cm)

Leucojum vernum
Z4 Like a tall snowdrop, with strap-shaped leaves.
‡12in (30cm) ↔8in (20cm)

Muscari latifolium
Z4-8 Broad leaves and bicolored spikes of flowers in pale and dark blue.
‡8in (20cm) ↔2in (5cm)

Narcissus 'Actaea'

Narcissus bulbocodium

Narcissus 'February Gold'

Narcissus 'Hawera'

Narcissus 'Ice Follies'

Narcissus 'Little Witch'
Z4 Golden-yellow flowers with reflexed petals.
‡9in (22cm)

Narcissus minor

Narcissus 'Passionale'

Narcissus triandrus

Scilla bifolia

Scilla mischtschenkoana 'Tubergeniana'

Scilla siberica
Z3 Bell-shaped flowers of cobalt blue above bright green leaves.
‡4–8in (10–20cm) ↔2in (5cm)

Tulipa 'Apeldoorn's Elite'
Z4 Rich yellow flowers feathered with red to give a subtle effect.
‡24in (60cm)

Tulipa 'Ballade'
Z4 Elegant flowers of rich pink with white petal edges and tips.
‡20in (50cm)

Tulipa 'China Pink'

Tulipa 'Maureen'
Z4 Oval, ivory-white flowers.
‡20in (50cm)

Tulipa 'Mrs John T. Scheepers'
Z4 Large flowers of pale yellow.
‡24in (60cm)

Tulipa 'Red Surprise'
Z4 Bright red, starry flowers.
‡8in (20cm)

Summer-Flowering Bulbs

Summer-flowering bulbs bring sparkle to gardens with their bright colors and exotic shapes. Unfortunately, many are not hardy in most of Canada, but they are not expensive; and most can be lifted in fall and kept in a frost-free place. Dahlias and gladioli are familiar to everyone, but modern lilies are easy to grow, too, and tigridias and hedychiums are even more exotic.

Allium giganteum

Allium karataviense

Allium sphaerocephalon
Z3 Slender stems topped with a red ball of small blooms.
↕20–30in (50–90cm)

Bletilla striata
Z5 Terrestrial orchid: a leafy plant with spikes of 1–6 small, pink flowers.
↕12–24in (30–60cm)

Canna 'Tropicana'
Z8 Orange flowers and foliage striped in red, pink, yellow, and green.
↕to 6ft (2m) ↔4ft (1.2m)

Crinum x powellii
Z8 Huge bulbs produce large leaves and long pink trumpet flowers.
↕5ft (1.5m) ↔12in (30cm)

Crocosmia 'Emily McKenzie'
Z6 Sword-shaped leaves and bright orange flowers marked with bronze.
↕24in (60cm) ↔3in (8cm)

Dahlia 'Bishop of Llandaff'

Dahlia 'Glorie van Heemstede'
Z8 Medium-sized bright yellow flowers shaped like waterlilies.
↕4½ft (1.3m) ↔18in (45cm)

Dahlia 'Jescot Julie'
Z8 Long-petaled flowers of orange and red colors.
↕3ft (1m) ↔18in (45cm)

Dahlia 'Pearl of Heemstede'
Z8 This waterlily dahlia has silvery-pink flowers.
↕3ft (1m) ↔18in (45cm)

Dracunculus vulgaris
Tender Min. temp. 35°F (2°C). Spotted stems support interesting leaves and huge, purple, unpleasantly scented flowers.
↕to 5ft (1.5m) ↔24in (60cm)

Eremurus 'Cleopatra'
Z5 Rosettes of straplike leaves and tall spikes of small soft orange flowers.
↕5ft (1.5m) ↔24in (60cm)

Eucomis bicolor
Z7 Rosettes of broad leaves below spikes of starry, cream, purple-edged blooms.
↕12–24in (30–60cm) ↔8in (20cm)

Galtonia candicans
Z5 Spikes of white, hyacinth-like flowers and strap-shaped leaves.
↕4ft (1.2m) ↔24in (60cm)

Gladiolus communis subsp. *byzantinus*

Gladiolus murielae

Gladiolus 'Green Woodpecker'
Z8 Greenish-yellow flowers with red
markings.
↕5ft (1.5m) ↔5in (12cm)

Hedychium coccineum
Z8 An exotic-looking plant with spikes
of tubular, scented, orange, pink, or
cream flowers.
↕10ft (3m) ↔3ft (1m)

Hedychium gardnerianum
Perennial Z8 Large heads of spidery,
showy, sweetly scented cream flowers.
↕6–7ft (2–2.2m)

Hedychium 'Tara'
Z8 A selection of *H. coccineum* with
deeper-colored flowers.
↕10ft (3m) ↔3ft (1m)

Ixia viridiflora
Tender Unusual pale turquoise-green
flowers on tall, wiry stems.
↕12–24in (30–60cm)

Leucojum aestivum 'Gravetye Giant'
page **343**

Lilium 'Black Dragon'
Z5 Tall stems carry pure white, scented
flowers that are deep maroon in bud.
↕5ft (1.5m)

Lilium 'Everest'
Z5 Large white flowers, heavily scented,
with dark spots, on tall stems.
↕5ft (1.5m)

Lilium henryi
page **347**

Lilium 'Karen North'
Z3 Elegant flowers with reflexed petals of
orange-pink with deeper spots.
↕3–4½ft (1–1.3m)

Lilium martagon var. *album*
page **348**

Lilium pyrenaicum
page **350**

Lilium regale
page **350**

Nectaroscordum siculum
Z5 Plants smell strongly of garlic and
produce loose umbels of pendulous cream
flowers marked dark red.
↕to 4ft (1.2m) ↔4in (10cm)

Rhodohypoxis baurii 'Tetra Red'
Tender Forms clumps or mats of bright,
squat, starry flowers.
↕↔4ft (10in)

Tigridia pavonia
Broad, spotted flowers in shades of red,
yellow, and white, each lasting one day.
↕5ft (1.5m) ↔4in (10cm)

Tropaeolum polyphyllum
Tender Min. temp. 35°F (2°C). Trailing
stems with finely divided gray leaves, and
bright yellow flowers.
↕2–3in (5–8cm) ↔to 3ft (1m)

Zantedeschia aethiopica
'Green Goddess'
page **577**

Fall-Flowering Bulbs

Bulbs and corms can provide color and interest when most plants are dying down. Most require full sun and well-drained soil if their flowers are to benefit from the last fine days of the year. Many do not fit easily with bulb production cycles and do not flower well until they are established in the garden, so they may need some effort to find in catalogs and nurseries.

Allium callimischon
Z6 Slender stems with white or pale pink flowers for dry soils.
↕4–14in (8–35cm) ↔2in (5cm)

Amaryllis belladonna
Z8 The dark stems support beautiful pink trumpets.
↕24in (60cm) ↔4in (10cm)

Colchicum speciosum 'Album'
page **167**

Colchicum 'Waterlily'
Z4 Beautiful white goblets appear without leaves.
↕7in (18cm) ↔4in (10cm)

Crinum x powellii 'Album'
page **183**

Crocus banaticus
page **186**

Crocus boryi
Z4 Each corm produces up to four pale lilac and cream flowers.
↕3in (8cm) ↔2in (5cm)

Crocus goulimyi
page **186**

Crocus kotschyanus
page **186**

Crocus medius
page **186**

Crocus ochroleucus
page **186**

Crocus pulchellus
page **186**

Crocus speciosus
Z3 Violet-blue, scented flowers with orange stigmas.
↕6in (15cm)

Cyclamen hederifolium
page **190**

Leucojum autumnale
page **343**

Lycoris squamigera
Z4 Foliage appears in spring and dies down. Bright pink stems of spidery flowers grow rapidly in fall.
↕↔18–24in (45–60cm)

Merendera montana
Z7 Starry lilac flowers; needs well-drained soil.
↕↔2in (5cm)

Nerine bowdenii
page **382**

Sternbergia lutea
Z7 Deep green leaves and bright yellow crocus-like flowers.
↕6in (15cm) ↔3in (8cm)

Tropaeolum tuberosum 'Ken Aslet'
Tender Min. temp. 35°F (2°C). Clambering stems with small leaves and yellow, hooded flowers.
↕6–12ft (2–4m)

Zephyranthes candida
Tender Clumps of narrow leaves and white, crocus-like flowers over many weeks.
↕4–8in (10–20cm) ↔3in (8cm)

Spring Bedding

When the last bedding plants of the season die down, it is time to replace them with young plants that will survive the winter and then flower in spring. Most of these are biennials, such as Canterbury bells, sweet Williams, and wallflowers. Add winter-flowering pansies for early color, especially in containers. Plant spring bulbs among the bedding plants for extra interest.

Bellis perennis 'Pomponette'

page 116

Campanula medium 'Calycanthema'
Biennial Z4 Cup-and-saucer Canterbury bells in pink, blue, and white.
‡to 30in (75cm)

Dianthus barbatus 'Auricula-eyed Mixed'
Biennial Z4 Traditional sweet Williams with flowers zoned in white, pink, and maroon.
‡to 24in (60cm)

Erysimum cheiri 'Cloth of Gold'
Biennial Z3 Bright yellow, scented flowers.
‡18in (45cm)

Erysimum cheiri 'Fireking Improved'
Biennial Z3 Orange-red flowers.
‡18in (45cm)

Erysimum cheiri 'Prince Primrose Yellow'
Biennial Z3 Dwarf type with large flowers.
‡12in (30cm)

Hyacinthus orientalis 'Fondant'
Bulb Z5 Pure pink-colored flowers.
‡10in (25cm)

Hyacinthus orientalis 'Pink Pearl'

page 296

Hyacinthus orientalis 'Violet Pearl'
Bulb Z3 Amethyst-colored flowers.
‡10in (25cm)

Myosotis 'Spring Symphony Blue'
Biennial Z4 The blue flowers associate well with most spring bulbs.
‡6in (15cm)

Polyanthus Primroses

page **448**

Tulipa 'Halcro'
Bulb Z4 Large, deep salmon-red flowers.
‡28in (70cm)

Tulipa 'Oranje Nassau'
Bulb Z4 Fiery flowers in shades of red and scarlet.
‡12in (30cm)

Tulipa 'Spring Green'

page **557**

Viola 'Felix'
Biennial Z6 Yellow and purple, "whiskered" flowers on tufted plants.
‡6in (15cm)

Viola 'Rippling Waters'
Biennial Z6 Large flowers of dark purple edged with white in spring.
‡6in (15cm)

Viola Ultima Series
Biennial Z6 Wide range of colors on plants that flower through mild spells.
‡6in (15cm)

Summer Bedding

Although bedding out on the grand scale will probably never be as popular as it was in Victorian times, most gardeners find room for plants that grow and flower quickly once planted out. Although most are not tolerant of frost, some are annuals and others are tender perennials. Most also have a long flowering period and, even if only for one season, are excellent value.

Ageratum houstonianum 'Pacific'
Annual Compact plants with dense heads of purple-blue flowers.
‡8in (20cm)

Antirrhinum majus Sonnet Series
Annuals page 30

Begonia 'Pin Up'
Perennial page 115

Begonia Olympia Series
Tender perennials Compact, large-flowered bedding begonias.
‡↔8in (20cm)

Callistephus 'Matsumoto Scarlet'
Annual Upright plant with semi-double flowers, good for cutting.
‡30in (75cm) ↔18in (45cm)

Catharanthus roseus 'Grape Cooler'
Tender perennial Annual vinca. Pink flowers with a rose eye all summer.
‡12in (30cm) ↔18in (45cm)

Celosia argentea 'Century Yellow'
Tender perennial Feathery plumes of flowers that dry well and keep their color.
‡18in (45cm) ↔12in (30cm)

Celosia argentea Big Chief Mix
Tender perennial Cockscomb-like crests of flowers in a range of colors.
‡40in (100cm) ↔15in (37cm)

Dahlia 'Coltness Gem'
Tender perennial Reliable, single-flowered dahlias in clear, bright colors.
‡↔18in (45cm)

Diascia rigescens
Perennial page 20◄

Gazania 'Daybreak Bronze'
Tender perennial Daisy-like flowers with a distinct darker zone in the center. Cold tolerant.
‡8in (20cm) ↔10in (25cm)

Impatiens Deco Series
Annuals Large, bright flowers on plants with dark green leaves.
‡↔ to 8in (20cm)

Lobelia 'Compliment Scarlet'
Perennial Z4 Bold plant with green foliage and large scarlet flowers on tall spikes.
‡30in (75cm) ↔12in (30cm)

Lobelia 'Crystal Palace'
Annual page 354

Lobelia erinus 'Mrs Clibran'
Annual A compact plant with white-eyed, bright blue flowers.
‡4–6in (10–15cm)

Nicotiana 'Lime Green'
Annual page 383

Nicotiana x sanderae Domino Series
Annual page 49◄

Pelargonium Multibloom Series
Perennials page 408

Pelargonium Video Series
Perennials page 408

Penstemon 'Beech Park'
Perennial Z8 Large pink and white
trumpets throughout summer. Sometimes
sold as 'Barbara Barker'.
30in (75cm) ↔ 18in (45cm)

Petunia 'Mirage Reflections'
Annual Weather-resistant multiflora
petunias in pastel colors with darker veins.
12in (30cm) ↔ 24in (60cm)

Phlox drummondii 'Tapestry'
Annual Wide range of pastel colors and
bicolors on bushy plants.
20in (50cm) ↔ 15in (38cm)

Polemonium 'Lambrook Mauve'
Perennial   page 440

**Portulaca grandiflora
Sundial Series**
Annuals Sun-loving plants with brilliant
flowers and petals like satin.
4in (10cm) ↔ 6in (15cm)

Rudbeckia hirta 'Rustic Dwarfs'
Annual Mixture of fall shades on large,
dark-eyed flowers.
to 24in (60cm)

Salpiglossis sinuata Casino Series
Annuals   page 52

Salvia coccinea 'Lady in Red'
Annual Bushy plants bear slender spikes
of small but showy red flowers all summer.
16in (40cm)

Salvia farinacea 'Victoria'
Annual The small, deep blue flowers
are crowded on spikes held well above
the leaves.
to 24in (60cm) ↔ to 12in (30cm)

Salvia fulgens
Subshrub   page 506

Salvia pratensis Haematodes Group
Perennial   page 478

Salvia splendens Sizzler Series
Annuals Early-flowering plants with
blooms in colors from red to lavender
and white.
8–10in (20–25cm)

Tagetes patula 'Disco Orange'
Annual Weather-resistant, single flowers.
8–10in (20–25cm)

Tagetes 'Zenith Red'
Annual Marigold with double red flowers.
12in (30cm)

Verbena 'Peaches and Cream'
Annual Seed-raised spreading plants with
peach-colored flowers that fade to cream.
12in (30cm) ↔ 18in (45cm)

Zinnia elegans 'Red Sun'
Annual Bushy plant that is wind-
and mildew-tolerant. Double flowers
4in (10cm) across.
20in (50cm) ↔ 18in (45cm)

Variegated Herbaceous Plants

Variegation may be restricted to a narrow rim around the edge of a leaf, or it may be more spectacular. Regular patterning with white, cream, or gold may help define the shape of large leaves, but random streaks and splashes can make some plants look unhealthy. Remember that plants may revert back to their plain form: always remove any shoots with plain green leaves.

Aquilegia vulgaris
Vervaeneana Group
Perennial Z3 Leaves are marbled and splashed with yellow and green, below white, pink, or blue flowers.
↕3ft (1m) ↔18in (45cm)

Arabis procurrens **'Variegata'**
Perennial page 95

Armoracia rusticana **'Variegata'**
Perennial Z5b Deep-rooted plants with large leaves heavily splashed with white, especially in spring.
↕3ft (1m) ↔18in (45cm)

Astrantia major **'Sunningdale Variegated'**
Perennial page 108

Brunnera macrophylla **'Hadspen Cream'**
Perennial page 124

Coreopsis **'Calypso'**
Perennial Z4 Narrow leaves edged with gold; yellow flowers with a red zone.
↕↔15in (38cm)

Gaura lindheimeri **'Corrie's Gold'**
Perennial Z6 White flowers on delicate stems; small gold-edged leaves.
↕5ft (1.5m) ↔3ft (1m)

Hemerocallis fulva **'Kwanzo Variegata'**
Perennial Z3 Arching leaves with bright white stripes, and occasional double orange flowers.
↕30in (75cm)

Hosta **'Fortunei Albopicta'**
Perennial page 29

Hosta **'Golden Tiara'**
Perennial page 29

Hosta **'Great Expectations'**
Perennial Z4 Glaucous green, puckered leaves with broad yellow centers, and grayish-white flowers.
↕22in (55cm) ↔34in (85cm)

Hosta **'Shade Fanfare'**
Perennial page 292

Hosta sieboldii var. *elegans*
Perennial page 292

Hosta **Tardiana Group 'Halcyon'**
Perennial page 29

Hosta **'Undulata Univittata'**
Perennial page 29

Hosta venusta
Perennial page 293

Hosta **'Wide Brim'**
Perennial page 293

Houttuynia cordata **'Chameleon'**
Perennial Z5b Vivid leaves in shades of cream, green, and red, and small, white flowers.
↕to 6–12in (15–30cm) or more ↔indefinite

Iris laevigata **'Variegata'**
Perennial page 310

Iris pallida **'Variegata'**
Perennial page 320

amium galeobdolon
'Herman's Pride'
Perennial Z3b Spreading ground cover with silver-veined leaves and yellow flowers.
6in (15cm) ↔ 3ft (1m)

amium maculatum **'White Nancy'**
Perennial page **333**

ysimachia punctata **'Alexander'**
Perennial Z4 Creeping plant with spires of yellow flowers, and white-edged foliage tinged pink in spring.
3ft (1m) ↔ 2ft (60cm)

Mimulus luteus **'Variegatus'**
Perennial Z8 Creeping plant with yellow flowers and pale green leaves edged with white.
12in (30cm) ↔ 18in (45cm)

Miscanthus sinensis **'Variegatus'**
Ornamental grass Z4b Narrow leaves with cream and green stripes. Feathery seedheads in fall.
6ft (2m) ↔ 4ft (1.2m)

Molinia caerulea **'Variegata'**
Ornamental grass page **374**

Persicaria virginiana
'Painter's Palette'
Perennial Z5 Bright foliage splashed with white and marked with red and brown, on red stems. Variegation comes true from seed.
16–48in (40–120cm) ↔ 24–56in (60–140cm)

Phalaris arundinacea **'Picta'**
Ornamental grass page **415**

Phlox paniculata **'Pink Posie'**
Perennial Z3 Compact, strong-growing phlox with white-edged leaves and pink flowers.
30in (75cm) ↔ 24in (60cm)

Phormium cookianum subsp. *hookeri* **'Tricolor'**
Evergreen perennial page **424**

Physostegia virginiana **'Variegata'**
Perennial Z3b Upright plant with grayish leaves edged with white, and deep pink flowers.
↕30in (75cm) ↔ 24in (60cm)

Pleioblastus viridistriatus
Bamboo page **439**

Pulmonaria rubra **'David Ward'**
Perennial Z5 Coral-red flowers in spring, and large leaves broadly margined with white.
↕16in (40cm) ↔ 3ft (1m)

Saxifraga stolonifera **'Tricolor'**
Evergreen perennial Z7 A slightly tender plant with round leaves edged with white and pink.
↕↔12in (30cm)

Sisyrinchium striatum **'Aunt May'**
Perennial Z8 Upright fans of narrow, gray leaves edged with cream, and spikes of cream flowers.
↕↔ to 20in (50cm)

Symphytum x uplandicum **'Variegatum'**
Perennial page **537**

Veronica gentianoides **'Variegata'**
Perennial Z4 Mats of deep green leaves margined with white, and spikes of small, pale blue flowers.
↕↔18in (45cm)

Vinca major **'Variegata'**
Perennial page **569**

Variegated Trees and Shrubs

While flowers usually have a short season, foliage provides color for at least half the year—and all year if evergreen. Variegated shrubs increase that interest with their bright coloring, and some have flowers that complement the foliage. Many variegated evergreens are useful to brighten shady areas and are good in pots and containers; they are also popular with flower arrangers.

Acer campestre 'Carnival'
Tree Z4b Pink-splashed leaves.
↕25ft (8m) ↔15ft (5m)

Acer negundo 'Flamingo'
Tree page 65

Acer palmatum 'Butterfly'
Shrub or small tree page 66

Acer platanoides 'Drummondii'
Tree page 69

Acer pseudoplatanus 'Leopoldii'
Tree Z5b The leaves are pink at first in spring, then speckled with yellow.
↕↔30ft (10m)

Aralia elata 'Variegata'
Tree page 96

Berberis thunbergii 'Rose Glow'
Shrub page 118

Buddleja davidii 'Harlequin'
Shrub Z5b Striking leaves edged with white, and purple flowers.
↕↔8ft (2.5m)

Buddleja davidii 'Santana'
Shrub Z5b Mottled foliage in shades of green and yellow, and purple flowers.
↕↔8ft (2.5m)

Buxus sempervirens 'Elegantissima'
Evergreen shrub page 127

Camellia x *williamsii* 'Golden Spangles'
Evergreen shrub Z8 Bright pink flowers and gold-splashed leaves.
↕↔8ft (2.5m)

Ceanothus 'Pershore Zanzibar'
Evergreen shrub Z8 Fast-growing, with fluffy blue flowers in late spring, and lemon yellow and bright green foliage.
↕↔8ft (2.5m)

Cornus alba 'Elegantissima'
Shrub Z2 Dark red stems with gray-green leaves, edged with white, that turn pink in fall.
↕↔10ft (3m)

Cornus alba 'Spaethii'
Shrub page 17

Cornus alternifolia 'Argentea'
Shrub Z4 Tiers of horizontal branches, clothed with small leaves that are edged with white.
↕10ft (3m) ↔8ft (2.5m)

Cornus mas 'Variegata'
Shrub Z5 After producing yellow flowers in spring, the plant is bright with white-edged leaves.
↕8ft (2.5m) ↔6ft (2m)

Cotoneaster atropurpureus 'Variegatus'
Shrub page 177

Daphne x *burkwoodii* 'Carol Mackie'
Semi-evergreen shrub Z5 New leaves are edged with yellow that fades to white in time.
↕↔3ft (1m)

Elaeagnus pungens 'Maculata'
Evergreen shrub page 214

uonymus fortunei 'Silver Queen'
vergreen shrub   page 232

uchsia magellanica var. *gracilis*
Variegata'
hrub Z7 The leaves are colored in smoky
inks and grays, with small, red and
urple flowers.
10ft (3m) ↔ 6–10ft (2–3m)

ledera helix 'Glacier'
vergreen climber   page 278

Hibiscus syriacus 'Meehanii'
hrub Z6 Sun-loving. Purple-blue flowers;
eaves with broad white edges.
10ft (3m) ↔ 6ft (2m)

Hydrangea macrophylla 'Tricolor'
hrub Z6 Gray-green leaves marked with
hite, and pale pink flowers.
5ft (1.5m) ↔ 4ft (1.2m)

ex x altaclerensis 'Lawsoniana'
vergreen shrub   page 303

igustrum lucidum 'Excelsum
uperbum'
vergreen shrub   page 346

Osmanthus heterophyllus
Variegatus'
vergreen shrub Z7 Holly-like leaves
ith broad yellow margins, and fragrant,
ny flowers in fall.
↔ 8ft (2.5m)

Philadelphus coronarius
Variegatus'
hrub   page 417

Philadelphus 'Innocence'
hrub Z4 Arching shrub with creamy-
ellow leaves and semidouble white flowers.
10ft (3m) ↔ 6ft (2m)

Pieris 'Flaming Silver'
vergreen shrub Z5b Acidic-soil-loving
lant with narrow foliage, edged with
hite, that is pink in spring.
↔ 8ft (2.5m)

Pseudopanax lessonii 'Gold Splash'
Evergreen shrub   page 458

Rhamnus alaternus
'Argenteovariegata'
Evergreen shrub   page 466

Rhododendron
'President Roosevelt'
Evergreen shrub Z8 Weakly branching,
acidic-soil-loving shrub with gold-
splashed leaves and red flowers.
↕↔ 6ft (2m)

Sambucus nigra 'Pulverulenta'
Shrub Z4b Bright, slow-growing shrub
for part-shade with young leaves heavily
splashed with white.
↕↔ 6ft (2m)

Symphoricarpos orbiculatus
'Foliis Variegatus'
Shrub Z4 Leaves margined with yellow,
small flowers and conspicuous red fruit.
↕↔ 6ft (2m)

Syringa vulgaris 'Dappled Dawn'
Shrub Z2 Leaves are irregularly splashed
with gold. Flowers are pale lilac.
↕15ft (5m) ↔ 10ft (3m)

Weigela 'Florida Variegata'
Shrub   page **573**

Gold-Leaved Plants

Gold-leaved plants bring a splash of sunshine to the garden. In contrast to plants with variegated leaves, most fully gold-leaved plants are rather prone to scorch in full sun so are best in light shade. But avoid dark shade, or the leaves may become lime green. Some plants are gold for only a part of their growth; their young, gold tips fade to green, but this contrast is still pleasing

Acer cappadocicum 'Aureum'
Tree Z6b The leaves unfurl yellow in spring, turn green in summer, and then turn gold in fall.
↕50ft (15m) ↔30ft (10m)

Acer shirasawanum 'Aureum'
Tree Z6b The bright yellow leaves turn red in fall.
↕↔20ft (6m)

Begonia 'Tiger Paws'
Perennial

Calluna vulgaris 'Beoley Gold'
Evergreen shrub

Carex elata 'Aurea'
Ornamental grass

Carex oshimensis 'Evergold'
Ornamental grass

Chamaecyparis lawsoniana 'Minima Aurea'
Conifer Z6 Small evergreen, conical shrub with lime green and gold foliage.
↕3ft (1m)

Chamaecyparis lawsoniana 'Stardust'
Conifer Z6 Yellow, fernlike foliage.
↕50ft (15m) ↔25ft (8m)

Chamaecyparis obtuse 'Crippsii'
Conifer Z5b A slow-growing tree with gold foliage.
↕50ft (15m) ↔25ft (8m)

Choisya ternata 'Sundance'
Evergreen shrub

Cornus alba 'Aurea'
Shrub Z2 Beautiful soft gold foliage that is prone to sunscorch on dry soils.
↕↔3ft (1m)

Cortaderia selloana 'Aureolineata'
Ornamental grass

Erica arborea 'Albert's Gold'
Evergreen shrub Z7b Attractive, upright habit, with gold foliage but few flowers.
↕6ft (2m) ↔32in (80cm)

Erica carnea 'Foxhollow'
Evergreen shrub

Erica carnea 'Westwood Yellow'
Evergreen shrub Z6 Upright habit, with yellow foliage, and pale pink flower in winter.
↕8in (20cm) ↔12in (30cm)

Erica × stuartii 'Irish Lemon'
Evergreen shrub

Fagus sylvatica 'Dawyck Gold'
Tree

Fraxinus excelsior 'Jaspidea'
Tree Z5 The winter shoots are yellow, as are the leaves in spring and fall.
↕100ft (30m) ↔70ft (20m)

Fuchsia 'Genii'
Shrub

Gleditsia triacanthos 'Sunburst'
Tree

Hakonechloa macra 'Aureola'
Ornamental grass

Hedera helix 'Buttercup'
Evergreen climber   page 278

Hosta 'Sum and Substance'
Perennial   page 293

Humulus lupulus 'Aureus'
Climbing perennial   page 294

Ilex crenata 'Golden Gem'
Evergreen shrub Z7 Compact, small-
leaved shrub with bright gold leaves and
sparse, black berries.
3ft (1m) ↔ 4–5ft (1.2–1.5m)

Iris pseudacorus 'Variegatus'
Perennial   page 310

Laurus nobilis 'Aurea'
Evergreen shrub   page 336

Lonicera nitida 'Baggesen's Gold'
Evergreen shrub   page 355

Origanum vulgare 'Aureum'
Perennial herb   page 390

Pelargonium crispum 'Variegatum'
Perennial   page 404

Philadelphus coronarius 'Aureus'
Deciduous shrub Z3 Gold young leaves
turning green-yellow in summer; white
fragrant flowers in early summer.
8ft (2.5m) ↔ 5ft (1.5m)

Phormium 'Yellow Wave'
Perennial   page 426

Ribes sanguineum 'Brocklebankii'
Shrub   page 477

Robinia pseudoacacia 'Frisia'
Tree   page 479

Salvia officinalis 'Kew Gold'
Evergreen subshrub Z6 Aromatic
golden leaves sometimes flecked with
green; mauve flower spikes in summer.
8–12in (20–30cm) ↔ 12in (30cm)

Sambucus racemosa
'Sutherland Gold'
Shrub Z3 Finely divided foliage of
bright yellow that is best when plants
are regularly pruned.
↕↔ 6ft (2m)

Spiraea japonica 'Goldflame'
Shrub   page 533

Dark and Purple Foliage

The primary value of dark foliage in the garden is as a foil to other plants, though many are very beautiful in their own right. An adjacent purple-leaved plant makes gold, variegated, and silver plants look even more brilliant and is the perfect foil for white, pink, yellow, and orange flowers. Most purple-leaved plants develop their best color in full sun, looking dull and greenish in shade

edera helix 'Atropurpurea'
vergreen climber

euchera micrantha var.
iversifolia 'Palace Purple'
erennial

phiopogon planiscapus
Nigrescens'
erennial

enstemon digitalis 'Husker Red'
erennial Z3 Semi-evergreen perennial
ith red and purple foliage and pale
nk flowers.
20–30in (50–75cm) ↔12in (30cm)

hysocarpus opulifolius 'Diablo'
hrub

runus x *cistena*
hrub

runus virginiana 'Shubert'
hrub or small tree Z2 Dark green leaves
early spring that quickly turn purple.
30ft (10m) ↔25ft (8m)

heum palmatum
'Atrosanguineum'
erennial

osa glauca
pecies rose

alvia officinalis
'urpurascens Group
vergreen shrub

ambucus nigra 'Guincho Purple'
hrub

edum telephium
'Atropurpureum Group
erennial

radescantia pallida 'Purpurea'
ender perennial This sprawling
lant has bright purple leaves and
mall pink flowers.
8in (20cm) ↔16in (40cm)

Viburnum sargentii 'Onondaga'
Shrub Z3b Upright-growing shrub with
purple leaves that turn red in fall, and
pale pink flowers.
‡6ft (2m)

Viola riviniana 'Purpurea'
Perennial Z6 Low-growing plant
with small purple leaves and flowers.
Seeds profusely.
‡4–8in (10–20cm) ↔8–16cm (20–40cm)

Vitis vinifera 'Purpurea'
Climber

Weigela florida 'Foliis Purpureis'
Shrub

Silver Foliage

Most plants that have silver leaves have adapted to hot, sunny climates, and these are plants for full sun in the garden. They are also adapted to low rainfall in many cases, so they can form the basis of a drought garden or gravel garden. Their color makes them ideal to associate with pink and white flowers, and with purple foliage. In addition, many have fragrant leaves.

Acacia baileyana
Tender shrub The foliage is less fine than *A. dealbata* but steely gray; the flowers are bright yellow.
‡15–25ft (5–8m) ↔10–20ft (3–6m)

Acca sellowiana
Tender evergreen shrub Green leaves with silver reverses, flowers with fleshy, red and white edible petals.
‡6ft (2m) ↔8ft (2.5m)

Anaphalis triplinervis
Perennial Z3 Clump-forming plant with silver-gray leaves and white flowers in late summer.
‡32–36in (80–90cm) ↔18–24in (45–60cm)

Anaphalis triplinervis 'Sommerschnee'
Perennial   page 88

Antennaria microphylla
Perennial   page 93

Anthemis punctata subsp. cupaniana
Perennial   page 93

Artemisia alba 'Canescens'
Perennial Z5b Very finely divided gray leaves that form a feathery mass.
‡18in (45cm) ↔12in (30cm)

Artemisia ludoviciana 'Silver Queen'
Perennial   page 101

Artemisia pontica
Evergreen perennial Z6 A creeping perennial that has masses of upright stems with feathery leaves that form a mounded clump.
‡16–32in (40–80cm) ↔indefinite

Atriplex halimus
Shrub Z7b Slightly tender, but wind-tolerant, fast-growing plant with small, shiny, silver leaves.
‡6ft (2m) ↔8ft (2.5m)

Brachyglottis 'Sunshine'
Evergreen shrub   page 12

Cedrus atlantica Glauca Group
Conifer Z6 The blue Atlas cedar in time becomes a large, magnificent specimen tree with blue-gray foliage.
‡130ft (40m) ↔30ft (10m)

Convolvulus cneorum
Evergreen shrub   page 16

Cytisus battandieri
Shrub   page 19

Dianthus 'Becky Robinson'
Perennial   page 204

Dianthus 'Haytor White'
Perennial   page 204

Elaeagnus 'Quicksilver'
Evergreen shrub   page 215

Erica tetralix 'Alba Mollis'
Evergreen shrub   page 221

Eucalyptus gunnii
Evergreen tree   page 229

Halimium 'Susan'
Evergreen shrub   page 269

Hebe pimeleoides 'Quicksilver'
Tender evergreen shrub Ground-hugging
shrub with tiny silver leaves and pale
lilac flowers.
‡12in (30cm) ↔24in (60cm)

Hebe pinguifolia 'Pagei'
Evergreen shrub   page 243

Hebe 'Red Edge'
Tender evergreen shrub Spreading, low
shrub with red-edged gray leaves.
‡18in (45cm) ↔24in (60cm)

Helianthemum 'Wisley Primrose'
Evergreen shrub   page 281

Helichrysum splendidum
Perennial   page 282

Helictotrichon sempervirens
Ornamental grass   page 283

Lavandula x *intermedia*
Dutch Group
Shrub   page 338

Perovskia 'Blue Spire'
Shrub   page 412

Pyrus salicifolia 'Pendula'
Tree   page 464

Romneya coulteri
Perennial Z7 Vigorous, suckering plant
with coarsely toothed silver leaves and
white, yellow-centered flowers.
‡6ft (2m) ↔indefinite

Salix 'Boydii'
Shrub   page 501

Salix lanata
Shrub   page 503

Salvia argentea
Perennial   page 504

Salvia discolor
Perennial   page 505

Santolina chamaecyparissus
Evergreen shrub   page 513

Sedum spathulifolium 'Cape Blanco'
Perennial   page 521

Senecio cineraria 'Silver Dust'
Evergreen shrub   page 54

Senecio cineraria 'White Diamond'
Evergreen shrub Z7 The almost white
leaves resemble oak leaves in shape.
‡12–16in (30–40cm) ↔12in (30cm)

Senecio viravira
Tender shrub Min. temp. 35°F (2°C).
The finely divided leaves are carried on
sprawling stems that eventually produce
creamy, pompon flowers.
‡24in (60cm) ↔3ft (1m)

Stachys byzantina 'Countess
Helen von Stein'
Perennial Z3b Wide, almost oval leaves
covered with silvery hairs.
‡18in (45cm) ↔3ft (1m)

Verbascum bombyciferum
Perennial   page 561

Plants for Spring Color

Spring is a frantic time in the garden, and at times it seems that every plant is trying to flower. The earliest flowers are demure and adapted to survive any snows, sleet, and wind, but soon, flowers are bigger and bolder, and the yellows, white, and blues of the spring bulbs are joined by masses of pink cherry blossoms, showy magnolias, rhododendrons, clematis, and wisteria.

Acer pseudoplatanus **'Brilliantissimum'**
Tree page **69**

Anemone ranunculoides
Perennial page **92**

Arabis caucasica **'Rosea'**
Alpine Z3 Mat-forming plant, can trail over a low wall with pale pink flowers in spring.
‡6in (15cm) ↔20in (50cm)

Aubrieta x cultorum **'Whitewell Gem'**
Alpine Z4 Trailing plant with double purple flowers.
‡2in (5cm) ↔24in (60cm)

Bergenia purpurascens
Perennial Z3b Bold, leathery leaves turn red in cold weather, and clusters of bright, purplish flowers open in spring.
‡18in (45cm) ↔12in (30cm)

Caltha palustris
Perennial page **131**

Camellia x williamsii cultivars
Evergreen shrubs pages **136–137**

Chaenomeles speciosa **'Moerloosei'**
Shrub page **148**

Clematis alpina
Climber Z4 The blue, bell-shaped flowers have white centers and are followed by fluffy seedheads.
‡6–10ft (2–3m)

Clematis **'Frances Rivis'**
Climber page **160**

Clematis **'Markham's Pink'**
Climber page **160**

Clematis montana var. *rubens*
Climber page **160**

Corydalis solida
Bulbous perennial Z4 Pink flowers are held above feathery, gray foliage.
‡10in (25cm) ↔8in (20cm)

Corylopsis pauciflora
Shrub page **174**

Daphne cneorum
Evergreen shrub Z2b Very fragrant rose pink flowers on a low, spreading shrub.
‡8in (20cm) ↔18in (45cm)

Daphne tangutica
Evergreen shrub Z6 The tips of shoots are studded with fragrant, pink and white flowers in late spring.
‡↔3ft (1m)

Dicentra **'Luxuriant'**
Perennial Z4 Lobed leaves and clusters of red flowers over a long season.
‡12in (30cm) ↔18in (45cm)

Dodecatheon meadia
Perennial Z5 A clump-forming plant with clusters of magenta-pink flowers that resemble cyclamen.
‡16in (40cm) ↔10in (25cm)

Epimedium x rubrum
Perennial page **216**

Epimedium x *versicolor* 'Sulphureum'
Perennial Z4 Evergreen, clump-forming plant with divided leaves and pretty, pale yellow flowers.
↕↔12in (30cm)

Euphorbia x *martinii*
Evergreen subshrub   page 234

Euphorbia polychroma
Perennial   page 235

Forsythia x *intermedia* 'Lynwood Variety'
Shrub   page 240

Forsythia 'Northern Gold'
Shrub Z4 Upright shrub with bright yellow flowers at the ends of the branches. An Ottawa introduction.
↕8ft (2.5m) ↔5ft (1.6m)

Fothergilla major
Shrub   page 241

Hepatica nobilis
Perennial   page 287

Magnolia 'Elizabeth'
Shrub   page 364

Magnolia x *loebneri* 'Merrill'
Shrub   page 364

Magnolia x *soulangeana* 'Lennei'
Tree Z5b Beautiful tree of spreading habit with large, deep purple flowers.
↕↔20ft (6m)

Magnolia stellata
Tree   page 365

Malus floribunda
Tree   page 368

Phlox subulata 'Scarlet Flame'
Perennial Z3 Low spreading, makes a good ground cover with red flowers.
↕4in (10cm) ↔20in (50cm)

Pieris japonica 'Mountain Fire'
Evergreen shrub Z5b Acidic-soil-loving shrub with white flowers and red new growth becoming bronze, and then green.
↕12ft (4m) ↔10ft (3m)

Primula veris
Perennial   page 451

Primula vialii
Perennial Z4 Short-lived perennial with dense heads of lilac flowers blooming from contrasting red buds.
↕12–24in (30–60cm) ↔12in (30cm)

Prunus avium 'Plena'
Tree   page 456

Prunus glandulosa 'Alba Plena'
Shrub   page 453

Prunus 'Kanzan'
Tree   page 456

Prunus padus 'Colorata'
Tree   page 456

Prunus 'Shirofugen'
Tree   page 457

Prunus tenella
Shrub Z2 Small shrub with masses of bright rose pink flowers that appear before the leaves.
↕↔5ft (1.6m)

Prunus 'Ukon'
Tree   page 457

Pulmonaria rubra
Perennial   page 459

Rhododendron species and cultivars
Shrubs   pages 470–476

Syringa vulgaris 'Agincourt Beauty'
Shrub Z2 Long trusses of large, sweetly scented, purple blooms.
↕20ft (7m) ↔15ft (5m)

Wisteria floribunda 'Rosea'
Climber Z6 Long racemes of pale pink flowers cascade from this vigorous plant.
↕28ft (9m)

Plants for Summer Color

In gardens the summer months are often dominated by bedding, but there are many bright-flowered perennials at their best. There are fewer shrubs in flower in mid-summer than in spring, but an important exception is the rose, without which gardens would be much poorer. There are roses for every part of the garden, from lofty climbers to spreading groundcovers.

Anchusa azurea 'Loddon Royalist'
Perennial   page 89

Aquilegia vulgaris 'Nora Barlow'
Perennial   page 95

Buddleja davidii 'Dartmoor'
Shrub Z5b The flowers, borne in unusually large, branched clusters, are a rich reddish-purple color.
‡10ft (3m) ↔15ft (5m)

Buddleja globosa
Shrub   page 126

Campanula lactiflora 'Loddon Anna'
Perennial   page 139

Clematis 'Bees' Jubilee'
Climber   page 161

Clematis x durandii
Perennial Z5 Non-climbing hybrid that sprawls through other plants, with large, blue flowers.
‡3–6ft (1–2m)

Clematis 'Gipsy Queen'
Climber Z3 Velvety, purple flowers with red anthers throughout summer.
‡10ft (3m)

Clematis 'Perle d'Azur'
Climber   page 165

Digitalis lanata
Perennial Z3 Leafy stems with densely packed, small cream flowers.
‡24in (60cm) ↔12in (30cm)

Erica cinerea 'Velvet Night'
Evergreen shrub Z5 Dark foliage is highlighted by deep purple flowers.
‡24in (60cm) ↔32in (80cm)

Erica vagans 'Mrs D.F. Maxwell'
Evergreen shrub   page 221

Fuchsia hardy types
Shrubs   page 244

Genista pilosa 'Vancouver Gold'
Shrub Z5 Spreading shrub with vivid yellow flowers freely produced.
‡18in (45cm) ↔3ft (1m)

Geraniums, hardy, large
Perennials   pages 260–261

Hemerocallis cultivars
Perennials   page 286

Hydrangea serrata 'Bluebird'
Shrub   page 300

Hypericum 'Hidcote'
Shrub   page 301

Bearded Iris
Perennials   page 316–319

Iris laevigata
Perennial   page 210

Iris sibirica 'Gatineau'
Perennial Z3 Clump-forming plant with narrow foliage and bright blue flowers.
‡3ft (1m) ↔12in (30cm)

Lathyrus latifolius 'White Pearl'
Climber Z4 This herbaceous perennial has pure white, scentless flowers.
‡6ft (2m)

Oenothera fruticosa 'Fyrverkeri'
Perennial   page 386

Papaver orientale 'Cedric Morris'
Perennial   page 399

Penstemon cultivars
Perennials   pages 410–411

Philadelphus 'Buckley's Quill'
Shrub Z4 Upright shrub with fragrant
white flowers that have narrow petals.
‡6ft (2m) ↔4ft (1.2m)

Phlox maculata 'Alpha'
Perennial   page 421

Photinia x fraseri 'Red Robin'
Evergreen shrub   page 427

Platycodon grandiflorus
Perennial   page 406

Potentilla fruticosa
'Coronation Triumph'
Shrub Z2b Arching shrub with large, bright
yellow flowers for most of the summer.
↔4ft (1.2m)

Potentilla 'Gibson's Scarlet'
Perennial   page 443

Rosa 'Champlain'
Shrub Z3 A dwarf, free-flowering
selection with dark red flowers and
good disease resistance.
‡↔3ft (1m)

Rosa 'Cuthbert Grant'
Shrub Z3 Fragrant, semidouble, crimson
flowers with a repeat bloom in early fall.
‡4ft (1.2m) ↔3ft (1m)

Rosa 'John Davis'
Climbing shrub Z3 Bright pink flowers
with a spicy scent in clusters. Free
flowering and disease resistant.
‡8ft (2.4m) ↔4ft (1.2m)

Rosa 'Just Joey'
Hybrid tea rose   page 481

Rosa 'Many Happy Returns'
Floribunda rose   page 483

Rosa 'Morden Blush'
Shrub Z2b A low-growing rose with good
disease tolerance. The pale pink flowers
are produced continually all summer.
‡3ft (1m) ↔4ft (1.2m)

Rosa 'Sweet Dream'
Patio rose   page 489

Roses, Old Garden
Deciduous shrubs   pages 492–493

Salvia nemorosa 'Ostfriesland'
Perennial Z4 Slender spikes of violet-blue
flowers all summer.
‡18in (45cm) ↔12in (30cm)

Salvia x sylvestris 'Mainacht'
Perennial   page 511

Spiraea nipponica 'Halward's Silver'
Shrub Z3 Small erect shrub with copious
white flowers that cover the branches.
‡↔3ft (1m)

Thalictrum delavayi
'Hewitt's Double'
Perennial   page 542

Tradescantia x andersoniana
'J. C. Weugelin'
Perennial   page 550

Tradescantia x andersoniana
'Osprey'
Perennial   page 550

Weigela 'Minuet'
Shrub Z5 Compact shrub with purple-
tinged foliage and pink flowers with
a yellow throat.
‡30in (75cm) ↔4ft (1.2m)

Weigela 'Rumba'
Shrub Z3b Spreading shrub with purple-
edged leaves and dark red flowers. Good
repeat blooming.
‡3ft (1m) ↔4ft (1.2m)

Plants for Fall Color

Fall is a season of great change in the garden, and although many annuals and perennials continue their summer display, it is the colors of leaves and fruits (see also pp.618–19) that most capture the imagination. This should be the most spectacular time of all in the garden, as borders erupt in fiery orange and red shades before the more somber displays of winter.

Acer grosseri **var.** *hersii*
Tree   page 64

Acer palmatum 'Bloodgood'
Small tree   page 66

Acer palmatum 'Garnet'
Shrub   page 66

Acer rubrum 'October Glory'
Tree   page 70

Acer tataricum subsp. *ginnala*
Shrub   page 70

Amelanchier lamarckii
Large shrub   page 87

Anemone hupehensis
'September Charm'
Perennial Z4 Pale pink flowers on neat growth.
↕24–36in (60–90cm) ↔16in (40cm)

Aster amellus 'King George'
Perennial   page 104

Aster ericoides 'Pink Cloud'
Perennial Z4 The bushy plants are covered with small, pink flowers.
↕3ft (1m) ↔12in (30cm)

Ceanothus x *delileanus*
'Gloire de Versailles'
Shrub   page 145

Clematis 'Alba Luxurians'
Climber   page 164

Clematis 'Duchess of Albany'
Climber   page 164

Clematis tangutica
Climber Z2 Vigorous climber with bright yellow bell-like flowers from mid-summer on, and attractive fluffy seeds.
↕20ft (6m) ↔10ft (3m)

Cornus kousa var. *chinensis*
Tree   page 171

Cortaderia selloana
'Sunningdale Silver'
Ornamental grass   page 173

Cotinus 'Grace'
Shrub   page 177

Dahlia cultivars
Perennials   pages 194–195

Euonymus alatus
Shrub   page 230

Euonymus europaeus 'Red Cascade'
Shrub   page 231

Euphorbia polychroma
Perennial   page 235

Fraxinus nigra 'Fallgold'
Deciduous tree Z2b Upright tree with dark green leaves that turn golden in fall and no fruit. Does well in wet soils.
↕50ft (15m) ↔25ft (8m)

Fuchsia 'Mrs. Popple'
Shrub   page 244

Gentiana septemfida
Perennial   page 257

Ginkgo biloba
Tree **Z3** This deciduous conifer has broad leaves that turn butter yellow before they drop in fall.
‡to 100ft (30m) ↔25ft (8m)

Helianthus 'Loddon Gold'
Perennial   page **281**

Hibiscus syriacus 'Oiseau Bleu'
Shrub   page **288**

Indigofera amblyantha
Shrub   page **307**

Liquidambar styraciflua 'Worplesdon'
Tree   page **352**

Liriodendron tulipifera
Tree   page **352**

Liriope muscari
Perennial   page **353**

Malus 'John Downie'
Tree   page **368**

Nandina domestica
Shrub   page **377**

Nyssa sylvatica
Tree   page **385**

Parthenocissus tricuspidata
Climber   page **401**

Phygelius capensis
Shrub   page **428**

Prunus sargentii
Tree   page **457**

Prunus x *subhirtella* 'Autumnalis Rosea'
Tree   page **457**

Pseudolarix amabilis
Tree **Z6** A deciduous conifer that is grown for its attractive conical shape and golden fall color.
‡50–70ft (15–20m) ↔20–40ft (6–12m)

Rhus typhina 'Dissecta'
Shrub   page **477**

Rudbeckia fulgida var. *deamii*
Perennial **Z3b** Daisylike flowers of orange, with black centers.
‡24in (60cm) ↔18in (45cm)

Rudbeckia laciniata 'Goldquelle'
Perennial   page **500**

Salvia uliginosa
Perennial   page **511**

Schizostylis coccinea 'Sunrise'
Perennial   page **518**

Sedum 'Ruby Glow'
Perennial   page **520**

Sedum spectabile 'Iceberg'
Perennial **Z4** Fleshy, pale-leaved plant with pure white flowers.
‡12–18in (30–45cm) ↔14in (35cm)

Sorbus reducta
Shrub   page **531**

Sorbus x *thuringiaca* 'Fastigiata'
Deciduous tree **Z5** A good upright tree with orange to copper fall color and red fruits. Not as prone to fire blight as other mountain ashes.
‡25ft (7.5m) ↔15ft (5m)

Tricyrtis formosana
Perennial **Z5** Erect stems with glossy leaves, and pale pink, starry flowers with darker spots.
‡32in (80cm) ↔18in (45cm)

Viburnum plicatum 'Mariesii'
Shrub   page **568**

Vitis coignetiae
Climber   page **572**

Plants for Winter Interest

Gardeners who do not think that anything happens in gardens in winter miss out on some of the most exciting plants of all: some bear flowers; others have highly attractive bark in winter; and many evergreens come into their prime. Many grow happily in shady positions, and this is the ideal place to plant a winter garden, preferably by a door or from where it can be viewed.

Acer griseum
Tree   page 64

Acer pensylvanicum 'Erythrocladum'
Deciduous tree   page 68

Asplenium scolopendrium
Cristatum Group
Evergreen fern Z4 Erect, leathery fronds with broadened, irregular tips, which look bold in winter.
‡18in (45cm) ↔24in (60cm)

Aucuba japonica 'Crotonifolia'
Evergreen shrub   page 110

Bergenia 'Ballawley'
Perennial   page 120

Calluna vulgaris 'Robert Chapman'
Heather   page 130

Caragana arborescens 'Walker'
Weeping tree Z2 Narrow thread-like foliage and yellow flowers in summer and a very columnar weeping habit that gives winter interest.
‡to 8ft (2.5m) (depending on graft stock)
↔3ft (1m)

Chamaecyparis obtusa 'Nana Aurea'
Conifer Z5 This dwarf conifer is rounded with a flat top and yellow foliage.
‡6ft (2m)

Chimonanthus praecox 'Grandiflorus'
Shrub   page 152

Clematis cirrhosa var. *balearica*
Climber Z8 This evergreen climber has pale cream, bell-shaped flowers that are fragrant.
‡8–10ft (2.5–3m)

Cornus alba 'Sibirica'
Shrub   page 169

Cornus mas
Shrub or small tree   page 171

Cornus mas 'Aurea'
Shrub Z4 Masses of tiny yellow flowers in winter followed by chartreuse spring foliage that turns green in summer.
‡↔15ft (5m)

Cyclamen cilicium
Tuberous perennial   page 189

Cyclamen coum Pewter Group
Bulb   page 190

Daphne bholua 'Gurkha'
Shrub   page 196

Erica carnea 'Ann Sparkes'
Evergreen shrub   page 219

Erica carnea 'Pink Spangles'
Evergreen shrub Z5 This bright heather has flowers that are pink and white as they first open.
‡6in (15cm) ↔18in (45cm)

Erica carnea 'Vivellii'
Evergreen shrub   page 219

Erica x *darleyensis* 'Furzey'
Evergreen shrub Z5 Small shrub with dark foliage and deep pink flowers.
‡12in (30cm) ↔24in (60cm)

Erica x *darleyensis* 'J. W. Porter'
Evergreen shrub Z5 Deep green foliage tipped with cream and red in spring, and deep pink flowers.
‡12in (30cm) ↔24in (60cm)

Hamamelis x intermedia cultivars
Shrubs

Helleborus argutifolius
Perennial

Helleborus niger
Perennial

Helleborus x nigercors
Perennial

Ilex aquifolium 'Golden Milkboy'
Tree

Ilex x meserveae 'Blue Princess'
Shrub

Iris unguicularis
Perennial

Juniperus communis 'Repanda'
Conifer Z2 The foliage of this ground-hugging conifer is often bronze in winter.
↕8in (20cm) ↔3ft (1m)

Kerria japonica
Shrub Z5 Deciduous shrub with yellow flowers in summer and bright green shoots. Does well in part shade.
↕5ft (1.6m) ↔4ft (1.2m)

Lonicera sempervirens
Shrub

Mahonia x media 'Lionel Fortescue'
Tender evergreen shrub Min. temp. 35°F (2°C). Divided leaves with leaflets like holly leaves and upright spikes of bright yellow flowers.
↕15ft (5m) ↔12ft (4m)

Mahonia x media 'Winter Sun'
Tender evergreen shrub Min. temp. 35°F (2°C). The appeal of this prickly, upright shrub is its scented yellow winter flowers.
↕15ft (5m) ↔12ft (4m)

Pulmonaria rubra
Evergreen perennial

Rubus thibetanus
Shrub

Salix babylonica var. *pekinensis* 'Tortuosa'
Tree

Salix hastata 'Wehrhahnii'
Shrub

Skimmia japonica 'Nymans'
Evergreen shrub Z7 This spreading shrub is female and bears good clusters of red berries.
↕3ft (1m) ↔6ft (2m)

Stachyurus praecox
Shrub

Symphoricarpos x doorenbosii 'White Hedge'
Shrub Z5 Suckering shrub of upright habit with white berries.
↕6ft (2m) ↔indefinite

Viburnum x bodnantense 'Dawn'
Shrub

Viburnum farreri
Shrub

Viburnum tinus 'Eve Price'
Evergreen shrub

Berrying Plants

If birds do not enjoy the feast as soon as they ripen, berries can enhance the garden for many months. Red berries are most common, but there are black, white, yellow, pink, blue, and even purple berries, to be included in almost any garden. Pale berries look best against a dark background such as an evergreen hedge, and red berries are attractive against a wintery, sunny sky.

Actaea alba
Perennial Z4 Clump-forming plant with divided leaves and fluffy flowers followed by pearly, white berries with black eyes.
‡3ft (1m) ↔18–24in (45–60cm)

Ampelopsis brevipedunculata
Vine Z5 Climber with three-part leaves and fruit that turn from green, through purple, to porcelain blue.
‡↔25ft (7.5m)

Arbutus unedo f. *rubra*
Evergreen tree Z7 The pink flowers and red, globular fruits are both at their best in fall.
‡↔25ft (8m)

Arum italicum subsp. *italicum* 'Marmoratum'
Perennial   page **102**

Berberis dictyophylla
Shrub Z6b This deciduous shrub is at its best in winter when the white shoots are studded with red berries.
‡6ft (2m) ↔5ft (1.5m)

Berberis x *stenophylla* 'Corallina Compacta'
Evergreen shrub   page **117**

Berberis verruculosa
Evergreen shrub   page **119**

Callicarpa bodinieri var. *giraldii* 'Profusion'
Shrub   page **128**

Celastrus orbiculatus
Climber Z4 Strong-growing climber with yellow fall color and yellow fruits opening to reveal red seeds.
‡46ft (14m)

Clerodendron trichotomum var. *fargesii*
Shrub Z6 Fast-growing plant with fragrant white flowers and turquoise berries set against red calyces.
‡↔15ft (5m)

Cornus 'Norman Hadden'
Evergreen tree Z8 Some leaves turn yellow and drop each fall, when the cream and pink flowers are followed by large red fruits.
‡↔25ft (8m)

Cotoneaster conspicuus 'Decorus'
Evergreen shrub   page **178**

Cotoneaster 'Rothschildianus'
Evergreen shrub Z8 An arching shrub with golden-yellow berries in fall after white flowers in summer.
‡↔15ft (5m)

Crataegus viridis 'Winter King'
Deciduous tree Z5 White flowers in spring, flaking bark for winter interest and persistent red fruits.
‡20ft (6m) ↔15ft (4.5m)

Euonymus planipes
Shrub Z5 The foliage is bright red in fall and falls to reveal red capsules containing orange seeds.
‡↔10ft (3m)

Gaultheria mucronata 'Wintertime'
Evergreen shrub — page 252

Hippophae rhamnoides
Shrub — page 289

Hypericum kouytchense
Shrub — page 302

Ilex aquifolium & cultivars
Evergreen shrubs — pages 304–305

Ilex x meserveae 'Blue Angel'
Evergreen shrub Z5 Compact, slow-growing shrub with glossy, dark, bluish-green leaves and red berries.
‡12ft (4m) ↔6ft (2m)

Ilex verticillata 'Winter Red'
Shrub Z3 Deciduous shrub with white flowers in spring and masses of small red berries in winter.
‡8–10ft (2.5–3m) ↔10ft (3m)

Lonicera nitida 'Baggesen's Gold'
Evergreen shrub — page 355

Lonicera periclymenum
'Graham Thomas'
Climber — page 356

Malus baccata 'Columnaris'
Deciduous tree Z2b A slender tree with white flowers in spring and red or yellow fruits that hang on well and attract birds.
‡30ft (9m) ↔5ft (1.6m)

Physalis alkekengi
Perennial Z4 Creeping plant with upright stems: orange lanterns containing orange berries follow white flowers.
‡24–30in (60–75cm) ↔3ft (1m)

Pyracantha 'Cadrou'
Evergreen shrub Z7 Spiny shrub with white flowers and red berries, resistant to scab.
‡↔6ft (2m)

Rosa 'Fru Dagmar Hastrup'
Shrub rose — page 496

Rosa 'Geranium'
Shrub rose Z6 Arching, prickly stems with neat red flowers and large, long red hips.
‡8ft (2.5m) ↔5ft (1.5m)

Rosa glauca
Species rose — page 496

Rosa rugosa 'Jens Munk'
Species rose Z2 Semidouble pink flowers and good red fruit on a disease-free plant.
‡6ft (2m) ↔4ft (1.2m)

Sambucus racemosa
'Sutherland Gold'
Shrub Z3 Divided yellow leaves in summer and clusters of small, red berries.
‡↔10ft (3m)

Skimmia japonica 'Fructu Albo'
Evergreen shrub Z7 Neat evergreen with white flowers and bright, white fruits.
‡24in (60cm) ↔3ft (1m)

Sorbus aria 'Lutescens'
Tree — page 530

Sorbus hupehensis var. *obtusa*
Tree — page 530

Tropaeolum speciosum
Perennial climber — page 553

Viburnum davidii
Evergreen shrub — page 567

Viburnum opulus 'Xanthocarpum'
Shrub — page 568

Conifers for Small Gardens

Conifers provide an amazing range of shapes, sizes, colors, and textures. They can be used to give upright accents in borders, as dense screens, and for evergreen groundcover. They tolerate most soils but many varieties, except yew, need sun. Many change color with the seasons and are especially brilliant in early summer when new growth contrasts with older foliage.

Abies balsamea **Hudsonia Group**
Conifer Z2 This very dwarf form grows into a rounded shrub and does not bear cones.
‡24in (60cm) ↔ 3ft (1m)

Abies koreana **'Silberlocke'**
Conifer Z4b Attractive twisted foliage that reveals the silver reverse to the needles, and attractive cones.
‡30ft (10m) ↔ 20ft (6m)

Abies lasiocarpa **'Compacta'**
Conifer Z2b Slow-growing conical tree with blue-gray leaves.
‡10–15ft (3–5m) ↔ 6–10ft (2–3m)

Abies nordmanniana
'Golden Spreader'
Conifer Z5b Dwarf, slow-growing plant with bright gold foliage.
‡3ft (1m) ↔ 5ft (1.5m)

Chamaecyparis lawsoniana
'Chilworth Silver'
Conifer Z5b Slow-growing conical shrub with silver-gray foliage.
‡5ft (1.5m)

Chamaecyparis lawsoniana
'Ellwood's Gold'
Conifer page 149

Chamaecyparis obtusa
'Nana Gracilis'
Conifer page 150

Cryptomeria japonica
'Elegans Compacta'
Conifer page 187

Cryptomeria japonica
'Vilmoriniana'
Conifer Z5b Forms a tight ball of foliage that is green in summer but bronze in winter.
‡↔ 18in (45cm)

Juniperus chinensis **'Blaauw'**
Conifer Z4 Forms a dense, upright shrub with blue-gray leaves.
‡4ft (1.2m) ↔ 3ft (1m)

Juniperus chinensis **'Obelisk'**
Conifer Z4 Grows slowly into an interesting, upright shape with bluish-green leaves.
‡8ft (2.5m) ↔ 24in (60cm)

Juniperus communis **'Compressa'**
Conifer page 325

Juniperus x pfitzeriana
'Wilhelm Pfitzer'
Conifer page 325

Juniperus procumbens **'Nana'**
Conifer page 326

Juniperus scopulorum **'Blue Heaven'**
Conifer Z2 Neat in habit, with blue leaves and a conical shape.
‡6ft (2m) ↔ 24in (60cm)

Juniperus squamata **'Blue Star'**
Conifer page 326

Juniperus squamata **'Holger'**
Conifer Z4 Spreading evergreen with bluish foliage that contrasts with the yellowish new growth.
‡↔ 6ft (2m)

Microbiota decussata
Conifer Z3 Spreading conifer with fine foliage that turns bronze in winter sun.
↕3ft (1m) ↔indefinite

Picea abies 'Nidiformis'
Conifer Z2b This slow-growing plant grows outward to form a "nest" in the center of the plant.
↕5ft (1.5m) ↔10–12ft (3–4m)

Picea glauca var. albertiana 'Conica'
Conifer page **432**

Picea mariana 'Nana'
Conifer page **433**

Picea pungens 'Koster'
Conifer page **433**

Pinus mugo 'Mops'
Conifer page **436**

Pinus parviflora 'Adcock's Dwarf'
Conifer Z5b A dwarf cultivar of the Japanese white pine, with grayish leaves.
↕6ft (2m)

Pinus sylvestris 'Beuvronensis'
Conifer Z2 A rounded, dwarf cultivar of the Scots pine.
↕3ft (1m)

Taxus baccata 'Dovastonii Aurea'
Conifer page **541**

Taxus baccata 'Fastigiata Aureomarginata'
Conifer Z6 Upright accent plant with yellow-margined leaves, and red-fleshed (poisonous) berries.
↕10–15ft (3–5m) ↔3–8ft (1–2.5m)

Taxus baccata 'Fastigiata'
Conifer page **542**

Taxus baccata 'Repens Aurea'
Conifer Z6 This spreading form of yew has golden leaves.
↕↔3–5ft (1–1.5m)

Taxus x *media* 'Wardii'
Conifer Z5 A fast growing conifer with dark green foliage and red fruits.
↕6ft (2m) ↔15ft (4.5m)

Thuja occidentalis 'Holmstrup'
Conifer page **543**

Thuja occidentalis 'Rheingold'
Conifer page **544**

Thuja occidentalis 'Smaragd'
Conifer Z2b A dwarf, conical bush with bright green leaves.
↕3ft (1m) ↔32in (80cm)

Thuja orientalis 'Aurea Nana'
Conifer page **544**

Thuja plicata 'Stoneham Gold'
Conifer page **545**

Tsuga canadensis 'Jeddeloh'
Conifer page **553**

Trees for Small Gardens

Trees add shade and character to gardens, but large forest trees should never be planted in small gardens or too near homes. Beech, oaks, and ash may be cheap to buy, but it is best to look for small trees that will give interest over a long period during the year. Consider the shade they will cast: dense evergreens can create areas that are dry and dark, where little will grow.

Acer palmatum cultivars
Deciduous trees or large shrubs
pages 66–67

Amelanchier x grandiflora **'Ballerina'**
Deciduous tree page 87

Betula utilis var. *jacquemontii*
Deciduous tree page 122

Cercis siliquastrum
Deciduous tree page 147

Cornus alternifolia
Deciduous tree or large shrub Z3b Attractive small tree with upturned branch tips, white flowers in spring and black fruit.
↕20ft (6m) ↔25ft (7.5m)

Cornus **'Eddie's White Wonder'**
Deciduous tree Z7 Multistemmed tree that bears deep purple, small flowers surrounded by large white bracts.
↕20ft (6m) ↔15ft (5m)

Crataegus laevigata **'Paul's Scarlet'**
Deciduous tree page 181

Euonymus europeaus **'Red Cascade'**
Deciduous tree page 231

Laburnum x watereri **'Vossii'**
Deciduous tree page 332

Magnolia **'Heaven Scent'**
Deciduous tree Z4b Goblet-shaped pink flowers, with white interiors, in spring and early summer.
↕↔30ft (10m)

Malus coronaria **'Charlottae'**
Deciduous tree Z4 Fragrant, semidouble, pale pink flowers in spring.
↕↔28ft (9m)

Malus sargentii
Deciduous tree Z5 A very small spreading tree with white spring flowers, red fruits and good disease resistance.
↕6ft (1.8m) ↔10ft (3m)

Prunus maackii
Deciduous tree Z2b Pyramidal tree becoming rounded with age with attractive white flowers in spring, black fruit in late summer, and coppery bark for winter interest.
↕30ft (9m) ↔25ft (7.5m)

Prunus serrula
Deciduous tree page 455

Pyrus calleryana **'Chanticleer'**
Deciduous tree page 463

Salix **'Erythroflexuosa'**
Deciduous tree Z4b Semi-weeping tree with twisted, orange-yellow shoots.
↕↔15ft (5m)

Sorbus **'Joseph Rock'**
Deciduous tree page 531

Styrax japonicus
Deciduous tree page 536

Syringa reticulata **'Ivory Silk'**
Deciduous tree Z2 Fragrant creamy flowers after the common lilacs have bloomed. Attractive speckled bark and mildew resistant.
↕25ft (7.5m) ↔20ft (6m)

Hedge Plants with Attractive Foliage

Formal hedging plants must be tolerant of regular clipping. Those that have one flush of growth each year, such as yew, need clipping only once a season, unlike privet, which may require trimming two or three times, Evergreens are most popular, but deciduous plants still reduce wind speed, and are often cheaper. Dimensions below are ultimate sizes.

Buxus sempervirens 'Suffruticosa'
Evergreen shrub   page **127**

Caragana aurantiaca
Shrub Z2 Small shrub that makes a good hedge even on poor soils. Can be cut back hard if it gets over-large.
‡4ft (1.2m)

Chamaecyparis lawsoniana
'Lanei Aurea'
Conifer   page **149**

Cotoneaster lucidus
Shrub Z2 An upright plant with shiny dark green foliage that turns red in fall. Pink flowers and black fruit.
‡18ft (2.4m) ↔6ft (1.8m)

x *Cupressocyparis leylandii*
'Haggerston Grey'
Conifer   page **188**

Fagus sylvatica
Deciduous tree Z5b European beech and its purple form retain their dead leaves in winter if trimmed to 2m (6ft).
‡80ft (25m) ↔50ft (15m)

Ligustrum ovalifolium 'Aureum'
Evergreen shrub Z7 Good choice where a bright yellow hedge is required, and regular clipping is possible.
‡↔12ft (4m)

Physocarpus opulifolus 'Diablo'
Shrub   page **431**

Pinus strobus
Conifer Z2b Soft green needles but needs pruning often. Will not re-grow from old wood.
‡80ft (24m) ↔50ft (15m)

Prunus x cistena
Deciduous shrub   page **453**

Prunus laurocerasus
'Otto Luyken'
Evergreen shrub   page **454**

Prunus tomentosa
Shrub Z2 A tall shrub that can be kept as a fairly low hedge and still flower and fruit.
‡9ft (2.7m) ↔12ft (3.5m)

Quercus imbricaria
Tree Z4b Shiny green leaves in summer turn brown and stay all winter to fall in spring. An excellent hedge.
‡↔50ft (15m)

Taxus baccata
Evergreen tree   page **541**

Thuja occidentalis
Conifer Z3 The most widely used hedging plant in eastern Canada, it can be kept as a medium-sized hedge with an annual trim.
‡40ft (12m) ↔15ft (4.5m)

Flowering Hedges

Flowering hedges add much more than structural elements and security to the garden: they can become a focus of attention. Many flowering shrubs that tolerate pruning can be used but, because of the pruning required to maintain flowering at its best, they may not be suitable for dense, formal hedges, or for boundary hedges where year-round screening is required.

Escallonia 'Apple Blossom'
Evergreen shrub   page 226

Forsythia x *intermedia* 'Lynwood Variety'
Shrub   page 240

Fuchsia 'Riccartonii'
Shrub   page 244

Hypericum 'Rowallane'
Shrub Z7 Semi-evergreen, bearing clusters of yellow, cupped flowers in summer on arching stems.
↕6ft (2m) ↔3ft (1m)

Lavandula angustifolia 'Hidcote'
Evergreen shrub   page 337

Lonicera x *xylosteoides* 'Clavey's Dwarf'
Shrub Z2 A low, rounded shrub with white flowers in early summer and red berries in fall.
↕15ft (1.6m) ↔3ft (1m)

Osmanthus x *burkwoodii*
Evergreen shrub   page 391

Philadelphus coronarius 'Aureus'
Shrub Z3 Golden yellow foliage that may scorch in full sun on poor soil, and fragrant white flowers.
↕8ft (2.5m) ↔5ft (1.5m)

Potentilla fruticosa 'Primrose Beauty'
Shrub   page 442

Prunus x *cistena*
Shrub   page 453

Rhododendron 'Hinomayo'
Evergreen shrub   page 468

Ribes sanguineum 'Pulborough Scarlet'
Shrub   page 478

Rosa 'Buff Beauty'
Modern shrub rose   page 494

Rosa 'Champlain'
Shrub Z3 A dwarf, free-flowering selection with dark red flowers and good disease resistance.
↕↔3ft (1m)

Rosa 'Chinatown'
Floribunda rose   page 482

Rosa x *harisonii* 'Harison's Yellow'
Shrub Z2 A tall, spiny rose with an upright habit that makes a good barrier hedge. Semidouble yellow flowers in spring and dark red fruits.
↕6ft (2m) ↔4ft (1.2m)

Spiraea japonica 'Anthony Waterer'
Shrub   page 533

Spiraea x *vanhouttei*
Shrub   page 534

Syringa pubescens subsp. *microphylla* 'Superba'
Shrub   page 538

Viburnum dilatum 'Catskill'
Shrub Z5b Clusters of white flowers in spring and bright red, persistent fruit. Leaves turn orangey-copper in fall.
↕5ft (1.6m) ↔8ft (2.6m)

Spiny Hedges

There are places in the garden, usually around the edges, where the physical barrier of a hedge is not enough, and plants with spines are needed to ensure privacy and prevent the access of animals. Though these plants have many advantages, pruning and clipping must be done carefully, and dropped twigs can cause more discomfort in the future when weeding at the base.

Berberis darwinii
Evergreen shrub page 116

Berberis x ottawensis 'Superba'
Shrub page 117

Berberis x stenophylla
Evergreen shrub Z6b Long, arching shoots are covered with small orange flowers in spring, and spines all year.
‡10ft (3m) ↔15ft (5m)

Berberis thunbergii
Shrub Z4 Spiny stems have purple leaves that turn red before falling.
‡3ft (1m) ↔8ft (2.5m)

Crataegus crus-galli
Tree Z2 A small tree with long thorns that can be kept short as a hedge. White flowers produce persistent dark red fruits.
‡20ft (6m) ↔25ft (7.5m)

Crataegus monogyna
Tree Z4b The singleseed hawthorn forms a quick-growing spiny hedge, but is not as attractive as some other varieties of hedge.
‡30ft (10m) ↔25ft (8m)

Ilex aquifolium & cultivars
Evergreen shrubs pages 304–305

Mahonia japonica
Evergreen shrub page 366

Mahonia x media 'Buckland'
Evergreen shrub page 367

Poncirus trifoliata
Shrub Z5b Angular green shoots with vicious spines, fragrant white flowers, and orange-like fruits in fall.
‡↔15ft (5m)

Prunus spinosa
Tree Z5b The blackthorn is a dense shrub, with white spring flowers and sloes in fall.
‡15ft (5m) ↔12ft (4m)

Pyracantha 'Orange Glow'
Evergreen shrub page 462

Pyracantha 'Watereri'
Evergreen shrub page 463

Rosa glauca
Species rose page 496

Rosa rugosa 'Jens Munk'
Species rose Z2 Thickets of prickly stems with pink flowers followed by small red hips.
‡6ft (2m) ↔4ft (1.2m)

Rosa rugosa 'Therese Bugnet'
Species rose Z2 A vigorous bush that makes an impenetrable hedge with dark pink fragrant flowers and red fruit.
‡↔6ft (2m)

Groundcovers for Sun

Many plants with creeping, trailing, or clump-forming habits can be planted to form a groundcover in sunny gardens. However, most will only suppress new weeds, and very few will actively smother existing weeds, so clear the soil of all perennial weeds before you plant. When planting, mix different plants to create interest, and add a few taller plants to prevent a flat effect.

Alchemilla mollis
Perennial   page 81

Artemisia stelleriana
'Boughton Silver'
Perennial Z4 Divided, evergreen, silver foliage that forms dense mats.
‡6in (15cm) ↔ 12–18in (30–45cm)

Campanula glomerata **'Superba'**
Perennial   page 138

Ceanothus thyrsiflorus var. *repens*
Evergreen shrub   page 145

Dicentra **'Stuart Boothman'**
Perennial   page 208

Erica x *darleyensis* **'Jenny Porter'**
Evergreen shrub   page 219

Genista lydia
Shrub   page 255

Geranium **'Johnson's Blue'**
Perennial   page 259

Geranium x *oxonianum*
'Wargrave Pink'
Perennial   page 261

Hosta **'Fortunei Aureomarginata'**
Perennial   page 291

Juniperus squamata **'Blue Carpet'**
Conifer Z4b Low-growing plant with shoots that lift from the ground at a gentle angle.
‡12–18in (30–45cm) ↔ 5–6ft (1.5–1.8m)

Lamium maculatum **'White Nancy'**
Perennial   page 333

Osteospermum jucundum
Perennial   page 392

Persicaria vaccinifolia
Perennial   page 414

Phalaris arundinacea **'Picta'**
Perennial grass   page 415

Phlomis russeliana
Perennial   page 418

Phlox subulata
'McDaniel's Cushion'
Alpine Z3b Mossy foliage is covered with starry, pink flowers in late spring.
‡2–6in (5–15cm) ↔ 20in (50cm)

Potentilla megalantha
Perennial   page 443

Rosa groundcover types
Shrubs   pages 490–491

Sempervivum ciliosum
Alpine   page 524

Thymus **'Silver Queen'**
Subshrub   page 547

Veronica gentianoides
Perennial   page 564

Viola **'Nellie Britton'**
Perennial   page 571

Groundcovers for Shade

Shade is often considered to be a problem, but there are lots of plants to use as groundcovers that do not need full sun. However, the more dense the shade, the less choice there is. Luckily, those that tolerate the worst conditions are evergreen, though slow growing. In less hostile conditions, many of these plants will quickly spread: an excellent alternative to grass under trees.

Adiantum venustum
Fern   page 76

Ajuga reptans 'Catlin's Giant'
Perennial Z4 Very large, purple leaves and tall, blue flower spikes.
‡8in (20cm) ↔24–36in (60–90cm)

Bergenia 'Silberlicht'
Perennial   page 120

Convallaria majalis
Perennial   page 167

Cotoneaster dammeri
Evergreen shrub Z4 Spreading shrub with white flowers and red berries.
‡8in (20cm) ↔6ft (2m)

Epimedium x *perralchicum*
Perennial   page 216

Euonymus fortunei
'Emerald Gaiety'
Evergreen shrub Z5 Bushy, with white-edged leaves tinted pink in winter.
‡3ft (1m) ↔5ft (1.5m)

Euphorbia amygdaloides
var. *robbiae*
Perennial   page 233

Gaultheria procumbens
Evergreen shrub   page 253

Geranium macrorrhizum 'Spessart'
Perennial Z3b Mats of scented foliage tinted with purple in fall, and pale pink flowers in summer.
‡20in (50cm) ↔24in (60cm)

Geranium sylvaticum 'Album'
Perennial Z4 Deeply lobed leaves and small, white flowers. For moist soil.
‡30in (75cm) ↔24in (60cm)

Hedera hibernica
Evergreen climber   page 277

Heuchera 'Red Spangles'
Perennial   page 288

Hosta 'Frances Williams'
Perennial   page 291

Omphalodes cappadocica
Perennial   page 387

Pachysandra terminalis
Perennial   page 394

Sanguinaria canadensis 'Plena'
Perennial Z3b Large glaucous leaves and white, double flowers. For moist soil.
‡6in (15cm) ↔12in (30cm)

Tiarella cordifolia
Perennial   page 547

Tolmiea menziesii 'Taff's Gold'
Perennial   page 548

Trachystemon orientalis
Perennial Z7 Large, rough, heart-shaped leaves and borage-like flowers.
‡12in (30cm) ↔3ft (1m)

Vinca minor 'Argenteovariegata'
Perennial Z3 Pale blue flowers among gray-green and cream leaves.
‡6in (15cm) ↔3ft (1m)

Plants with Scented Foliage

While flowers tend to have sweet, fruity perfumes, leaf scents tend to be more spicy or resinous, though some, especially scented geraniums, mimic other plants. Some plants waft their perfume onto the air, and others need gentle stroking. It is likely that these plants evolved their scents to make themselves less appealing to insect pests; gardeners find them irresistible.

Amicia zygomeris
Perennial Z8 Unusual plant, related to beans, with gray-green foliage that smells of cucumber when crushed.
‡7ft (2.2m) ↔4ft (1.2m)

Calocedrus decurrens
Conifer Z6b Columnar tree with sweetly scented foliage when crushed.
‡70–130ft (20–40m) ↔6–28ft (2–9m)

Calycanthus floridus
Shrub Z5 Large leaves with a spicy scent; brick red flowers that smell fruity.
‡10ft (3m) ↔12ft (4m)

Cercidiphyllum japonicum
Tree page 146

Chamaemelum nobile 'Treneague'
Perennial Z6 This non-flowering form of chamomile hugs the soil, and its foliage smells fruity when gently crushed.
‡4in (10cm) ↔18in (45cm)

Cistus ladanifer
Evergreen shrub Z7 The dark green leaves are sticky and fragrant; the flowers are white with a yellow eye.
‡6ft (2m) ↔5ft (1.5m)

Helichrysum italicum
Evergreen shrub Z7 Narrow, silver foliage on a small shrub that smells of curry.
‡24in (60cm) ↔3ft (1m)

Houttuynia cordata 'Flore Pleno'
Perennial Z5 A rather invasive, creeping plant with purplish leaves that have a strong citrus smell when crushed.
‡6–12in (15–30cm) ↔indefinite

Lavandula angustifolia 'Twickel Purple'
Evergreen shrub page 337

Lavandula stoechas
Shrub Z8 The purple flowerheads are topped with purple bracts.
‡↔24in (60cm)

Magnolia salicifolia 'Wada's Memory'
Shrub page 365

Melissa officinalis 'Aurea'
Perennial Z3b Form of lemon balm with yellow splashes on the leaves.
‡3ft (1m) ↔18in (45cm)

Mentha suaveolens 'Variegata'
Perennial Z5 Variegated apple mint has a pleasant fragrance and showy leaves.
‡3ft (1m) ↔indefinite

Monarda 'Cambridge Scarlet'
Perennial page 342

Monarda 'Scorpion'
Perennial Z3b Whorls of bracts and violet flowers on tall, leafy stems.
‡5ft (1.5m) ↔3ft (1m)

Origanum laevigatum
Perennial page 357

Origanum laevigatum
‘Herrenhausen’
Perennial page 390

Pelargoniums, Scented-Leaved
Perennials pages **404–405**

Perilla frutescens var. *crispa*
Annual page **412**

Perovskia atriplicifolia
Shrub Z5 The upright stems carry tiny, blue flowers in fall, but the grayish leaves are fragrant all summer.
↕4ft (1.2m) ↔3ft (1m)

Perovskia ‘Blue Spire’
Subshrub page **412**

Prostanthera cuneata
Tender evergreen shrub Small, mint-scented leaves and pretty white flowers in summer.
↕↔12–36in (30–90cm)

Prostanthera rotundifolia
Tender shrub Mint-scented leaves are smothered in lilac flowers in spring.
↕6–12ft (2–4m) ↔3–10ft (1–3m)

Pseudotsuga menziesii
Conifer Z5 A large tree with resinous foliage.
↕80–160ft (25–50m) ↔20–30ft (6–10m)

Ptelea trifoliata ‘Aurea’
Tree Z3b The gold foliage and bark are strongly scented.
↕15ft (5m)

Rosa eglanteria
Species rose Z6 Very thorny, arching shoots with small pink flowers, and foliage that smells of apples when wet or in high humidity.
↕↔8ft (2.5m)

Rosmarinus officinalis
‘Silver Spires’
Evergreen shrub Z7 The culinary rosemary, but with silver variegated foliage on an upright plant.
↕3ft (1m) ↔24in (60cm)

Salvia discolor
Shrub page **505**

Salvia officinalis ‘Icterina’
Subshrub page **508**

Skimmia x *confusa* ‘Kew Green’
Evergreen shrub page **527**

Plants with Scented Flowers

Fragrance is too often forgotten when planting a garden. Yet there are as many shades of fragrance as there are of colors: they can affect mood, take you back to your childhood, or whisk you off to a far-off land with a single sniff. The most strongly scented flowers are often white or insignificant in appearance, but they have evolved to make their presence felt in other ways.

Abelia chinensis
Shrub Z7 Spreading, with heads of small pale pink flowers in late summer.
↕5ft (1.5m) ↔8ft (2.5m)

Buddleja alternifolia
Shrub   page 124

Camellia 'Inspiration'
Evergreen shrub   page 131

Camellia japonica
'Adolphe Audusson'
Evergreen shrub   page 132

Camellia japonica 'Elegans'
Evergreen shrub   page 132

Chimonanthus praecox
'Grandiflorus'
Shrub   page 152

Chimonanthus praecox 'Luteus'
Shrub Z7 Pale yellow flowers scent the late winter air.
↕12ft (4m) ↔10ft (3m)

Choisya ternata
Evergreen shrub   page 153

Clematis montana var. *grandiflora*
Climber   page 160

Convallaria majalis
Perennial   page 167

Daphne bholua 'Gurkha'
Shrub   page 196

Daphne tangutica Retusa Group
Evergreen shrubs   page 196

Dianthus 'Doris'
Perennial   page 204

Erica erigena 'Golden Lady'
Evergreen shrub   page 219

Hamamelis (Witch Hazels)
Shrubs   pages 270–271

Hemerocallis citrina
Perennial Z3 A tall species with bright yellow, lemon-scented flowers in early summer.
↕5ft (1.6m) ↔4ft (1.2m)

Hosta 'Honeybells'
Perennial   page 292

Iris, Bearded (many)
Perennials   pages 316–319

Jasminum officinale
'Argenteovariegatum'
Climber   page 324

Lathyrus odoratus
Annual   page 335

Lilium Pink Perfection Group
Bulb   page 349

Lonicera caprifolium
Climber Z7 The Italian honeysuckle has pink and cream, fragrant flowers in summer.
↕20ft (6m)

Lonicera periclymenum 'Belgica'
Climber Z4b In early summer this honeysuckle produces creamy yellow flowers streaked with maroon.
↕22ft (7m)

Lonicera periclymenum
'Graham Thomas'
Climber   page 356

Magnolia grandiflora 'Goliath'
Evergreen tree   page 363

Mahonia x *media* 'Charity'
Evergreen shrub   page 367

Matthiola longipetala
subsp. *bicornis*
Annual   page 46

Mirabilis jalapa
Tender perennial   page 47

Narcissus triandus
Bulb   page 379

Nicotiana 'Lime Green'
Tender perennial   page 383

Osmanthus x *burkwoodii*
Evergreen shrub   page 391

Paeonia lactiflora
'Sarah Bernhardt'
Perennial   page 396

Philadelphus 'Beauclerk'
Shrub   page 416

Philadelphus 'Belle Etoile'
Shrub   page 416

Phlox paniculata 'White Admiral'
Perennial Z4 Large heads of pure white
flowers with a sweet, peppery scent,
borne in summer.
↕3ft (1m)

Pittosporum tenuifolium
Evergreen shrub   page 437

Primula florindae
Perennial   page 446

Rhododendron 'Spicy Lights'
Shrub Z4 Deciduous azalea with dark
orange flowers that have a spicy fragrance.
↕5ft (1.5m) ↔4ft (1.2m)

Rosa 'Arthur Bell'
Floribunda rose   page 482

Rosa 'Blessings'
Hybrid tea rose   page 480

Rosa 'Graham Thomas'
Modern shrub rose   page 495

Rosa 'Peace'
Hybrid tea rose   page 481

Sarcococca hookeriana var. *digyna*
Evergreen shrub   page 515

Skimmia japonica 'Rubella'
Evergreen shrub   page 527

Syringa meyeri 'Palibin'
Shrub   page 537

Syringa vulgaris 'Madame Lemoine'
Shrub   page 539

Ulex europaeus 'Flore Pleno'
Evergreen shrub Z7 Spiny bush that
has a few of its double flowers, scented
of coconut, open almost all year.
↕8ft (2.5m) ↔6ft (2m)

Viburnum x *burkwoodii* 'Park
Farm Hybrid'
Evergreen shrub Z6 Upright shrub with
bronze new leaves and deep pink, scented
flowers in late spring.
↕10ft (3m) ↔6ft (2m)

Viburnum carlesii 'Aurora'
Shrub Z5b Pink flowers in late spring,
opening from red buds.
↕↔6ft (2m)

Plants for Paving

Plants help break up large expanses of paving or gravel. The clean surface also helps prevent the flowers of small plants from becoming splashed with soil and reflects heat back up. Few plants tolerate being stepped on; use only the toughest, such as thymes and chamomile, where there is heavy foot traffic. Less busy areas can be home to dwarf shrubs and alpines.

Acaena **'Blue Haze'**
Perennial Z7 A vigorous, spreading perennial with divided, gray-blue leaves and round, white flowerheads followed by red burrs.
‡4–6in (10–15cm) ↔3ft (1m)

Acaena microphylla
Perennial   page 63

Achillea ageratifolia
Perennial   page 71

Aethionema **'Warley Rose'**
Shrub   page 78

Ajuga reptans **'Atropurpurea'**
Perennial   page 81

Anthemis punctata
subsp. *cupaniana*
Perennial   page 93

Arenaria montana
Perennial   page 98

Armeria juniperifolia
Subshrub   page 100

Campanula cochlearifolia
Perennial   page 138

Chamaemelum nobile **'Treneague'**
Perennial Z6 This non-flowering form of chamomile hugs the soil, and its foliage smells fruity when gently crushed.
‡4in (10cm) ↔18in (45cm)

Dianthus **'Pike's Pink'**
Perennial   page 205

Diascia **'Joyce's Choice'**
Perennial Z7 Early-flowering, with long spikes of pale, apricot-pink flowers in summer.
‡12in (30cm) ↔18in (45cm)

Erigeron karvinskianus
Perennial   page 222

Erinus alpinus
Perennial   page 222

Helianthemum
'Rhodanthe Carneum'
Evergreen shrub   page 280

Lysimachia nummularia **'Aurea'**
Perennial   page 361

Penstemon rupicola
Dwarf shrub Z4 Tiny compared to border penstemons: evergreen, with leathery leaves and small, tubular deep pink flowers in early summer.
‡4in (10cm) ↔18in (45cm)

Phlox subulata **'Candy Stripe'**
Perennial Z3 Evergreen perennial with bright pink and white striped flowers.
‡4in (10cm) ↔20in (50cm)

Phlox subulata **'Marjorie'**
Perennial   page 423

Pratia pedunculata
Perennial Z6 Mildly invasive creeping plant with tiny leaves and star-shaped, pale blue flowers in summer.
‡½in (1.5cm) ↔indefinite

Saponaria ocymoides
Perennial page 514

Sedum acre 'Aureum'
Perennial Z4 Rather invasive succulent
with tiny shoots and leaves that are
yellow when young, and yellow flowers.
‡2in (5cm) ↔24in (60cm)

Sedum kamtschaticum 'Variegatum'
Perennial page 520

Sedum spathulifolium 'Purpureum'
Perennial page 521

Sedum spurium 'Schorbuser Blut'
Perennial page 522

Soleirolia soleirolii 'Aurea'
Tender perennial A surprisingly vigorous
plant with bright lime green, tiny leaves
that form mounds and cushions.
‡2in (5cm) ↔3ft (1m)

Stachys byzantian 'Primrose Heron'
Perennial Z3b Woolly, pointed leaves
that are a pale yellow at first, becoming
gray-green as they mature.
‡8in (20cm) ↔24in (60cm)

Thymus polytrichus
subsp. *britannicus* **'Albus'**
Subshrub Z6 A mat-forming woody plant
with hairy leaves and white flowers.
‡2in (5cm) ↔24in (60cm)

Thymus pulegioides
'Bertram Anderson'
Evergreen shrub page 546

Thymus serpyllum 'Pink Chintz'
Perennial Z4 Trailing stems that root as
they grow, with grayish leaves and pink
flowers loved by bees.
‡10in (25cm) ↔18in (45cm)

Thymus serpyllum var. coccineum
Subshrub page 546

Thymus 'Silver Queen'
Evergreen shrub page 547

Viola 'Jackanapes'
Perennial page 571

Waldsteinia ternata
Perennial Z3 Spreading by runners, this
makes a thick mat that is evergreen in
mild climates. Bright yellow flowers
in summer and strawberry-like fruits.
‡4in (10cm) ↔24in (60cm)

Architectural Plants

Every garden needs plants that are larger than life, with the sort of shape or texture that cannot be ignored. Too many of these plants can be visually overwhelming, with their bold leaves and spiky shapes, but if carefully placed among less flashy plants, they become the focus of a view or a feature in a border. Make use of light and shade to emphasize bold silhouettes.

Macleaya x *kewensis* **'Kelway's Coral Plume'**
Perennial page 362

Melianthus major
Perennial page 372

Miscanthus sinensis **'Flamingo'**
Ornamental grass page 373

Paeonia delavayi
Shrub page 395

Perovskia atriplicifolia
Shrub Z5 Upright, gray-leaved stems with small blue flowers in late summer. Long flowering season.
↕4ft (1.2m) ↔3ft (1m)

Phormium cookianum subsp. *hookeri* **'Cream Delight'**
Perennial page 424

Phormium tenax
Perennial page 425

Phormium tenax **Purpureum Group**
Perennials page 426

Phyllostachys aurea
Bamboo Z5 The golden bamboo: yellow-brown canes and yellow-green leaves.
↕6–30ft (2–10m) ↔indefinite

Phyllostachys nigra
Bamboo page 430

Phyllostachys nigra f. *henonis*
Bamboo page 431

Pleioblastus variegatus
Bamboo page 438

Prunus **'Amanogawa'**
Tree Z6 Very slender, upright growth, and semidouble pink flowers in spring.
↕25ft (8m) ↔12ft (4m)

Prunus **'Kiku-Shidare-Zakura'**
Tree page 454

Robinia pseudoacacia **'Frisia'**
Tree page 479

Rodgersia aesculifolia
Perennial Z5 Creeping rhizomes produce clumps of large leaves like those of horse chestnuts, and pink flowers.
↕6ft (2m) ↔3ft (1m)

Sorbaria tomentosa var. *angustifolia*
Shrub Z6 A spreading shrub with feathery leaves, red stems, and fluffy, white flowerheads.
↕↔10ft (3m)

Stipa gigantea
Ornamental grass page 535

Trachycarpus fortunei
Palm page 549

Viburnum plicatum **'Pink Beauty'**
Shrub Z5b A spreading shrub with horizontal tiers of branches, covered with white flowers turning to pink.
↕10ft (3m) ↔12ft (4m)

Woodwardia radicans
Fern Z8 A large, evergreen fern with huge, arching fronds.
↕6ft (2m) ↔10ft (3m)

Yucca filamentosa **'Bright Edge'**
Shrub page 575

Yucca flaccida **'Ivory'**
Shrub page 576

Yucca gloriosa
Evergreen shrub Z8 Erect trunks with gray-green narrow, sharp-tipped leaves, and large clusters of white flowers.
↕↔6ft (2m)

Shrubs and Climbers for Shaded Walls

Some walls or fences are sunless nearly all year, but the even temperatures and often moist soil suits ivies, climbing hygrangeas, and some shrubs. Walls that receive only morning sun can be a problem in colder climates: rapid thawing can damage shoots and flowers, as with magnolias. However, this is the perfect site for some clematis, climbing roses, chaenomeles, and honeysuckles.

Akebia quinata
Semi-evergreen climber Z5b Twining stems with dark green, divided leaves and scented, purple flowers in spring.
‡30ft (10m)

Camellia x williamsii
'Francis Hanger'
Evergreen shrub Z8 Glossy leaves form a good foil to the white, golden-centered flowers.
‡↔5ft (1.5m)

Chaenomeles speciosa **'Geisha Girl'**
Shrub Z5b Bushy plant with semidouble flowers of pale apricot pink.
‡↔5ft (1.5m)

Clematis **'Carnaby'**
Mid-season clematis Z4 Compact climber with large pink flowers, with a deeper center on each petal.
‡8ft (2.5m) ↔3ft (1m)

Clematis **'Helsingborg'**
Early clematis Z4 Masses of dainty, deep purple-blue flowers are followed by fluffy seedheads.
‡2–3m (6–10ft) ↔1.5m (5ft)

Clematis **'Henryi'**
Mid-season clematis

Clematis **'Minuet'**
Late-season clematis

Clematis **'Nelly Moser'**
Mid-season clematis

Clematis **'Niobe'**
Mid-season clematis

Clematis **'Venosa Violacea'**
Late-season clematis

Codonopsis convolvulacea
Perennial climber

Corylopsis pauciflora
Shrub

Cotoneaster horizontalis
Shrub

Daphne odora **'Aureomarginata'**
Evergreen shrub Z8 Low-growing, mounded shrub with leaves edged with gold, and pale pink, fragrant flowers.
‡↔5ft (1.5m)

Euonymus fortunei
'Emerald 'n' Gold'
Evergreen shrub

Forsythia suspensa
Shrub

Garrya elliptica **'James Roof'**
Evergreen shrub

Hedera canariensis
'Gloire de Marengo'
Evergreen climber Z8 Silvery green leaves variegated with white, and tinged pink in winter.
‡12ft (4m)

Hedera colchica **'Dentata'**
Evergreen climber

Hedera colchica **'Sulphur heart'**
Evergreen climber

Hedera helix 'Goldheart'
Evergreen climber Z6 Red stems with
deep green leaves marked with a central
gold splash.
‡25ft (8m)

Hydrangea anomala
subsp. *petiolaris*
Climber   page 296

Jasminum humile
Evergreen shrub Z7 Sparsely branched,
arching shrub with bright yellow flowers
in summer.
↔8ft (2.5m)

Jasminum nudiflorum
Shrub   page 323

Kerria japonica 'Pleniflora'
Shrub Z5b Vigorous, upright plant with
slender, green stems and double orange/
gold flowers.
‡↔10ft (3m)

Lonicera japonica 'Halliana'
Evergreen climber Z6 Strong-growing
climber with scented white flowers that
age to yellow.
‡30ft (10m)

Muehlenbeckia complexa
Tender climber Min. temp. 35°F (2°C).
Masses of threadlike, dark, twisting stems
with tiny violin-shaped leaves.
‡10ft (3m)

Parthenocissus henryana
Climber   page 401

Parthenocissus quinquefolia
Climber Z2b Vigorous, deciduous climber
with leaves divided into five leaflets that
take on vivid red shades in fall.
‡50ft (15m)

Pileostegia viburnoides
Evergreen climber Z7 Oblong, dark green
leaves and clusters of fluffy, white flowers.
‡20ft (6m)

Pyracantha 'Harlequin'
Evergreen shrub Z8 Prickly shrub with
white-variegated leaves, white flowers,
and red berries.
‡5ft (1.5m) ↔6ft (2m)

Rosa 'Albéric Barbier'
Rambler rose   page 486

Rosa 'Dublin Bay'
Climbing rose   page 484

Rosa 'Handel'
Climbing rose   page 485

Rosa 'Mermaid'
Climbing rose Z6 Strong, thorny climber
with dark, shiny leaves and single,
primrose yellow flowers.
‡20ft (6m)

Schizophragma integrifolium
Climber Z8 Large climber with toothed,
dark green leaves and showy white flowers.
‡40ft (12m)

Plants for Sunny Walls

Reserve the warmest, sunniest garden walls to grow plants that are slightly tender in your climate. However, these sites can also be very dry, especially if the border is narrow and in the shadow of a roof, and it may be difficult to establish plants. Walls that receive only the morning sun are more gentle to plants, which may grow more quickly because there may be more moisture.

Abelia 'Edward Goucher'
Semi-evergreen shrub   page 60

Abelia floribunda
Evergreen shrub   page 60

Abelia x grandiflora
Semi-evergreen shrub   page 61

Abelia x grandiflora
'Francis Mason'
Evergreen shrub Z6 Yellow and dark green leaves; pale pink flowers in late summer.
↕↔6ft (1.5m)

Actinidia kolomikta
Climber   page 75

Alonsoa warcsewiczii
Perennial   page 86

Ampelopsis brevipedunculata
Climber Z4 Grow this for its berries which change from green, through yellow and lilac, to a bright porcelain blue.
↕↔25ft (7.5m)

Callistemon citrinus 'Splendens'
Evergreen shrub   page 129

Campsis x tagliabuana
'Madame Galen'
Climber   page 140

Carpenteria californica
Evergreen shrub   page 142

Ceanothus 'Autumnal Blue'
Evergreen shrub   page 144

Ceanothus 'Concha'
Evergreen shrub Z8 Dark blue flowers.
↕↔10ft (3m)

Cestrum parqui
Shrub Z8 Clusters of lime green, tubular, night-scented flowers in summer.
↕↔6ft (2m)

Clematis cirrhosa 'Freckles'
Early clematis Z6 Purple-tinted, cream-spotted leaves; bell-shaped winter flowers.
↕8–10ft (2.5–3m) ↔5ft (1.5m)

Clematis 'Etoile Violette'
Late-season clematis   page 165

Clematis 'Jackmannii'
Late-season clematis   page 165

Clematis 'Lasurstern'
Mid-season clematis   page 162

Clematis rehderiana
Late-season clematis   page 165

Clematis 'The President'
Mid-season clematis   page 163

Clematis viticella 'Purpurea Plena Elegans'
Late-season clematis   page 165

Clianthus puniceus
Evergreen shrub   page 166

Cytisus battandieri
Semi-evergreen shrub   page 191

Eccremocarpus scaber
Climber   page 212

Escallonia 'Langleyensis'
Evergreen shrub   page 227

Fremontodendron 'California Glory'
Shrub   page 242

Hedychium gardnerianum
Perennial Z8 Large heads of spidery,
sweetly scented cream flowers.
↔6–7ft (2–2.2m)

Ipomoea indica
Climber   page 309

Jasminum x stephanense
Climber Z8b Fast-growing, with clusters
of pink, fragrant flowers in summer.
‡15ft (5m)

Lapageria rosea
Climber   page 333

Lonicera x brownii
'Dropmore Scarlet'
Climber Z3 A very hardy climber with
tubular red flowers from mid-summer
to fall.
↔15ft (4.5m)

Lonicera x italica
Climber   page 355

Lonicera x tellmanniana
Climber   page 357

Magnolia grandiflora 'Exmouth'
Evergreen shrub   page 362

Passiflora caerulea
Climber   page 402

Phygelius
Shrubs   pages 428–430

Rhodanthemum hosmariense
Subshrub   page 467

Ribes speciosum
Shrub Z8 Spiny shrub with bristly stems,
small glossy leaves, and pendulous red
flowers resembling fuchsias.
‡↔6ft (2m)

Roses, climbing
Deciduous climbers   pages 484–485

Solanum crispum 'Glasnevin'
Climber   page 528

Solanum laxum 'Album'
Climber   page 528

Thunbergia grandiflora
Climber   page 545

Trachelospermum jasminoides
Evergreen climber   page 549

Vestia foetida
Tender shrub Min. temp. 35°F (2°C).
A short-lived plant with unpleasantly
scented leaves and prolific, pendulous
yellow flowers.
‡6ft (2m) ↔5ft (1.5m)

Vitis 'Brant'
Climber Z8 An ornamental grape with
green leaves that turn red in fall. Bears
edible black grapes.
‡22ft (7m)

Wisteria floribunda 'Alba'
Climber   page 574

Wisteria floribunda 'Lawrence'
Climber Z4 The hardiest of all wisterias,
this variety has pale blue flowers with
a white keel.
‡60ft (18m)

Wisteria sinensis
Climber   page 575

Wisteria sinensis 'Sierra Madre'
Evergreen shrub Z6b Attractive cultivar
with bicolored, fragrant flowers.
‡28ft (9m)

Zauschneria californica 'Dublin'
Perennial   page 577

Plants for Bees and Butterflies

Plants that will attract these fascinating
and useful garden visitors usually have
simple, tubular, or daisylike flowers,
especially in pinks and purples; avoid
double-flowered varieties. Butterflies
also like fruity scents. Remember that
their caterpillar stage needs different
food plants. For example, milkweed
and some of its relatives in the genus
Asclepias feed monarch caterpillars.

Ageratum houstonianum
'Blue Horizon'
Annual This has many small flowers
forming a ball-like head on tall, sturdy
stems. Good weather resistance.
‡30in (75cm) ↔12in (30cm)

Allium schoenoprasum **'Forescate'**
Perennial Z3 Ornamental chives with
abundant heads of pink flowers.
‡24in (60cm)

Artemesia ludoviciana
'Silver Queen'
Perennial   page 101

Asclepias tuberosa
Perennial Z4 Thick, upright stems
support small heads of bright orange
flowers followed by interesting seedheads.
‡4ft (1.2m) ↔24in (60cm)

Aster **'Andenken an Alma Pötschke'**
Perennial   page 104

Aster x *frikartii* **'Mönch'**
Perennial   page 105

Buddleja davidii cultivars
Shrubs   page 125

Caryopteris x *clandonensis*
'Heavenly Blue'
Shrub   page 142

Ceanothus **'Puget Blue'**
Evergreen shrub Z8 Mass of fine foliage
covered with mid-blue flowers.
‡↔2.2m (7ft)

Centaurea montana
Perennial Z3 A mat-forming plant with
toothed leaves and blue flowers from
spring to mid-summer. Provides nectar
for many early butterflies.
‡18in (45cm) ↔24in (60cm)

Clethra alnifolia
Shrub Z4b An upright, deciduous shrub
with upright spikes of bell-shaped flowers
in late summer.
‡↔8ft (2.5m)

Cytisus x *beanii*
Shrub   page 192

Digitalis purpurea
'Sutton's Apricot'
Biennial Z4 Tall foxglove with pale
apricot-pink flowers in summer.
‡3–6ft (1–2m)

Echinacea purpurea
Perennial Z3b Large, daisylike flowers
with pink petals and dark centers.
‡3ft (1m) ↔18in (45cm)

Echium vulgare **'Blue Bedder'**
Annual Z5 Bushy plant with bristly,
grayish green leaves and soft blue
flowers.
‡↔18in (45cm)

Eryngium planum
Perennial Z4 Steely blue, branched stems
with small, light blue, spiky flower heads
emerge from evergreen leaf rosettes.
‡36in (90cm) ↔18in (45cm)

Eupatorium maculatum
Perennial   page **232**

Hoheria glabrata
Tree   page 290

Hyssopus officinalis
Evergreen shrub Z2 Green leaves and
spikes of blue flowers in summer.
24in (60cm) ↔ 3ft (1m)

Lamium orvala
Perennial Z5 A choice, clump-forming
plant that does not creep, with large
leaves and purplish flowers in spring.
24in (60cm) ↔ 12in (30cm)

Lavandula angustifolia
'Loddon Pink'
Evergreen shrub Z6 Compact shrub with
gray leaves and spikes of pale pink flowers.
18in (45cm) ↔ 24in (60cm)

Leucanthemum x superbum
'Wirral Supreme'
Perennial   page 342

Ligustrum amurense
Shrub Z5 A dense shrub with short spikes
of strangely scented white flowers in
late spring.
↕ ↔ 15ft (5m)

Lunaria rediviva
Perennial Z5 Pale lilac, fragrant flowers
are followed by translucent seedheads.
24–36in (60–90cm) ↔ 12in (30cm)

Malva moschata f. *alba*
Perennial   page 370

Mentha longifolia Buddleja Mint
Group
Perennial Z5 Tall stems of grayish leaves
and heads of pink flowers.
↕ ↔ 3ft (1m)

Monarda 'Croftway Pink'
Perennial   page 375

Origanum laevigatum
'Herrenhausen'
Perennial   page 390

Papaver orientale 'Cedric Morris'
Perennial   page 399

Prunella grandiflora 'Loveliness'
Perennial   page 452

Puschkinia scilloides
Bulb Z4 A small bulb with very pale blue
flowers in small clusters, each with a
darker blue central stripe. Much visited
by bees in early spring.
↕ ↔ 8in (20cm)

Rosmarinus officinalis 'Miss
Jessopp's Upright'
Evergreen shrub   page 498

Rudbeckia fulgida var. *sullivantii*
'Goldsturm'
Perennial   page 500

Sedum 'Herbstfreude'
Perennial Z3b Upright, unbranched
stems with pale green, fleshy leaves,
and deep pink flowers in flat heads in
late summer. Also sold as 'Autumn Joy'.
↕ ↔ 24in (60cm)

Solidago 'Goldenmosa'
Perennial   page 529

Tagetes 'Naughty Marietta'
Annual   page 55

Thymus serpyllum var. *coccineus*
Perennial   page 546

Vernonia noveboracensis
Perennial Z5 Upright perennial with
toothed leaves and fluffy heads of
red-purple or white flowers in late
summer and fall.
↕ 6ft (2m) ↔ 24in (60cm)

Plants to Attract Garden Birds

Native and visiting birds will visit gardens to feed on a wide variety of plants, especially those bearing berries and seeds (see also pages 618 and 647). Unfortunately, their feeding necessarily means that the food source—and the attractive fall display—does not last long, so it is worth offering them a variety of plants and providing extra food on a regular basis.

Acer negundo
Tree Z2 A rather weedy species that will survive poor conditions and provide seeds for winter birds.
‡50ft (15m) ↔30ft (10m)

Amelanchier x grandiflora **'Ballerina'**
Tree or shrub page 87

Atriplex hortensis var. *rubra*
Annual page 30

Berberis thunbergii
Shrub Z4 Green leaves and small, yellow flowers in summer become red leaves and berries in fall.
‡6ft (2m) ↔8ft (2.5m)

Celastrus scandens
Climbing vine Z3 A vigorous native climber with bright orange fruit that open to show the red seeds.
‡↔30ft (10m)

Cornus florida **'Cherokee Chief'**
Tree page 170

Cotoneaster lacteus
Evergreen shrub page 179

Cotoneaster simonsii
Shrub page 179

Crataegus x lavallei **'Carrierei'**
Tree page 182

Cynara cardunculus
Perennial page 191

Elaeagnus angustifolia
Shrub Z2 Deciduous shrub or small tree with silvery leaves, scented yellow flowers, and olive-like fruit in fall.
‡↔20ft (6m)

Helianthus annuus **'Music Box'**
Annual Multicolored sunflowers that produce heads of seeds that may be harvested to feed birds in later months.
‡28in (70cm) ↔24in (60cm)

Ilex aquifolium **'Handsworth New Silver'**
Evergreen shrub page 305

Ilex verticillata
Shrub Z3b Small, spreading shrub with entire leaves, inconspicuous flowers, and bright red fruit in early winter. Does best in moist locations.
‡↔15ft (5m)

Lonicera periclymenum **'Serotina'**
Climber page 324

Mahonia aquifolium
Evergreen shrub Z4b A suckering shrub with spiny leaves, and yellow flowers followed by black berries.
‡3ft (1m) ↔5ft (1.5m)

Malus x zumi **'Golden Hornet'**
Tree page 369

Miscanthus sinensis
Ornamental grass Z4 This grass forms clumps of long, arching leaves and silver or pink flowerheads in late summer.
‡8ft (2.5m) ↔4ft (1.2m)

Onopordum nervosum
Biennial Z6 A large, silvery, prickly plant with thistlelike purple flowers.
‡8ft (2.5m) ↔3ft (1m)

Parthenocissus quinquifolia
Vine page 401

Prunus virginiana
Tree Z2 A spreading tree with pendent spikes of small white flowers followed by black berries.
‡50ft (15m) ↔30ft (10m)

Pyracantha 'Mohave'
Evergreen shrub Z6 Dense, spiny growth with dark green leaves and bright red berries.
‡12ft (4m) ↔15ft (5m)

Rhus typhina
Shrub page 477

Ribes odoratum
Shrub Z2 Weakly branched shrub with yellow clove-scented flowers in spring, and black berries in late summer.
‡↔6ft (2m)

Rosa pimpinellifolia
Species rose Z3 This very spiny bush has single white flowers followed by purplish-black hips.
‡3ft (1m) ↔4ft (1.2m)

Sambucus nigra 'Aureomarginata'
Shrub Z4 Fast-growing plant for any soil, with yellow-edged leaves, white flowers, and heads of black elderberries.
‡↔20ft (6m)

Silybum marianum
Biennial Z5 Rosettes of spiny leaves, veined with white; prickly mauve seedheads and thistle seeds.
‡5ft (1.5m) ↔24–36in (60–90cm)

Sorbus aucuparia 'Fastigiata'
Tree Z4 Upright, with red berries in late summer after white spring flowers.
‡25ft (8m) ↔15ft (5m)

Viburnum trilobum
Shrub Z2 Strong-growing shrub with white flowers in summer, bright fall color and red berries.
‡15ft (5m) ↔12ft (4m)

Vitis vinifera 'Purpurea'
Climber page 572

Plants to Attract Hummingbirds

Aquilegia McKana Hybrids
Perennial Z3 A short-lived strain that is easy to grow from seed. The long spurred flowers are in a wide range of colors.
‡30in (75cm) ↔24in (60cm)

Campsis x tagliabuna 'Madame Galen'
Vine page 140

Hemerocallis citrina
Perennial Z3 A tall daylily with bright yellow, lemon-scented flowers that bloom for several weeks.
‡5ft (1.6m) ↔36in (1m)

Lonicera tatarica
Shrub Z2 A bushy, deciduous shrub with grayed leaves and white, pink, or red flowers in early summer, followed by scarlet to yellow berries.
‡12ft (4m) ↔8ft (2.5m)

Monarda 'Cambridge Scarlet'
Perennial page 374

Nicotiana alata 'Nicki Series'
Annual A dwarf strain with flowers fragrant during the day, in shades of red, pink, white, and green.
‡18in (45cm) ↔15in (39cm)

Flowers for Cutting

It is useful to be able to cut flowers from the garden, either to use on their own or to add to bought flowers. Many annuals are grown especially for cutting, but other garden plants can supply flowers for the house without spoiling the display. To produce many smaller stems for cutting, pinch out the shoots of free-branching plants such as asters and delphiniums in early summer.

Achillea 'Coronation Gold'
Perennial page 71

Aconitum 'Bressingham Spire'
Perennial page 74

Aster 'Little Carlow'
Perennial page 106

Aster pilosus var. *pringlei* 'Monte Cassino'
Perennial Z4 Thin stems of narrow, upright habit, forming a dense bush with needle-like leaves and small white flowers.
‡3ft (1m) ↔12in (30cm)

Astilbe 'Fanal'
Perennial page 107

Astrantia major 'Shaggy'
Perennial Z3b The bracts around the flower clusters are longer than usual.
‡12–36in (30–90cm) ↔18in (45cm)

Baptisia australis
Perennial page 111

Calendula 'Fiesta Gitana'
Annual page 33

Callistephus chinensis Ostrich Plum Series
Annual page 33

Campanula lactiflora 'Prichard's Variety'
Perennial Z3b Compact, with heads of violet-blue flowers in mid-summer.
‡30in (75cm) ↔18in (45cm)

Campanula persicifolia 'Chettle Charm'

Perennial Z3b Deep green foliage and white, blue-tinted flowers.
‡3ft (1m) ↔12in (30cm)

Chrysanthemums
Perennials pages 154–157

Clematis 'Vyvyan Pennell'
Climber page 163

Crocosmia x *crocosmiiflora* 'Solfaterre'
Perennial page 183

Dahlia
Tender perennial pages 194–195

Delphinium 'Bellamosum'
Perennial Z3b Well-branched stems with thin spikes of deep blue flowers.
‡1–1.2m (3–4ft) ↔45cm (18in)

Delphinium 'Bruce'
Perennial page 198

Delphinium 'Sungleam'
Perennial page 201

Dendranthema rubellum 'Clara Curtis'
Perennial Z4 Sprawling perennial with purple-pink flowers in early fall. May still be listed as *Chrysanthemum rubellum* in some catalogs.
‡30in (75cm) ↔24in (60cm)

Dianthus (Border Carnations)
Perennials page 203

Dianthus 'Coronation Ruby'
Perennial Z5 Clump-forming perennial with pink and ruby red clove-scented flowers.
‡38cm (15in) ↔30cm (12in)

Eryngium x *tripartitum*
Perennial   page 224

Geum 'Mrs J. Bradshaw'
Perennial Z4 Hairy leaves, wiry branched
stems, and double scarlet flowers.
‡40–60cm (16–24in) ↔ 60cm (24in)

Gladiolus Hybrids
Tender bulb Sword-like foliage and
slender spikes of open-faced flowers
in a wide range of colors.
‡ to 48in (1–2m)

Iris Bearded
Perennial   pages 316–319

Kniphofia 'Royal Standard'
Perennial   page 330

Lathyrus odoratus (Sweet Peas)
Annual climbers   page 335

Leucanthemum x *superbum*
'Wirral Supreme'
Perennial   page 342

Liatris spicata
Perennial Z4 This forms a rosette of
leaves from which rises a dense spike
of purple or white fluffy flowers that
open from the top downwards in summer.
‡5ft (1.5m) ↔ 18in (45cm)

Narcissus 'Merlin'
Bulb   page 381

Narcissus 'White Lion'
Bulb Z4 Double, white flowers too heavy
to stand up outside; best when cut.
‡16in (40cm)

Osteospermum 'Whirligig'
Subshrub   page 49

Paeonia lactiflora 'Sarah Bernhardt'
Perennial   page 396

Penstemon
Perennial   pages 410–411

Phlox maculata 'Alpha'
Perennial   page 421

Phlox maculata 'Omega'
Perennial Z3b Conical heads of fragrant,
small white flowers with a deep pink eye.
‡36in (90cm) ↔ 18in (45cm)

Physostegia virginiana 'Vivid'
Perennial   page 432

Rosa 'Alexander'
Hybrid tea rose   page 480

Rosa 'Iceberg'
Floribunda rose   page 483

Rosa 'Royal William'
Hybrid tea rose   page 481

Rosa 'Silver Jubilee'
Hybrid tea rose   page 481

Roses, Modern Shrub
Deciduous shrubs   pages 494–495

Rudbeckia fulgida var. *sullivantii*
'Goldsturm'
Perennial   page 500

Rudbeckia laciniata 'Goldquelle'
Perennial   page 500

Scabiosa caucasica 'Clive Greaves'
Perennial   page 517

Schizostylis coccinea 'Sunrise'
Perennial   page 518

Solidago 'Goldenmosa'
Perennial   page 529

Solidaster x *luteus* 'Lemore'
Perennial Z5 This generic hybrid produces
heads of yellow daisylike flowers.
‡36in (90cm) ↔ 12in (30cm)

Tanacetum coccineum 'Brenda'
Perennial   page 540

Tulipa 'Sorbet'
Bulb Z4 Late blooms are pale pink with
carmine streaks and flashes.
‡24in (60cm)

Veronica spicata subsp. *incana*
Perennial   page 565

Flowers for Drying

Dried flowers prolong the beauty of summer throughout the year. Many are easy to grow and dry, by simply hanging them upside down in a shady, airy position. Many flowers can be used if dried in warm sand or silica gel, then kept in a dry atmosphere. Select young, unblemished flowers that are not fully open, then remove most of the leaves before tying them into bunches.

Achillea filipendulina 'Gold Plate'
Perennial   page 72

Achillea 'Moonshine'
Perennial   page 73

Amaranthus hypochondriacus
'Green Thumb'
Annual Plants produce upright, branched spikes of pale green flowers.
‡24in (60cm) ↔12in (30cm)

Astrantia maxima
Perennial   page 108

Bracteantha Bright Bikini Series
Annuals   page 123

Catananche caerulea 'Major'
Perennial Z4 Cornflower-like flowers of papery texture on wiry stems above narrow, grayish leaves.
‡20–36in (50–90cm) ↔12in (30cm)

Centaurea cyanus 'Florence Pink'
Annual Upright-growing annual with a bushy habit and pink flowers.
‡14in (35cm) ↔18in (45cm)

Consolida ajacis Giant
Imperial Series
Annual Larkspur producing elegant spires of flowers: essentially annual delphiniums.
‡2–3ft (60–90cm) ↔14in (35cm)

Cortaderia selloana
'Sunningdale Silver'
Ornamental grass   page 173

Echinops ritro
Perennial   page 213

Hydrangea macrophylla cultivars
Shrubs   page 298

Hydrangea serrata 'Bluebird'
Shrub   page 300

Limonium sinuatum 'Art Shades'
Perennial Z8 Usually grown as annuals, with crispy flowers in shades of pink, salmon, orange, pink, and blue.
‡24in (60cm) ↔12in (30cm)

Limonium sinuatum 'Forever Gold'
Perennial   page 351

Nigella damascena 'Mulberry Rose'
Annual Feathery foliage with purplish-pink flowers, and inflated seed pods.
‡18in (45cm) ↔9in (23cm)

Rhodanthe manglesii 'Sutton's Rose'
Annual Wiry plants with grayish leaves and white or pink flowers with a strawlike texture.
‡24in (60cm) ↔6in (15cm)

Sedum spectabile 'Brilliant'
Perennial   page 522

Plants with Ornamental Seedheads

Although they may lack the bright colors of the flowers, there is much beauty to be enjoyed in the seedheads of plants. Some may be cut and preserved to decorate the home, while others can be left in the garden to bring straw or bronze tones to the winter scene; they look especially good when covered with frost or snow until birds pull them apart in their hunt for food.

Allium cristophii
Bulb   page 83

Astilbe chinensis var. *pumila*
Perennial Z3b Pink flower spikes become rust-brown as they age.
‡10in (25cm) ↔ 8in (20cm)

Clematis 'Bill Mackenzie'
Climber   page 164

Clematis macropetala 'White Swan'
Climber Z1 Compact and early-flowering. Blooms are white with silver seedheads.
‡3ft (1m)

Cotinus coggygria
Shrub Z4b Green leaves in summer that turn scarlet in fall, with feathery, smoke-like seedheads.
‡15ft (5m)

Dictamnus albus var. *purpureus*
Perennial   page 209

Echinops ritro
Perennial   page 213

Hydrangea paniculata 'Grandiflora'
Shrub   page 299

Hyoscyamus niger
Annual Extremely poisonous plant with sinister, veined flowers and beautiful seedheads resembling shuttlecocks.
‡2–4ft (60–120cm) ↔ 3ft (1m)

Iris foetidissima
Perennial Z6 Pale blue and brown flowers develop into green pods that split in fall to reveal orange seeds.
‡12–36in (30–90cm) ↔ 12in (30cm)

Iris foetidissima 'Variegata'
Perennial   page 314

Lunaria annua
Annual   page 45

Nigella orientalis 'Transformer'
Annual Bushy annual with finely divided leaves and small yellow flowers that produce umbrella-like seed pods.
‡18in (45cm) ↔ 9–12in (22–30cm)

Paeonia ludlowii
Shrub   page 396

Papaver somniferum
'Hen and Chickens'
Annual The single flowers are followed by curious pods that are surrounded by a ring of tiny pods.
‡4ft (1.2m) ↔ 12in (30cm)

Physalis alkekengi
Perennial Z4 Vigorous and suckering with bright orange, "Chinese lantern" fruits in fall.
‡24–30in (60–75cm) ↔ 36in (90cm)

Scabiosa stellata 'Drumstick'
Annual Wiry-stemmed and hairy with pale lilac flowers and round, crispy seedheads.
‡12in (30cm) ↔ 9in (23cm)

Typea minima
Aquatic perennial Z3 Narrow rush-like foliage and dark brown poker-like seedheads. Gather as soon as formed to prevent them shedding during winter.
‡30in (75cm) ↔ 18in (45cm)

Cottage Garden-Style Plants

The idealized image of a cottage garden is in summer with bees lazily buzzing around roses, lilies, hollyhocks, and peonies, but in fact the authentic cottage garden was a glorious mixture because it contained old-fashioned plants discarded by wealthier gardeners. Cottage garden flowers are often scented, usually herbaceous, and always evocative of a gentler age.

Alcea rosea 'Nigra'
Biennial Z4 The "black-flowered" hollyhock.
‡6ft (2m) ↔24in (60cm)

Calendula 'Fiesta Gitana'
Annual page 33

Campanula 'Burghaltii'
Perennial Z4 Mounds of mid-green leaves and tubular grayish-blue flowers.
‡24in (60cm) ↔12in (30cm)

Campanula persicifolia 'White Cup and Saucer'
Perennial Z3b Pure white flowers are bell-shaped with a white, circular disk, like a saucer, below the bloom.
‡36in (90cm) ↔12in (30cm)

Campanula portenschlagiana
Perennial page 139

Delphiniums
Perennials pages 198–201

Dianthus 'Gran's Favourite'
Perennial page 204

Dicentra spectabilis
Perennial page 207

Eryngium alpinum
Perennial page 223

Eschscholzia californica
Annual page 228

Geranium macrorrhizum 'Album'
Perennial Z4 Scented, evergreen leaves and white flowers in summer.
‡20in (50cm) ↔24in (60cm)

Geranium x *oxonianum* 'A.T. Johnson'
Perennial Z4 This clump-forming plant has silvery-pink flowers.
‡↔12in (30cm)

Geranium sanguineum 'Album'
Perennial Z4 A compact plant with divided leaves and white flowers.
‡8in (20cm) ↔12in (30cm)

Geranium sylvaticum 'Mayflower'
Perennial page 261

Geum 'Lady Stratheden'
Perennial page 262

Lavatera, Annuals
Annuals page 340

Lilium candidum
Bulb page 346

Lupinus Band of Nobles Series
Perennial Z8 A good seed mixture with tall spikes of bicolored flowers.
‡5ft (1.5m) ↔30in (75cm)

Lupinus 'The Chatelaine'
Perennial Z5 Tall spires of bicolored flowers in deep pink and white.
‡36in (90cm) ↔30in (75cm)

Lychnis chalcedonica
Perennial page 359

Paeonia lactiflora 'Bowl of Beauty'
Perennial page 395

Paeonia officinalis 'Rubra Plena'
Perennial page 397

Papaver orientale 'Beauty of Livermere'
Perennial page 398

Papaver orientale 'Mrs. Perry'
Perennial Z3b Salmon-pink flowers with petals like satin above coarse foliage.
‡30in (75cm) ↔24–36in (60–90cm)

Papaver rhoeas Shirley Mixed
Annuals page 399

Phlox 'Kelly's Eye'
Perennial page 421

Phlox paniculata cultivars
Perennials page 422

Primula 'Wanda'
Perennial page 452

Rosa 'Ballerina'
Patio rose page 488

Rosa 'Fantin-latour'
Old garden rose page 493

Rosa 'Gertrude Jekyll'
English shrub rose page 495

Rosa xanthina 'Canary Bird'
Shrub rose page 497

Saxifraga x urbium
Perennial Z7 Mats of evergreen leaf rosettes and sprays of dainty, white flowers in late spring.
‡12in (30cm) ↔indefinite

Scabiosa caucasica 'Miss Willmott'
Perennial page 517

Schizostylis coccinea 'Sunrise'
Perennial page 518

Verbascum 'Cotswold Beauty'
Perennial page 561

Verbascum 'Pink Domino'
Perennial Z4 Dark green leaves give rise to unbranched stems of rounded, deep pink flowers.
‡4ft (1.2m) ↔12in (30cm)

Viola cornuta
Perennial page 570

Plants for a Rock Garden

Rock gardens are good places to grow small plants, raising them closer to observers' eyes. But the raised beds also allow the soil to be tailored to suit these plants, which often require perfect drainage or specific soil mixes. Most of the plants below are easily grown and require no special treatment, making them yet more attractive: rock gardening can be an addictive hobby.

Hot Color Schemes

A grouping of plants in warm, vivid colors looks best in full sunlight; if your garden can offer a really sunny spot, take care when choosing an assortment of plants that they will all enjoy the heat.

Mixing in some plants with dark bronze and purple foliage (see p.606) will heighten the fiery effect. Remember that hot colors jump toward the eye and can make spaces seem smaller.

Alonsoa warscewiczii
Perennial   page **86**

Arctotis x hybrida 'Flame'
Tender perennial Reddish-gold daisy flowers with silver petal backs and silver-gray leaves. 'Mahogany' and 'Red Magic' are also recommended.
‡18–20in (45–50cm) ↔12in (30cm)

Astilbe 'Fanal'
Perennial   page **107**

Bassia scoparia f. trichophylla
Annual Feathery leaves that start off green, then turn fiery red, aging to purple over the summer.
‡1–5ft (0.3–1.5m) ↔12–18in (30–45cm)

Begonia 'Illumination Orange'
Perennial   page **114**

Calendula 'Fiesta Gitana'
Annual   page **33**

Callistemon citrinus 'Splendens'
Evergreen shrub   page **129**

**Campsis x tagliabuana
'Madame Galen'**
Climber   page **140**

Canna 'Tropicana'
Bulb Z8 Orange flowers and foliage striped in red, pink, yellow, and green.
‡to 6ft (2m) ↔4ft (1.2m)

Carthamus tinctoria 'Orange Gold'
Annual Clusters of bright, thistlelike tufted flowers, good for drying.
‡12–24in (30–60cm) ↔12in (30cm)

**Chrysanthemum 'Amber
Yvonne Arnaud'**
Perennial   page **154**

Chrysanthemum 'Wendy'
Perennial   page **156**

Coreopsis tinctoria 'Sunrise'
Annual Upright stems among clumps of mid-green leaves bearing solitary, daisy-like flowers attractive to bees.
‡24in (60cm) ↔12in (30cm)

Coreopsis verticillata 'Grandiflora'
Perennial Z3b Loose clusters of dark yellow flowers in early summer.
‡24–32in (60–80cm) ↔18in (45cm)

Crocosmia 'Lucifer'
Perennial   page **184**

Dahlia 'Hamari Gold'
Perennial   page **195**

Dahlia 'Zorro'
Perennial   page **195**

Diascia 'Rupert Lambert'
Perennial Z7 Mat-forming, with spikes of spurred, deep warm pink flowers from summer to fall.
‡8in (20cm) ↔20in (50cm)

Eschscholzia californica
Annual   page **228**

Heliopsis 'Goldgefieder'
Perennial Z4 Double daisy-like golden yellow flowerheads with a green center, on stiff stems with coarse leaves.
‡36in (90cm) ↔24in (60cm)

Iris 'Apricorange'
Perennial page 316

Iris 'Sun Miracle'
Perennial page 319

Kniphofia 'Bee's Sunset'
Perennial page 329

Ligularia 'Gregynog Gold'
Evergreen shrub page 345

Lonicera etrusca 'Donald Waterer'
Climber Z8 Dark, red-bloomed stems and buds, bright orange berries.
‡12ft (4m)

Lychnis chalcedonica
Perennial page 359

Mimulus cupreus
'Whitecroft Scarlet'
Perennial Z8 Spreading stems with tubular, scarlet summer flowers.
‡4in (10cm) ↔6in (15cm)

Papaver orientale 'Aglaia'
Perennial Z3b Salmon colored flowers with cherry-pink shading at the petal bases.
‡18–36in (45–90cm) ↔24–36in (60–90cm)

Papaver orientale 'Leuchtfeuer'
Perennial Z3b Orange flowers with black blotches at the petal bases, silvery leaves.
‡18–36in (45–90cm) ↔24–36in (60–90cm)

Pelargonium 'Voodoo'
Perennial page 408

Penstemon 'Chester Scarlet'
Perennial page 411

Penstemon 'Schoenholzeri'
Perennial page 411

Persicaria amplexicaulis 'Firetail'
Perennial Z4 Robust clump-forming plant with tall, bright red "bottlebrush" flowerheads on upright stems.
‡↔to 4ft (1.2m)

Phormium 'Sundowner'
Perennial page 425

Phygelius x *rectus* 'Devil's Tears'
Shrub page 429

Potentilla 'Gibson's Scarlet'
Perennial page 443

Rhododendron 'Spek's Orange'
Deciduous shrub page 471

Rosa, **many**

Rudbeckia fulgida var. *sullivantii*
'Goldsturm'
Perennial page 599

Salvia coccinea 'Pseudococcinea'
Perennial page 505

Tithonia rotundifolia 'Torch'
Annual Upright, strong growing plant with bright orange-red single flowers freely produced.
‡6ft (2m) ↔18in (45cm)

Tropaeolum majus
'Hermine Grashoff'
Annual climber page 552

Veltheimia bracteata
Bulbous perennial page 560

Cool Color Schemes

Cool blues, purples, and creamy whites always look elegant and can be used to create an illusion of distance. As dusk falls, cool colors appear to glow in the fading light, a bonus in gardens used for evening entertaining. Mix in plenty of lush foliage to cool down summer heat still further; for a lighter, brighter look, choose some plants with gray and silvery leaves (see p.608).

Aeonium haworthii
Succulent   page 76

Ageratum 'Blue Danube'
Annual Low, bushy plants covered in fluffy lavender-blue flowers. Deeper blue 'Blue Horizon' is also recommended.
↕8in (20cm) ↔12in (30cm)

Allium caeruleum
Bulb   page 82

Anchusa azurea 'Loddon Royalist'
Perennial   page 89

Aruncus dioicus
Perennial   page 102

Baptisia australis
Perennial   page 111

Camassia leichtlinii
Bulb Z5 Bears spires of star-shaped, greenish white flowers in spring.
↕8in (20cm) ↔12in (30cm)

Campanula glomerata 'Superba'
Perennial   page 138

Centaurea cyanus 'Blue Diadem'
Annual Deep blue cornflower.
↕8–32in (20–80cm) ↔6in (15cm)

Clematis x durandii
Perennial Z5 A non-climbing species that produces its blue flowers for most of the summer. It needs staking or a shrub to grow through.
↕6ft (2m) ↔2ft (60cm)

Convolvulus sabatius
Trailing perennial   page 168

Cyananthus lobatus
Perennial   page 189

Cynara cardunculus
Perennial   page 191

Delphinium 'Giotto'
Perennial   page 199

Delphinium 'Lord Butler'
Perennial   page 200

Delphinium 'Thamesmead'
Perennial   page 201

Echinops ritro subsp. *ruthenicus*
Perennial Z4 Metallic blue globe thistle with silvery, cobwebby leaves.
↕24–36in (60–90cm) ↔18in (45cm)

Eryngium bourgatii 'Oxford Blue'
Perennial Z4 Silver-veined spiny leaves and branching stems of blue thistle flowers with silver bracts.
↕6–18in (15–45cm) ↔12in (30cm)

Eryngium x tripartitum
Perennial   page 224

Galtonia viridiflora
Bulb Z8 In late summer, bears spires of snowdroplike greenish-white flowers among gray-green straplike leaves.
↕to 3ft (1m) ↔4in (10cm)

Hebe albicans
Shrub   page 272

Heliotropium arborescens
Tender perennial Popular summer
bedding with purple, very fragrant flowers.
↕2–3ft (60–100cm) ↔12–18in (30–45cm)

Hosta 'Love Pat'
Perennial   page **292**

Hydrangea macrophylla
'Nikko Blue'
Shrub Z6 A hortensia type with rounded
blue flowers and vigorous growth.
↕6ft (2m) ↔8ft (2.5m)

Ipheion 'Rolf Fiedler'
Bulb Z5 Star-shaped blue flowers and
blue-green leaves in spring.
↕4–5in (10–12cm)

Iris 'Orinoco Flow'
Perennial   page **317**

Iris sibirica 'Smudger's Gift'
Perennial   page **311**

Iris sibirica 'Uber den Wolken'
Perennial   page **311**

Lavandula x *intermedia*
Dutch Group
Shrub   page **338**

Linum narbonense 'Heavenly Blue'
Perennial Z5 Forms clumps covered with
saucer-shaped pale blue flowers, each
lasting a single day.
↕12–24in (30–60cm) ↔18in (45cm)

Molucella laevis 'Pixie Bells'
Annual Pale green leaves and flower spires
conspicuous for the pale green, shell-like
calyces surrounding each tiny flower.
↕24–36in (60–90cm) ↔9in (23cm)

Myosotis 'Bouquet'
Annual Floriferous, compact blue
forget-me-not. The dwarf 'Ultramarine'
is also recommended.
↕4–8in (12–20cm) ↔6in (15cm)

Nepeta x *faassenii* 'Dropmore'
Perennial Z3 A plant with gray foliage
and blue flowers freely produced on
arching stems.
↕24in (60cm) ↔18in (45cm)

Phlox paniculata 'Le Mahdi'
Perennial   page **422**

Pulmonaria saccharata
Argentea Group
Evergreen perennial   page **460**

Ruta graveolens 'Jackman's Blue'
Shrub Z5 Gray-blue feathery leaves; the
dull yellow flowerheads can be trimmed
off to the benefit of the foliage. Be very
careful when handling this plant: contact
with foliage may cause an allergic sun-
activated reaction.
↕↔24in (60cm)

Salvia cacaliifolia
Perennial   page **504**

Salvia guaranitica 'Blue Enigma'
Perennial   page **506**

Scabiosa caucasica 'Clive Greaves'
Perennial   page **517**

Thalictrum delavayi
'Hewitt's Double'
Perennial   page **542**

Veronica 'Shirley Blue'
Perennial Z4 Gray-green, hairy leaves
and spires of saucer-shaped blue flowers
from late spring to mid-summer.
↕12in (30cm)

Plants for White Gardens

Single-color gardens are popular with many gardeners, and the most planted are white gardens, perhaps because so many white flowers are also scented. Consider also leaf color and foliage, including variegated, silver, and gray-leaved plants. To relieve the sameness of the scheme, it is often helpful to add a few cream or pale blue flowers—these will actually enhance the effect.

Anemone blanda 'White Splendour'
Bulb   page 90

Anemone x hybrida
'Honorine Jobert'
Perennial   page 91

Astilbe 'Irrlicht'
Perennial Z3b The coarsely cut dark foliage is a good contrast to the upright, white, fluffy flowers.
↕↔18in (50cm)

Clematis 'Marie Boisselot'
Climber   page 162

Cosmos bipinnatus 'Sonata White'
Annual   page 176

Crambe cordifolia
Perennial   page 181

Crocus sieberi 'Albus'
Bulb   page 185

Dahlia 'Hamari Bride'
Tender perennial This semi-cactus dahlia has pure white flowers and is popular for exhibition.
↕4ft (1.2m) ↔2ft (60cm)

Delphinium 'Sandpiper'
Perennial   page 201

Deutzia setchuenensis
var. *corymbiflora*
Shrub Z7 Masses of white flowers are produced on a bush with brown, peeling bark.
↕6ft (2m) ↔5ft (1.5m)

Dicentra spectabilis 'Alba'
Perennial   page 207

Digitalis purpurea f. *albiflora*
Biennial   page 210

Echinacea purpurea 'White Lustre'
Perennial Z3 The stiff stems have creamy white flowers with golden cones.
↕32in (80cm) ↔18in (45cm)

Erica carnea 'Springwood White'
Evergreen shrub   page 219

Erica tetralix 'Alba Mollis'
Evergreen shrub   page 221

Gillenia trifoliata
Perennial   page 263

Gypsophila paniculata
'Bristol Fairy'
Perennial   page 266

Hoheria sexstylosa
Evergreen tree   page 290

Hosta plantaginea
Perennial Z4 Pale green leaves and strong stems of fragrant white flowers in fall.
↕24in (60cm) ↔36in (90cm)

Hydrangea arborescens 'Annabelle'
Shrub   page 297

Hydrangea paniculata 'Floribunda'
Shrub   page 299

Hydrangea quercifolia
Shrub   page 300

Iris 'Christmas Time'
Perennial Z3 The ruffled, white flowers have red beards.
‡41in (1.1m) ↔12in (30cm)

Iris confusa
Bulbous perennial   page 312

Iris sibirica 'Crème Chantilly'
Perennial   page 310

Iris sibirica 'Harpswell Happiness'
Perennial   page 311

Iris sibirica 'Mikiko'
Perennial   page 311

Lunaria annua var. *albiflora*
Biennial Z4 The white-flowered form of common honesty.
‡3ft (90cm) ↔12in (30cm)

Magnolia stellata
Shrub   page 365

Malus 'Sugar Tyme'
Tree Z4 Fragrant, white flowers in spring and persistent red fruit in fall.
‡20ft (6m) ↔15ft (5m)

Malva moschata f. *alba*
Perennial   page 370

Narcissus 'Empress of Ireland'
Bulb   page 380

Paeonia obovata var. *alba*
Perennial Z6 A choice plant with rounded, grayish leaflets and pure white flowers, most attractive in bud.
‡↔24–28in (60–70cm)

Papaver orientale 'Black and White'
Perennial   page 398

Physostegia virginiana 'Summer Snow'
Perennial Z3b Pure white flowers in spikes on upright stems.
‡4ft (1.2m) ↔24in (60cm)

Pulmonaria 'Sissinghurst White'
Perennial   page 460

Pulsatilla vulgaris 'Alba'
Perennial   page 462

Ranunculus aconitifolius 'Flore Pleno'
Perennial   page 465

Rosa 'Iceberg'
Floribunda rose   page 483

Rosa 'Madame Hardy'
Shrub rose   page 493

Rosa 'Rambling Rector'
Rambler rose   page 487

Rubus 'Benenden'
Shrub   page 499

Sanguinaria canadensis 'Plena'
Perennial Z3b Cup-shaped flowers in early spring with several rows of petals.
‡6in (15cm) ↔12in (30cm) but spreads slowly.

Trillium grandiflorum
Perennial   page 551

Tulipa 'Purissima'
Bulb Z4 The compact stems carry very large, pure white flowers in mid-spring.
‡14in (35cm)

Viburnum plicatum 'Summer Snowflake'
Shrub Z6 Small shrub with horizontal branches and flat heads of white flowers in summer.
‡↔10ft (3m)

Zantedeschia aethiopica
Perennial   page 576

Plants for Clay Soil

Clay soil is difficult to dig, either wet or dry. It is prone to harbor slugs, and it is slow to warm up in spring; it is often described as a cold soil. However, it is usually rich in nutrients, and if plenty of organic matter is added it can be very fertile. Plants to avoid are those from upland areas, such as alpines, or those on the borderline of hardiness in your climate.

Clematis **'Polish Spirit'**
Climber Z2 Small, single, purple flowers with red anthers. Late-flowering.
‡15ft (5m) ↔ 6ft (2m)

Cornus sericea **'Flaviramea'**
Shrub page 172

Deutzia x *elegantissima* **'Rosealind'**
Shrub page 202

Filipendula purpurea
Perennial page 239

Forsythia ovata **'Ottawa'**
Shrub Z3b Bright yellow flowers in early spring. This variety is hardier than most and flowers to the top most years.
‡6ft (1.8m) ↔ 5ft (1.5m)

Geranium psilostemon
Perennial page 261

Helenium **'Moerheim Beauty'**
Perennial page 279

Hemerocallis **'Stella de Oro'**
Perennial page 286

Hydrangea paniculata **'Kyushu'**
Shrub Z4 Erect cultivar with glossy leaves and large creamy white flowers.
‡10–22ft (3–7m) ↔ 8ft (2.5m)

Iris sibirica cultivars
Perennials page 311

Mahonia aquifolium **'Apollo'**
Evergreen shrub page 366

Narcissus **'Jumblie'**
Bulb page 379

Persicaria campanulata
Perennial Z6 Small clusters of pink, bell-shaped flowers on spreading stems.
‡36in (90cm)

Philadelphus **'Manteau d'Hermine'**
Shrub page 417

Potentilla fruticosa **'Tangerine'**
Shrub Z3 Twiggy, with yellow flowers flushed red throughout summer.
‡3ft (1m) ↔ 5ft (1.5m)

Quercus palustris
Tree page 464

Rosa **'Amber Queen'**
Floribunda rose page 482

Solidago **'Goldenmosa'**
Perennial page 529

Spiraea japonica **'Anthony Waterer'**
Shrub page 533

Symphytum **'Goldsmith'**
Perennial Z6 This spreading plant has heart-shaped leaves edged in gold, with pale blue, cream, and pink flowers.
↔ 12in (30cm)

Syringa vulgaris
'Katherine Havemeyer'
Shrub page 539

Plants for Sandy Soil

The advantages of sandy soils include the ability to dig, hoe, and prepare them during much of the year because they drain quickly after rain. However, water drains through quickly, taking nutrients with it, so it is important to dig in organic matter to improve the soil structure, retain moisture, and improve fertility. Silver-leaved and slightly tender plants are very suitable.

Aesculus parviflora
Shrub   page **78**

Buddleja davidii 'White Profusion'
Shrub   page **125**

Calluna vulgaris 'Darkness'
Evergreen shrub   page **130**

Caragana pygmea
Shrub Z2 A rounded bush with yellow flowers in early summer. Can be cut back hard and will re-grow from the base.
‡4ft (1.2m)

Centranthus ruber
Perennial Z4 A somewhat sprawling plant with heads of fragrant pink, red, or white flowers. Flowers from late spring into summer.
‡3ft (1m)

Echinops bannaticus 'Taplow Blue'
Perennial   page **213**

Erica cinerea 'Eden Valley'
Evergreen shrub   page **220**

Eryngium x *oliverianum*
Perennial   page **223**

Gladiolus communis
subsp.*byzantinus*
Bulb   page **263**

Kniphofia 'Little Maid'
Perennial   page **330**

Lavatera x *clementii* 'Rosea'
Shrub   page **339**

Limnanthes douglasii
Annual   page **351**

Oenothera macrocarpa
Perennial   page **386**

Penstemon 'Hidcote Pink'
Perennial Z7 Spikes of small, tubular, pink flowers. Good in bedding.
‡24–30in (60–75cm) ↔18in (45cm)

Penstemon pinifolius
'Mersea Yellow'
Evergreen shrub Z5 Dwarf, spreading, with yellow flowers in summer.
‡16in (40cm) ↔10in (25cm)

Persicaria affinis 'Superba'
Perennial   page **413**

Persicaria bistorta 'Superba'
Perennial   page **414**

Potentilla fruticosa 'Daydawn'
Shrub   page **442**

Potentilla nepalensis
'Miss Willmott'
Perennial   page **444**

Robinia pseudacacia 'Frisia'
Tree   page **479**

Santolina rosmarinifolia
'Primrose Gem'
Evergreen shrub   page **513**

Shepherdia argentea
Shrub Z1 An attractive silver foliage: small, yellow flowers and red edible berries.
‡15ft (4.5m) ↔12ft (3.5m)

Yucca flaccida 'Ivory'
Shrub   page **576**

Plants for Alkaline Soils

The majority of plants will grow in soil that is neutral or slightly alkaline, but some positively prefer more alkaline soil. These include plants that are just as important as the rhododendrons and camellias of acidic soils and include delphiniums, clematis, and dianthus. But quality of soil is important: it must be improved with organic matter, as poor, thin soils are difficult to plant.

Aquilegia vulgaris 'Nivea'
Perennial   page 94

Aster novae-angliae
'Harrington's Pink'
Perennial Z3   page 104

Buddleja 'Pink Delight'
Shrub Bright pink flowers are produced on thick, conical spikes.
‡10ft (3m) ↔15ft (5m)

Buddleja davidii 'Royal Red'
Shrub   page 125

Buddleja x *weyeriana* 'Sungold'
Shrub Z7 Spikes of golden yellow flowers in summer.
‡12ft (4m) ↔10ft (3m)

Canna 'President'
Tender perennial   page 34

Cercis siliquastrum
Tree   page 147

Chaenomeles speciosa 'Nivalis'
Shrub Z5b A variety of Japanese quince with pure white flowers in spring.
‡8ft (2.5m) ↔15ft (5m)

Clematis 'Comtesse de Bouchaud'
Climber   page 165

Clematis 'Praecox'
Climber Z4 This unusual hybrid is a scrambler, with a frothy mass of tiny white and blue flowers.
‡6–10ft (2–3m)

Clematis 'Miss Bateman'
Climber   page 162

Convallaria majalis var. *rosea*
Perennial Z3 This lily of the valley has dusky pink flowers; familiar sweet scent.
‡9in (23cm) ↔12in (30cm)

Cornus mas
Evergreen shrub   page 171

Cotoneaster sternianus
Evergreen shrub   page 180

Crocus Spring flowering
Bulbs   page 185

Delphinium 'Blue Nile'
Perennial   page 198

Deutzia scabra 'Pride of Rochester'
Shrub Z6 The stems have attractive, peeling, brown bark, but the chief merit is the scented, double, pale pink flowers.
‡10ft (3m) ↔6ft (2m)

Dianthus alpinus
Perennial Z3b Cushions of gray foliage and scented flowers in pink shades.
‡3in (8cm) ↔4in (10cm)

Dianthus deltoides
Perennial Z3b Mats of deep green leaves are covered with small pink flowers for several weeks in summer.
‡8in (20cm) ↔12in (30cm)

Dianthus 'Monica Wyatt'
Perennial   page 205

Dicentra spectabilis
Perennial   page 207

Euonymus europaeus 'Red Cascade'
Shrub   page 231

Fraxinus excelsior
Tree Z4b Deciduous spreading tree with dark green leaves that turn yellow in fall. Tends to seed freely.
‡100ft (30m) ↔70ft (20m)

Fraxinus ornus
Tree Z6 Bushy, round-headed tree with showy white flowers and bright, purple fall color.
‡↔50ft (15m)

Fuchsia 'Heidi Ann'
Tender shrub An upright, bushy plant with double lilac and cerise flowers.
‡↔18in (45cm)

Fuchsia 'Prosperity'
Tender shrub A vigorous plant with crimson and pink double flowers.
‡↔18in (45cm)

Galanthus 'Magnet'
Bulb page 250

Helianthemum 'Jubilee'
Shrub Z5 Small shrub with bright green leaves and double yellow flowers.
‡8in (20cm) ↔12in (30cm)

Helleborus orientalis
Perennial Z5 Nodding flowers in shades of pink, white, and green are produced in early spring.
‡↔18in (45cm)

Ilex aquifolium 'Silver Queen'
Evergreen tree page 305

Magnolia x kewensis
'Wada's Memory'
Shrub page 365

Magnolia 'Ricki'
Shrub page 365

Magnolia salicifolia
'Wada's Memory'
Shrub page 365

Magnolia x soulangeana
'Rustica Rubra'
Shrub page 365

Magnolia wilsonii
Shrub page 365

Morus nigra
Tree Z8 The black mulberry is a long-lived, picturesque tree with tasty fruit.
‡40ft (12m) ↔50ft (15m)

Philadelphus 'Sybille'
Deciduous shrub Z5 Arching shrub with cup-shaped, intensely fragrant white flowers in early summer.
‡4ft (1.2m) ↔6ft (2m)

Prunus 'Okame'
Tree page 456

Prunus 'Taihaku'
Tree page 457

Prunus tenella 'Fire Hill'
Shrub Z2 Deep pink, single flowers cover the upright branches in spring.
‡↔5ft (1.5m)

Pulsatilla vulgaris
Perennial page 461

Ribes alpinum
Shrub Z2 An upright shrub that makes a good hedge in sun and shade and is pollution tolerant.
‡↔6ft (2m)

Spiraea x vanhouttei
Shrub page 534

Syringa vulgaris 'Charles Joly'
Shrub page 538

Verbascum 'Cotswold Beauty'
Perennial page 561

Plants for Acidic Soil

Acidic soils contain low quantities of calcium, a nutrient found in limestone, but some of the most beautiful plants, including rhododendrons, heathers, and pieris, have adapted to grow well only in soils where it is deficient. Most also benefit from light shade and rich soil. Where soil is not ideal, grow plants in large pots or other containers of acidic soil.

Acer japonicum 'Aconitifolium'
Shrub   page 65

Acer palmatum var. *dissectum*
Shrub Z5b The finely cut leaves turn yellow in fall, on a mounded shrub.
‡6ft (2m) ↔10ft (3m)

Acer palmatum 'Seiryu'
Shrub Z6 An upright shrub with divided leaves that turn orange in fall.
‡6ft (2m) ↔4ft (1.2m)

Camellia 'Leonard Messel'
Evergreen shrub   page 134

Camellia sasanqua 'Narumigata'
Evergreen shrub   page 135

Camellia x *williamsii* 'Debbie'
Evergreen shrub Z8 The semidouble flowers are deep pink.
‡6–15ft (2–5m) ↔3–10ft (1–3m)

Cassiope 'Edinburgh'
Evergreen shrub   page 143

Clethra alnifolia
Shrub Z4b Long panicles of fragrant white flowers in July when few other shrubs are blooming, and good yellow fall color.
‡6ft (1.8m) ↔5ft (1.5m)

Cornus alternifolia
Tree or shrub Z3b Flat heads of white flower in spring give clusters of black fruit that attract birds on top of the horizontal branches.
‡20ft (6m) ↔25ft (7.5m)

Crinodendron hookerianum
Evergreen shrub   page 182

Daboecia cantabrica 'Bicolor'
Evergreen shrub   page 193

Daboecia cantabrica 'William Buchanan'
Evergreen shrub   page 193

Enkianthus campanulatus
Shrub   page 215

Erica arborea var. *alpina*
Evergreen shrub   page 218

Erica arborea 'Estrella Gold'
Evergreen shrub Z8 Fragrant white flowers appear among the lime green foliage and yellow shoot tips.
‡4ft (1.2m) ↔30in (75cm)

Erica ciliaris 'Corfe Castle'
Shrub   page 220

Erica ciliaris 'David McLintock'
Shrub   page 220

Erica cinerea 'C.D. Eason'
Shrub   page 220

Erica cinerea 'Fiddler's Gold'
Shrub   page 221

Erica cinerea 'Windlebrooke'
Shrub   page 220

Erica erigena 'W. T. Ratcliff'
Evergreen shrub Z7 A compact plant with green foliage and white flowers.
‡30in (75cm) ↔22in (55cm)

Eucryphia x *nymansensis*
'Nymansay'
Evergreen shrub page 230

Fothergilla major
Shrub page 241

Halesia caroliniana
Tree Z5 White bell-shaped flowers hang
in clusters below the branches in spring
and give inflated brown pods.
‡30ft (9m) ↔ 35ft (10.5m)

Hamamelis x *intermedia* 'Pallida'
Shrub page 271

Hydrangea macrophylla 'Blue Wave'
Shrub Z6 This lacecap provides a delicate
but showy display, with large and small
blue flowers in each head.
‡5ft (1.5m) ↔ 6ft (2m)

Iris douglasiana
Perennial page 313

Kalmia latifolia
Shrub page 327

Leiophyllum buxifolium
Perennial page 341

Lithodora diffusa 'Heavenly Blue'
Evergreen shrub page 353

Magnolia liliiflora 'Nigra'
Shrub page 363

Meconopsis betonicifolia
Perennial page 371

Meconopsis grandis
Perennial page 371

Nyssa sylvatica
Tree page 385

Pieris 'Forest Flame'
Evergreen shrub page 434

Pieris japonica 'Blush'
Evergreen shrub page 435

Primula pulverulenta
Perennial page 450

Quercus rubra
Tree Z3 An oak that grows well in city
conditions, with reddish young foliage
and good fall color.
‡↔ 60ft (18m)

Rhododendron 'Beethoven'
Evergreen azalea page 468

Rhododendron 'Dora Amateis'
Dwarf rhododendron page 476

Rhododendron 'Ginny Gee'
Dwarf rhododendron Z6b A compact
plant bearing pink flowers that fade
almost to white with age.
‡↔ 24–36in (60–90cm)

Rhododendron impeditum
Dwarf rhododendron Z5 Gray-green
leaves are almost hidden by lavender-blue
flowers in spring.
‡↔ 24in (60cm)

Rhododendron 'Palestrina'
Evergreen azalea page 469

Rhododendron 'Rose Bud'
Evergreen azalea page 469

Rhododendron 'Vuyk's Rosyred'
Evergreen azalea page 469

Skimmia japonica 'Rubella'
Evergreen shrub page 527

Tamarix tetranda
Shrub page 540

Trillium grandiflorum
Perennial page 551

Vaccinium corymbosum
Shrub page 558

Vaccinium glaucoalbum
Shrub page 559

Vaccinium vitis-idaea
Koralle Group
Shrubs page 559

Plants for Poor Soil

While it is true that most plants grow better in well-prepared soil, there are some that grow well in poor soil that has not had much preparation or cultivation. Many annuals evolved to take advantage of open sites, disappearing as the soil improves and larger plants invade the area, so they are a good choice, but there are shrubs and perennials that will also survive.

Achillea 'Moonshine'
Perennial   page **73**

Artemisia abrotanum
Shrub Z5 Small shrub with green, finely divided, pleasantly fragrant leaves.
‡↔3ft (1m)

Buddleja davidii 'Empire Blue'
Shrub   page **125**

Ceanothus 'Blue Mound'
Evergreen shrub   page **144**

Cistus x *purpureus*
Evergreen shrub   page **159**

Cytisus x *praecox* 'Allgold'
Shrub   page **192**

Daphne mezereum
Shrub Z4 Fragrant pink flowers in early spring and poisonous red berries in fall.
‡4ft (1.2m) ↔3ft (1m)

Eschscholzia caespitosa 'Sundew'
Annual Neat, low-growing, with divided gray leaves and yellow flowers.
‡↔6in (15cm)

Festuca glauca 'Blaufuchs'
Ornamental grass   page **238**

Gaillardia 'Dazzler'
Perennial   page **249**

Genista lydia
Shrub   page **255**

Hebe ochracea 'James Stirling'
Evergreen shrub   page **274**

Iberis sempervirens
Evergreen shrub   page **302**

Kolkwitzia amabilis 'Pink Cloud'
Shrub   page **331**

Lathyrus latifolius
Climber   page **334**

Lavandula angustifolia 'Twickel Purple'
Evergreen shrub   page **337**

Lavatera, Shrubs
Shrubs   page **339**

Phlomis fruticosa
Evergreen shrub   page **418**

Potentilla fruticosa 'Elizabeth'
Shrub   page **442**

Robinia hispida
Shrub   page **478**

Santolina chamaecyparissus 'Lemon Queen'
Evergreen shrub Z7 Silver, feathery foliage; small, round, pale yellow flowers.
‡↔12in (60cm)

Thymus vulgaris 'Silver Posie'
Evergreen shrub Z4 Thyme with variegated leaves and pink flowers.
‡6–12in (15–30cm) ↔16in (40cm)

Plants for Wet Soil

Waterlogged, badly drained soils are inhospitable places for most plants. Roots need to breathe, and if all the air spaces within the soil are filled with water, most roots rot and only marginal or aquatic plants can survive. However, if the soil is permanently moist, there are many beautiful plants that will thrive, and they may survive flooding if it is only for a few days.

Alnus glutinosa 'Imperialis'
Tree   page 85

Astilbe 'Sprite'
Perennial   page 107

Betula nigra 'Heritage'
Tree Z3 Attractive bark that flakes to reveal a pale inner bark. Good pest resistance.
‡50ft (15m) ↔ 40ft (12m)

Cardamine pratense 'Flore Pleno'
Perennial Z4 Double-flowered lady's smock with pink flowers in spring.
‡↔ 8in (20cm)

Chamaecyparis pisifera 'Boulevard'
Conifer   page 151

Cornus alba 'Sibirica'
Shrub   page 169

Darmera peltata
Perennial   page 197

Euphorbia griffithii 'Dixter'
Perennial Z5 Orange fall bracts.
‡30in (75cm) ↔ 3ft (1m)

Filipendula rubra 'Venusta'
Perennial   page 240

Fraxinus nigra 'Fallgold'
Tree Z2b An upright selection with lasting fall color.
‡35ft (10.5m) ↔ 25ft (7.5m)

Fritillaria meleagris
Bulb   page 243

Ilex verticillata 'Winter Red'
Shrub Z3b A deciduous holly with bright red berries that last well into winter.
‡6ft (1.8m) ↔ 4ft (1.2m)

Iris pseudacorus
Perennial   page 310

Iris versicolor
Perennial   page 310

Larix laricina
Deciduous conifer Z1 This native larch will grow well in wet or dry soils. It has a good yellow fall color.
‡60ft (18m) ↔ 26ft (75m)

Ligularia 'Gregynog Gold'
Perennial   page 345

Lobelia cardinalis 'Queen Victoria'
Perennial   page 354

Lysimachia clethroides
Perennial   page 361

Matteuccia struthiopteris
Fern   page 370

Mimulus cardinalis
Perennial   page 373

Osmunda regalis
Fern   page 392

Primula candelabra types
Perennials   page 450

Primula denticulata
Perennial   page 444

Rodgersia pinnata 'Superba'
Perennial   page 479

Plants for Hot, Dry Sites

As problems of water supply become more acute, consider plants that have low water requirements. Often, these have silvery or small leaves, and some are fragrant, so the garden can still be interesting through the year. They look attractive growing through gravel, an effective mulch to retain soil moisture. In addition, many establish quickly and are evergreen and low maintenance.

Abutilon vitifolium
'Veronica Tennant'
Shrub   page **62**

Acanthus spinosus
Perennial   page **63**

Agave victoriae-regina
Perennial   page **80**

Allium **'Globemaster'**
Bulb   page **83**

Armeria juniperifolia **'Bevan's Variety'**
Perennial   page **100**

Artemisia **'Powis Castle'**
Perennial   page **101**

Artemisia schmidtiana **'Nana'**
Perennial Z3b An evergreen that forms a feathery, silver carpet with small yellow flowerheads in summer.
↕3in (8cm) ↔12in (30cm)

Ballota pseudodictamnus
Evergreen shrub   page **111**

Ceanothus **'Cascade'**
Evergreen shrub Z8 The arching branches bear masses of powder blue flowers in late spring.
↕↔12ft (4m)

Cedronella canariensis
Tender perennial The slightly sticky leaves are aromatic; produces small clusters of mauve flowers in late summer.
↕4ft (1.2m) ↔24in (60cm)

Ceratostigma plumbaginoides
Perennial   page **146**

Cistus x aguilarii **'Maculatus'**
Evergreen shrub   page **158**

Convolvulus cneorum
Evergreen shrub   page **168**

Cytisus battandieri
Shrub   page **191**

Cytisus x kewensis
Shrub Z7 Arching stems are covered with cream flowers in spring.
↕12in (30cm) ↔5ft (1.5m)

Cytisus multiflorus
Shrub Z8 An upright shrub at first, then spreading, with masses of small white flowers.
↕10ft (3m) ↔8ft (2.5m)

Dianthus **'Haytor White'**
Perennial   page **204**

Dictamnus albus var. *purpureus*
Perennial   page **209**

Dierama pulcherrimum
Perennial Z7b Clumps of grasslike leaves produce arching stems of pendent, pink, bell-shaped flowers.
↕3–5ft (1–1.5m) ↔24in (60cm)

Eryngium bourgatii
Perennial Z5 Silver-veined spiny leaves form clumps with branching stems of steely blue prickly flowerheads.
↕6–18in (15–45cm) ↔12in (30cm)

Plants For Damp Shade

A border that has damp soil and is in shade for much of the day is a useful place to grow woodland plants without having to plant a woodland. Without the drying effect of the trees, the soil will support a greater range of plants; those native to the Himalayas and South America should thrive, especially if the soil is acidic. It is also a good site for hellebores, lilies, and ferns.

Plants for Dry Shade

The dry shade under trees is not a hospitable place for most plants. Those that survive best are spring-flowering bulbs that disappear underground in summer before the soil dries out. Some evergreens and winter-flowering plants also survive. Even these require good soil preparation and careful watering and feeding for several seasons until they are well established.

Alchemilla mollis
Perennial   page **81**

Asplenium scolopendrium
Fern   page **103**

Aucuba japonica 'Rozannie'
Evergreen shrub Z7 Cultivar with green leaves; the flowers are bisexual and self-fertile, resulting in many red berries.
‡↔3ft (1m)

Bergenia cordifolia
Perennial Z3b The large, rounded, evergreen leaves make a good ground-cover; pink flowers in spring are showy.
‡24in (60cm) ↔30in (75cm)

Dryopteris filix-mas
Fern   page **211**

Euonymus fortunei
'Emerald 'n' Gold'
Evergreen shrub   page **231**

Galanthus nivalis 'Flore Pleno'
Bulb   page **250**

Hedera helix 'Little Diamond'
Evergreen climber   page **278**

Helleborus foetidus 'Wester Flisk'
Perennial Z6 Deep red stems, finely divided leaves, and red-edged green flowers.
‡24in (60cm) ↔3ft (1m)

Iris foetidissima
Perennial Z6 Purple and brown flowers, and orange seeds in winter.
‡12–36in (30–90cm)

Iris foetidissima 'Variegata'
Perennial   page **314**

Kerria japonica 'Golden Guinea'
Shrub   page **328**

Lamium galeobdolon
'Hermann's Pride'
Perennial Z3b Arching stems marked silver, and pale yellow flowers.
‡18in (45cm) ↔3ft (1m)

Liriope muscari
Perennial   page **353**

Pachysandra terminals 'Variegata'
Evergreen perennial   page **394**

Rhododendron 'Cecile'
Shrub   page **470**

Rubus tricolor
Evergreen shrub Z8 The creeping stems are covered with decorative red bristles, and the leaves are deep green.
‡24in (60cm) ↔6ft (2m)

Symphytum officinale 'Variegatum'
Perennial Z4 Spreading perennial with hairy leaves edged with white, and pink flowers in summer.
‡5ft (1.5m) ↔6ft (2m)

Vinca minor 'Atropurpurea'
Perennial   page **570**

Vinca minor 'Gertrude Jekyll'
Evergreen shrub Z3b A low ground cover with compact growth and white flowers from mid-summer to fall.
‡4in (10cm) ↔36in (90cm) or more

Plants for Exposed Situations

Gardens exposed to strong winds, especially cold ones, make gardening difficult. Choose compact varieties that require less staking, and avoid large-leaved plants that may be damaged. Late-flowering cultivars will not be caught by spring frosts. Protect plants with netting when planting and in winter to reduce damage, and plant hedges and screens as windbreaks.

Acer rubrum 'October Glory'
Tree   page **70**

Arctostaphylos uva-ursi
Ground cover   page **98**

Aster alpinus
Perennial   page **103**

Betula pendula 'Youngii'
Perennial   page **121**

Calluna vulgaris 'Kinlochruel'
Evergreen shrub   page **130**

Crataegus x mordenensis 'Snowbird'
Small tree Z3 Double white flowers in spring and bright red fruit and bronzy foliage in fall.
↕↔20ft (6m)

Dianthus gratianopolitanus
Perennial Z4 Low-growing mats of gray foliage and solitary pink flowers.
↕6in (15cm) ↔16in (40cm)

Erica carnea 'Vivelli'
Evergreen shrub   page **219**

Erica x watsonii 'Dawn'
Evergreen shrub   page **221**

Genista tinctoria
Woody ground cover Z3 A low, spreading shrub with upright branches covered with small yellow flowers in spring.
↕↔36in (90cm)

Philadelphus 'Snowbelle'
Shrub Z4 Scented, double white flowers in clusters on upright branches.
↕4ft (1.2m) ↔3ft (1m)

Pinus cembra
Conifer Z2 This pine does not shed its lower branches and makes a dense green column.
↕35ft (10.5m) ↔20ft (6m)

Potentilla fruticosa 'Abbotswood'
Shrub   page **442**

Prunus maackii
Tree Z2b Clusters of white flowers in spring give cherries that attract birds. Peeling cinnamon brown bark is attractive in winter.
↕30ft (9m) ↔25ft (7.5m)

Sambucus nigra 'Guincho Purple'
Shrub   page **512**

Spiraea japonica 'Goldflame'
Shrub   page **533**

Spiraea japonica 'Shirobana'
Shrub Z3 Mounds of foliage are dotted with pink, white flowerheads, all summer.
↕24in (60cm) ↔36in (90cm)

Spiraea nipponica 'Snowmound'
Shrub   page **534**

Tamarix tetrandra
Shrub   page **540**

Viburnum opulus 'Roseum'
Shrub Z2b Erect, fast-growing shrub with globular heads of white flowers in summer.
↕↔12ft (4m)

Plants that Withstand Salt

In coastal regions, gales can blow salt-laden winds far inland at any time of the year. Salt is also used to clear snow from winter roads, and the salt-laden spray can drift afar and affect dormant plants by desiccating the foliage of evergreens and altering the chemical balance of the soil. The ability of plants to recover varies greatly. The following seem to be reasonably salt-tolerant.

Acer platanoides 'Crimson King'
Perennial page 68

Aesculus hippocastanum
'Baumannii'
Tree Z4b Dark green finger-like leaves and double white and pink flowers in late spring.
‡50ft (15m) ↔ 40ft (12m)

Armeria maritima
'Dusseldorf Pride'
Evergreen perennial Z4 A clump-forming plant with grass-like foliage and heads of pink flowers on wiry stems in late spring.
‡↔ 8in (20cm)

Caragana arborescens
Shrub or small tree Z2 A very tough plant that can be cut back almost to the ground if it becomes over large.
‡20ft (6m) ↔ 9ft (3m)

Choisya ternata
Evergreen shrub page 153

Crambe maritima
Perennial Z5 Silver-blue leaves, giant heads of white flowers followed by seed pods.
‡↔ 24in (60cm)

Elaeagnus angustifolia
Tree or large shrub Z2b Silvery foliage, sweetly scented yellow flowers in early summer and edible but mealy fruit.
‡15ft (4.5m) ↔ 12ft (3.5m)

Euonymus alatus
Shrub page 230

Fraxinus americana 'Autumn Purple'
Tree Z4 A conical tree with leaves that turn red to purple in fall.
‡60ft (18m) ↔ 40ft (12m)

Hydrangea macrophylla 'Altona'
Shrub page 298

Hydrangea macrophylla
'Geoffrey Chadbund'
Shrub Z6 Lacecap; deep red flowers.
‡3ft (1m) ↔ 5ft (1.5m)

Lonicera x *heckrottii* 'Goldflame'
Climber Z5 A vigorous climber with tubular flowers, orange-red outside and yellow within all summer.
‡15ft (5m)

Picea pungens 'Koster'
Conifer page 433

Prunus virginiana 'Shubert'
Tree Z2 A small tree with leaves that open green and turn a reddish purple. It has white flowers and cherries that birds will eat.
‡25ft (8m) ↔ 20ft (6m)

Robinia pseudoacacia 'Frisia'
Tree page 479

Senecio cineraria 'Silver Dust'
Biennial page 54

Syringa reticulata 'Ivory Silk'
Large shrub or tree Z2 Creamy white fragrant flowers in summer and a speckled bark that gives winter interest.
‡25ft (8m) ↔ 20ft (6m)

Syringa vulgaris 'Madam Lemoine'
Shrub page 539

INDEX

J

ACKNOWLEDGMENTS

The publisher would like to thank the following for their kind permission to reproduce the photographs:
Key: a-above; b-below/bottom; l-left; r-right; c-center; ca-center above; cl-center left; cr-center right; br- below/bottom right; bc-below/bottom center; t-top; tc-top center; tr-top right

6 Marianne Majerus Garden Images. 12 GAP Photos: Marcus Harpur. 28 Unwins Seeds Ltd (c). 29 Photos Horticultural (t); Garden Picture Library: Friedrich Strauss (b). 30 Garden World Images: Lee Thomas (b). 31 GetStock.com: Paroli Galperti (t); Thompson & Morgan (b) 32 Thompson & Morgan (t). 34 Garden World Images (t); A–Z Botanical: Peter Etchells (c). 35 Thompson & Morgan (t) (c); A–Z Botanical: Christer Andreason (b). 36 Garden Picture Library: Jerry Pavia (c). 37 Garden Picture Library: J.S. Sira (t); Juliette Wade (b). 38 Unwins Seeds Ltd (b); Thompson & Morgan (c). 39 Thompson & Morgan (t); Photos Horticultural (c); Garden World Images: Trevor Sims (b). 40 GAP Photos: Visions (t); Unwins Seeds Ltd (t). 41 Garden World Images (t); Garden Picture Library: John Glover (c). 42 Suttons Seeds (c). 43 Garden World Images (t) (c). 45 Photos Horticultural (t). 46 Suttons Seeds (c). 47 Unwins Seeds Ltd (b); Thompson & Morgan (c). 48 Unwins Seeds Ltd (t); Thompson & Morgan (c); A–Z Botanical: Dan Sams (b). 49 Unwins Seeds Ltd (c). 50 John Glover (t); Suttons Seeds (c). 51 Unwins Seeds Ltd (t). 52 Thompson & Morgan (c). 53 Thompson & Morgan (c). 55 Thompson & Morgan (b).

57 Suttons Seeds (t); Thompson & Morgan (b). 60 GAP Photos: Martin Hughes-Jones (b). 63 GAP Photos: Elke Borkowski (t). 64 Marianne Majerus Garden Images (t) (b). 79 GAP Photos: Richard Bloom (b); J.S. Sira (t). 80 Alamy Images: Steffen Hauser/botanikfoto (b). 85 Getty Images: Nacivet (b). 86 Alamy Images: Holmes Garden Photos (b). 87 GAP Photos: Christina Bollen (t). 88 GAP Photos: Richard Bloom (b). Marianne Majerus Garden Images (b). 97 GAP Photos: Maayke de Ridder (b). 100 GAP Photos: Geoff Kidd (t). 104 GAP Photos: Martin Hughes-Jones (t). 109 Garden World Images: Francoise Davis (b). Getty Images: Jayme Thornton (t). 110 GAP Photos: Jonathan Buckley (t). 114 GAP Photos: Visions (tr). 115 Garden World Images: Gilles Delacroix (tc). 129 Garden World Images: Gilles Delacroix (tr). 132 GAP Photos: S&O (tr). 142 GAP Photos: Mark Bolton (b). 145 GAP Photos: Dave Bevan (b). 146 Garden World Images: Gilles Delacroix (b). 149 The Garden Collection: Pedro Silmon (bl). 150 The Garden Collection: Derek Harris (b). 151 GAP Photos (t). 159 Getstock.com: Harold R. Stinnette Photo Stock (b). 170 Garden World Images: MAP/Arnaud Descat (b). 176 GAP Photos: Marcus Harpur (b); The Garden Collection: Liz Eddison (t). 180 Derek Gould (t). 181 GAP Photos: Gerald Majumdar (t). 182 Harpur Garden Library (t). 187 GAP Photos: Martin Hughes-Jones (t). 188 Garden World Images: MAP/Frédéric Didillon (t).

194 Caroline Reed (tl). 195 Andrew Lawson (ca). 202 Photolibrary: Andrea Jones (t). 210 Getty Images: Rob Whitworth (b); Elaine Hewson (t). 213 Caroline Reed (t). 225 Clive Nichols (t). 230 The Garden Collection: Torie Chugg (t). 232 GAP Photos: Dave Bevan (t). Garden World Images: Gilles Delacroix (b). 237 Garden Exposures Photo Library (t). 238 GAP Photos: Visions (b). 244 A–Z Botanical: Geoff Kidd (br). 251 GAP Photos: Geoff Kidd (b). 256 Garden World Images: Glenn Harper (t). 259 Marianne Majerus Garden Images (bc). 261 Marianne Majerus Garden Images (cr). 266 GAP Photos: J.S. Sira (t). 269 Photolibrary: J.S. Sira (t). 279 Caroline Reed (t). 283 GAP Photos: John Glover (b). 284 The Garden Collection: Nicola Stocken Tomkins (b). 285 GAP Photos: Martin Hughes-Jones (b). 294 Garden World Images: MAP/Frédéric Tournay (b). 296 GAP Photos: Howard Rice (t). 303 Clive Nichols (tr). 307 Garden World Images: Trevor Sims (tr). 311 GAP Photos: J.S. Sira (tc). 321 GAP Photos: J.S. Sira (b). 332 Garden World Images: Gilles Delacroix (b). 336 GAP Photos: Lee Avison (t). 344 GAP Photos: Friedrich Strauss (t). 351 Photolibrary: Paroli Galperti (t). 357 Garden World Images: Gilles Delacroix (t). 358 Garden World Images: Lee Thomas (t). 369 Marianne Majerus Garden Images (b). 370 GAP Photos: John Glover (b). 371 Marianne Majerus Garden Images (b). 372 GAP Photos: Ron Evans (b). 373 Getty Images: Richard Bloom (b). 374 GAP Photos: Jo Whitworth (t).

379 Harpur Garden Library (br). 380 Marianne Majerus Garden Images (cl). 390 Photolibrary: Chris Burrows (b). 397 GAP Photos: Jo Whitworth (b). 399 Clive Nichols (b). 403 Alamy Images: William Tait. 416 GAP Photos: Martin Hughes-Jones (b). 423 GAP Photos: Adrian Bloom (b). 426 GAP Photos: Neil Homes (t). 431 GAP Photos: Martin Hughes-Jones (b). 434 GAP Photos: J.S. Sira (t); Garden Picture Library: J.S. Sira (tl). 444 Marianne Majerus Garden Images (b). 452 GAP Photos: Visions (b). 454 GAP Photos: Pernilla Bergdahl (t). 461 GAP Photos: Martin Hughes-Jones (t). 464 GAP Photos: Martin Hughes-Jones (b). 480 Photolibrary: Dennis Davis (tr). 484 GAP Photos: Dave Bevan (l). 498 GAP Photos: Neil Holmes (t). 503 Marianne Majerus Garden Images (b). 508 GAP Photos: Rob Whitworth (t). 513 GAP Photos: Jo Whitworth (t). Marianne Majerus Garden Images (b). 515 Garden World Images: Philip Smith (b). 526 GAP Photos: Martin Hughes-Jones (b). 540 Marianne Majerus Garden Images (t). 541 GAP Photos: Richard Bloom (t). 543 Photolibrary: John Glover (b). 547 GAP Photos: Visions (t). 548 GAP Photos: Howard Rice (t). 558 Garden World Images: Ashley Biddle (t). 570 GAP Photos: Martin Hughes-Jones (b). 574 Alamy Images: Frank Paul (b). 561 Harry Smith Collection (br).

All other images © Dorling Kindersley For further information see: www.dkimages.com

PUBLISHER'S ACKNOWLEDGMENTS

Dorling Kindersley would also like to thank:

Text contributors and editorial assistance Geoff Stebbings, Candida Frith-Macdonald, Simon Maughan, Andrew Mikolajski, Sarah Wilde, Tanis Smith, James Nugent, and Tina Jindal; at the Royal Horticultural Society, Vincent Square: Susanne Mitchell, Karen Wilson and Barbara Haynes

Design assistance Wendy Bartlet, Ann Thompson
DTP design assistance Louise Paddick
Additional picture research Charlotte Oster, Sean Hunter; special thanks also to Diana Miller, Keeper of the Herbarium at RHS Wisley
Index Ella Skene

First Edition
Project Editor Simon Maughan
Editor Tracie Lee
Art Editor Ursula Dawson
Managing Editor Louise Abbott
Managing Art Editor Lee Griffiths
DTP Design Sonia Charbonnier
Production Mandy Inness
Picture Research Sam Ruston, Neale Chamberlain

Canadian Publishing Team
Editor Julia Roles
Project Editor Ian Whitelaw
Editor-in-chief Trevor Cole

Revised Edition
RHS Editor Simon Maughan
RHS Consultant Leigh Hunt
Picture Research Sarah Hopper
Editor Fiona Wild

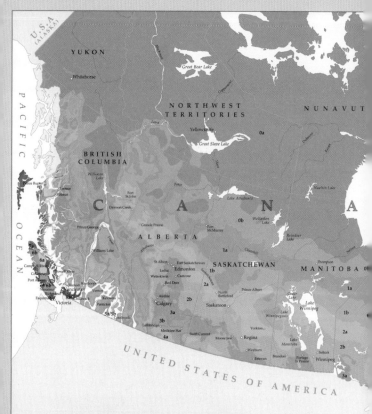

Based on the Plant Hardiness Zones of Canada 2000 map developed by Natural Resources Canada and Agriculture and Agri-Food Canada, this map indicates the different zones in Canada where various types of trees, shrubs, and flowers will most likely survive. Ranging from 0 (the harshest) to 8 (the mildest), there are 9 major zones split into 17 subzones.

Reproduced with the permission of the Minister of Public Works and Government Services Canada, 2003.